NATIONS OF THE MODERN WORLD

ARGENTINA

H. S. Ferns
Professor of Political Science,
University of Birmingham

AUSTRALIA

O. H. K. Spate
Director, Research School of Pacific Studies,
Australian National University, Canberra

AUSTRIA

Karl R. Stadler
Professor of Modern and Contemporary History,
University of Linz

BELGIUM

Vernon Mallinson
Professor of Comparative Education,
University of Reading

BURMA

F. S. V. Donnison
Formerly Chief Secretary to the Government of
Burma; Historian, Cabinet Office, Historical
Section 1949–66

CEYLON

S. A. Pakeman
Formerly Professor of Modern History, Ceylon
University College; Appointed Member, House
of Representatives, Ceylon, 1949–52

CYPRUS

H. D. Purcell
Professor of English,
University of Libya, Benghazi

DENMARK

W. Glyn Jones
Reader in Danish, University College, London

MODERN EGYPT

Tom Little
Managing Director and General Manager of
Regional News Services (Middle East) Ltd,
London

ENGLAND

John Bowle
Professor of Political Theory, Collège d'Europe,
Bruges

FINLAND

W. R. Mead
Professor of Geography, University College
London

NIGERIA	Sir Rex Niven *Administration Service of Nigeria, 1921–54* *Member, President and Speaker of Northern* *House of Assembly, 1947–59*
PAKISTAN	Ian Stephens *Formerly Editor of* The Statesman *Calcutta and Delhi, 1942–51* *Fellow, King's College, Cambridge, 1952–58*
PERU	Sir Robert Marett *H.M. Ambassador in Lima, 1963–67*
POLAND	Václav L. Beneš *Professor of Political Science,* *Indiana University* Norman J. G. Pounds *Professor of History and Geography,* *Indiana University*
SOUTH AFRICA	John Cope *Formerly Editor-in-Chief of* The Forum *and South Africa Correspondent of* The Guardian
SOVIET UNION	Elisabeth Koutaissoff *Professor of Russian, Victoria University,* *Wellington*
SPAIN	George Hills *Formerly Correspondent and Spanish* *Programme Organizer, British Broadcasting* *Corporation*
SUDAN REPUBLIC	K. D. D. Henderson *Formerly of the Sudan Political Service and* *Governor of Darfur Province, 1949–53*
TURKEY	Geoffrey Lewis *Senior Lecturer in Islamic Studies, Oxford*
YUGOSLAVIA	Muriel Heppell and F. B. Singleton

AUSTRIA

AUSTRIA

By
KARL R. STADLER

PRAEGER PUBLISHERS
New York · Washington

BOOKS THAT MATTER

Published in the United States of America in 1971
by Praeger Publishers, Inc.,
111 Fourth Avenue, New York, N.Y. 10003

© 1971 in London, England, by Karl R. Stadler

Library of Congress Catalog Card Number: 69-12307

Printed in Great Britain

Preface

THIS IS NOT A survey of Austrian affairs, though it tries to present a general picture of the country and its people, but essentially the work of a contemporary historian. As such it is history with a difference, in that it concentrates on the formative influences that have made Austrians into what they are today, places their story in the regional context of East-Central Europe, and draws liberally on the political and social sciences for motivation and elucidation.

But it is also a book which presents a thesis, and the reader will have to judge whether the author has succeeded in establishing it. The thesis is that throughout her history Austria was a state without a nation, and that it took the turbulent events of the last half-century to awaken a sense of national purpose among a people bitterly divided on all major issues. The decisive influence of the seven years of German occupation in creating the remarkable degree of national consciousness evident today has for long been the author's research interest, and much evidence from new sources is presented here for the first time in English.

In more than twenty years of teaching at Nottingham University the author has repeatedly discussed with colleagues and students the issues raised in this book. Now, after his return to Austria, his work at this new university has enabled him to see things more clearly than they appear from a distance, and to clear up some of the misconceptions about Austria so widespread in the English-speaking world. It remains for the author to thank all those, too numerous to mention, with whom he has discussed individual topics and who have drawn his attention to additional books or documents. His colleagues at Linz, Dr Gerhard Botz and Dr Hans Hautmann, have given invaluable assistance on certain points and with the maps and the Index. Last, and by no means least, he must put on record how much this book owes to the patience and co-operation of his wife. Needless to say, his views and judgements are his responsibility alone.

Linz
April 1970   KARL R. STADLER

9

Abbreviations

Agitprop 'Agitation and Propaganda'
BDC Berlin Document Center
BDM Bund deutscher Mädel
BRD Bundesrepublik Deutschland
Cominform Information Bureau of Communist and Workers'
  Parties
Comintern Communist International
DAF Deutsche Arbeitsfront
DDR Deutsche Demokratische Republik
DDSG Donau-Dampfschiffahrtsgesellschaft
DFP Demokratisch-Fortschrittliche Partei
EEC European Economic Community
EFTA European Free Trade Association
EWG Europäische Wirtschaftsgemeinschaft (EEC)
FPÖ Freiheitliche Partei Österreichs
Gestapo Geheime Staatspolizei
HJ Hitler Jugend
IAEO International Atomic Energy Organization
IfZ Mü Institut für Zeitgeschichte, München
IMT International Military Tribunal (Nuremberg)
Kommandatura Soviet Military Command in Vienna
KPÖ Kommunistische Partei Österreichs
NDP Nationaldemokratische Partei
NSDAP Nationalsozialistische Deutsche Arbeiterpartei
ÖAAB Österreichischer Arbeiter- und Angestelltenbund
O 5 Austrian Freedom Movement
ÖGB Österreichischer Gewerkschaftsbund
OKW Oberkommando Wehrmacht
ÖVP Österreichische Volkspartei
RIIA Royal Institute of International Affairs
RSHA Reichssicherheitshauptamt
RS (Ö) Revolutionäre Sozialisten (Österreichs)
SA Sturm-Abteilung
SD Sicherheitsdienst (of the SS)
SMV Sowjetische Mineralölverwaltung

SPD Sozialdemokratische Partei Deutschlands
SPÖ Sozialistische Partei Österreichs
SS Schutz-Staffel
UNIDO United Nations Industrial Development Organization
USIA Administration for Soviet Property in Austria
VO Volksopposition
WDU (later VDU) Wahlpartei, earlier Verband der Unabhängigen
WLB Weltanschaulicher Lagebericht

Contents

List of Illustrations

Maps

Acknowledgements

THE AUTHOR AND PUBLISHERS wish to express their thanks to the staffs of the Press Offices of the Federal Chancellery in Vienna and of the City of Vienna who provided many photographs for selection for this book and located some not on their files.

The copyright of the individual illustrations is held by the following:

Bildarchiv der österreichischen Nationalbibliothek: 4, 6
Bundespressedienst: 1, 2, 7, 13, 14, 15, 16, 18, 19, 23, 24
Dokumentationsarchiv des österreichischen Widerstandes: 8, 9, 11
Foto Hilscher: 5, 10
Grünzweig, Vienna: 22
Pressestelle der Stadt Wien: 12, 20, 21, 25, 26
SPÖ: 17
Verein für Geschichte der Arbeiterbewegung: 3

Chapter 1

Austria and the Austrians

THIS BOOK IS NOT really about Austria but about the Austrians. 'Austria' has undergone too many changes in her history – from the 'Ostmark' of the later Babenbergs, the private domains of the Habsburgs, the 'Austrian Empire' and 'Austria–Hungary' to the Republic of Austria, Hitler's *Ostmark* (soon broken up into the 'Alpine and Danubian *Gaue*'), and finally the Second Republic. The only sensible course, then, is to look at the people who live in this country.

Like every other nation they are the product of geography and history, that is, of the conditions and circumstances they were born into, and of the use they made of their opportunities through the ages. Because they did not inhabit a self-contained little island, but were situated on one of Europe's major crossroads where Teuton and Latin, Slav and Magyar, met and intermingled, and because the interests and policies of their rulers involved them in the affairs of a whole continent, which affected their outlook and their traditions, some reflections on the course of Austrian history may be of use even to the general reader who only wishes to acquaint himself with the Austria of today.

This is the more important since the frequent misreading of Austrian history has often led to the wrong assumptions about land and people, and consequently to wrong decisions and bad policies. There are three principal misconceptions abroad which have all been reflected in the momentous developments of the last hundred years, if they are not still current today. The first concerns the ethnic origins of the Austrian people, who are not simply one of the Teutonic tribes even though their early culture and their speech link them with the Bayuvarians. The migration and the settlements of many different peoples, the effects of peaceful colonization and of hostile invasions, though well documented, have never been given sufficient weight in assessing the country's ethnic nature. In consequence, Austrians have been represented as a branch of the German family that should be brought back into the Reich.

Even more substantial is the second error, the habit of seeing Austrian history as part of German history. With the Habsburgs as

19

'Holy Roman Emperors', and the long-standing contest for the mastery of Germany (which Francis Joseph I eventually lost to Bismarck), it is perhaps understandable that historians preoccupied with dynastic policies and diplomatic activities should fail to notice the emergence of a national entity with its own political and social concepts and perspectives. The neglect of these aspects of Austrian history again furthered the view of Austria as a German land to be 'liberated' or reunited with the main body if the opportunity arose.

There is yet another notion which occasionally haunts historical writing: the alleged mission of Austria as an outpost of Germandom against Slavs and other barbarians pressing against the Reich from the East. The present ideological division of the European continent adds topicality to this dangerous view, which is at best based on a half-truth. Austria certainly defended Central Europe from Magyars and Turks, and she subjected Slav peoples to Habsburg rule – not for the sake of Germandom or any other anachronistic fancy, but for dynastic reasons. In fact, the Habsburgs could not have retained their possessions without taking the ruling strata of these lands into partnership, and in the decades before the Great War imperial governments often depended on the non-German nationalities for parliamentary majorities against their German-speaking subjects. Of Habsburg 'missions' there never was any dearth, as A. J. P. Taylor noted:

> In the sixteenth century they defended Europe from the Turk; in the seventeenth century they promoted the victory of the Counter-Reformation; in the eighteenth century they propagated the ideas of the Enlightenment; in the nineteenth century they acted as a barrier against a Great German national state.[1]

To see Austria cast in the role of a spearhead against the Slav belt, now communist-dominated, because of an imagined historic mission, is arrant nonsense.

This is not to deny that German historians and nationalist propagandists have occasionally succeeded in persuading numbers of Austrians of the truth of these propositions. The superior social organization and greater technical skills of Germans as against Slavs, coupled with the community of language and culture, facilitated the process of identification with 'the Germans' regardless of constitutional realities. A misreading of the significance of the revolution of 1848 created a feeling of solidarity with German progressive thought among liberals and Socialists, and the success of Bismarck in creating the German Reich added admiration for power

[1] A. J. P. Taylor, *The Habsburg Monarchy 1809–1918* (London, 1967 edn), p. 12.

politics, compared with which the muddle and indecisiveness of Austrian policies seemed petty and shameful. And finally, the rivalry between Austria and Russia culminating in the First World War, and Hitler's invasion of the Soviet Union in the Second, could be represented as the defence of the European heartland from the sinister East.

The present book will have no truck with any of these notions. Its thesis is that ethnically, culturally, and politically Austria is nobody's errant offspring or lost province but a nation *sui generis*. She has no special mission other than to live at peace with her neighbours, whom she has got to know rather well in centuries of shared history, and if her present position on the dividing-line of two rival political systems enables her to provide a meeting-place for politicians and scholars and traders from both camps and the larger world besides, so much the better for all concerned.

The Land and the People

Geographically, the most significant feature of Austria is her position across some of the most important highways of Europe. In the west, the Brenner line connects south Germany with the north Italian plains. In the east, the prehistoric 'amber road' runs southward from the Vistula and Oder rivers across the Danube and the eastern Alps to the northern tip of the Adriatic. North of the Alps the Danube provides a great waterway from west to south-east, and at the intersection of that river and the 'amber road' a settlement arose which was to become one of Europe's great cities – Vienna.

Geologically, the country is made up of the Bohemian massif (10 per cent of the Federal territory), the Alpine forelands (30 per cent), and the Alps proper or 'eastern Alps' (60 per cent). In this mountainous state only about one-third of the total territory is less than 500 metres above sea-level (mainly the provinces around Vienna), while nearly 40 per cent lies above 1,000 metres, including the 3,797-metre Grossglockner massif. Western Austria, part of the south, and a central area extending from the lake district near Salzburg to isolated blocks on the fringe of the Vienna basin are of a high Alpine character with majestic forms shaped by snow, ice, and wind. The wide fringes of the Alps, the Bohemian woods, the Bohemian massif sloping down towards the Danube, and stretches along the river where it cuts its way through the mountains are of a sub-alpine character, while the massif itself is in the shape of a high plateau. The hilly regions of the Weinviertel, parts of Burgenland and Styria, the Klagenfurt basin, and the Alpine forelands contain open fertile areas, and finally the few plains of any size such as the Vienna basin, the Marchfeld, and the lowlands around Lake

Neusiedl already resemble the eastern steppe. Almost the whole of Austria belongs to the river system of the Danube which empties into the Black Sea.

The climate of Austria presents some curious contrasts. As a result of the prevalent direction of the winds, most precipitation comes from the west and the amount decreases from west to east. The driest areas (500 to 600 millimetres annually) are in the Vienna basin and the wine and wood districts adjoining, the wettest (2,000 to 3,000 millimetres) in the Bregenz woods and the central lake district. The highest mountain ranges, however, especially in Carinthia, are reached by air which has already lost much of its humidity; thus the weather there is dry and clear. Their height, of course, affects the temperature. The mean annual temperatures decrease with an increase in altitude, and they are higher in the continental dry lowlands of eastern Austria than at the same altitudes in western Austria. In the Marchfeld region and the northern Burgenland the mean annual temperature rises to nearly 10°C, and in the lowlands of south-eastern Austria it is over 9°C. On the other hand, it drops below 0°C above 2,100 metres, and at 3,000 metres it is minus 5·6°C.

These differences in altitude, topography, and climate, and the interplay of these factors in the different zones, have resulted in each region – often even neighbouring localities – bearing quite different characters, to which human enterprise has further contributed. As a result, the overall characteristics of a zone are only statistically true; field and settlement patterns, economic organization and hence living standards, and even religious affiliations and political loyalties can in no way be deduced from the framework nature has provided, though a glance at a physical map will explain the fierce local patriotism and the regional loyalties which in the Republic of Austria have found their political expression in a tenacious federalism directed against the centralism of Vienna.

Of the total surface of Austria, almost 39 per cent is covered by forests; pastures account for 26 per cent; and only 19 per cent is arable; hence the importance to the economy of timber (10 to 11 million cubic metres annually), of milk and milk products as well as livestock, and of agricultural products in general. Austrian agriculture supplies the greater part of domestic demand and even exports quantities of milk, cheese, and butter, while augmenting certain deficiencies by imports from North America (bread grains), Italy and eastern Europe (fruit, vegetables, and eggs), and Denmark and eastern Europe for poultry.

One of the earliest causes of settlement in Austria was, next to trade routes and communications, the country's mineral wealth.

Styria is one of the great iron-producing regions of Europe, accounting for 94 per cent of Austria's total of 3·5 million tons mined. The mining of non-ferrous metal ores was also considerably expanded after the war, lead-zinc ores, mostly in Carinthia, amounting to almost 200,000 tons, while in the mining of crude magnesite Austria is leading world production with 1·5 million tons. The mining of china clay (330,000 tons) and of salt (200,000 tons) is also of considerable importance. The Hallstatt salt-mine has been in continuous operation for some 2,500 years; place names containing the Celtic word for salt – *Hall* – or the German word *Salz* (such as Hall, Hallein, Hallstatt, or Salzburg and Salzkammergut) are an indication of the importance of their chief products.

There is one serious deficiency, though: hardly any of the output of Austria's coal-mines (4·6 million tons) consists of bituminous coal; it is practically all lignite. To offset this lack, there is the enormous volume of hydro-electric power supplied by Alpine rivers and reservoirs. More than two-thirds of electricity generated by water-power comes from run-of-the-river plants, one-third from storage plants in the mountains. In the winter months, when water-levels are low, thermal plants offset the decline in supplies, and they use Austrian lignite. As elsewhere, electrification has made great strides since the war: output by water-power has quadrupled, that by thermal plants has increased tenfold. A well-developed grid-system has brought power to even the smallest village, and some is even exported to neighbouring countries. Since Austria's first atom reactor for the production of electric power, at Zwentendorf near Vienna, will not be operative until 1975, the traditional methods will have to do for a long time yet. And finally, there is oil and natural gas. When production was started in 1932 at Zistersdorf near Vienna at the level of 100 tons of crude oil, few could foresee the potentialities of this new industry. Before the German invasion output went up to 33,000 tons, but after the *Anschluss* production was stepped up to the million-ton range and beyond. During the Allied occupation, with the Russians having taken over the oilfields under the title of 'German assets', this became one of the thorniest problems in Austrian politics, but since 1955 the oil industry has been a major factor in the country's recovery. Production of oil now stands at 2·7 million tons, and of natural gas at 1·6 million cubic metres, with estimated extractable reserves of 35 million tons and 15,000 million cubic metres, respectively.

These natural factors are reflected in Austria's economic structure and the occupation of her inhabitants. Taking the population as a whole, including families and dependants, it will not surprise us to learn that almost 40 per cent derive their living from industry and industrial trades and only 16·5 per cent from agriculture and forestry. Commerce and transport account for 13·5 per cent, the public services and the professions each for 5 per cent, while 20 per cent live on pensions of various kinds. Looked at in another way, considering only employed persons, the share of agriculture and forestry has dropped over the last thirty years from 32 to 23 per cent, while that of industry has risen from 33 to 43 per cent. How this came about, and what the consequences were, will be considered in a later chapter.

What of the people themselves? When the Austrian Republic was carved out of the old Empire in 1918, it counted 6·42 million inhabitants, a number that had risen to only 6·75 million twenty years later, on the eve of the German invasion. No statistics exist for the war years; the loss of some 250,000 Austrian Jews, killed or forced to emigrate by the new rulers, and the death of some 380,000 Austrians at the fronts and in air raids have to some extent been compensated for by the admission of large numbers of 'Folk Germans' and refugees from eastern Europe. By the time of the 1961 census the seven-million mark had been topped; the estimated population in 1970 is 7·42 million.[2]

As a result of a history in the course of which peoples of vastly different characteristics swept over the country, settled, and intermingled; and which later, under the Habsburgs, turned the multinational Empire into a melting-pot of races, the Austrians are an extremely mixed people, as even a fleeting acquaintance will confirm. According to E. H. Buschbeck,[3] at least four basic anthropological types are recognizable among them. There is first the tall, strongly-built type with a short head characteristically flattened at the back, strong nose and jaw, and a rich growth of dark hair, which usually occurs in the mountainous parts of Yugoslavia and is therefore called 'Dinaric'. The second is tall and slim, has an elongated head, face, and hands, fair hair and blue or grey eyes, and is called 'Nordic'. Many shaded crossbreeds of these types form the bulk of the population, though there is also the 'Alpine' type, short, thickset, with round head and face and dark hair, eyes, and complexion, and lastly, especially in the eastern parts of Austria, the 'East-Baltic' type: medium-sized with broad head and face, angular jaw and broad, turned-up nose, light-complexioned and often fair-haired – in short, the type very common among the Slavs. Only rarely is the 'pure' type encountered in Austria; the great

---

[2] All figures in this section from *Statistisches Handbuch für die Republik Österreich*, Statistisches Zentralamt (Vienna, 1969), and *Introducing Austria*, by the same office (Vienna, 1968).

[3] E. H. Buschbeck, *Austria* (London, 1949), ch. II.

majority of people combine the features of two or more races, and the large influx of 'Folk Germans' from Czechoslovakia, Hungary, Romania, and Yugoslavia, whose names and features suggest a similar process of assimilation, strengthen this impression.

The major reason for considering Austria a 'German' state has been the fact that the language spoken in Austria is German: standard High German in writing, apart from slight differences in vocabulary, and 'Austro-Bavarian' in pronunciation, with strong local dialects which make communication difficult even among Austrians, especially since the dialect spoken in Vorarlberg is Alemannic (as in Switzerland), which has also influenced the Tyrolese speech, while the idiom spoken in the towns along the Danube (including Vienna) shows phonetic traces of early Franconian settlers. Little more than 100,000 Austrians declare their mother tongue as Czech or Slovak (Vienna), Croat (Burgenland and Styria), or Slovene (Styria and Carinthia) – sad remnants of the great Slav family which played a big part in the earlier history of eastern Austria.

Early History

The records of prehistory on Austrian soil are sparse and of fairly recent date. The earliest traces are of pre-Neanderthal man – a mere 180,000 years ago. Only the last few thousand years are better 'documented': we know, for instance, that in the last Ice Age Austria was populated by a race of reindeer hunters, who have left us an outstanding sculptured fertility symbol, the 'Venus of Willendorf'. Around 1400 B.C. the native inhabitants were overrun by invasions from the North and West. Archæological finds point to the co-existence of Balkan and north and west European cultures in a population called Veneto-Illyrian. When this was subdued by the first Celtic invasion, about 400 B.C., the result seems again to have been less drastic than one might have assumed, for side by side with the new Celtic names of settlements, rivers, and mountains, others continued with their old Illyric names. Probably as a result of the first Teutonic incursions from Scandinavia in the second century B.C., the Celts of Carinthia moved into the north Italian plain, which led to Roman counter-moves aimed at strengthening the northern frontiers and eventually extending the Empire eastward. Even then, however, Roman rule never extended north of the Danube, where Teutonic tribes held sway; the river was the great moat, the frontier between two worlds.[4]

For the first century and a half of our time, the *Pax Romana*

[4] For the early history of Austria cf. especially sections I–IV of Karl Ziak (ed.), *Unvergängliches Österreich* (Vienna, 1958).

ruled in the country, and as elsewhere it was a period of progress and prosperity. The establishment of a large number of settlements, eleven of which became self-governing cities (including Vienna, St Pölten, Enns, Wels, Salzburg, Leibnitz, Spittal, Lienz, and Bregenz), a network of roads, and the exploitation of the country's mineral resources, as well as general trade, all contributed to the flowering of what is rather disparagingly called 'Roman provincial culture'. The Romanization of the Celtic and the Raetian population proceeded apace together with the adoption, beside the official cult, of various oriental cults (where Mithras and Isis seem to have been particularly popular) and eventually of Christianity. But after the death of Emperor Marcus Aurelius at Vienna in the year 180 the decline set in, with Germanic invasions from the North and West, and the Huns from the East. The latter's conquest, in A.D. 433, of the province of Pannonia, as well as their later incursions, does not seem to have been as destructive of civilization as their bad name suggests. The death of Attila and their great defeat twenty years later forced their withdrawal down the Danube, and their place was taken by western Germanic tribes of settled peasants.

But it was in the following century that the ethnic pattern for early Austria began to form: the incursions of the Bayuvarians from the north-west and of the Avars from the East. Around A.D. 530 the former – part of the Markomannian tribe which had settled in Bohemia – crossed into what is now Bavaria and, faced by the powerful Franks in the West, turned south across the Brenner and east as far as the river Traisen in present-day Lower Austria. Simultaneously the Avars, Central Asian horsemen like the Huns, swept into the open spaces in the East and south-east and settled various Slavonic subject peoples in their wake, from Lower Austria through Styria to Carinthia. There were conflicts between Bayuvarians and Slavs, but on the whole it seems to have been a peaceful process, for in early documents Bayuvarian and Slavonian freemen appear together as witnesses; had the latter been conquered, they would have been turned into serfs. In fact there is evidence that early in the seventh century Bavaria was under the strong cultural (and presumably political) influence of the Avar realm. A Slav rising under King Samo against their Avar overlords, however, led to a short-lived period of peaceful colonization and economic prosperity in eastern and southern Austria's Slav belt, but with Samo's death in 665 the Avars advanced again, reconquered Pannonia as far as the eastern Alps, and pushed their Mongolian–Turkish outposts up to the rivers Kamp and Thaya; the Slav tribes in Bohemia, Moravia, and in the Alps were once more reduced to a state of semi-vassalage.

Hard-pressed by the kingdom of the Franks in the West, and the Avars in the East, the Bayuvarians spent the next hundred years in the attempt to shake off their Franconian masters and at the same time push their frontiers deeper into Lower Austria. Duke Tassilo in particular appears to have had close relations with the Avars, there is mention of an alliance with them, and he is eventually brought to heel by Charlemagne, not least because of his association with these 'enemies of the realm'. To Charlemagne the empire of pagan nomads to the east rightly appeared as a serious challenge both to his dynastic interests and to the establishment of Christianity, and the great campaign against the Avars which began in 791 led after a few years to the destruction of their power; deprived of their herds and compulsorily settled, the remnants of this warlike people soon disappeared. Bavarian nobles and churches were endowed with lands, large numbers of Bavarian peasants followed the armies and settled among the original Slav peasants. With the destruction of the Avars the course of Austrian history was determined for the next several centuries: incorporated in the Reich, with Germanic settlers soon to predominate and Christianity established and spreading, this 'Eastern March' between the rivers Enns and Raab with indeterminate frontiers was soon to be referred to in one document as 'marca orientalis', forerunner of the term *Ostmark*.

However, a new challenge arose from the East which was to bring about the end of the Carolingian Reich and a half-century of warfare, before Austria emerged as a distinct political entity. Another wave of Ural-Altaic horsemen, the Magyars, swept into the Hungarian plain; they are first mentioned in a skirmish near 'Wenia' (Wien, Vienna) in 881. Twenty-six years later they destroyed a whole Bavarian army and the road to the West lay open to them. But their control of eastern Austria, and their forays into Bavaria and beyond, did not materially change the economic and cultural structure of the existing civilization, based as it was on firm settlements; the *Nibelungenlied*, one of the greatest epic poems in any language, with its (German) margrave at Pöchlarn on the Danube in Lower Austria who owes allegiance to distant Magyar overlords, bears witness to this. After several attempts that were only partly successful the new German kingship of the Saxon dynasty decisively defeated the Magyar horsemen on the river Lech near Augsburg in 955, and this event which at last brought security to the south-east of the Reich is held to be the real beginning of Austria. In fact, forty-one years later, on All Saints' Day 996, Otto III, grandson of the victor of Lech, endowed the bishop of Freysing with lands in the 'region usually referred to as *Ostarichi*' – the *Ostreich*, or *Österreich*. It must therefore have been a March with an established name with which Leopold of Babenberg was endowed in 976; he was the first of the Austrian Babenbergs who ruled for 270 years, first as margraves and later as dukes. In fact, when the provisional National Assembly in 1918 looked for a substitute for the Habsburg imperial colours of black-and-yellow, it chose red-white-red, the colours of the last Babenbergs, for the new republic.

The rule of the Babenbergs – which confirmed the separate territorial organization of the Austrian lands and at the same time created new links with the Orient, partly through the Crusades and on account of the marriages of three dukes with Byzantine princesses – ended with the death in battle of Frederick 'the Fighter' in 1246. As this event almost coincided with the end of the Hohenstaufen dynasty, when Germany embarked on the thirty years' interregnum without a royal authority at the centre, the Austrian Estates elected as their duke Przemisl Ottakar, king of Bohemia, thus bringing the first Austro–Bohemian union into being. Since by force and by treaty he added Styria, Carinthia, and most of Carniola, and also had designs on Hungary, we can see here the first plans for a great union of the Alpine, Sudeten, and Carpathian lands, and all that was needed for their realization was the kingship of Germany. But in 1273 the crown went to Count Rudolf of Habsburg, head of a wealthy and influential family in south-west Germany, who called upon Ottakar to surrender the duchies of Austria, Styria, and Carinthia; after various negotiations and treaties the Bohemian sought to force the issue by the sword, and was killed in battle north of Vienna in 1278. But recognizing that the power of kingship depended on the wealth and influence of the royal family, Rudolf immediately set about the task of strengthening his *Hausmacht*, the 'Domain of Austria', by enfeoffing his own sons with the vacant duchies of Austria and Styria (while Carinthia went to a faithful supporter, and Bohemia to Ottakar's son).

This marked the beginning of the association between the House of Habsburg and Austria which was to last for 640 years: two hundred years of consolidation of their *Hausmacht*, two hundred years of expansion, and a century each of 'concentration' and of belated modernization against a background of political decline. Not once in the fifty years since the expulsion of Charles Habsburg in 1918 has there been a real chance of restoration for a dynasty which somehow does not seem to fit into the twentieth century.

The Habsburgs

We have seen why for reasons of defence against foreign invasions (Huns, Avars, Magyars) the Eastern March from the start required

a tighter military organization, a more centralized system of government, than was necessary in other provinces of the realm. Since
these pressures continued for several centuries, with the Turks as the
new challengers, the Habsburg policy of consolidation and expansion continuously brought new peoples under their rule who had
not yet overcome the feudal stage and formed themselves into
nationalities; this explains the delay in the development of a national
consciousness and the desire for independent nation states such as
were emerging in western Europe. Nevertheless, since the Habsburgs
were in origin a German dynasty and the inhabitants of Vienna and
the original *domus Austriae* were predominantly Germans, a certain
identity of interests existed throughout their long association which
anchored the dynasty securely to the original Danubian and Alpine
provinces.[5]

Although divided administratively in two regions, the Habsburg
domain underwent a significant expansion in the fourteenth century.
Between 1335 and 1375 Carinthia and the Tyrol, Istria and parts of
Vorarlberg, were peacefully acquired, while a few years later
Trieste joined voluntarily, seeking protection from Venice. Duke
Rudolf IV at the same time vied with King Charles IV, his father-
in-law, as to which of their capitals – Vienna and Prague, respectively – was to be the greater city; this competition led to the
rebuilding of St Stephen's Cathedral in Vienna and the establishment of Vienna University, the second in Germany after Prague's
Charles University. Early in the fifteenth century Albrecht II again
for a short while ruled over Bohemia, and also over Hungary, which
was the first time such a union had come about. He was also the
first to acquire the crowns of the German realm and of the Holy
Roman Empire (which had become increasingly identified), symbol
of the universal monarchy of the Middle Ages which became
virtually hereditary in the House of Austria between 1437 and 1806.
Neither dignity denoted much power; a certain political influence –
and even greater obligations at a time when the great national states
of the West and the German princes sought to limit the importance
of these offices. But luck was with the Habsburgs – or their mastery
of 'the weapon of dynastic marriage'. 'Bella gerant alii, tu felix
Austria nube': in three generations the House of Habsburg acquired
three great heritages. Of the great Burgundian monarchy the
French seized Burgundy proper when the male line died out in
1477, while Flanders, Brabant, and Holland went to Mary of Burgundy whose husband was Maximilian of Austria, German king and
heir to the Habsburg dominions and the Imperial Crown. After the
loss of their possessions in Switzerland this was ample compensation,

[5] For the contrary view cf. Taylor, op. cit., ch. I.

for it gave the Habsburgs a stake in the most advanced region of
Europe of that time. In 1496 their son Philip married Juana, heiress
to the Spanish monarchy (sister of Henry VIII's Catherine of
Aragon), thus adding Spain to the family domain. While this may
not seem to have affected Austria very much, for the now enormous
Habsburg heritage had to be divided between Charles V (ruler over
the Netherlands, Spain, and the Indies, and most of Italy – 'the
Reich in which the sun never set') and his younger brother
Ferdinand I, who took over the archduchy of Austria, relations
between the two courts remained very close: their common concern
was the paramountcy of the House of Habsburg, their enemy the
French monarchy, their duty the defence of Catholicism. But
Ferdinand also was brother-in-law to Ludovic Jagiello, last of the
Jagellon kings of Bohemia and Hungary, upon whose death in 1526
in the battle of Mohacs against the Turks Ferdinand succeeded to
the vacant crowns. Three years later the Turks staged their first
great siege of Vienna (the second was in 1683), but though they
were repulsed here they held most of Hungary for over a century.

The battle of Mohacs was an important event in the history of
the region. It ended, for nearly four centuries, the national independence of the Magyars and their discontent, which even the Compromise of 1867 could not pacify, contributed materially to the
weakness and eventually the doom of the Empire. For the Habsburgs the year 1526 was the beginning of their great Danubian base,
a tripartite political entity which was to mould the three nations –
Austrians, Bohemians, and Hungarians – and later accessions into
the multi-national Empire of our own century. And finally, with
this event the Habsburgs became Europe's standard-bearers against
the Turks, Austria the main bastion against further Turkish expansion. It has been said that the Turkish invasions spoilt the Habsburg
plans for dominating Germany; but it could also be argued that the
Turks prevented them from making the attempt, which would
probably have been no more successful than that of their Hohenstaufen and Luxembourg predecessors. Thus, by providing them
with a 'mission', the Turks may have saved the Habsburgs and
enabled them to survive into the twentieth century. The growing
weakness and eventual collapse of the Ottoman – as of the Romanov
– Empire removed the last *raison d'être* of the Danubian monarchy
as understood by the Habsburgs.

But we are anticipating. If external enemies had threatened the
monarchy in the first half of the sixteenth century, disintegration
was the danger in the second half. The Estates of the various lands
fought for their independence and for the privileges of their aristocratic members. Peasant unrest, the first rumblings of the great

upheaval which was to culminate in the movement known as the Reformation, the strength of the Hussite movement in Bohemia, the spread of Protestantism in the remnant of Hungary and in the German lands, all these presented the Habsburgs with problems which they solved in their own fashion. Basically it was the alliance

The Empire under Charles V (mid-sixteenth century)

of the Jesuits and the dynasty, aided by aristocratic selfishness and lack of leadership among their enemies, which defeated Protestantism in Central Europe. Following the ruling of the Augsburg Diet of 1555 that princes could determine the religion of their subjects ('cuius regio, eius religio'), Austria – which had overwhelmingly turned Protestant – was restored to the 'true faith' at the price of much oppression, cruel slaughter, and mass emigration. The Counter-Reformation succeeded, not by any spiritual reform of the

Church, but by the power of the sovereign; for the next 300 years
the Catholic Church remained the handmaiden of Austria's ruling
classes, just as the ambivalent attitude of the Protestant minority
towards the state had its origins in those events.

While Habsburg Hungary succumbed easily, eastern Hungary
under Turkish suzerainty preserved its Calvinism, as a weapon for
future use. But it was in Bohemia that the conflict had the most
far-reaching consequences. In the battle of the White Mountain in
1620 historic Bohemia was destroyed, Czech Hussite culture was
replaced by the cosmopolitan culture of the Baroque, the civilization of the Counter-Reformation. The native nobility was dis-
possessed or driven into exile; two-thirds of the landed estates
changed hands; the revived Diet lost all its rights, for now Bohemia
became a 'hereditary land' like the German provinces, and the
Bohemian nation was submerged until its promising renewal in
1918. The power and prestige of the imperial cause was soon dissipated, however, in a last attempt to subdue Germany as well.
French and Swedish intervention ended the Habsburg dream of
German unity through the Holy Roman Empire, and the Peace of
Westphalia in ending the Thirty Years War also ended all hopes of
Habsburg predominance outside their own domain.

But there was important work to be done yet in the south-east.
In a last fling of vigour the Turkish Empire, which stretched to
within 70 miles of Vienna and had a pasha ruling at Buda, once
again attacked the Habsburgs with French encouragement. The
famous two-month siege of Vienna in 1683 by 200,000 Turkish
troops under the command of the Grand Vizier, Kara Mustapha,
was beaten off and the Turks were pursued hotfoot through the
length and breadth of Hungary. By the first Peace of 1699 all of
Hungary and most of Transylvania, and by the second Peace of
1718 the Banat, Belgrade, and part of Wallachia were added to the
Habsburg domain. Trouble with the recalcitrant Magyars was soon
settled by means of the first of many 'Compromises', under which
they recognized the Habsburg as their king and he recognized their
constitution and privileges. Hungary thus preserved her separateness, her feudal Diet and autonomous local government, and above
all the privileges of her landed class; her spokesman in 1711 was the
ancestor of the Count Michael Károlyi who 207 years later attempted
to save Hungary by proclaiming the end of the Habsburg monarchy.

The beginning of the eighteenth century saw the last great
dynastic conflict, between the Habsburgs and the Bourbons, and the
last success of Habsburg expansion in the West. In the War of the
Spanish Succession, which disposed of the Spanish Empire after the
extinction of the Spanish branch of the House of Austria and in

which Austria, Britain, and Holland were ranged against Louis XIV, the Austrian Habsburgs gained in the Treaties of Utrecht and Rastatt (1713–14) the southern Low Countries, Milan, and for a time the kingdom of Naples. This not merely enhanced the prestige of the House of Austria but also added a new element to a Court and a capital city already known for their international, even cosmopolitan, character; now men from Belgium and Lombardy joined the new upper class which developed in the imperial service – notably in the army as a result of the Turkish and Spanish Succession Wars, but also in the administration and in the diplomatic service.

Italians like Piccolomini, Montecuccoli, Pallavicini, Colloredo; Germans like Ludwig of Baden, Mansfeld, the Schönborns; the French-speaking Charles of Lorraine; Spaniards like Gallas; Scots and Irishmen like Butler, O'Donnell, Taaffe; Walloons like Tilly: they all served side by side with Austrian and Bohemian families like Waldstein, Trauttmansdorf, the Starhembergs, and the Harrachs. Best known of all, perhaps, abroad as the companion in arms of Marlborough, and in Austria as the hero of a popular song celebrating his exploits against the Turks, was Prince Eugene of Savoy, Italian by birth and educated at the Court of Louis XIV, whose Vienna palace, the Belvedere, is still one of the delights of the capital. Their names fill the history books, but through the palaces they built and the streets named after them they still seem somehow a living reality, token of the supra-national character of Court and city. They – and the artists, chaplains, secretaries, and servants they brought with them or attracted – superimposed the dazzling cosmopolitan, specifically Austrian, character on a civilization which might otherwise have remained provincial German.

Consolidation and Modernization

The eighteenth century was a time of concentration and consolidation. Since Charles VI, Emperor since 1711, had no male heir and the Habsburg lands were in the same danger of partition as the Spanish Empire, he settled the succession by a fundamental constitutional law, the Pragmatic Sanction, on his daughter Maria Theresa while at the same time asserting the indivisibility of the monarchy. Thus the Habsburg domain changed from a collection of disconnected sovereignties into a clearly defined Empire, with the approval of each of the Diets of the Habsburg lands and the agreement of most foreign powers obtained (in some cases) at a considerable price. This included treaties and pledges which involved Charles in a series of wars that cost him his son-in-law's heritage of Lorraine, as well as the kingdoms of Naples and Sicily (while the gain of Tuscany, Parma, and Piacenza at least rounded off his Italian possessions), and eventually even Belgrade and Little Wallachia reverted to the Turks. Austria's bid for colonial trade through the East India Company at Ostend – part of the Emperor's determined policy of encouraging industry and commerce – had to be sacrificed to Britain in return for recognition.

But all his efforts seemed to be in vain, and on his death in 1740 Maria Theresa found herself beset by enemies on all sides, notably Prussia's Frederick II, who seized Silesia. The long-drawn-out struggle which followed, involving almost the whole of Europe, brought about, or confirmed, new alignments. It brought Russia on to the European scene as an active power. The traditional line-up, Austria and Britain versus France, was replaced by a combination of Austria and France versus Prussia and Britain, whereby Britain contributed not a little towards the new role of Prussia as a European power. The German Empire was reduced to a shadowy existence, its smaller principalities maintaining an uneasy balance between Prussia, Austria, and France. Only Austria emerged strangely unchanged in political substance, though strengthened in cohesion and more clearly identified with her role in south-eastern Europe.

Maria Theresa was the first modern ruler of Austria. Her internal reforms may have been dictated by the need for efficiency comparable to that of Prussia, but they were imbued with a different spirit: not as 'the first servant of the state' (Frederick), but as 'mother of her country', the Empress did evince a concern for the welfare of the people which was as yet unknown in the age of absolutism. Her administrative reforms translated Charles's legal unity into practice; the 'Empire', which used to be the Court and the army, was now given a bureaucratic machine, strictly controlled at the centre, to hold it together. An 'Austrian State Council' for the Empire and a joint 'Bohemian–Austrian Office' for the Hereditary Lands and Bohemia were established; the administration of the lands was reorganized in such a way that agents of the central body supervised its working independent of provincial Diets; and at the local level the rule of the landed gentry was replaced by government-appointed district officers. Together with the reform of the administration of justice and of finance, these measures brought into being a class of able and honest civil servants, always underpaid yet filled with a sense of duty and loyalty towards their sovereign, which was the backbone of the new imperial system. Three new departments at the centre dealt with financial and economic affairs, and inevitably taxation was increased – and extended to make the nobility and the clergy as well as church lands liable.

The much-needed codification of the law took place in the sixties and seventies, when torture was abolished; a forerunner of the Ministry of Education was set up and communes were obliged to provide elementary schools in 1773 – the start of universal education in Austria; a syllabus was issued for secondary schools, and finally the universities were changed from domains of the Jesuits to modern secular institutions. Likewise, in spite of the Empress's deep religiosity (not to say bigotry), the relations of Church and state were ordered in such a way that the paramount position of the state was safeguarded. Only Hungary escaped the reforms, since Maria Theresa could not afford a head-on clash like the battle of the White Mountain with the Czechs. Hungary therefore retained her Chancery and her own administration, together with her gentry in full control; every advance in Austria made Hungary appear more backward politically and socially. Whether she had a choice or not, by arresting her reforms at the frontier of Hungary Maria Theresa was the founder of dualism.

In her eldest son, Joseph II, we encounter the most attractive representative of the Enlightenment among the rulers of the time, a radical in his methods, more tolerant and humanitarian than his mother but without her sure touch and patience. A child of his time, though always in advance of it, he sought to make state authority the instrument of progress, and many of his measures proved too advanced for his people and had to be withdrawn. But his great judicial, ecclesiastical, and social reforms could not be undone: a three-tier system for the judiciary consisting of local courts, courts of appeal, and a supreme court; freedom of worship for Protestants and Jews, and the dissolution of those monasteries that did no useful work like teaching or nursing the sick, about one-third of the 2,163 religious houses; and the abolition of serfdom, which secured freedom of movement, of marriage, and the free choice of occupation, coupled with security of tenure for most of the owners of peasant holdings. This latter policy was unique even among enlightened rulers, and it is held to have ensured the survival of peasant communities (and hence of peasant nations) in east-central Europe.

Where he failed was in his larger designs for a centralized state. Most of his legislation was carried through by letters patent; not even the Hungarian Estates were summoned, while he replaced that country's administration by German officials and refused to recognize its privileges. In 1784 German was introduced as the language of administration throughout the Empire, even in Hungary where Latin had been used; and this decision, a typical case of a rationalist expedient without any nationalist or racist undertones, not only provoked much opposition but produced an unexpected effect:

> Since government officials and judges in the lower courts had to use the native idiom of the Emperor's subjects, they were forced to learn these languages themselves, and since elementary education was also provided in the local tongue, the Slav languages became increasingly important and contributed to the national awakening of these peasant communities. Thus Joseph II, the head of the centralized state, became the father of federalism and nationalism,

as an Austrian historian wrote, adding that as the executor of the ideas of the Enlightenment Joseph II was 'the most important monarch of all who occupied the Austrian throne'.[6] When Joseph died in 1790 he was sure he had failed completely. Leopold II, his brother, who succeeded him for the short period of two years, was more of a pragmatist and yielded to pressures more readily, especially from the Hungarians. In fact, in his dealings with that country he concluded the second of those 'Compromises' which the Hungarian nobles forced upon Austria to preserve their privileges, at least until 1848. But the spirit of 'Josephinism' – centralist, secular, progressive, or even liberal, and sometimes daringly unorthodox – survived the period of the French wars and the reaction which followed it.

For this was the principal effect of the Napoleonic Wars upon Austria: they once again gave Austria a 'mission' in Europe, which was the defence against revolution and, long after France had been defeated, against the ideas that had originally produced it. Presiding over this bastion of conservatism and legitimacy was Francis II, Leopold's untalented pedestrian son, the first half of whose long reign was spent in warfare or diplomatic intrigue against the French, while the second half, inspired by Metternich, served the ends of reaction through the instrumentality of the 'Holy Alliance'.

After the three wars of coalition with different allies which, in spite of occasional victories, failed to stem the French tide sustained by the first people's army in modern history and by Napoleon's military genius, Austria tried to go it alone in a 'war of liberation', with similar results. Francis now used the more familiar Habsburg weapon of dynastic marriage, and his young daughter Marie-Louise was sacrificed to obtain Napoleon's favour and a breathing-space for Austria. If it had not been for the Corsican's boundless

---

[6] Robert Endres, 'Das Zeitalter der Reformen' in *Unvergängliches Österreich*, p. 297.

ambition, the Austrian attempt at armed mediation after the disaster in Russia and the new Prussian–Russian alliance might have saved him both throne and country. As it was, his refusal brought Austria into the coalition and the battles of Leipzig and Waterloo sealed his fate.

The Congress of Vienna did not only dance; it also conducted a lot of business, such as attempting to put the political clock back to before 1789 as well as confirming the new relationships of the powers as they developed during twenty-two years of war and crisis. Austria emerged stronger and more consolidated than she had been for a long time. Wisely, she made no attempt to recover the distant Nether-lands (Belgium forming part, until 1830, of the new kingdom of Holland) or her former possessions in south-west Germany, known as the *Vorlande*, which went to Bavaria, Württemberg, and Baden. The provinces she had lost in various campaigns were restored to her, so that apart from the losses to Italy after 1859 and 1866 and the acquisition of Bosnia–Herzegovina her territory remained fairly constant until the dissolution in 1918. The new 'Austrian Empire', proclaimed by Francis in 1804 when he also adopted the title of Francis I, 'Emperor of Austria', extended from Lake Constance to the Bukovina, from Venetia and Dalmatia in the South to Galicia and Silesia in the North. The emptiness of the 'Holy Roman Empire' had been further demonstrated when Napoleon forced the western and southern German principalities into the Rhine League, where-upon Francis resigned the title of Holy Roman Emperor in 1806, thus ending its thousand-year history. The Congress did not attempt to resurrect the Empire; instead, Germany became a loose associa-tion of sovereign states under Austria's presidency, 'powerful for defence, powerless for offence', as Metternich put it. Prussia's great accession of strength, however, by the acquisition of the Rhine Province, Westphalia, and half of Saxony, laid the basis of her future predominance.

For Austria's internal development the following period, up to the revolution of 1848, was one of political repression and economic progress. Under two reactionary rulers – Francis I was succeeded in 1835 by his weak-minded son Ferdinand I – absolutism reigned supreme. The Estates lost all practical importance (except in Hungary), all government business was concentrated in the Emperor's Secretariat, the civil service functioned without initiative or inspiration from above; Austria was 'administered, but not ruled', as Metternich complained, and the people were plagued by a ubiquitous police system and a capricious censorship. But this also was the time of Austria's industrial revolution, with iron, engineer-ing, and textile industries springing up and communications vastly expanding. A new bourgeois society came into being which, denied a share in public affairs, turned to the arts and to things of the mind. The famous Biedermeier style of life, following on the classical tradition of Haydn and Mozart, embraced Beethoven, Schubert and Strauss, Grillparzer, Raimund, and Nestroy on the stage, the painters Waldmüller and Danhauser, as well as the first steam-engine, the Danubian Steamship Company, and the first horse-drawn railway from Linz to Budweis. It also saw the spread of liberal ideas in opposition to Metternich's police state and the policy of national oppression practised by the Holy Alliance. Inspired first by the ideals of Young Germany and of Young Europe, they soon find expression in the lyrics of Lenau and Anastasius Grün, and even the new working class appears sporadically as an ally.

The discontent of the people in general, and of the nationalities in particular, aggravated by the economic depression of 1847, needed only a spark to set the Empire alight. This spark was provided by the news of the February Revolution in Paris. On 13 March 1848 Vienna rose in revolt, with the students in the lead, and before the elemental resolve of the populace the whole structure of absolutism seemed to collapse like a house of cards. Metternich fled to London, the Court to Innsbruck where, in December, Ferdinand at last abdicated and eighteen-year-old Archduke Francis, his nephew, acceded to the throne as Francis Joseph I. Meanwhile, however, the revolution appeared to have failed; some of its immediate gains – freedom of the press and abolition of censorship; trial by jury; the arming of the population and formation of a 'National Guard' – were soon revoked. The promise of ministerial responsibility was more difficult to carry out; after three successive governments within two months had come to grief over this, a single Chamber and universal franchise were at last offered, and the first Austrian Parliament was elected and met in July. In addition to the famous *Lex Kudlich*, which abolished the hereditary rights of landlords in jurisdiction and administration, the labour service, and the insecurity of peasant tenants, the Parliament, now removed to Kremsier, drafted a constitution for 'a modern, multi-national state according to the wishes and with the consent of the nations', based on the fundamental rights of the citizens and the nationalities. Before a vote could be taken, however, this Parliament was dissolved by force on 7 March 1849.

For in the meantime things had not gone too well: in Vienna, the revolutionaries divided against themselves when the bourgeoisie found itself faced with the far-reaching social and economic demands of the workers. Encouraged by this split, the Court pro-

ceeded to crush the national revolutions in Mil
Hungary,

> to mobilize the new nations ['geschichtslose
> the historic nations: it holds down the Po
> Ruthenian peasants; it combines with the
> after the defeat of the radical wing . . . agai
> Germans; it incites the Slavs and Rom
> particularly the Croats under Ban Jellacic, to armeᴅ ᴿᵉᵇᵉˡ
> against the Magyars...[7]

Vienna attempts to prevent the departure of a regiment to Hungary, and in the rioting War Minister Count Latour is killed, whereupon Prince Windischgrätz and Jellacic take the city and wreak vengeance on its radical elements. The Hungarian rising is quelled with the assistance of a Russian army (under the terms of the Holy Alliance) by General Haynau (whom brewery-workers in East London were to attack on the occasion of an official visit). Again the victors show no mercy: nine generals are hanged and four are shot, Premier Battyány is executed, countless officers are sentenced to long terms of imprisonment, and the names of Kossuth and other fugitives are nailed on the gallows.

The events of 1848–49 marked the temporary eclipse of liberalism and nationalism, but the issues fought over in those tumultuous months were only shelved for a short time, and each of the contestant groups was soon to reappear with its claims: the bourgeoisie which needed liberal policies for the development of the economy; the working class which fought for social justice; the nationalities which demanded equality, autonomy, and eventually their freedom. One final aspect of 1848 needs to be discussed, which was possibly the most relevant to the character of the Austrian state and its future: the relations between Austria and Germany.

Pan-Germanism, the *grossdeutsch* movement, was the child of the revolution of 1848. While German nationalists had been dreaming of an all-German Reich as early as the time of the Napoleonic Wars, it was only discontent with the Austrian system which caused such notions to spread in the Habsburg Empire, principally among students and professional men. With the revolution spreading throughout Germany, an opportunity seemed to present itself, and a German National Assembly, with Austrian representatives, was convened at Frankfurt. It was soon evident that serious tactical – and political – divisions existed among the delegates. The *grossdeutsch* faction proposed the restoration of the German Reich with a Habsburg Emperor; the *kleindeutsch* party sought the expulsion

[7] Otto Bauer, *Geschichte Österreichs* (Vienna, 1911), p. 22.

Austria from a Germany united under the Hohenzollern; while the Democrats, the 'left wing', stood for a German Republic between the North and the Baltic Seas and the Adriatic, with independent national states for Hungarians, Poles, and Italians. Since Habsburg and Hohenzollern interests could not be reconciled, and since the bourgeoisie was not prepared to overthrow the dynasties, a united democracy for all German-speaking regions was ruled out; in fact, the Austrian delegates withdrew when a *kleindeutsch* draft constitution was adopted according to which no part of the future Reich was to be united with non-German provinces in a single state. Since 1848 was probably the last chance of a voluntary union between Austria and Germany, it is tempting to speculate on the course history might have taken if the voting had gone the other way. As it was, her rejection at Frankfurt, confirmed by Bismarck in 1866, forced Austria to turn towards the East and south-east, with important consequences for the national identification of the majority of Austrians. There were those, however, who still preferred a *kleindeutsch* solution, and they called themselves *grossdeutsch*, and later National Socialists; later they were to play a disastrous part in the Republic of Austria. Incidentally, the king of Prussia contemptuously rejected the dignity offered to him – partly because Austria was too strong to be humbled with impunity, partly because he would not treat with a revolutionary body. Thus, the 'revolution from below' having failed, it was left to Bismarck to unify Germany by a 'revolution from above'.

Dualism and After

Inside the Habsburg Empire the next thirty years were a period of trial and error in search of a suitable form of government; no fewer than eight constitutions were tried out in two decades. In varying forms and combinations the issue was always the same: absolute versus representative government, centralism versus federalism, conservatism versus liberalism. The details are of interest only to the student of constitutional history, but the broad outline is as follows: the victory of the counter-revolution ushers in a ten-year period called 'neo-absolutism' which comes to an end with the wars in Italy, when Austria suffers great losses. She is left with only two Italian possessions, Venetia (and this only for another seven years) and Trieste and Istria, which she retains till 1918. The foundation of the Kingdom of Italy as well as the lost war are serious blows to her prestige and her exchequer. The resultant crisis leads to the beginnings of constitutional government under liberal auspices. The Habsburgs had defeated political liberalism in the revolution, but they were compelled to adopt a liberal economic

policy: they abolished duties between Austria and Hungary, removed mercantilist restrictions on imports, lowered protective
tariffs, expanded posts and railways, established freedom of trade,
and freed the sale of land. The constitutional enactments of 1860
and 1861 went some way towards satisfying the requirements of the
liberal bourgeoisie, but not nearly far enough. It took another defeat,
this time at the hands of the Prussians in 1866, before the next
advance towards modern government could be made.

Defeated by the Prussians in the battle of Königgrätz (Sadowa),
Austria had to consent to the dissolution of the German Confederation and to 'new arrangements in Germany without the participation
of the Austrian Empire' – in short, the Prussian-dominated North
German Federation. At the same time she had to yield up Venetia
to Italy. By these decisions both the German and the Italian questions were settled *against* the interests of Austria. But more was to
come: under the impact of this defeat the last historic 'Compromise'
was concluded with Hungary in 1867, which was to remain the
constitutional basis until 1918. It split the 'Austrian Empire', now
called 'Austria–Hungary', into two halves: 'The Kingdoms and
Lands represented in Parliament' (i.e. Austria) and Hungary, also
referred to as 'Cisleithania' and 'Transleithania', the latter being
the 'lands of the crown of St Stephen'. Foreign affairs, defence, and
the finance for both were to be a common concern, with Hungary
contributing 30 per cent of the expenses, while economic matters
were to be adjusted every tenth year. There was to be no joint
Parliament at the centre, but 'Delegations' of the Austrian and
Hungarian Parliaments. The Compromise established the system of
dualism and it was 'liberal' in that it was not autocratic; but by
surrendering Austria to the German bourgeoisie and Hungary to
the Magyar gentry the crown was inviting early trouble with the
classes excluded from power by reasons of social position or of race.
The main Compromise is paralleled by minor 'compromises' on
both sides: in Austria the German liberals combine with the Polish
aristocracy against the interests of the Polish and Ruthenian peasants
in Galicia, and in Hungary the Magyars co-operate with the Croats.
Otto Bauer's observation sums it up neatly:

> The 'Compromise' is an understanding among the ruling classes
> of the historic nations (Germans, Magyars, Poles, Croats) against
> the mass of their fellow-nationals (whom the curial franchise
> excludes from power) *and* against the newer nations (the Czechs,
> Slovenes, and Ruthenes in Austria, and the Slovaks, Serbs, and
> Romanians in Hungary).[8]

[8] Otto Bauer, op. cit., p. 29.

The Franco–Prussian War of 1870, which finally killed all hopes of 'revenge for Sadowa', interrupted only briefly the period of liberal rule which lasted for another eight years, when it was succeeded by a combination of feudal magnates and the petty bourgeoisie. In most material respects Austrian liberalism had laid the foundations of the modern state: constitutional enactments on ministerial responsibility and civil liberties, including laws on the press, on associations and assemblies; electoral reform which substituted direct elections (albeit based on property qualifications) for indirect elections through the Diets; the final separation of the judiciary from the administration; the revocation of the Concordat; and the introduction of universal elementary education from the sixth to the fourteenth years. Since all these measures represented compromises, there was nothing final about them; and the working classes had to await the dissolution of the monarchy before their basic demands were met; but much of this legislation has stood the test of time and is still, with appropriate changes and additions, the law of the land. If only the liberals had also been able to initiate a solution to the national problem, and the federalist conservatives had been less backward-looking, the whole of Central Europe would have benefited from the creative genius displayed in this age.

Just as absolutism had prepared the way for the liberal régime, in the same way liberalism produced the very forces which were to overthrow it. The short-lived boom after the Franco–Prussian War, with the reckless promotion of new companies and feverish speculation, led to the great crash of 1873 and years of depression. The increasing dependence of small manufacturers, artisans, and peasants on finance capital led to the first stirrings of reactionary, corporatist, and anti-semitic ideas, while the industrial working class was brought into ever sharper opposition to capitalist exploitation. Social reform became the slogan both of the clerical forces, such as Vogelsang's 'Christian socialism', and of the emergent labour movement which first organized itself, in 1867, in educational circles and now openly proclaimed its socialist class aims. Liberalism, discredited by the depression and increased taxation, and compromised by its share in the speculation fever, was faced with a barrage of demands for the protection of small entrepreneurs, traders, and farmers, and for factory legislation. A section of the young labour movement, which was now split into 'moderates' and 'radicals', adopted terroristic methods and thus provided a justification for increased persecution of socialism.

Foreign affairs played into the hands of the anti-liberal forces. Since Austria–Hungary had maintained neutrality during the Franco–Prussian War and had accepted Prussian hegemony in the new Reich, there was no longer any need for Bismarck to fear the Empire; on the contrary, he now needed Austria as an ally against France. His support at the Congress of Berlin (1878), which ended the Russo–Turkish War, for the Austrian occupation of Bosnia–Herzegovina paved the way for the defensive treaty between the two countries which was concluded in the following year and was expanded into the Triple Alliance when Italy also joined in 1882. This policy was not to the liking of the liberals (who opposed the Bosnian adventure), and with the support of the crown they were replaced by the Taaffe cabinet which rested on a combination of feudal magnates from Bohemia, the Polish gentry, conservative Czechs, and German and South Slav Clericals.

Thus the year 1879 ushered in a period which can best be described with the title of one of Karl Renner's earlier works, 'The struggle of the Austrian nationalities for power in the State', or, less elegantly, in Taaffe's words, a policy of 'muddling along'. From now on governments depended on transient groupings of parties and nationalities, usually including Poles and clericals, sometimes Czechs, for their majorities. These divergent interests prevented any kind of clear-cut decision, for every concession a particular group wrung from the government resulted in demands for similar concessions elsewhere, or else for 'compensation'. That in spite of fundamental political and national divisions Austria still continued to be governed efficiently was due to the unsung labours of the civil service; that legislation kept in step with requirements the country owed to its numerous and intelligent jurists; and that the economy, science and technology developed rapidly, as if to catch up on missed opportunities, was the result of international contacts and pressures. Of the rich story of Austrian life up to the outbreak of the Great War we shall consider only those aspects which have a direct bearing on the events of 1914–18 and on the problems of the First Republic.

The defeat of liberalism brought a new element on to the parliamentary scene: the modern mass parties. A series of reforms of the franchise, one per decade, was designed to activate the petty-bourgeois following of the clericals and their allies both among Germans and the nationalities; thus the reform of 1882 which brought in all those (males) who paid 5 florins per annum in direct taxes, a sum which was lowered to 4 florins in 1896, when provision was made for an additional seventy-two members to be elected on a general franchise as distinct from the privileged franchise of the four traditional curias. As a result of socialist pressure, and no doubt frightened by the first (abortive) revolution in Russia in 1905, the Beck government in the following year introduced universal (male), equal, direct, and secret suffrage (although constituencies were arranged in such a way that the Germans, while numbering about 30 per cent of the total population of Austria, were assured of 45·2 per cent of the seats in Parliament).

The beneficiaries were at first right-wing parties preaching radical, anti-capitalist policies. The German nationalists, on the basis of a radical programme adopted at Linz in 1880, assumed influence and notoriety under Georg von Schönerer, who openly professed his loyalty to the Hohenzollern Emperor in Berlin as against the Habsburg Emperor in Vienna. He started a 'Los von Rom' (away from Rome) anti-clerical agitation in order to facilitate union with the Protestants of Prussia and reviled the Jews, and even though his movement lost ground after about 1900, it is a measure of his success that, Pan-Germanism apart, his great rival, Karl Lueger, adopted much of his social demagogy and anti-semitism for his 'Christian Social Party'. Not surprisingly, Hitler paid his tribute to both men in *Mein Kampf*.

Also to benefit from the widened franchise were the Socialists. Kept down by vicious legislation and judicial terror, and bitterly divided among themselves, they were at last given leadership and a sense of direction by Victor Adler, a young Jewish doctor whose humanitarian instincts were roused by the condition of the working class which he encountered in the course of his profession. Founded as the Social Democratic Workers' Party in 1889, they gained 14 seats in the parliamentary elections of 1897 on a restricted franchise, and eighty-seven on the universal franchise ten years later. But such was the force of national feeling in Austria that even this party, in spite of its theoretical internationalism, had to be organized as an alliance of autonomous national parties, and at its Brno Conference in 1899 it adopted a programme of national autonomy for the peoples of Austria–Hungary. This did not prevent a split in the Czech section of the party, in 1911, between those who, in common with non-socialist Czechs, wanted no lead from Vienna, and the rest who preferred continued co-operation.

For the question of national rights became ever more urgent, and the political upheavals in the Parliament at Vienna were reflected in the situation existing in the Crown Lands. The few concessions offered after 1879, such as the re-establishment of bilingual administration in the Bohemian lands, and of Polish administration in Galicia, and even the division of the Charles University in Prague into a Czech and a German university, could not prevent the new national and social radicalism from deadlocking business in the Diets – and eventually in the Vienna Parliament, where the new franchise provided Czechs and others with innumerable occasions for obstruction. That matters were even worse for the nationalities in the Hungarian half of the Dual Monarchy was irrelevant to those represented in Vienna; against furious German opposition they demanded from the government the satisfaction of their national *and economic* needs.

But this was the last thing the government was able and prepared to do. On the throne since 1848, Francis Joseph had grown old and tired, incapable of the mental effort required to see the alternatives and of the energies needed to decide on a policy. In the 'Lands of the Bohemian Crown', the antagonism between Germans and Czechs might have been overcome by the solution which worked in Moravia and which was 'cultural autonomy', but neither side produced a man great enough to fight for it. The situation of the South Slavs was even more complicated, for they were divided up between Austria and Hungary, with Bosnia–Herzegovina under joint administration. Here Serbia was actively encouraging dissident tendencies, while Russia provided the Pan-Slav ideology. It may be that Archduke Francis Ferdinand knew the solution when he dreamt of a 'trialist' organization replacing the dualist system, although his unlovable, bigoted, and reactionary nature made him an unlikely saviour of the Empire, even if he had not been assassinated at Sarajevo.

For the real key to a settlement did not lie in the South, where a pacific and constructive policy could have retained the loyalty of the Catholic, anti-Serb Croats and Slovenes, but in the North, where industrialization had raised Bohemia and Moravia to the Austrian level of economic importance and prosperity and the Czech demand for autonomy had become ever more persistent. Unfortunately for them – and for all the Danubian nations, as it turned out subsequently – their economic position, based on great mineral wealth and a skilled and industrious population, and the high rate of investment in the mining and engineering industries, made them far too valuable for Vienna to contemplate a genuine partnership. As late as 1911 Otto Bauer had warned: 'Austria will become a federation of autonomous nations, or it will cease to exist';[9] three years later she had started on her road to extinction.

[9] Otto Bauer, op. cit., p. 46.

Chapter 2

The End of the Monarchy

AFTER THE ALARUMS AND excursions of the sixties and seventies the Empire settled down into a pattern largely devised by Bismarck. Bound to Germany by the treaty of 1879, the Habsburgs abandoned all aspirations beyond southern and eastern Europe. The Triple Alliance of 1882 brought Italy into the fold, while the Mediterranean Treaty of 1887 was a token of Austria's interest in the maintenance of the *status quo* in the eastern Mediterranean. The renewal by Austria of the Three-Emperors' League, with Germany and Russia, in 1881 and 1884, and treaties with Serbia (1881) and Romania (1883), underlined her new role in the East and south-east. In fact, relations with Russia, which had been seriously strained in the eighties, improved in the nineties and made possible two agreements on Balkan questions in 1897 and 1903. What, then, went wrong with this system of defensive pacts and agreements which were to have guaranteed stability and peace?

The Central Powers blamed the Franco–Russian Alliance of 1894, the French blamed the policy of Bismarck (though he had left office in 1890); others blamed military alliances, armaments and their manufacturers; Lenin blamed capitalist imperialism; and psychologists the pugnacity of human nature. But, as A. J. P. Taylor has pointed out,

> The worst of such general theories is that they will explain almost anything. The very things that are blamed for the war of 1914 – secret diplomacy, the balance of power, the great continental armies – also gave Europe a period of unparalleled peace . . . If we are going to probe far back into history, it is no good asking, 'What factors caused the outbreak of war?' The question is rather, 'Why did the factors that had long preserved the peace of Europe fail to do so in 1914?'[1]

There is no answer to this question that would command general acceptance. In the particular case of Austria–Hungary it was undoubtedly the shortcomings of Court and government, aristocratic

[1] *The Listener* (12 August 1954).

46

indolence and racial arrogance, the determination to teach that upstart Serb nation a lesson; it was not anticipated that a local police action would be swamped in a general war of the powers.

When in 1908 Austria turned the occupation of Bosnia–Herzegovina into annexation she used the revolution of the Young Turks as an excuse; a more valid reason was the hostility of Serbia which the new dynasty of the Karageorgević (1903) had turned from an economic dependency of the Empire into a fiercely nationalist state. While the Bosnian crisis deepened the rift between Triple Alliance and Triple Entente, Serbia's success in the Balkan War of 1912 further heightened her self-assurance. But this is not to say that she bore any responsibility for the events of 28 June 1914 when Francis Ferdinand and his wife were shot dead in Bosnia. Their very presence was a provocation of the Serbs, but far from being encouraged, the young Bosnian Serbs who plotted and executed the assassination were a serious embarrassment to the Serb government which was only just recovering from the last Balkan War and had not yet absorbed the newly-gained lands. The Austrian decision to punish Serbia, whatever her excuses and apologies, was the first step to world war, and it was taken by Count Berchtold, the Austro–Hungarian Foreign Minister.

He needed his ally's approval, and on 5 July William II agreed; Austria must act against Serbia, he said, even at the risk of war with Russia. Now William often said very foolish things, but that Bethmann Hollweg, his Chancellor, also approved, without seeking counsel and weighing the consequences, places an even greater responsibility on this man, for without German support Austria would not have dared to move, especially since Serbia agreed to nearly all the demands in the Austrian ultimatum. Of course the Germans were bluffing; they believed that the Russians would let Serbia be chastised, because their army could not be properly equipped until 1917 and the French army was in process of reorganization, while the German army was at the height of its strength.

On 28 July Austria declared war on Serbia, and two days later Russia decreed a general mobilization. This was little more than a diplomatic gesture, for her armies would not be ready for at least six weeks, and in any case Russia had no aggressive plans in Europe. On the other hand, she could not allow the Balkans, and so Constantinople and the Straits, to be controlled by the Central Powers. Now Germany asked Russia to stop mobilizing, and, when she refused, declared war on her on 1 August. At the same time France was asked for a pledge of neutrality and the surrender of her principal fortresses as security; her evasive replies led to a declaration of war on her also. Germany was bent on getting the first blow in, following the lines of the famous Schlieffen Plan, according to which Germany must knock out France in the first six weeks and then turn all her power against Russia. To get at the French, the German armies had to go through Belgium, a neutral country; and it was the invasion of Belgium which brought Great Britain into the war – a nation to which the German generals had never given a thought. Eventually what was planned as a short, sharp Balkan campaign turned into a world-wide conflagration.

Austria's contribution to the cause of the Central Powers is a matter for debate. The first Austrian offensive against the Russians failed; the Tsarist armies swept into Galicia, but could be prevented from continuing into Hungary, and were in fact thrown back in the spring of 1915. As in the West, the fighting here developed into a war of position on several sectors of the front and over considerable periods of time, which even the great Brussilov offensives in Galicia and the Bukovina in the latter half of 1916 could not change. For the rest of the war the Eastern Front was dominated by the Germans, militarily and politically; there were divisions over the future of Poland, which the Central Powers had proclaimed an independent kingdom (November 1916); peace with the independent Ukraine and the promise of grain deliveries seemed to offer a much-needed respite (February 1918); and the Treaty of Brest-Litovsk (March 1918) imposed on the new Bolshevik régime bore the mark of the German victors, with Austria–Hungary as a mere bystander.

In the South, the main campaign was not concluded until the end of 1915, when Serbia and Montenegro admitted defeat. Bulgaria had joined the Central Powers in 1915, while Romania joined the Allies in the following year, both in the hope of acquiring territories their neighbours held. Italy, likewise, had taken almost a year before she abandoned her neutrality; the Allied offer of the Brenner frontier with Austria, Istria, and parts of Dalmatia decided the issue. Here, too, even the bloodiest battles produced few results, although it took Allied reinforcements to prevent an Italian rout after the great Austrian victory at Caporetto in October 1917. By the time of the Armistice, on 3 November 1918, even the Austrian front against Italy was crumbling.

It was inevitable that as the likelihood of a quick victory receded and a long war of attrition loomed ahead, and the Germans, moreover, let their Austro–Hungarian allies feel their superiority, despondency spread among the people. Arthur Henderson's famous dictum that 'while Germany has failed to conquer her enemies, she has conquered her allies'[2] was appreciated by politicians and even by

[2] Quoted in *The New Europe* (18 January 1917), p. 30.

members of the new Emperor's entourage. In November 1916 Francis Joseph I had at last been buried and Charles I found himself faced with a desperate situation. The war exacted a heavy toll and conditions in the industrial regions became ever more difficult. With Parliament suspended since March 1914 by the premier, Count Stürgkh, strict censorship of the press, and close supervision of all political activities, the task of the labour leaders to counteract the growing radicalization of the masses was not made any easier; the assassination of Stürgkh by Friedrich Adler, radical son of the socialist leader, in October 1916, had been a warning for the ruling class, which the events in Russia further underlined.

Supported by his Foreign Minister, Count Czernin, the young Emperor made several honest but ineffectual attempts to find a way out of the war for his country. Contact was established with Clemenceau, who was connected by marriage with a prominent liberal family in Vienna; Prince Sixte of Bourbon-Parma, brother of the Empress and an Allied officer, acted as intermediary between Paris and Vienna; Count Mensdorff had conversations with General Smuts; and Austrian and French agents continued to meet on Swiss soil until the end of February 1918. All this is often quoted as evidence of Charles's pacific intentions. What is rarely mentioned are the terms which the Austrian government proposed and which were either unacceptable or came too late. Caught in the web of a complicated domestic power structure, with the forces of class and nationality delicately poised, constantly exposed to the blackmailing tactics of the Magyar gentry, and now subjected to the dictates of the German High Command, the various diplomatic exchanges with the neutrals, Pope Benedict XV, and President Wilson, in retrospect look like the last desperate struggles of drowning men. The increasing strength of the Western democracies, the elemental force of the national movements, and the new challenge of Russian socialism were more than a match for Habsburg diplomacy.

The Emperor's belated offer, in his Manifesto of 16 October, to reorganize the Austrian half of the Empire on a federal basis no longer interested the nationalities, since Wilson had already recognized the Czecho-Slovak National Council as a belligerent government. Only the Magyars acted: they declared Hungarian independence in personal union with Austria. Wilson's note of 20 October, which stipulated independence for all the Austro–Hungarian nations, sealed the fate of the Empire. On the following day the German members of the Austrian Parliament (elected in 1911) met in the *Landhaus* in Vienna and constituted themselves as the 'Provisional National Assembly of the independent State of German-Austria'. Its three presidents, representing the German-nationalist,

the Christian Social, and the Social Democratic parties, together
with twenty members formed the 'State Council' which carried out
the functions of a Head of State, as well as those of a government,
until, on 30 October, a cabinet of 'state secretaries' under Karl
Renner as 'state chancellor' was formed. In the next few days,
Count Michael Károlyi was to head a government of an independent Hungary, and a Czechoslovak and a South Slav state came
into being. Thus, as Gordon Shepherd wrote, 'the boldest blueprint
ever drawn up in the Hofburg to rebuild the Empire was used
instead as its demolition order'.[3] The Emperor withdrew from
Vienna, declaring that he wished for 'no share in the business of
government', and on 11 November offered to accept in advance the
form of government German Austria wanted to adopt. Thereupon
the National Assembly on the following day proclaimed Austria a
democratic republic, and until 1934 the Twelfth of November was
celebrated as Austria's national day.

Unlike the new national states of the Northern and Southern
Slavs, the new Austria had in fact nothing to celebrate: she had not
suffered national oppression and had accepted the dynasty as her
traditional head. Only the left wing of the Social Democrats – part
of which now broke away from the parent body and formed the
Communist Party – had entertained republican views; the right-
wing leadership, notably Adler and Renner, had so far adapted
themselves to the existing order that the description of them as 'His
Imperial Royal Majesty's Social Democrats' ('k.u.k. Sozialdemo-
kraten') was not entirely undeserved. Now, however, when the
dynasty ceased to have any useful function, and the desperate
masses of returning soldiers and starving townspeople needed an
explanation for their undeserved suffering and a symbol of hope for
the future, the dynasty – which was soon to be expelled from the
country – provided the one, and the Republic the other.

It was different with the right-wing parties and their following,
who had identified themselves, albeit with reservations on particular
issues, with the Empire and the social order it represented. Monarchist sympathies remained strong with the peasantry and the petty
bourgeoisie, who were frightened by the Marxist terminology and
the radical policies of the Socialists; capitalists, landowners, and
investors mourned the loss of their properties in the succession states,
and together with the aristocracy – which was deprived of its
privileges and titles – the bureaucracy, and the officer class, they
hoped for the restoration of their former glory. They were not
prepared to accept the responsibility of the Empire for the national
and social revolutions which had broken out all around them, but

[3] Gordon Shepherd, *The Austrian Odyssey* (London, 1957), p. 67.

instead blamed the Allies for having wantonly and deliberately destroyed Austria–Hungary. This allegation, which has even been repeated by historians in other countries, deserves refutation.

Allied War Aims

There is ample evidence in the mass of documentation now available that the disruption of the Habsburg Empire formed no part of the policy of the major Allies throughout the greater part of the war. As Professor Lord, an American historian, noted:

> The Allies had certainly had little serious intention of disrupting Austria. . . The traditional belief that Austria was a 'European necessity', the illusion that she could serve as a bulwark against the expansion of Germany towards the south-east or of Russia towards the Adriatic, the hope that she might be detached from Germany and persuaded to make a separate peace, the fear that the disappearance of the monarchy would lead only to the 'Balkanization' of Central Europe and to chaos worse confounded – such ideas seem to have predominated at London, Paris, and perhaps Washington, even down to the last year of the war.[4]

There was no specific reference to Austria–Hungary in statements issued by the British and French governments in November and December 1914. By the Treaty of London with Italy in April 1915 the Allies committed themselves to satisfying Italian territorial demands, and this seemed reasonable to Colonel House, who had made a study of the European situation for President Wilson and mentioned as reasonable peace terms 'an independent Poland' and 'the cession of Italian-speaking regions' to Sir Edward Grey.[5]

In the winter of 1916–17 a German approach caused President Wilson to request a detailed statement of war aims from both sides, and the Allied reply listed among other points 'the liberation of Italians, Slavs, Rumanians and Czecho-Slovaks from foreign domination', but what precisely this meant is not clear. It could presumably be interpreted as some kind of autonomy inside Austria–Hungary, for Lord Robert Cecil had stated in the Commons as late as 24 August 1917 that Britain was 'not pledged to the *form* of liberation'.[6] *The New Europe*, however, a journal devoted to the

[4] C. H. Haskins and R. H. Lord, *Some Problems of the Peace Conference* (Cambridge, 1920), pp. 206–7.
[5] C. Seymour, *The Intimate Papers of Colonel House* (London, 1926), II, p. 170.
[6] H. W. V. Temperley (ed), *A History of the Peace Conference* (London, 1921), I, pp. 171–2.

cause of the oppressed nationalities, had no doubt that the disruption of the Empire was in fact 'implied in a whole series of public pledges and private engagements',[7] while a Foreign Office memorandum submitted in the winter of 1916 discussed the following possibility:

> Let the Slav provinces of Austria constitute themselves into a Southern Slav state; let the German provinces of Austria be incorporated in the German Empire; let Bohemia be linked up to Poland; and let Hungary be formed of the purely Magyar portions of the country into an independent State . . .[8]

That this was not government policy, however, is shown by Lord Bryce's request to Colonel House a week later:

> If there were a chance that Germany would yield up Lorraine, and Austria the Trentino, and the Turks Armenia, he would be glad to know of it. These, he felt, were the concessions essential to stability and security in Europe.[9]

Similar differences of opinion as existed in government circles in London and Paris characterized the situation in Russia. The first proclamation to the peoples of Austria–Hungary issued by the Commander-in-Chief after the outbreak of war spoke only of 'the restoration of law and justice' and expressed the wish that the Habsburg peoples might prosper and 'live in peace and amity with their neighbours'. On 14 September 1914 Foreign Minister Sazonov informed the British and French ambassadors that he wanted to see Austria become a trialist state consisting of the hereditary lands of Austria and the kingdoms of Bohemia and Hungary, the monarch to be Emperor of Austria only, and king of the other two lands. The Tsar, on the other hand, as early as November 1914 considered the dissolution of Austria–Hungary necessary.[10] This was also the view of the new democratic government in March 1917, for whom Foreign Minister Milyukov declared:

> The establishment of the Czechoslovak State will set a limit to the aggressive German plans towards the Slav Countries. German Austria, as well as Hungary, must be kept within its ethnographical frontiers. The Italians will be united with Italy, the Rumanians with Rumania, and the Ukrainian territories will

[7] *The New Europe* (18 January 1917).

[8] D. Lloyd George, *The Truth about the Peace Treaties* (London, 1938), I, pp. 31 ff.

[9] Seymour, op. cit., II, p. 422.

[10] Merrit Abrash, 'War Aims toward Austria-Hungary; the Czechoslovak Pivot', in *Russian Diplomacy and Eastern Europe 1914–1917* (New York, 1963), pp. 78–123.

coalesce with our Ukraine. The natural problems propounded by history demand also the unification of all the Yugoslav regions.

Edward Beneš, subsequently Foreign Minister and then President of Czechoslovakia, who claims this declaration as a success for Czech exile diplomacy, was less successful in Italy, where Foreign Minister Sonnino told him as late as October 1917 that 'Italy was not concerned with dividing up the Habsburg Empire'.[11]

When on 4 December 1917 President Wilson recommended to Congress a declaration of war on Austria–Hungary he spoke of her as 'a vassal of the German Government' and of the need to deliver her peoples 'from the impudent and alien dominion of the Prussian military and commercial autocracy'. He stressed, however, that he did not wish to 'impair or to rearrange' the Empire, but simply to see 'that their affairs are left in their own hands in all matters, great or small'.[12]

The year 1918 opened with Lloyd George's statement of British war aims on 5 January when he denied that Britain was fighting to 'destroy Austria–Hungary', but admitted that in his view 'the consent of the governed must be the basis of any territorial settlement in this war.' As with President Wilson, the 'break-up of Austria–Hungary is no part of our war aims... [but]... genuine self-government on true democratic principles [must be] granted to those Austro-Hungarian nationalities who have long desired it.'[13]

This speech, Wickham Steed wrote, was made 'under the influence of the pro-Austrian tendencies in England', but was not to be taken seriously:

> An hour after making this speech, and before its text was available, Mr Lloyd George sent for me. 'I have not been able to go as far as you would like about Austria,' he said, 'but you will find that my speech goes a good way; and, for tactical reasons, it is important that it should not be opposed in the press. There is a good deal of tactics in it and a little Bolshevism, but, on the whole, I think you will find it sound.'[14]

And Beneš was told by Bissolati, an Italian Minister, that as early as September 1917 Lloyd George had said to him that in this matter – the future of Austria–Hungary – his opinion was the same as Gladstone's. 'Austria has already done so much harm in the world that it must be destroyed.'[15]

[11] Edward Beneš, *My War Memoirs* (London, 1928), pp. 176, 505 n.
[12] Temperley, op. cit., I, pp. 171–2.
[13] ibid., p. 90.
[14] H. Wickham Steed, *Through Thirty Years* (London, 1924) II, p. 180.
[15] Beneš, op. cit., p. 212.

Yet Lloyd George quoted in his Memoirs what General Smuts had replied to Count Mensdorff's question about Allied intentions towards Austria–Hungary:

> We had no intention of interfering in her internal affairs, but we recognized that if Austria could become a really liberal Empire in which her subject peoples would, as far as possible, be satisfied and content, she would become for Central Europe very much what the British Empire had become for the rest of the world. She would become a league of Free Nations, very largely free from the taint of militarism, and she would have a mission in the future even greater than her mission in the past . . . peoples not now directly within her orbit might be drawn to her in future by the attractions of her new policy.[16]

A little Bolshevist tactics? Hardly, though it may have looked like it to the Austrians twelve months later. The fact was simply that Allied statesmen were divided on this as on many other issues. Whether he knew it or not, President Wilson agreed with Smuts rather than with Lloyd George when he uttered his famous and ill-fated Fourteen Points in the address of 8 January 1918, the relevant points of which are:

> *Nine.* A readjustment of the frontiers of Italy should be effected along clearly recognizable lines of nationality.
> *Ten.* The peoples of Austria–Hungary, whose place among the nations we wish to see safeguarded and assured, should be accorded the freest opportunity of autonomous development.

It was followed in Point Eleven by rather vague proposals regarding the Balkan states, whose future position was dependent on the uncertain future of the Empire. Point Eleven was the only paragraph shown to any representative of the Allied governments and was taken to Vesnić, head of the Serbian mission. He criticized it strongly because the break-up of Austria–Hungary was not demanded.[17]

> This news depressed the President. But, on the advice of House, he did not change his original statement. He could not advocate the partitioning of the Habsburg dominion without strengthening the bonds between Berlin and Vienna . . .[18]

---

[16] Lloyd George, *War Memoirs* (London, 1936), V, pp. 2464–5.
[17] C. Seymour, *American Diplomacy during the World War* (Baltimore, 1934), p. 287.
[18] G. S. Viereck, *The Strangest Friendship in History* (London, 1933), pp. 212–13.

But Wilson within a few months completely changed his mind. Perhaps he came to recognize that Austria could not be prised loose from Germany, that the exiled leaders of the nationalities had a case for independence, and that anyway the Allies needed the support of the eastern Europeans against both the Central Powers and Bolshevik Russia. On 29 May he announced that he had followed with great interest the proceedings of the 'Congress of Oppressed Nationalities' held at Rome in April, and when Austria tried to interpret this as a mere declaration in favour of autonomy, he stated on 28 June that in his government's view 'all branches of the Slav race should be completely free from German and Austrian rule'.[19]

The process of disintegration proceeded apace. After the recognition of the Czech National Council as a belligerent government Wilson refused an Austrian request for discussions on 'the basic principles of a peace', since he had made these abundantly clear; and when he finally received an Austrian request for an armistice to be followed by negotiations on the basis of the Fourteen Points, the 'Four Principles', and the 'Five Particulars', he replied on 18 October that Point Ten with its demand for 'autonomous development' no longer held good:

> Since that sentence was written ... the Government of the United States has recognized that a state of belligerency exists between Czecho-Slovaks and the German and Austro–Hungarian Empires, and that the Czecho-Slovak National Council is a *de facto* belligerent government, clothed with proper authority to direct the military and political affairs of the Czecho-Slovaks. It has also recognized in the fullest manner the justice of the national aspirations of the Yugo-Slavs for freedom. The President is therefore no longer at liberty to accept a mere 'autonomy' of these peoples as a basis of peace, but is obliged to insist that they, and not he, shall be the judges of what action on the part of the Austro–Hungarian Government will satisfy their aspirations and their conception of their rights and destiny as members of the family of nations.[20]

This, in fact, is the refutation of Austrian – and German – accusations that the Central Powers were induced to lay down their arms by the promise of fair terms, only to find that they no longer applied, or had been superseded by harsher conditions; they did *not* make peace when the Fourteen Points were published, but tried to improve their position for another nine months, during which new

[19] Temperley, op. cit., I, pp. 198–9.
[20] ibid., p. 371.

commitments were entered into by the Allied Powers and more sacrifices demanded of the peoples. Whether the peace settlement was wise or not, the leaders of the Central Powers cannot be acquitted of their share of the responsibility for it. If the Allies cannot be convicted of malice, there still remains the charge of negligence: they ought to have considered the consequences before they encouraged the ambitions of the exiled leaders of the nationalities and thereby incited nationalist passions which destroyed a large and viable state. This, too, is a view which will not stand up to closer inspection, as the records prove. The danger of 'Balkanization' loomed very large in all considerations of the Austrian question, and the memoirs of Beneš, Masaryk, and others describe very vividly the uphill struggle of the exiles before they were given a hearing. Only one thing was certain from the start: that the victims of Austrian aggression (like Serbia) and those nations that had thrown in their lot with the Allies (like Italy and Romania) would, in the event of victory, be compensated at the expense of the Empire; but this is what alliances are for.

We have already seen, in our discussion of Austria's constitutional history, what the obstacles were that prevented the various peoples from forming a real partnership; they were the very special traditions of the dynasty; the recognition of Magyar privileges; and the fierce conflict between the nationalism of the historic nations (Germans, Magyars) and of the 'unhistoric', newer nations like Czechs and South Slavs. It is still possible to agree with Professor Lord's definition of the secret of Habsburg success:

> The Emperor Francis I congratulated himself that his peoples were alien to each other and detested one another: each race could therefore be used as a jailer for some other race. 'From their antipathies springs order', he declared, 'and from their mutual hatred the general peace.' . . . Francis Joseph might adopt as an official slogan *Viribus Unitis*, but his practice was based much more upon the traditional maxim, *Divide et Impera*. . .[21]

But 'mutual hatred' in the nineteenth century was based on nationalism, and we must now turn to a consideration of this phenomenon.

The Problem of Nationality

When the Royal Institute of International Affairs in 1939 commissioned a report on nationalism from a study group, the authors saw fit to preface their findings with a 'Note on the Use of Words',

[21] Haskins and Lord, op. cit., pp. 204–5

which has not lost its usefulness with the passage of time.[22] They wrote that the term 'nation' could on the one hand be used synonymously with 'state' or 'country' to mean a society united under one government, even though the implications of 'nation' are never precisely those of 'state' since

> 'nation' calls attention to those persons who compose a political community, 'State' to the sovereign power to which they owe an allegiance and which holds sway over the territory which they inhabit.

But 'nation' could also be used to denote an aggregation of individuals united by other, as well as political, ties – ties commonly of race, religion, language, or tradition, and this sense of 'nation' is often contrasted with 'state'. Its derivatives also present no problems: 'nationality' as an equivalent of 'membership of a State' (and in the particular context of the Habsburg monarchy and its *Nationalitäten* 'a people potentially but not actually a nation'); and 'nationalism' as a consciousness, on the part of individuals or groups, of membership in a nation, or of a desire to forward the strength, liberty, or prosperity of a nation. In this book the English words 'nation', 'state', 'nationality', and 'nationalism' are used in precisely these senses, as are their exact German equivalents: *Nation, Staat, Nationalität,* and *Nationalismus.*

Difficulties arise over 'people' and its nearest – and far more emotive – German equivalent *Volk,* of which Hugh Seton-Watson has said that there is a vast difference between the Latin word 'nation', with its background of Roman Church and law and modern Enlightenment, and the Germanic word 'folk', with its suggestion of dark emotions, tribal loyalties, and Teutonic forests.[23]

'People', says the RIIA study, is a wider term which can cover, in addition to nation, the members of the political unit, the state, and of the ethnological unit, 'the race', as well as being an apt name for any aggregation of individuals which cannot be described by the other terms. But the term *Volk,* in addition to embracing the equivalents of 'the common people' and 'sovereign people', has in the last century acquired a special significance for which there is no equivalent in English (except in such terms as 'folk art' or 'folklore'). It denotes a body of people of common or similar physical (and therefore spiritual) descent with a subjective will to live together based on certain objective facts in their past. *Volk* is organic

[22] *Nationalism. A Report by a Study Group of Members of the RIIA* (London, 1963), pp. xvi–xx. Chatham House, London, is the headquarters of the RIIA.

[23] Hugh Seton-Watson, 'Fascism, Right and Left', *Journal of Contemporary History,* I/1 (1966), p. 189.

content, whereas *Staat* is merely form or organization. Even so, the noun *Volk* has many unemotive, neutral connotations, unlike the adjective *völkisch* which has become a political term *par excellence*. It all but replaced the term *national* as indicating a right-wing nationalist position, and acquired overtones of irrational mystical significance. The fact that, in German, *national* is a bookish word, looking and sounding foreign, while *völkisch* is of Teutonic origin and intelligible to the uneducated, may have contributed to its popularity in nationalist circles. (It is irrelevant in this context – and not wholly explicable – that the Nazi Party had two such foreign loanwords in its name, and used others for newly created offices and institutions.)

Modern nationalism derives from the French Revolution which placed the source of sovereignty in the people. It is a difficult case to counter, for in the last resort it rests on the simple notion of justice. 'Once the fact is granted', Albrecht-Carrié has written, 'that such a thing as, say, a Polish people exists, it would take some moral and intellectual contortions to proceed to contend that such a people should be ruled by Germans or Russians.'[24]

This 'universal' principle stresses the rational commitment of the individual to his polity – coupled with the recognition of the right of other polities to the same freedom. Unfortunately there is another strand as well: a romantic, often mystical conception of a nation's uniqueness, its special qualities and history, reinforced by the darker mysteries of blood and race. The perversion of the universal principle by the French Revolution – the application of force to 'free' others – led to the growth of the second strand in modern nationalism, notably in the German states where it eventually culminated in the frenzied mass-surrender to 'uniqueness' which was the Third Reich.[25] Only in this context is K. R. Minogue's definition of nationalism as 'a political movement depending on a feeling of collective grievance against foreigners'[26] or indeed the more far-reaching contention of an American psychologist 'that a common hate is one of the most frequently effective factors in making and uniting a nation' justified.[27]

Possibly because he was a Central European himself the late Professor Frederick Hertz, in his *Nationality in History and Politics*, has provided a very clear discussion of the issues which we encoun-

[24] R. Albrecht-Carrié, *The Unity of Europe. An Historical Survey* (London, 1966), p. 187.
[25] For a discussion of this conflict cf. J. L. Talmon, *The Unique and the Universal* (London, 1966).
[26] K. R. Minogue, *Nationalism* (London, 1967), p. 25.
[27] W. Pilsbury, quoted F. Hertz, *Nationality in History and Politics* (London, 1944), p. 37.

ter in a consideration of the concept of nation as it applies to Austria.[28] He rightly dismissed as inadequate all definitions based exclusively on *objective factors* like language, race, territory, etc., because all too frequently they could be used by nationalists for justifying annexations without regard to the people's wishes. The inadequacy of such objectivist theories has led to political theorists defining nationality as a community formed by the will to be a nation – *a subjectivist view* which 'corresponded to the striving of Liberals for freedom and to the democratic concept of a popular will expressed by the majority'. He quotes John Stuart Mill's definition of the essence of nationality as 'the mutual sympathy of its adherents' and Ernest Renan's 'daily plebiscite', a community of will, but while accepting the subjectivist definition insists on the need for very careful formulation. Mill's 'mutual sympathy' is more likely to take the form of contempt for the mass of the people, as in the case of Hitler, and devotion to national aims. (Or, as Minogue has pointed out, 'Nationalism . . . appears to be a love for an abstraction of the nation, and that abstraction may have none but the most tenuous connection with the concrete national life.'[29]) Likewise, the 'will to be a nation' is often not a rational desire but a multitude of feelings and vague ideas unsupported by objective factors like territory. Hence,

> the mere will does not yet make a nation. A nation cannot be founded like a company or a club. It is a community of fate . . . brought together and moulded by historical events and natural factors.

It follows that national consciousness is a specific kind of group consciousness, extending from a subconscious, latent state of mind to a clear-cut ideology (where, we might add, it becomes truly dangerous through its cultivation of the twin myths of the noble descent of the nation and of its great mission). Also, of the four principal 'national aspirations' listed by Hertz – unity, freedom, individuality, and distinction – it can be said that they, too, extend from the natural and reasonable to the intolerant and aggressive, as when freedom is held to include freedom from influences regarded as non-national or anti-national and leading to their suppression, or when the striving for distinction becomes a striving for domination.

If we now apply these concepts to Austria we find that while most objective factors point in the direction of Germany, subjectively there is both the 'daily plebiscite' and the 'mutual sympathy', a consciousness which is certainly not ideological. But 'national consciousness' is very difficult to define; it may be more helpful to

[28] ibid., pp. 11–21.　　　　　　[29] Minogue, op. cit., p. 23.

look at that equally elusive concept, 'national character'. In a very thoughtful essay Walter P. Metzger points to a curious conflict:[30] historians, he writes, will shy away from generalizations about national character because the subject has been contaminated by the claims of chauvinists and racists; if, following Edmund Burke, one cannot indict an entire people, then one cannot depict an entire people. Yet, in spite of our formal objections, we do refer to Frenchmen and Germans as 'distinctive aggregates of human beings', as members of groups to which psychological labels can be attached. Thus, 'scholarly practice accepts what scholarly theory renounces', but this may well be due to problems of definition.

Metzger quotes two typical objections: Boyd C. Shafer, who denies (in his critical study of nationalism, *Nationalism, Myth and Reality*) that character can be classified by nationality because men are basically alike; and Adam de Hegedus (in his critique of patriotism, *Patriotism or Peace*), because every individual is unique. Since both authors believe that there can be national art, drama, and literature, and national political institutions, why not then national character as well? 'The answer lies not in the realm of fact but rather in the realm of meanings: to these writers, character is, by definition, either idiosyncratic or universal.'

This preference for definition over classification raises the problem of the exact meaning of the term 'character', for which there has been a variety of suggestions through the years: 'social role and essential being, patterned traits and unitary traits, normative connotations and neutral connotations' – and *national* character subsumed all that character denoted, with the leap from the individual to the group bringing additional meanings into play: 'collective soul', 'folk genius', 'group mind', etc. Two attempts are quoted at fashioning conceptual models to illuminate these elusive terms. There are Kardiner and Fromm who, after revising the Freudian model which made no provision for a character common to social groups, came to the conclusion that, in Metzger's words, 'the common character is not the disembodied spirit of the group but a likeness in the makeup of the members . . . a product of ubiquitous socializing processes'.

The historian who is not also a psychologist can find no difficulty in accepting either this notion of 'likeness', or else, equally plausibly, Metzger's 'dramaturgical model' which says, in effect, that every society requires its members to play standardized roles depending on age, sex, class, and occupation. Though all societies have roughly

[30] Walter P. Metzger, 'Generalizations about National Character: An Analytical Essay', in Louis Gottschalk (ed.), *Generalization in the Writing of History* (Chicago, 1963), pp. 77–102.

the same goals, such as security, continuity, health, etc., they 'evolve different instrumental roles and weave different characteristic plots'. Put to the test of our knowledge of different nations, this is surely borne out by our experience: for a nation is more than a government and power system, it is also a community of people exposed to common experiences. Hence, 'growing up and living in one country rather than in another is a matter of characterological importance', but it is not the only (or necessarily the most significant) factor, for members of a nation are simultaneously members of regional, occupational, and other groups as well. No factor in isolation accounts for a national difference, but many factors in combination – religion, occupation, education, and the rest – do.

The historian of culture comes to very similar conclusions if he accepts the ethnologist's definition of culture as *all learned behaviour* or, more precisely, as 'patterns, explicit and implicit, of and for behaviour, acquired and transmitted by symbols, constituting the distinctive achievement of human groups'.[31] This concept of culture embraces not only the thematic patterns of art and religion but the structure of language, the character of science and philosophy, and finally 'modal personality types', that is, the averages on which different groups in a society tend to converge, which is Alex Inkeles' attempt to avoid the controversial concept of national character.[32]

To avoid difficulties of nomenclature alternative terms have been suggested to replace 'national character', such as 'national tradition'. Frederick Hertz criticizes this, for 'the mentality of a nation is not merely a matter of tradition, it is also conditioned by its social structure and by powerful individuals'. His own suggestion, though, 'national mentality', would also appear too narrow because stressing the rational or cerebral component. This is strange, for Hertz does not underestimate the instinctive and emotional aspects of modern nationalism, which he describes as a union of mental primitiveness and the instruments offered by the progress of science and technology, and of which he rightly says that, in spite of the intellectual character of most of the leadership, 'its doctrines as a rule denounced reason and exalted emotions and instincts'.[33] It is probably legitimate therefore to assume that nationalism is both a survival of primeval barbarism and the product of modern society – the self-assertion of 'the cave-man within us' (Hanbury Hankins), and 'a

[31] Clyde Kluckhohn, *Culture and Behavior* (New York, 1962), p. 73.
[32] Alex Inkeles, 'Some Observations on Culture and Personality Studies' in Kluckhohn and Murray (edd.), *Personality in Nature, Society and Culture* (New York, 1956), pp. 577–90.
[33] op. cit., pp. 41, 270–1.

social neurosis' (Caroline Playne), the 'growth of aggressiveness due to social disintegration' (Karl Mannheim).

At the end of their inquiry into the nature of nationalism the authors of the Chatham House report examined the relation of nationalism to other forms of group feeling: 'Is nationalism something *sui generis*, or is it merely a variant of the feeling which binds together Londoners, Trade Unionists, cricketers, or Wesleyan Methodists?' Their findings were that, while an obvious relationship existed in respect of the emotional impulse underlying both, the important difference lay in the peculiar features of a nation that distinguished it from other groups. For the nation is a community and not an association, and it covers a comprehensive range of human activities instead of confining itself to a single end, or related groups of ends. It has a width and depth lacking in other groups – except, possibly, the old type of *Weltanschauungspartei*, now rapidly disappearing, where ideology provided a closed system of practical politics and emotional uplift; it is concerned with power or influence *vis-à-vis* other nations similarly constituted, with which it has to co-exist. A nation is therefore a specific type of group, and a characteristic system of beliefs (or ideology) has grown up around it which is quite unlike that of any other group:

> The nation is the political unit, and nationalism the group symbol, of the present stage of civilization . . . those concerned with the conduct of international affairs in the present epoch can only take the nation as a fact (without assuming that it will be eternal) . . .[34]

'Staatsidee' and Pan-Germanism

The growth of national consciousness in a people normally finds its expression in a nationalist movement and, eventually, in the establishment of a power system based, no longer on the old principles of legitimacy, but on the national idea. In established states the same process can be observed, except that the national idea is used to buttress the existing power structure which may still rest on the legitimacy of the dynasty. Whenever this happens in states with heterogeneous populations the predominant race (often, though not necessarily, the race of the dynasty) demands of the other ethnic groups that they identify themselves with the 'people of state' in language and religion, or that they at least abandon their claim to separateness. Hugh Seton-Watson[35] quotes the classical examples of

[34] RIIA, *Nationalism*, pp. 329, 340.

[35] Hugh Seton-Watson, *Nationalism and Communism* (London, 1964), p. 20, and 'Nationalismus und Nationalbewußtsein' in *Österreichische Osthefte* 8/1 (January 1966), pp. 1–15.

the policy of russification under Alexander III and Nicholas II, and of magyarization in Hungary between 1867 and 1918, as well as the attempts at a *staatlicher Nationalismus* in the succession states after 1918, all of which failed. Against this there were the three empires which did not try to solve the problems of multi-national states by means of a secular ideology of state – the Ottoman and British Empires, and Austria–Hungary. The Habsburg Emperors, in the 'Austrian' part of their dominions, made no attempt to identify themselves with the nationalism of any one of their peoples: 'Loyalty to the dynasty remained until the end the only claim, and the only non-material bond holding the diverse subjects together.' The dissolution of the Empire destroyed the stability of Central Europe, and the new Austria 'was torn between the Danube basin to which it was linked by history and economic interests, and the German-speaking community whose culture it shared'. (It is not too far-fetched to discover a parallel in Britain's position between the Commonwealth and Europe, as indeed quite a number of traditions and experiences were common to both empires.) Lewis Namier's classic judgement:

> The Habsburgs were the one dynasty which had never linked up its fate with that of any single nation; they had a capital and a territorial base, but no nationality; they developed schemes territorially coherent, though devoid of all national idea. Their instincts were purely proprietary, the one meaning of an Austrian State to them was that they possessed it; to the outside world that it existed. For the few, and mostly interested, exponents of an Austrian State, its existence was an aim in itself; and this was the pivot of all that there was in the alleged Austrian *Staatsidee*[36] –

no longer strikes us, half a century afterwards, as quite so condemnatory as the author intended and his contemporaries took it to be. There were good historical reasons for this development, though. Commenting on the rejection of nationalism by the Habsburgs, Hugh Seton-Watson in a recent paper on 'Super-national Monarchy and National State'[37] pointed to the fact that in the old *Erbländer* (hereditary lands) an Austrian nation might well have grown up in the same way as a French nation developed in the lands of the French monarchy, for

the differences between Ile de France, Brittany, Burgundy and

[36] H. W. V. Temperley (ed.), *A History of the Peace Conference*, IV, p. 59.
[37] Read at the International Symposium 'Herbst 1918. Die Auflösung des Habsburgerreiches und die Neuordnung Europas' held at Vienna, 21–25 October 1968.

Languedoc in the fourteenth century were hardly less than the differences between Styria, Tyrol and Bohemia, and the methods used by the kings of France to bring new lands and peoples under their control were far more cruel than any used by the Habsburgs.

As a result of such methods French and English nations had grown around the French and English monarchies long before the eighteenth century developed the doctrine of the nation. No such process occurred in Austria, for

> the Habsburgs, preoccupied by the problems of Germany, Spain, Italy and the Netherlands, did not regard Austria and Bohemia as especially important. Requiring the support of subjects in so many lands, they could not afford to antagonize them by imposing a centralized state at the expense of regional autonomies. . . By the time of Joseph II it was too late to create a centralized state, let alone an Austrian nation: Czech, Hungarian, Italian and even Rumanian national aspirations were already a reality. All that could now be done was to put loyalty to the supernational dynasty above all else.

Unfortunately this construction did not stand up to the pressures of nationalism; as Michael Balfour observes, the dynasty

> signally failed to rouse a consolidating spirit of loyalty among the miscellaneous peoples inhabiting their domain. Less than a third of the Habsburg Empire was included in the German Confederation, set up as a loose association in 1815, and of the twelve millions which were so included, almost half were Slavs.[38]

The establishment of an Austrian *Kaiserreich* in 1804, and the formal demise of the defunct Holy Roman Empire through the abdication of Francis I in 1806, is now seen by some historians as the potential turning-point in Austrian history: shorn of her distant possessions and consolidated as a Central European power, Austria could now have severed her last remaining links with Germany. That this course was not adopted, and that Austria continued to interfere in German affairs – notably in obstructing the desire for German unity – until she was forcibly removed from the scene by Prussia, was to prove the fatal weakness in her new position. It gave rise to the *deutschnational* conviction that Austria had a part to play in Germany, and that this was prevented by external forces: Napoleon in 1806, Bismarck in 1866, and Clemenceau and Wilson in 1918. At the same time, opposition to Habsburg absolutism, and

---

[38] *The Kaiser and his Times* (London, 1964), pp. 16 f.

an understandable reaction to the relative backwardness and paro-
chialism of Austria, made the liberal bourgeoisie incline towards
Germany, while Francis Joseph I ('I am a German Prince') unwittingly gave support to this trend.

It is unnecessary in this connection to argue the point about the
preferment allegedly shown to the German-speaking people of
Austria – whether this was deliberate policy or, more likely, due to
their greater economic and intellectual power; nor is it material
whether the oppression, social and cultural, of the other nationalities was such as to warrant their increasingly militant attitude.
The fact is that the series of blows to Habsburg prestige and power,
leading to their expulsion from Germany and the loss of most of
their Italian dominions, coupled with the *Ausgleich* they were
compelled to conclude with Hungary, raised national passions to
such a point that the survival of the Empire began to appear in
doubt. Yet Michael Balfour's contention that 'any widespread
demand for self-government on a national basis was . . . in the long
run incompatible with the effective functioning and even the very
existence of the Austro–Hungarian state'[39] is valid only if appeasement of the Magyars (and of the *deutschnational* element in the
Empire) were placed above satisfaction of Slav aspirations for a
democratic federation.

Quite apart from these very real difficulties there is no evidence
that Court and government entertained any such reforming notions.
This is not to say, however, that no plans for the reorganization of
the Empire existed. The last few decades before the Great War
resounded with talk of federal solutions and measures of decentrali-
zation, and some legislation was even passed to meet the demands
of various ethnic groups. It is not without significance that Francis
Ferdinand, impatiently biding his time until death removed the
obstacle to the fulfilment of his ambitions, gathered round him
some very remarkable men who discussed and published plans for
imperial reform. A recent study by a conservative historian, after a
survey of the various projects discussed, even goes so far as to suggest that the Empire was on the best way to a complete reorganization when external forces intervened and destroyed what could have
become a pillar of strength and stability in Central Europe. . . .[40]

But apart from these scholarly exercises there were two significant
political forces in the Empire which had clear notions of the reme-
dies needed to cure its ills. That their plans were mutually exclusive
is beside the point; they seemed plausible at the time, and either

[39] op. cit., p. 26.
[40] Wilhelm Böhm, *Konservative Umbaupläne im alten Österreich* (Vienna,
1967).

could have been realized. These forces were the Social Democrats
with their programmes of national autonomy, either territorial or
personal, and the Pan-Germans who, inspired by the growing power
of the Hohenzollern Reich across the border, dreamt of the union
of the Teutonic peoples against their enemies – Jews, clericals, and
Slavs.

Languages and Peoples of the Habsburg Empire, 1867–1918

While the strength of national feeling is understandable in a
people living under foreign rule, it is not so clear why some German-
speaking Austrians should have developed such a particularly
aggressive and irrational creed, unless we consider, with Hugh
Trevor-Roper, nationalism as the expression of wounded nationality:

> the cry of men who have suffered great national defeat, or whose
> nationality is denied, or who live insecurely on exposed national
> frontiers, surrounded, and in danger of being swamped, by
> foreigners . . . In Germany, it is on the raw edges that we find

chronic nationalism, among the Sudetenlanders and the Austro-Germans, insecure among Czechs and South Slavs, or the Baltic Germans, insecure among the North Slavs.

And he notes a curious detail:

> All the great nationalist leaders have been only half-national themselves. Their followers may be – generally are – true nationals. . . But the leaders, it is well known, tend to be marginal in their nationality, perhaps inspired by secret doubts of their nationality. The leader of the Irish nationalists in the last century was wholly English, in this, half-Cuban. Napoleon was not French nor Stalin Russian. Hitler was an Austrian, not a German. . .[41]

Whatever the number of genuine Nazis among the 530,000 party members in Austria by the end of the Second World War, there can be no doubt that German Austria was the original home of a particularly virulent and cruel brand of National Socialism, not because of some particular 'national characteristic', but because of her ethnic situation.

There is yet another aspect which explains the German-nationalist fixation of many Austrians: this is the psychological effect of the widespread intermarriage between the races both in Vienna as the centre of the multi-national monarchy and in the regions bordering on Slav areas of settlement. The Viennese psychologist Wilfried Daim has pointed out that

> the children of such 'mixed' marriages can either *productively* overcome or *pathologically* be broken by the in-between position in which they find themselves. They overcome it productively if they love both peoples as they love both their parents. . . But there is also the pathological side of their position which manifests itself in complete identification with one side only, and a sense of shame with regard to the other side. Paradoxically, such people become the apostles of pure race, of keeping German blood pure – even if they bear a Czech or Ukrainian name.[42]

Hitler, himself of mixed origins, is a case in point: his hatred of Vienna, that 'Stadt der Blutschande'[43] and 'Rassenbabylon', is a

[41] H. R. Trevor-Roper, *Jewish and other Nationalism* (London, 1962), pp. 12–13, 20–21.
[42] Wilfried Daim, 'Die Nation – in österreichischer Sicht', in *Die österreichische Nation: Zwischen zwei Nationalismen* (Vienna, 1967), p. 19.
[43] An interesting example of Hitler's linguistic weakness: *Blutschande* means 'incest', which is the very opposite of what he meant – 'the shameful pollution of German blood with foreign'.

typical example of the need to overcompensate for an imagined blemish.

Historians of National Socialism have recently been looking into the peculiarly Austrian origins of the creed and its movement, particularly Whiteside in his useful account of the forerunners of Adolf Hitler's party.[44] Oddly enough, while most writers correctly see the origins in the unresolved national conflicts of the Empire, and especially in the conflict between Germans and Czechs, they adopt a narrowly materialistic interpretation which, moreover, often draws conclusions from insufficient evidence. It is of course true that one of the causes of Sudeten German associations (of workers and others) was the need to protect their interests against the influx of Czechs into German areas; but these interests were not always economic ones. Only the traditional contempt felt by many Germans for Slavs in general, and in this case for the socially and culturally inferior Czech immigrants in particular, can explain the bitterness of the controversies about Czech schools, bilingual notices, and place-names. A predominant ethnic group favoured by tradition and government saw its privileges threatened by the rise of a competitor and national rival, which, moreover, had the advantage of greater numbers on its side. Nor is it always true that Czech workers came prepared to accept lower wages than the Germans; there is also the opposite evidence of new industries in Lower and Upper Austria importing skilled Czech labour as foremen and under-managers, with unskilled workers recruited from the German-speaking peasantry as their social inferiors (which, if current research bears out first impressions, may in part account for the strength of *deutschnational* traditions in Upper Austria).

But what began as a social movement soon adopted the ideologies of German nationalism, from cultural romanticism to naked racism. Francis L. Carsten has done well to draw attention to the German component in the early history of National Socialism, especially the influence of writers like Lagarde, who more than balance the specifically Austrian contribution. As early as 1853 Lagarde advocated increased German settlement in the non-Germanic territories of the monarchy; later he wrote that only the 'Germanization of the peoples on our eastern borders' and the separation of Russia from the South Slavs could ensure the survival of Austria, Germany's natural ally, as a viable state. But Austria, too, needed to be 'Germanized': 'We don't need to be kind to Czechs and similar people: they are our enemies and must be treated accordingly. . . .' All the Slavs, Czechs, Hungarians, and Jews

[44] Andrew Gladding Whiteside, *Austrian National Socialism before 1918* (The Hague, 1962).

'hate us because they know that our life is their death, because they know that without us they are incapable of civilized existence, and yet they will not admit our superiority. . . .'[45]

This was the spirit that animated the followers of Georg Ritter von Schönerer, the man behind the *Linzer Programm* of 1882 which expresses the *deutschnational* perspectives of the time: creation of an independent unit of those parts of the Empire which had belonged to the German Confederation; preservation of its German character with German as the only official language; and a customs union and a special treaty to strengthen the alliance with Germany. On the other hand, all connections with Hungary – except the dynastic one – were to be severed, Galicia to be given autonomy, and Bosnia and Dalmatia to be annexed by Hungary.[46] This programme, which also contained a number of social and economic points, would probably not have altered the course of German and Austrian history if it had been adopted; but it was at least a logical alternative to the socialist concept – except that this world of the Pan-Germans was doomed, as Carsten points out: even without the Great War the Germans in Cisleithania – a minority of 35 per cent – could not for long have resisted the rising tide of Slav nationalism. Schönerer's own hope for the collapse of the Empire, with the German provinces joining the Reich, was perhaps a little more realistic, but it would have deprived Germany of her one dependable ally in the Pan-German scheme of conquest. Thus, unwittingly, *Deutschnationalismus* in Austria worked against the German interest; but it did worse to Austria:

> In the Habsburg Monarchy with its mixture of races pan-German propaganda was bound to be a destructive force, and even among the German minority its influence was rather small. But the sons of the pan-German corps students of the 'nineties became the fanatical Nazi students after 1918.[47]

However, the authorities whose duty it should have been to seek solutions steadfastly refused to acknowledge a need for them: loyalty to the dynasty was all the government considered necessary. The academic speculations Francis Ferdinand encouraged in his own circle, in particular the concept of a trialist solution, would also in retrospect seem to have been doomed, even if Sarajevo had

---

[45] Francis L. Carsten, *Der Aufstieg des Faschismus in Europa* (Frankfurt, 1968), pp. 29–30.

[46] Quoted Peter G. J. Pulzer, *The Rise of Political Anti-Semitism in Germany and Austria* (New York, 1964), p. 151.

[47] Carsten, op. cit., p. 47. This work is an expanded version of *The Rise of Fascism* (London, 1967).

not occurred, by the extremely reactionary and illiberal philosophy of the heir to the throne.

Having sown the seeds, Schönerer was overtaken by the dynamics of a radical plebeian movement: in 1903 the *Deutsche Arbeiterpartei* was founded without him, but by former associates of his. Eventually, under the leadership of Rudolf Jung, this party, with its racist-nationalist and 'socialist' programme, became the *Deutsche Nationalsozialistische Arbeiterpartei* and eventually merged with the Nazi Party in Munich. The nationalist movement, from Schönerer to Hitler, contributed materially to the prevailing lack of faith in Austria coupled with the uncritical adulation of Imperial Germany. Inevitably, the attitude of the Czechs towards all Germans, whether of the Reich or of Austria, was one of hostility and fear.

Into this atmosphere Hitler was drawn when, as a child, he attended the *Realschule* in Linz; there he conceived his life's work which he described on page 1 of *Mein Kampf* as the 'reunion of the two German states':

> Deutschösterreich muß wieder zurück zum großen deutschen Mutterlande . . . Gleiches Blut gehört in ein gemeinsames Reich.[48]

The hapless schoolmaster who taught him German, history, and geography, *deutschnational* in outlook but a loyal Austrian, to his embarrassment found himself commemorated in *Mein Kampf* as the man who had influenced the young Hitler, but he steadfastly refused any distinctions or invitations from the pupil who had only lasted three years before he left under a cloud and who was now German Chancellor. But the young historian who has retraced Hitler's early moves and contacted surviving contemporaries has also discovered the source of many of his convictions and prejudices, and even of his terminology.[49]

Linz in 1900–04 was a stronghold of the *Deutschnationale*, which was due to the nearness of the Bohemian border and considerable Czech immigration. It was the town where concerts given by the Czech violinist Jan Kubelik led to violent demonstrations and the sermons of a Czech preacher, Father Jurasek, to fierce protests. In this atmosphere secondary schools were the centres of nationalist agitation, but Hitler left too young to have joined any of the students' associations – nevertheless, the fact that his teacher of

[48] 'German Austria must return to the great German motherland . . . People of the same blood belong in the same Reich.'

[49] Eleonore Weber-Kandl, *Hitlers Österreichbild*, phil. dissertation (Vienna University, 1965).

religious knowledge, a priest, was a very unpopular man, and that the master who failed him in French was a Jew may well have contributed to his anti-clerical and anti-semitic attitudes. In Vienna Hitler lived in the street where the editorial offices of the Schönerer paper, *Das Alldeutsche Tagblatt*, which he undoubtedly read every day, were situated. From this paper Hitler lifted all the more vituperative terms for Austria which are to be found in *Mein Kampf*: 'Leichnam', 'Staatkadaver', 'Völkerkonglomerat', 'Völkerbabylon', 'Völkerbrei', 'monströse Staatsleiche', etc. Here he acknowledged his indebtedness to Schönerer as well as to Karl Lueger, the popular Catholic leader, from whom he learned the art of addressing mass meetings.

The Socialist Alternative

Against the dynastic principle, which ignored race and nationality, and the Pan-German concept based exclusively on race, Austrian Social Democrats developed a coherent scheme which combined the Marxist notion of class relationships with the realities of racial feeling. The problems such a policy raised are best illustrated by reference to that other Social Democratic Party operating in a multi-national Empire and also deriving its political strategy from Marxist thought – the Russian party.

In the beginning, Marxism was the enemy of nationalism. When they wrote *The Communist Manifesto* it seemed to Marx and Engels that national differences were rapidly disappearing before the growth of international capitalism. The workers had no fatherland; against the bourgeois International they needed a strong workers' International. In so far as Marx recognized the existence of nations he adopted a Western political point of view; thus he opposed aligning the German-speaking Alsatians with the German instead of the French section of the First International, as this would substitute 'an artificial contrivance of arbitrary lingual connexions' for 'the actual state and national connexions'.[50] He was distinctly hostile towards the lesser nationalities: movements such as those of the Czechs and Irish seemed to him unprogressive and counter-revolutionary. But as his hopes for revolution in the advanced nations receded, he came to look more favourably upon national movements as a step in the right direction. By 1872 he admitted that 'special regard must be paid to the institutions, customs and traditions of various lands'. In 1875 he emphasized the national

[50] S. F. Bloom, *The World of Nations, a Study of the National Implications in the work of Karl Marx* (1941), pp. 19, 38, 41, 201, 92, 88, quoted Cobban, *National Self-Determination* (2nd edn, London, 1948), whose argument I am following in this section.

setting of the class struggle: socialism must achieve its victory first
of all in particular countries. It was the attitude of the later Marx
which led straight to the national theories of Lenin and Stalin, not
a 'remarkable breakaway' from, but a 'natural development' of,
Marxist thought.

German and western European socialism had on the whole
tended to ignore or underestimate the force of nationalism, regarding national movements as merely a by-product of the victory of
capitalism over feudalism, and therefore essentially reactionary.
Lenin, however, did not deny that nationalism was normally associated with the rise of the middle classes to power, or that the
nation-state was the characteristic political form of the capitalist
period – but this did not lead him to the simplistic conclusion that
all nationalist movements were to be condemned. He divided the
nations of the world into three categories. In the advanced capitalist
countries of the West the progressive national movement of the
bourgeoisie had long ended and had turned into oppressive régimes.
In eastern Europe and Russia bourgeois democratic and nationalist
movements were now in progress and should be supported – as
should the incipient bourgeois nationalism of the colonial world.[51]
In his polemic against Rosa Luxemburg's view that so long as
capitalism existed the right of self-determination was an illusion,
he criticized her condemnation of the separation of Norway from
Sweden, which she described as 'merely a manifestation of peasant
and petty-bourgeois particularism'. He likewise applauded the victory of the Serbs and Bulgars in the Balkan Wars as the destruction
of Balkan feudalism – just as, for similar reasons, towards the end
of his life Marx had favoured Irish nationalism. National freedom
was, of course, not an end in itself, but it was desirable as a step
towards the future proletarian revolution.

Thus in 1903 the Russian Social Democratic Labour Party advocated under his influence the right of all nations in Russia to self-
determination, and for similar reasons he opposed the war of 1914
in which he saw only Serbia representing a genuine nationalist
element, which, however, was of no real significance in the general
conflict of rival imperialisms. And finally, there were his repeated
assertions, in 1917 and 1918, of the right of nations to self-determination. But the leading specialist of the party was Stalin, whose
approach was more systematic and who provided a more elaborate
treatment of the question. Stalin's definition was 'A nation is not a
racial or tribal, but a historically constituted, community of people',[52]

---

[51] V. I. Lenin, *Selected Works* (1936), V. pp. 257–60; IV, pp. 252–3, 426 n.
[52] J. Stalin, *Marxism and the National and Colonial Question* (2nd edn,
1936), pp. 5, 8, 19, 31, 57.

which in effect was the political, Western interpretation of the basis of nationality without identifying the nation with the state: 'A nation is a historically evolved, stable community of language, territory, economic life, and psychological make-up, manifested in a community of culture.' This, while not applying to Switzerland or Canada, was true enough of Central and eastern European conditions. Understanding the nation in this sense, he proclaimed its right of self-determination: 'Nations are sovereign, and all nations are equal.'

He added two important qualifications, though: (i) national rights do not include the right to the maintenance of reactionary institutions; and (ii) he attacked the national programme of the Austrian Social Democratic Party adopted at Brno in 1899, which proposed to divide the nationalities in the Austro–Hungarian Empire into separate units, each with its national autonomy, based on cultural connections, that is, on personal nationality, and not on territorial contiguity. Stalin criticized this project as 'an absolutely unjustifiable substitution of national autonomy for self-determination of nations'. The distinction he drew between this brand of national autonomy, which he condemned, and regional autonomy, which he advocated, shows the essentially political nature of his conception of self-determination. Regional autonomy, he said, 'does not deal with a fiction deprived of territory, but with a definite population inhabiting a definite territory'.

This, it must be admitted, was a weak point in Karl Renner's proposals for the reform of the Empire which we shall have to consider in greater detail. It is interesting to note, though, that in recent years a controversy has arisen in the Soviet Union over Stalin's definition as against Lenin's. It is pointed out, for instance, that it was not by accident that Lenin only wrote of the community of language, territory, and economic life, whereas Stalin added 'psychological make-up manifested in a community of culture'. That Lenin praised Stalin's pamphlet on *The National Question* is held to be immaterial, for this does not imply endorsement of every detail. On the other hand, the psychological aspect seemed so important to Stalin that he included it, not only in his original pamphlet of 1913, but also in a letter of 18 March 1929 and finally in the 1946 edition of his Collected Works.

Soviet scholars now criticize Stalin for using 'psychological make-up' as a criterion for nationality, as if there were no psychological differences between people living in a capitalist as opposed to a socialist society, and secondly for equating psychological make-up with national character; whereas man's temperament is the result of natural conditions, his character – and this includes his national character – is determined by his position in the system of social relationships. That this is no mere academic disputation but an attack on 'bourgeois nationalists' who proclaim the immutability and indeed the further development of national differences, is evident from the conclusion which speaks of the Soviet people becoming a 'new international community' in ever closer co-operation with the 'socialist nations of the socialist world system', with whom, in fulfilment of Marxist–Leninist predictions, it will eventually merge in 'a fully-matured communist society'.[53]

No such long-term perspectives engaged the attention of the Austrians, however: they had to find a practical solution to a concrete situation, and the one proposal which still attracts the attention of historians today was contained in Karl Renner's *Der Kampf der österreichischen Nationen um den Staat* (1902).

For a long time the Social Democrats, in spite of their Marxist origins turned into a reformist party by Adler, fought to maintain a supra-national party and, with it, the multi-national Empire. The number of industrial workers was increasing in all nationalities, particularly among the Czechs, but there were Polish, South Slav, Italian, and (organizationally separate) Hungarian sections of the Social Democratic Party as well. At the first Congress of the all-Austrian party, at Brno in 1899, they adopted their famous 'Nationality Programme' which demanded the reorganization of the monarchy into a federal state based on autonomous areas, with full guarantees for the protection of minorities. 'We know that we shall have to live with one another in this Austria', said a Sudeten German delegate, 'and there is nothing else to do but to find a way to prevent the collapse of Austria and to enable its natives to live together.'[54] The enormous difficulties which any attempted implementation of this programme would have presented were not lost on two of the most brilliant minds in the party, Renner and Bauer, who between 1902 and 1908 continued to study the problems involved and produced the works that must count among the classics on the nationality question in the monarchy.

To Renner as to Bauer, nationalism was transformed class-hatred, and as such it blocked cultural and economic progress by creating political tension. To overcome this blockage, its driving force had to be confined to the only sphere where it was legitimate, that is, culture and communication, and to achieve this, the whole state-structure had to be reorganized into different administrative strata:

---

[53] *Woprosi Istorii* (Moscow), 6/1966; also issues 1, 4, and 7 of the same year, quoted *Ost-Probleme* (Bonn) 2/19, 27 January 1967.

[54] Josef Seliger, quoted Arthur G. Kogan, 'The Social Democrats and the Conflict of Nationalities in the Habsburg Monarchy', *Journal of Modern History*, vol. 21 (1949), p. 207.

autonomous cultural units; larger geographic-economic units cross-ing the national borderlines; and finally the central political struc-ture of supra-national government.

It was Renner's significant contribution to Social Democratic thinking on the national question that he went beyond the less sophisticated concept of *territorial autonomy* for the various national groups in the Empire and advocated the idea of *personal autonomy*. According to this the citizen belonged to an autonomous national association of his co-nationals, irrespective of his domicile, and these national organizations would have their agencies all over the Empire. The importance of the scheme lies in the fact, as Robert Kann has pointed out,[55] that 'in thus separating national rights from the premise of a majority status within any specific territory, Renner attempts to do away altogether with the concept of national minorities and the need for specific protection'. Because a citizen would not, in questions of national (i.e., ethnic) interest, be subject to the laws of a different ethnic group among whom he may happen to live, but to those of his own supra-territorial national organiza-tion, the national issue in the multi-national state could be solved without clear-cut national territories or borders. In any case it was obvious, in the specific Austrian situation of frequently interspersed ethnic groups, that territorial autonomy would either have required the recognition of minorities, or else would lead to the disregard of the national interests of splinter groups.

That Lenin and Stalin preferred the cruder solution of the Brno programme and rejected Renner's ideas as a dangerous version of bourgeois nationalism disguised in socialist verbiage was under-standable: only the politically and economically autonomous national unit provided a base for converting national conflict into class struggle, whereas Renner's scheme would make peaceful pro-gress feasible. For different reasons, the rising tide of nationalism also ran counter to a rational scheme which sought to substitute national rights in a supra-national state to the idea of a national state proper with its powerful appeal to the emotions – but the strength of national separatism in the years before the war, and even up to 1917, when loyalty to the dynasty was still remarkably wide-spread, must not be overestimated.[56]

The other great Austro–Marxist work, Otto Bauer's *Nationali-*

[55] Robert A. Kann, 'Karl Renner (December 14, 1870 – December 31, 1950)', *Journal of Modern History*, vol. 23 (1951), pp. 244–9. Cf. also the same author's *The Multinational Empire* (New York, 1950), II, pp. 167–77.

[56] Cf. Z. A. B. Zeman, *The Break-Up of the Habsburg Empire* (London, 1961) and K. R. Stadler, *The Birth of the Austrian Republic* (Leyden, 1966) for evidence of reforming, as against revolutionary, tendencies among the nationalities.

tätenfrage und der Staat (1908), also aimed at persuading the 'historic nations' – German Austrians and Magyars – to recognize the force of the demands for equality which their Slav subjects were raising and which only constitutional reform could satisfy. At the same time, however, he warned the Slavs not to base their policies on expectations of a collapse of the monarchy in an international war; their duty was to conduct the struggle on the basis of existing political realities, as it was the duty of the working class to conduct the class struggle within the multi-national Empire. The book was written under the impact of the Russian Revolution of 1905, which Bauer hoped would influence and accelerate developments in Austria–Hungary; but the onset of reaction under Stolypin, and the Dual Monarchy's subsequent actions, particularly the occupation of Bosnia–Herzegovina, disappointed such hopes.

Renner's scheme has been disparagingly referred to as 'an amalgam of pious hopes'; but the failure of the Habsburgs and their advisers to put these ideas into general practice reflects on them rather than on Renner. Likewise, the authors of the Chatham House study[57] argue from hindsight when they write:

> The extension of the functions of the State in the modern age over ever-increasing spheres of activity makes the separation between 'political' and 'non-political', which is the basis of Renner's plan, more and more Utopian.

We are, after all, considering the situation in the first years of the century when pressures of this kind had only just begun to appear, and we are discussing interim solutions, for, as the report says, 'by removing some vexed questions from the sphere of controversy, the scheme offers a prospect of reducing national antagonisms and thus of creating an atmosphere in which assimilation will become easier'. One is nevertheless tempted to agree with Kann that Renner's proposals were made 'too late, indeed, half a century too late. The era of Kremsier, to whose legal philosophy they are closely related, might have adopted them enthusiastically; the era of integral nationalism just passed them by'[58] – even if one feels that this formulation fails to indicate the responsibility of the dynasty for not even trying to counteract the force of nationalism.

Many years later Renner reverted to the controversy of his younger years, and in a collection of papers published posthumously under the title *Die Nation: Mythos und Wirklichkeit* not only pointed to the remarkable success of the 1906 constitution for Moravia, which incorporated the personality principle and prac-

[57] op. cit., pp. 290–91.
[58] Kann, *Multinational Empire*, II, p. 166.

tically ended national strife, but also summed up his criticism of
the peace settlement of 1919 in Central Europe:

> The former Empire never pretended to be a national state, but
> the new succession states were falsely proclaimed as such, and a
> large part of the domestic difficulties which beset them is due to
> this pretence. The peace treaties did not solve the problem of
> multi-national states but transferred it from each of the big
> powers to several small states. . . .[59]

Unfortunately, it was not only the constitutional structure of the
monarchy and the unwillingness of the government which prevented
the necessary reforms; the virus of narrow nationalism – fed by lack
of sensibility and even arrogance among the German-speakers –
entered the labour movement at a very early date, and it was in the
relations between Vienna and the Czechs that the split occurred.
Since the Czech Social Democratic political organizations had
secured their autonomy as early as 1897, the trade unions now began
to demand the same independence for themselves, which was rejected as absurd by the centre. A resolution of the Copenhagen Congress of the International in 1910 upheld the Austrian preference for
supra-national unions, but a majority of Czech Socialists disagreed
and formed a separate Czech Social Democratic Party, although a
minority of 'Centralists' remained loyal to Vienna up to 1918.

No comparable difficulties arose in Vienna's relations with the
other national groups, which lacked the backing of large organizations in an advanced state of industrialization. Accordingly, when
the war broke out which they had warned against and refused to
take any responsibility for, the Austrian Social Democrats felt they
could not stand aside. To some, 4 August 1914 was 'Der Tag der
deutschen Nation';[60] to others the need to defend Central Europe
against Tsarist absolutism was paramount; but all felt that, revolution being out of the question, they had to stand by the working
class in the hard times that lay ahead. The dilemma was, as so often,
best expressed by Victor Adler speaking of their decision to vote for
the war credits:

> Inconceivable for a German to act otherwise. Inconceivable for
> a Social Democrat to do it without great pain, without a bitter
> struggle with himself and his every feeling.[61]

[59] Karl Renner, *Die Nation: Mythos und Wirklichkeit* (Vienna, 1964), pp.
101, 91.
[60] 'The Day of the German Nation' – title of the leading article in the
Vienna *Arbeiter-Zeitung* on 5 August 1914.
[61] Otto Bauer, Introduction to Victor Adler, *Aufsätze, Reden und Briefe*
(Vienna, 1929), VI, p. xxix.

There was a remarkable measure of national unity which included all but a few members of the Left. To Socialists of all nations, Tsarism had always appeared as the spearhead of counter-revolution, the inveterate foe of democracy and socialism. In Austria in particular it was feared that a Russian victory would bring Tsarist autocracy right into the heart of Central Europe and would destroy the achievements of the labour movement for generations. In this they were in good company; had not Marx and Engels looked upon Austria as a bulwark against Russian expansion into Europe, 'the only factor', as Marx wrote, 'which justifies the existence of Austria as a separate state'? And in the first few days of war this Russian steamroller had crushed the Austrian defences and threatened the heartlands of the Empire; now it was everyone's duty to help defend the fatherland.

Even Bauer, who was soon to become leader of the Left and life-long antagonist of Karl Renner in the party, took this duty very seriously. He was called up as an officer of the reserve and immediately found himself on the Russian Front, was promoted and decorated, and taken prisoner by the Russians. When he returned to Vienna three years later, in an exchange of prisoners, the international situation and conditions in the country had changed considerably. What had not changed were the incompetence of the Habsburgs and the perspectives of the socialist leadership. The deepening crisis of the Habsburg Empire, Allied propaganda, and finally the democratic revolution in Russia had transformed the demands of the nationalities for reforms into a revolutionary struggle for complete freedom. Instead of recognizing this change, and seeking to retain whatever links could be preserved, the party continued the policy of 'national unity', fascinated as it was by Renner's advocacy of the virtues of the 'supra-national state'.

This, Renner claimed, represented a higher stage of development than the national state; history had overtaken the nationality principle which was now no more than a 'reactionary utopia', for the future belonged to the great economic units of national states. Against the national freedom movements of the Slavs he advocated an 'Austro–Polish solution', a 'greater-Croat solution', a federation of Central and south-eastern European states in a 'Middle-Europe' inevitably led by Germany. Not surprisingly, this policy was opposed, not only by the Socialists of the Slav nations, but also within the German Austrian leadership, and it was this group which Bauer joined after his return to Vienna, since he had by now become convinced of the inevitability of the national revolution, and the only remaining question was the attitude the Socialists were to adopt towards these aspirations.

The nationality programme of the Left, for which he was largely responsible and which recognized the right of the nations to self-determination, was bitterly attacked by Renner as late as May 1918: 'These ideas', he wrote in *Der Kampf*, 'are conceived in the spirit of Mazzini and not in the spirit of Karl Marx.' However, as so often before – or since – the nations preferred the heady wine of nationalist dreams to the sober calculations of philosophers and economists. This left Austria no other choice but to seek union with Germany, a policy which was closely linked with Bauer as the first Foreign Minister of the Republic of Austria.

The Last Act

The factors that transformed the national struggle into a policy aimed at complete independence and sovereignty were listed by Otto Bauer five years later, when he wrote his classic, *The Austrian Revolution*:

At first the object was national autonomy within a federation of States under the sceptre of the Habsburgs. But two events of historic importance brought about by the war enabled the Slav peoples to aim at complete national sovereignty and complete destruction of the Habsburg Empire.

The first of these events was the Russian Revolution. So long as Russian Tsardom remained intact, the existence of the Austro–Hungarian Empire was a historical necessity. Had it been over-thrown, the Slav States which would have emerged from it would inevitably have become vassal states of Russia. Its downfall would therefore have established the domination of Tsardom over Europe. The Russian Revolution effected a complete change in the sentiments of the peoples of the Habsburg Monarchy. . .

[Its victory] encouraged the national revolution of the Czechs, the Poles and the Yugoslavs. . . The defeat of the German Empire ensured the victory of this revolution. So long as the German Empire remained intact, the Slav peoples themselves could not desire the downfall of the Monarchy. Only when the power of the German Empire on the Western Front was broken by superior forces could the revolution of the Czechs, the South Slavs, and the Poles be crowned with complete victory.[62]

When the Austrian Parliament reassembled in May 1917 after three years of suspension, the national leaders came forward with their revolutionary programmes:

[62] Otto Bauer, *The Austrian Revolution* (London, 1925), pp. 72–3. This is a shortened version of the original *Die österreichische Revolution* (Vienna, 1923), from which some of the quotations are taken.

The Czechs greeted the Russian Revolution 'with boundless admiration and enthusiasm', declared 'solemnly before the whole world the Czech people's will to freedom and independence', demanded the reshaping of the Monarchy into 'a federal state of free national states with equal rights' and, as a logical sequence, the joining up of the Czechs and Slovaks in a single unit. The leader of the Yugoslavs similarly demanded 'the union of all territories of the Monarchy inhabited by Slovenes, Croats and Serbs in an independent state organism, free from the rule of any foreign nation . . .' The Ruthenes passionately protested against East Galicia being kept in constitutional union with Polish territories or forced into it still further, demanded self-government for the Little Russian territories of the Monarchy and hinted at their fundamental unity with the Russian Ukraine.[63]

But there was still no sign that the ruling class understood the portents of events in Russia, flushed as it was with the diplomatic victory at Brest-Litovsk. Only the Social Democrats could read the writing on the wall, and their newspaper *Arbeiter-Zeitung* wrote on 2 March 1918 about the treaty imposed on the Russians that it

> promises independent statehood to the Finns, Esths, Letts, Lithuanians, Poles and Ukrainians. Even the German Nationalists in their mental blindness cannot seriously believe it will be possible to refuse statehood to the Czechs, when it is conceded to nations far inferior to them in wealth, culture and power. In the great world-league of free nations . . . there is no room for the old Austria; if Austria is to exist at all, it must change into a union of free nations. . .[64]

Now that the Socialists had abandoned as insufficient the scheme of cultural autonomy, the government at last discovered it and proposed it in March 1918, and as no one showed any interest a new proposal was discussed in August according to which four national states of Germans, Czechs, Yugoslavs, and Poles should be constructed within the framework of Austria. It met with a cool reception. 'Negotiations are of no use', stated the Czech Deputy Stanek,

> because our final aim could not be reached by negotiations . . . the time for negotiations is long past, and the times are much too serious for anyone to conduct valid negotiations with the Government . . . unless authorized by the Czech Parliamentary Union or the Czech National Council.

[63] Lewis Namier in Temperley, op. cit., IV, p. 78. His comment that *'in form* they still acknowledged the dynasty' is misleading, as we shall see later.
[64] ibid., pp. 80–1.

And his colleague Klofác added:

> In evil days we have not lost our head and threats could not
> break us. Nor shall we lose our heads now, and promises will not
> influence us. . . The Czech question cannot be discussed with the
> Vienna Government which stands by the Dual System. . . The
> different proposals of the Vienna Government are therefore of no
> interest to us.[65]

The Social Democrats made a last attempt in the session of
2 October when they proposed a statement of peace aims, which
provided for the establishment of a national curia for each of the
nationalities. These curias were to work out their own national
institutions as well as negotiate with the other nations in the Empire
on matters they wished to have in common, the government pledg-
ing in advance its support for the constitutional reforms on which
they had all agreed. While a commission was appointed to study
these proposals, Victor Adler, the veteran socialist leader who was
to die the day before the republic was proclaimed, summed up the
feeling of disgust with the rulers of Austria which by then had
spread far beyond the ranks of Social Democracy:

> . . . We do not wish for victory. I am afraid the peoples of Austria
> would have to fear an overwhelming victory of their side almost
> as much as a victory of the Entente. . .

And the Czech Klofác spoke, more in sorrow than in anger, this
epitaph on the Habsburg monarchy:

> . . . Austria could have become a new Switzerland, it could have
> been the bridge between East and West, North and South; it
> could also have won over the Balkan peoples. . .[66]

Thus the Habsburg Empire went to its doom, leaving behind no
constructive idea but only memories and unsatisfied longings. The
conservative camp was divided between Habsburg-traditionalists
and *Deutschtum*-fanatics; the socialist camp dreamt of becoming
part of the great German labour movement; neither had a plan or
much hope for the small and independent republican state which
they were to inherit.

[65] ibid., p. 88.
[66] *Stenographisches Protokoll*, 3 October 1918.

Chapter 3

The Peace of St Germain

WE HAVE ALREADY NOTED how the dissolution of the Empire and the establishment of independent national states led to the historic meeting in Vienna on 21 October 1918 of those members of the old Austrian Parliament who represented the German-speaking regions and who now constituted themselves as a Provisional National Assembly. They included, apart from the representatives of the hereditary Habsburg lands, members from Bohemia and Moravia, southern Styria, and the South Tyrol who had already in fact, if not in law, become citizens of the Czechoslovak Republic and the South Slav and Italian kingdoms. Significantly, the various German-nationalist parties formed the strongest faction, with 101 members, followed by the Christian Socials with 70 seats. Reflecting the limited franchise of 1911, the Social Democrats came a poor third with only 39 members, but this disproportion was soon corrected when the first genuinely Austrian and democratic elections were held on 16 February 1919 and the desires and hopes of a desperate and exhausted population focused on the two popular mass parties which have ever since represented the great majority of Austrians.

This time the Social Democrats obtained 72, the Christian Socials 69, and nine German-nationalist parties (who were eventually to merge and form the *Grossdeutsche Volkspartei* (Pan-Germans) and the anti-clerical *Landbund* Peasant Party) 26 seats, while three independents represented the Czech minority, the Zionist Jews, and that small remnant of the liberal bourgeoisie which was prepared to accept the republic without reservations. It was this Assembly that appointed the first regular government headed by Karl Renner, with his fellow-Socialists Otto Bauer in charge of Foreign Affairs, Julius Deutsch for the Army, and Ferdinand Hanusch for Social Affairs, while the right-wing parties retained the other Ministries. But the principal task of representing the new state *vis-à-vis* the Allies and obtaining the best possible terms for a peace treaty fell to Renner.

The Austrians had repeatedly urged the Allies to open negotiations so that they should know what their status, their territory, their assets, and their obligations were; but the Allies, understandably, were preoccupied with the German problem and had not been able to work out an agreement between France and Italy on the future of Central Europe. The Austrian delegation, which arrived in Paris on 14 May 1919, was soon made to feel that they represented a defeated country: they were confined to their quarters, in complete isolation from the Allies with whom they could only exchange written statements, while the representatives of the succession states were free to press their claims in direct contacts with statesmen and experts. Because the Austrians had no part in the drafting of the Treaty of St Germain, though they were asked for comments and in fact succeeded in obtaining a number of improvements, it was subsequently referred to, like the Treaty of Versailles, as a *Diktat*, a dictated peace. But twenty-seven years later, when he was once more President of a newly-established Austrian Republic, Renner saw their position at St Germain in a rather better light:

> The Austrian delegation after its arrival at St Germain settled down, admittedly behind barbed wire, but nevertheless with its own postal service, a telephone connection with Austria via the Eiffel Tower, and all desirable facilities for its task. Unlike the German delegation which lived near by at Versailles, we were from the first to the last day the guests of the French Republic, and were received with friendliness. . . . A world-famous Austrian who had earned the gratitude of the British Empire, Freiherr von Slatin, better known as Slatin Pasha, who had been governor of a district in the Sudan under Gordon, and a prisoner of the Mahdi for eleven years, and who was made Inspector-General of the Sudan by Kitchener after his escape and was knighted: this man had given up his position and had returned to Austria, so as not to be compelled to fight his own country. He had come with us to St Germain to support us at the negotiations. He sat behind barbed wire with us; on the other side, in Paris, sat Lord Balfour, his personal friend, as a member of the British delegation. To him Slatin addressed a letter claiming that it contradicted the English sense of fair play to base one's judgement on hearsay and to deny the accused the right to defend himself in person. In his reply Lord Balfour regretted the procedure adopted by the powers which Britain alone could not change, but he obtained information from us through Slatin.[1]

[1] Karl Renner, *Österreich, St. Germain, und der kommende Friede* (Vienna, 1946), pp. 4–6.

Slatin, in fact, met the Prisoners of War Commission to whom he submitted two series of requests regarding the repatriation of Austrian prisoners, and although they only acceded to one relatively minor request, their attitude cannot be said to have been unreasonable.[2] Renner then described the relative freedom under which the delegation worked; while there were only two face-to-face meetings with the Allied leaders, no censorship prevented the Austrian case from being published in the world's press and thus influencing public opinion, which may well have contributed to several territorial and – particularly – economic concessions being made.

When the first treaty draft was presented to the Austrians on 2 June, it contained four gaps: the future strength of Austria's military forces, where Allied views diverged considerably and ranged from 40,000 (Great Britain) to 15,000 (France), with a figure of 30,000 eventually agreed upon, and the choice between a popular militia and a professional army, which the Social Democrats feared as an instrument likely to be turned against them,[3] but which was adopted by the Allies. Then there were the questions of reparations and of the public debt, whose complexities required protracted study and negotiations; and finally the Political Clauses relating to Italy and to Yugoslavia. Here it was Italy which proved the main stumbling-block: before she would consent to the terms for Austria, she had to be satisfied in Fiume and on the Dalmatian coast, both territories claimed by Yugoslavia, and on the Brenner frontier, which conflicted with President Wilson's Fourteen Points. Also, while the main concern of the French was to keep Austria from joining Germany, Italy was more interested in preventing Austria, Czechoslovakia, Hungary, and Yugoslavia from forming a confederation which would be as much of a menace to her as the old Empire had been. Thus Italy seemed the most likely of the powers to support Austria's immediate aims: the *Anschluss* with Germany and the defence of the southern region (Carinthia and South Styria) against Yugoslavia. Only one problem remained open: the Italian claim to South Tyrol, which the Austrians tried to resolve by offering the permanent neutralization of the whole of the Tyrol, thus securing for themselves, as Bauer hoped, 'the support of at least one of the Great Powers at the Peace Conference'. When this plan miscarried with the ban on the *Anschluss* and the loss of South Tyrol Bauer resigned from the Foreign Office.

[2] *Papers relating to the Foreign Relations of the United States. 1919. The Paris Peace Conference* (henceforth quoted as *US Foreign Relations*) (Washington, 1942), VII, pp. 50–2.

[3] *Österreichisches Haus-, Hof- und Staatsarchiv* (henceforth quoted as HHSA), Fasz. 374, Z1–4980, p. 5.

For the final treaty draft presented to the Austrians on 20 July brought the realization that, a number of concessions apart, the Allies were adamant on the place they wished to see Austria occupy in the new order in Central Europe, and since Renner was a *persona grata* with them, it would be easier for him than for Bauer to secure much-needed help for Austria. Further Austrian counter-proposals led to insignificant improvements in the definitive text, which was handed over on 2 September and accepted by the National Assembly on the sixth, by 97 votes to 23, but declared to be 'unjust to national sentiment, disastrous in its political consequences, and impracticable economically'. It speaks well for the commonsense of the people and their leaders that this resentment was not allowed to interfere with the task of making the best of the remaining opportunities, and of improving relations with the victors; that Austria did not follow the example of neighbouring Hungary and abandon herself to a futile gesture of communist defiance, but adhered to democratic practices, was to have important political consequences after the Second World War.

Political Issues

Although public opinion in Austria had expected a hard peace, the actual terms of the treaty aroused a storm of protest. Every single decision on matters of principle went against Austria; concessions only changed details. It was to no avail that Renner had brought with him to St Germain a team of experts and a wealth of documentation to disprove Allied allegations, correct false assumptions, and suggest workable alternatives; for all the notice the peacemakers took of the Austrian Notes, they might never have been written – or so it appeared at the time. In actual fact, the Austrian documents were studied closely by the experts at Paris, their arguments were noted by the press and other interested parties, and their appeal to commonsense and justice was not lost on those responsible for keeping the country which they had just created alive.

Of the principal decisions that went against Austria, two established the framework of the treaty by forcing German Austria to accept responsibility for the monarchy's share of the 'war guilt' of the Central Powers, and by insisting on treating Austria as an 'enemy state', while the third denied to Austria that right of self-determination which it had been the Allies' purpose to see established in Europe. If only the German-speaking Austrians were responsible for the war, it followed that the other nationalities had had no share in it, which was hardly true. An Austrian Note of 16 June countered the Allied observation that many representatives

of the new republic had held office, or had been prominent in public
life, in the Empire; the diplomatic service at any rate was different:

> When the war was declared the portfolio in question was in the
> hands of Count Berchtold, a Hungarian subject assisted by
> Count Forgach, a Hungarian also, and by Baron Musulin, a
> Croat. Moreover, during the recent decades Austria–Hungary
> was represented almost exclusively by Hungarian or Bohemian
> diplomats; thus in 1914 almost all the ambassadorial posts were

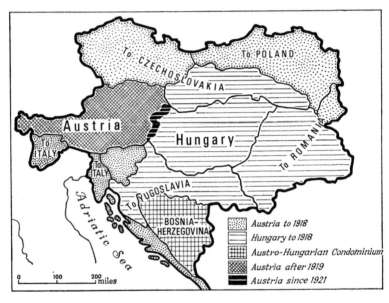

The Dissolution of Austria–Hungary

occupied by Hungarians, notably those at Paris, at St Petersburg,
at Berlin, at Rome, at Constantinople and at Tokio.

Since 1907, the Germans in the Austrian Chamber of Deputies
have been in a minority incapable of controlling votes without
joining some other national party. Consequently, the Austrian
governments have always been composed in part of Czechs, Poles
and sometimes of Slovenes.

There is some force in the Austrian contention, in the Note dated
2 July, that within 'the modest limits which the sovereign power of
the Monarch and the arbitrary will of the governing class' set to the

assent and collaboration of the people, the German Austrians were not alone in supporting the war, which was

> a war of Hungarians against Serbians, of Poles against their hereditary oppressors, especially against Russia, the would-be participator in the partition of Poland, a war of the Ukrainians against Czarism, of Croats and Slovenes on the one side against the Italians, their natural rivals in the Adriatic, on the other, for the predominance of the Catholic Yugo-Slavs over the orthodox peoples in the Balkans.[4]

This the Austrians proceeded to prove by submitting a selection of speeches made by leaders of the nationalities. The Poles, for instance, were shown to have been enthusiastic in their support of the war against Russia, and Polish members of the *Reichsrat* belonging to all parties were quoted as favouring 'an independent Polish State in association with Austria'. Among the South Slavs the hope prevailed that a Habsburg victory would mean South Slav unity under Catholic leadership, while an Italian victory would have led to the loss of yet more Slav territory. Monsignor Korosec, a Yugoslav Minister in 1919, had referred to Italy as the 'hereditary enemy in the South West' at the time when he was chairman of the South Slav group in the Austrian Parliament, and as late as June 1917 he had advocated a 'South Slav State within the Empire and under the dynasty', while the Diet of Carniola had gone on record denouncing the Pan-Slav agitation of Ante Trumbić, the Serb leader.

The position of the Czechs was different, but even here the great majority was in favour of maintaining the monarchy. Just as Czech deputies had voted for the occupation of Bosnia in 1878 – which German Austrian deputies had opposed – so there was in 1914 a school of thought which would have welcomed a Habsburg victory as likely to bring more Slavs under Austrian rule and thus to strengthen their position in the Empire. Among the signatories to the protest against the Allied declaration on the liberation of the Czechs was Stanek, now a Czech Minister, while his colleague in the government, Dr Stránský, had publicly declared himself in favour of the transformation of Austria–Hungary into a 'federative union of states'.[5]

Now none of this proved very much, for with a changing international situation politicians are allowed to change their minds – provided they do it in time and join the winning side. The treaty-makers shifted the argument from the leaders to their following:

[4] N. Almond and R. H. Lutz, *The Treaty of St. Germain* (Stanford, 1935), pp. 246–8.

[5] *Bericht über die Tätigkeit der deutschösterreichischen Friedensdelegation in St. Germain-en-Laye* (henceforth quoted as *Bericht*) (Vienna, 1919), vol. I.

It was not of their own will that [the nationalities] made war in the ranks of the soldiers of the Monarchy; they afterwards showed this by uniting with their alleged enemies who admitted them into their alliance[6]

– and since the Allies expressed themselves as satisfied with their war record, Austria had no case against them.

The other controversy concerned the status of the new republic as the successor of the Habsburg Empire or as a new state. The Austrian case was that the dissolution of the monarchy had left the nationalities without a state, whereupon they had proceeded to establish their own separate parliaments, governments, and armies, in short, had formed their own states (or else joined up with an existing state), and Austria was just one of them. While it was true that a change of government did not release a country from its obligations, the responsibility for the consequences of the war must be shared by all and not carried solely by the new Austria which 'has never declared war, never carried on war, and in relation with the Western Powers never occupied the position of a warring Power'. Indeed, the various commissions from the succession states now at work in Vienna were settling the estate left by the late Empire and dividing among themselves the rights and assets of this estate; it was a question not of making peace but of liquidating the former partnership; yet, in Paris, their governments adopted quite a different attitude regarding 'their obligations assumed in the past'.[7]

Perhaps illogically, the Allies settled for Wilson's formula, according to which Austria was both a new and an enemy state, the latter as 'that part of the Monarchy to which it stood in immediate succession'. This also settled the Austrian contention that it was properly a *State* Treaty and not a *Peace* Treaty that was being concluded; they were more successful with this argument in 1955. Yet another complication arose from the Austrian insistence on calling their new state *Deutsch-Österreich*, German Austria. Renner explained to Clemenceau that the name was 'expressly chosen to mark the difference between the former polyglot State, composed of nine nationalities, and the new Republic including only one of them';[8] but it undoubtedly also signalized the claim to all German-speaking regions and stressed the affinity with the German Republic. There was some apprehension among the representatives of the succession states, whom Lloyd George had suggested be consulted on the choice of name; the Yugoslavs objected because *German*

[6] *US Foreign Relations*, VII, p. 861.
[7] Almond and Lutz, op. cit., pp. 62–3.　　　　[8] ibid., p. 245.

Austria implied the existence of an Austria other than German, out-side the hereditary lands; and the Czechs feared that closer ties between Germany and Austria might strengthen pro-German senti-ment in their country. Even though Clemenceau agreed with Balfour that they could not prevent Austrians from calling them-selves *German* Austrians if they wished, the one and only gesture of defiance was soon abandoned, for there were far more important matters still to be settled where Allied goodwill was desperately needed.

For Austria, the right of self-determination had two distinct aspects. One concerned those German-speaking regions that were now claimed by Czechoslovakia, Yugoslavia, and Italy partly on historical grounds and partly for strategic reasons. The other was the right of the Austrian state to attach itself, under a special status, to the German Reich. We have already considered the emotional and cultural links that existed between the two countries, and have also seen how increasing dependence on the Reich for military assistance had produced resentment among Austrians of all ranks. (German contempt for the military qualities of Austrians – certain crack units excepted – created new problems after the *Anschluss* and during the Second World War.) Apart from the Pan-German parties, then, union with Germany was certainly not an article of faith; on behalf of the Social Democrats Victor Adler declared in Parliament on 21 October 1918:

> The German people of Austria is now to establish its own demo-cratic state . . . which will decide in full freedom the nature of its relationship with its neighbours and with the German Reich. It may unite with the neighbouring peoples to form a league of free nations – if this is the peoples' will. Should, however, the other nations reject such a union, or only be prepared to agree to it on conditions which do not meet the economic and political require-ments of the Austrian people, then German Austria will be com-pelled to attach itself to the German Reich as a federal unit [*Sonderbundesstaat*], as, left on its own, it would not be an eco-nomically viable state.[9]

It soon became obvious that the succession states were unwilling to agree to any kind of federation with Austria, and the decision was reached to declare Austria a constituent part of Germany. On 10 November Renner and Bauer visited Victor Adler, already on his deathbed (he died the following day), to obtain his approval of the text of the constitutional bill which was to be submitted to the party leaders on the 11th, and to Parliament on the 12th. Adler

[9] *Stenographisches Protokoll*, 21 October 1918.

agreed, and then he added: 'Still, they will have to come together again one day; it will be best for them. . .'[10] It was not only Austria's misfortune that this hope was never fulfilled.

It was not 'the voice of the blood' that attracted Socialists to Germany but political considerations (especially after the overthrow of the Hohenzollern dynasty on 9 November) and economic necessity, while Catholics and conservatives were opposed to the *Anschluss* with a Protestant, strongly socialist country, preferring to hope for the restoration of Danubian unity, with or without the Habsburgs.

The Allied camp was divided on this question; whereas the Anglo-Saxon Powers were prepared to accept the *Anschluss*, they allowed themselves to be persuaded by the French that it would not merely add to Germany's strength, but would seriously threaten the succession states. Czechoslovakia would be enclosed by Germans on three sides, Yugoslavia exposed to German pressure from the North, while Hungary with the open or secret support of the Reich would seek to retrieve the lands lost to her neighbours. By 22 April the issue was decided, when Clemenceau obtained the approval of the powers for an article in the German peace terms by which Germany would respect Austrian independence as 'inalienable except by consent of the Council of the League of Nations', and Austria was soon compelled to follow suit. Whether the Allied decision was wise or not will presumably be debated for ever. The infusion of Austrian *savoir-faire* into German politics, the high quality of Austria's political leadership, and the removal of an important item from the list of nationalist grievances are sometimes quoted as factors that might have altered the course of history in Central Europe. This, however, is assuming that the Treaties of Versailles and St Germain as such had an overwhelming part in the making of the Second World War – which is rather doubtful. That the same powers that banned the *Anschluss* of 1919, which would have preserved much of Austria's separateness, allowed the German invasion of 1938 to pass by with no more than paper protests, is quite another story.

The New Frontiers

The other violation of the right of self-determination concerned the frontiers and the territorial extent of the new republic. Here again the years of appeasement have left us with a number of myths which are uncritically accepted by writers. There is talk of the $3\frac{1}{2}$ million Austrians who came under foreign rule, and in defiance of geographical realities it is claimed that their inclusion in the republic would have made a viable unit of Austria. The decisions

10 Quoted *Die Zukunft*, 11/1948, p. 319.

are represented as having all gone against Austria, whereas in fact the considerable losses of territory to Czechoslovakia, and of the South Tyrol to Italy, were balanced by Austrian successes in Carinthia and western Hungary, the Burgenland. Perhaps understandably, only Austrian interests are considered and not enough attention is paid to the interests of her new neighbours.

But since the new national states in Central Europe were expected to take over the role of the three powers defeated in the war, and to provide the basis of the new order, they had to be provided with the necessary territory, defensible frontiers, and economic opportunities. If in addition to their national aspirations historic rights could be quoted (as in the case of the Bohemian kingdom), so much the better. Quite naturally, the Austrian delegation at St Germain fought for every square mile of territory inhabited by people who not only spoke German, but had expressed a wish to join Austria, especially the Sudeten Germans, but a glance at an ethnic map suffices to show how intolerable such a solution would have been for the Czechs, and how unmanageable for Austria. A more far-seeing policy on the part of the Czechs might have led to the adoption of the Austrian proposal to leave those parts of Bohemia and Moravia with Austria which adjoined the provinces of Upper and Lower Austria. This would at least have reduced the German minority of over 3 million people by about 360,000, and would have brought only 18,000 Czechs into Austria. Masaryk, in fact, had proposed an even more generous solution, under which around one million Sudeten Germans would have become Austrians;[11] but this had been two years earlier. Now, in 1919, the representatives of the new state demanded the historic frontiers against Austria, the national frontiers against Hungary (who had ruled Slovakia for centuries), and additional lands where it suited their economic or strategic interests – as for instance from Lower Austria, where the Austrians succeeded, however, in getting the original demand reduced from some 50,000 to 18,000 people.

All this may sound trivial, looked at in cold blood half a century later; but at the time Czech greed caused much bitterness, which Henlein and Hitler were to revive and exploit twenty years later. Austrian warnings that Czech plans were likely to transfer the nationality problems of the Empire to the new republic were disregarded and their statistics called 'mendacious'. Yet their prediction of the national composition of the new state, not counting the Polish minority – 62 per cent Czechs and Slovaks, 28 per cent Germans, 7 per cent Magyars, and 3 per cent Ruthenes – proved

[11] T. G. Masaryk, 'The Future Status of Bohemia', *The New Europe* (22 February 1917), pp. 171–2.

fairly accurate even ten years later, when the proportions were 67 per cent Czechs and Slovaks, 22 per cent Germans, 5 per cent Magyars, and 4 per cent Ruthenes.[12] Needless to say, the Anglo-Saxon statesmen at Paris were not very happy about all this, but allowed themselves eventually to be persuaded by French insistence and a pledge contained in a Czech Note:

> It is the intention of the Czechoslovak Government to create the organization of the State by accepting as a basis of natural rights the principles applied in the constitution of the Swiss Republic, that is, to make of the Czechoslovak Republic a sort of Switzerland, taking into consideration, of course, the special conditions in Bohemia.[13]

And Beneš himself spoke to the Council of Four of their general intention and policy to 'work out a constitutional system similar to that in operation in Switzerland'.[14] It is quite clear that Beneš envisaged such a system as the *ultimate aim* of Czech constitutional development and not as an immediate programme, and who would say that, but for the world economic crisis and the advent of the National Socialist régime in Germany, it would not have been realized? But it was no consolation for the Sudeten Germans at the time, whom the events of 1918–19 had transformed from a 'people of state' (*Staatsvolk*) into a minority under Slav rule.

The creditable achievements of Czechoslovakia in every sphere, and the general sympathy felt for that country in the tragic days of Munich, and then as a German 'protectorate', tend to obscure the basic weakness of a political structure which depended on a distant protector rather than on co-operation with its neighbours. While it is true to say that the Sudeten Germans had less cause for complaint than any other minority in Central Europe – except Austria's – Hitler could not have proceeded against the country in the way he did, with the tacit or open support of many Western statesmen, had there not been a widespread conviction of an injustice done in the settlement of 1919. The expulsion of the German minority after the Second World War, while probably final, has not really solved Czechoslovakia's problems: by throwing her back on the protection of the Soviet Union against German designs, she has paid for her national security with her political freedom.

As against the complexities of the Czech claims the Italian de-

---

[12] *Statistical Handbook of the Czechoslovak Republic* (London, n.d.) [1940?], p. 8.
[13] D. Hunter Miller, *My Diary at the Conference of Paris* (New York, 1924), XIII, pp. 68–70.
[14] *US Foreign Relations*, VI, p. 205.

mand for the Brenner frontier presented a clear-cut issue: were
strategic considerations to overrule one of the most important principles proclaimed by the Allies? In the Treaty of London Britain
and France had pledged themselves to support the Italian claim,
and in the hour of victory they considered themselves in honour

The Frontier with Czechoslovakia: the Sudeten Problem

bound, even though they hoped the United States – which had not
been a party to the treaty – would get them out of their dilemma.
In his Ninth Point President Wilson had only spoken of an adjust-
ment of Italy's northern frontier 'along the clearly recognizable
lines of nationality'; what made him change his mind, a mere
twelve months afterwards, will forever remain in doubt. The Italian
case was that even though defeat had removed the Dual Empire,
Italy's main adversary, she still needed protection against a powerful
bloc of 70 million Germans north of her territory which only a good

strategic frontier like the Brenner could provide. Wilson's advisers
accepted this view, especially since they reckoned with the union of
Austria with Germany; granting Italy the Brenner, while violating
a principle, would 'enormously enhance her security and reduce the
necessity of heavy armaments', and the 'complete autonomy' of the
province and freedom from military service would compensate
the population.

In spite of this assumption the U.S. intelligence section devised a
compromise based on a frontier 'midway between the linguistic line
and the line of the Treaty of London'. This would have brought
'only' 160,000 South Tyrolese (instead of 220,000) under Italian
rule – an improvement, the authors argued, on the Brenner line
which 'would simply throw the irredentist problem into Austrian
territory and would not lead to a lasting peace'. A British study,
however, came to the conclusion that Italy's security needs would be
satisfied with the linguistic frontier, apart from two minor correc-
tions where it might be necessary to enable the Italians to dominate
militarily the chief Austrian towns of Meran and Bozen.[15] Eventually, though, both the British and the French experts accepted the
American compromise proposal – only by this time the Italian–
Yugoslav conflict had become so embittered that Italy could only
be persuaded to adopt a more conciliatory line on the Adriatic
frontiers issue by still further appeasement at Austria's expense.
The President himself now sanctioned the surrender, but insisted on
calling it by a different name:

> Within certain limits he agreed that natural boundaries must be
> taken into consideration . . . the slope of the mountains not only
> threw rivers in a certain direction but tended to throw the life of
> the people in the same direction. These, however, were not strate-
> gic or economic arguments. . . Nature has swung a great boundary
> round the north of Italy. . . He had no great difficulty there in
> meeting the Italian views.[16]

So, with Nature herself on his side, he need have none of the
scruples to which Lloyd George still gave expression, for by now it
was not only the Brenner, but two additional areas as well, which
the Italians demanded – and received. An Austrian memorandum
traced the progression of Italian claims: in her negotiations with
the Empire, in April 1915, Italy would have been satisfied with the
Trentino and the Bozen basin as the price for her neutrality; in the
Treaty of London of the same month she was promised the Brenner

[15] Almond and Lutz, op. cit., pp. 337–41.
[16] ibid., pp. 335–7.

line if she went to war with Austria. In March 1919 she introduced hydrographic considerations and demanded the whole of the Adige basin, but not yet the basin of the Drave river, which was to appear in the 2 June draft. In this way, both Tarvis and the Sexten valley were also conceded.[17]

While the Austrian delegation conducted its losing battle for the language frontier, and even offered a 'Convention on the Neutrality of the Tyrol' under which both north and south would be completely demilitarized and, in the case of a conflict, occupied by Swiss troops, the Tyrolese Diet went further and declared its readiness to save the unity of the country by declaring it an 'independent neutral republic'.[18] None of this was any use; Italy was determined to round off her northern territory in the most advantageous way, but she did offer a large measure of local self-government to counteract the spirit of resistance among the population. The inevitable process of Italianization soon set in, but the worst outrages came with Mussolini's Fascist régime. Undermined in their economic basis, a stationary peasant community in a rapidly industrializing country, politically and ethnically in a permanent minority, the South Tyrolese have shown a remarkable degree of tenacity. Even Hitler's cynical deal with the Italian dictator in 1938, involving the 'resettlement' of the population in 'Greater Germany', failed to shift a mountain people deeply rooted in its soil and its traditions. If after the Second World War the Allies had been prepared to settle the issue on its local merits – all the easier since this time it was not a case of favouring an ally against an enemy state – they might have returned the South Tyrol to Austria and saved everybody concerned a great deal of trouble.

It so happened, however, that the same *sacro egoismo*, the ruthless pursuit of national interests at the expense of Italy's neighbours, was to work out to Austria's advantage in the other large dispute in which the new republic found itself involved: the struggle for Carinthia. For in this case Austria enjoyed the diplomatic and military support of the Italians, who were not suddenly moved by compassion or a sense of justice, but merely by the desire to weaken their Yugoslav neighbours.

The Yugoslav case resembled that of the Czechs in so far as they also based it on history: according to them, Carinthia had been two-thirds Slovene as late as 1850, and historic justice demanded that their original lands – Carinthia and South Styria – be restored to the Slovene people who were now united with their Croat and Serb brothers in the South Slav Kingdom. The present desires

[17] *Bericht*, II, pp. 208 f.
[18] *US Foreign Relations*, XII, pp. 307–8.

The Problem of the South Tyrol

and loyalties of the inhabitants, who had been forcibly 'Austrianized', should prove no obstacle, for after a few years of Slav independence they would regain their national consciousness. This, Archibald Coolidge, Head of the American Mission in Austria, sagely remarked, was the same argument as was used by the Germans in regard to French sentiment in Alsace in 1871,

> and history has shown the falsity of that argument. We are dealing with the way people feel now, not with the way they may be going to feel some day.[19]

[19] *US Foreign Relations*, XII, pp. 511–13.

It was a difficult choice to make, for while on the one hand there could be no doubt about the strength of the Slovene element, it was rather more difficult to ascertain what these people wanted. On account of their numerical weakness relative to German Austrians and their low social status the wave of national revival in the Slav nationalities had in their case not yet advanced beyond cultural to political demands, and assimilation had reduced their numbers still further.

Even before the treaty-makers had begun to take stock of the position, the Carinthian people went into action to defend the unity of their homeland. Remnants of the Austrian army and hastily assembled *Volkswehr* or local militias stopped the invading Yugoslavs until on American initiative a temporary boundary was fixed, to enable a field mission to investigate conditions. The mission came out strongly in favour of the Karawanken frontier, which made the Klagenfurt basin – with the exception of the parish of Seeland – into a compact geographical and economic unit, and as for the Slovenes in the population, they appeared to be largely in favour of remaining with Austria and resentful of the terroristic methods of the Yugoslav military and civilian authorities.[20] As regards South Styria, however, in the Marburg basin the German-speaking urban population was surrounded by a Slovene countryside which tended towards Yugoslavia. Here, as in the other Styrian region claimed by the Slovenes, Radkersburg, the Austrians pointed out that there were overwhelming German majorities of 75 to 80 per cent; that the river basins of Drau and Mur formed two economic units; and that the people concerned should be given the right of a free vote. After protracted negotiations among the Allies, however, the decision was reached that Marburg should go to Yugoslavia and Radkersburg stay in Austria while only the Klagenfurt basin should have a plebiscite.

What made the Klagenfurt plebiscite so memorable was the fact that it was one of the few post-war plebiscites which, thanks to inter-Allied supervision, presented a true picture of the people's wishes.[21] The Klagenfurt basin had been divided into two zones: Zone A, south of Klagenfurt and nearly 80 per cent Slovene-speaking, voted first on 10 October 1920, almost 60 per cent for Austria; this made a vote in Zone B, with Klagenfurt, superfluous for its outcome was a foregone conclusion. With the courage of despair the Yugoslavs, who had tried before to obtain control of the region by force and had nothing more to lose, invaded Zone A for

[20] ibid., pp. 500–10.
[21] Cf. in particular Sarah Wambaugh, *Plebiscites since the World War* (Washington, 1933), passim.

the last time, and it took a strongly-worded ultimatum from the ambassadors to get them out. Italy, who acted as protector of Austria's interests and her own, had assisted this development both in Paris and along the disputed frontiers; but the determination of the local population rising in defence of their homeland may well have contributed. It speaks for the commonsense of the Slovene-speaking Carinthians that they refused to listen to irredentist propaganda from across the frontier but decided instead to maintain their cultural identity while being loyal Austrians. (The renewed claim for 'Slovene Carinthia' made by Tito's government after the Second World War met with even less success than the first.) Nevertheless, the desperate efforts of the Yugoslavs were not without a certain tragic grandeur: with only a historic claim, which their own kin in Carinthia repudiated, fiercely attacked by their nearest 'ally' – Italy – while the Great Powers in Paris let them down, they only abandoned the contest when a continuation might have endangered the very existence of their new state.

In the case of Austria's other success – this time a real gain of territory – the situation was rather more complicated. Hungary's western province had since the days of the Turkish invasions been settled by farmers from Germany who had retained their speech and national consciousness. The repressive nationality policy of the Magyars had not spared this ethnic group, and long before the World War a movement for union with Austria had developed in the four west Hungarian *comitats* (or districts) of Pressburg, Wieselburg, Ödenburg, and Eisenburg, whence the name *Burgenland* for the new province was derived when it joined Austria at last. This movement, which now enjoyed official Austrian backing, met with fierce Hungarian opposition; after their extensive territorial losses to all their other neighbours, which they could not prevent and which reduced the 'Lands of the Crown of St Stephen' from a population of 20 million to just over eight, they were not prepared to lose another square mile, least of all to a weak and apparently defenceless country.

It became one of the lengthiest operations which the Peace Conference initiated: three and a half years from the dissolution of the Empire to the final settlement; and it engendered so much bitterness between the former associates that the outside world could well wonder how they had managed to live side by side in the same state. The reasons for the delays and crises are not far to seek. None of the powers supported Austria, for although she had the right of self-determination on her side, the Magyar gentry had influential connections in the Western capitals. Moreover, Hungary

soon began to enjoy the support of Italy who needed her as a
counterweight to France's allies in Central Europe, the so-called
'Little Entente'. Also, unlike Austria, Hungary had never been disarmed and could therefore defy Allied orders with impunity while
the Allies themselves were extremely reluctant to become involved in
any more military adventures and would not even allow Austria to
take military possession of a province they had just allotted her.
And finally, with the collapse of the short-lived Soviet Republic
under Bela Kun, during which the Allies had favoured Austria,
they were now supporting the extreme right-wing régime of Admiral
Horthy against the radical, socialist-led Austria.

The Slovene Question

The decision to enlarge one ex-enemy state at the expense of
another has often been criticized. All kinds of reasons have been
adduced – except the obvious one that in this case a principal war
aim could be realized without hurting an Allied or associated power.
It was first described as a Machiavellian move once and for all to
separate Hungary from Austria by the right-wing press in Vienna
which was more concerned with various plots to restore the Habsburgs and reunite the two countries than with the wishes of the
local population. This allegation was later given academic respectability by nationalist historians like Bibl and Soviet critics of the
Versailles system, who both call the Burgenland a *Zankapfel*, or
bone of contention, deliberately created by the Allies.

What really happened was far less diabolical. For months the Allies had no intention of disturbing long-established frontiers, and although the Austrian Parliament had first made its claim on 22 November 1918, the 2 June draft of the treaty made no mention of any frontier rectification or plebiscite, but on 12 May the Council of Ten had decided to arbitrate if any difficulty should arise over this frontier.[22] Again the Austrians bombarded the treaty-makers with memoranda which presented an incontrovertible case. Firstly, the river Leitha had been a purely administrative demarcation line, but by making it into a state frontier the Allies were now establishing a 'barrier from which commerce had been free since the time of the discovery of America' and were separating the three principal industrial centres in the region – Vienna, Wiener Neustadt, and Graz – from their 'kitchen-gardens' and their farms.

> Moreover, the Leitha frontier would place most sensitive points of our country within range of the artillery of our neighbours . . . Let us imagine, for an instant, that the frontier of France passes from Chantilly to Melun via Meaux, and that of England through Canterbury, and let the question be asked as to whether, under these circumstances, Paris or London could live in entire tranquillity . . .[23]

Then there was the nationality factor. In the four *comitats* there lived, according to the census of 1910, around 300,000 German-speakers who represented 68 per cent of the total population, while the rest consisted of Magyars (18 per cent), Croats (10 per cent), and Slovaks (3 per cent). But since the Czechs had already occupied Pressburg, which as Bratislava was to become the capital of Slovakia, Austria's claim was 'for the record' rather than with any hope of success. The next problem was the future of the Croat minority; as a distinct ethnic group between Germans and Magyars, were they to go to Austria or to Hungary? It was believed, correctly as it turned out, that they were, on the whole, pro-Austrian, but the plebiscite which Austria suggested would give them the opportunity of a choice. However, the Czechs had a different plan for the whole of the disputed territory: a 'Memoir' which they submitted to the Conference claimed that since Germans and Magyars had deliberately driven a wedge between North and South Slavs in the thirteenth and fourteenth centuries, this injustice should now be removed by establishing a 'corridor' between Czechoslovakia and Yugoslavia; such a solution would also serve the interests of peace by keeping Germans and Magyars apart.[24] However, this plan soon

---

[22] *Bericht*, I, pp. 130 f.   [23] Almond and Lutz, op. cit., p. 414.
[24] Wambaugh, op. cit., II, p. 274.

foundered on the determined opposition of the Allies; significantly, Yugoslavia – which was to have been the other beneficiary – was completely disinterested, but this did not prevent the Tito government in 1945 from demanding the liberation of the Burgenland Croats 'from the Austrian yoke'.

The rest of the story is too tedious to recount in detail; Sarah Wambaugh has written the definitive story of events leading up to the plebiscite in Ödenburg (Sopron), while German and Hungarian documents published since 1945 reveal the diplomatic intrigues – in which Austrian right-wing politicians were involved – that led to the loss of the capital of the province in a fraudulent inquiry presided over by the Italian General Ferrario. Considering the procedure one cannot but agree with Wambaugh that

> 'the majority for Hungary may really represent the wish of the inhabitants, or it may not' . . . As proper safeguards for a free and fair plebiscite were lacking, the vote is not convincing either one way or the other. Whether the failure of the Allies to protect the authenticity of the vote was due to European politics or to pressure of time, it is greatly to be regretted.[25]

While Austria never attempted to raise the issue again, the Hungarians did not give up so easily and in fact hoped as late as 1938 that the Germans would reward them for their co-operation by returning the Burgenland after the *Anschluss* – a request that received a very dusty answer. As the Nazi government were not particularly interested in the special character of this region they soon divided it up between its neighbours, Styria and Lower Austria, but such was the strength of local patriotism that it was restored to the status of a federal province (or *Land*) in 1945.[26]

Postscript on a Peace

Thus the territorial clauses of the Treaty of St Germain present a contradictory picture: the loss of the Sudetenland to Czechoslovakia, of the South Tyrol to Italy, and of some smaller territories to Yugoslavia; the gain of the Burgenland and the retention of Carinthia undivided; and lastly Vorarlberg was prevented from seceding both by Swiss hesitations and an Allied veto. What emerged was a new country, economically unbalanced and politically unstable, 'too small to live and too big to die', as Austrians maintained and many foreign observers feared. There was of course no question

[25] ibid., I, pp. 277–81, 288–97.
[26] For a discussion of St Germain, fifty years after, cf. K. R. Stadler, 'Fünfzig Jahre Vertrag von St. Germain', *Österreich in Geschichte und Literatur*, XIII/8, 1969, pp. 385–94.

of reparations; on the contrary, if Austria was to be kept alive she needed considerable supplies of food, coal, and raw materials, and her very survival became one of the first concerns of the League of Nations. That this dependence on foreign credits and goodwill exposed the country to political pressures goes without saying, but the particular misfortune of Austria was that her right-wing governments changed the foreign political orientation from a Western democratic one to increasing dependence first on Fascist Italy and then on Nazi Germany. And we may well agree with Erich Zöllner when in his monumental history of Austria he considers it the most ominous aspect of the peace settlement of 1919

> that it lasted only as long as democratic leaders of the defeated nations, notably Germany's, strove for improvements and alleviation by legitimate political means, while it quickly succumbed to the ruthlessness of aggressive dictatorship.[27]

The Peace, which we now know to have been only an armistice to be followed by an even more devastating war, has never ceased to be debated by historians as if to discover where we went wrong and how we can do better next time we have the chance. In this discussion the historic role and the achievements of the Danubian Empire occupy a special place since we are now confronted in Central and eastern Europe by another large imperial organization – the Soviet Union – taking up the story where the Habsburgs left off. This revival of interest half a century after the collapse of the old order is probably due to perplexity at the nature of a region which since the end of the Austro–Hungarian régime has defied all efforts to renew its former pattern and has refused to be federated or absorbed – whether in a Western framework of treaties and alliances as after 1918, under German leadership as in the thirties, or by Nazi or Soviet force as in the forties and fifties; and it does not appear that communism has provided a unifying drive in our time. Central Europe is simply not ready for unity. If Hans Kohn's observation that 'long-lasting historical forms which have a foundation in geographic realities sometimes reveal a strong tendency to reappear in new shapes and configurations' were ever to apply to the Danubian Empire, then the time is obviously not yet. For the moment, and for the foreseeable future, Central Europe remains a geographical and not a political concept.[28]

If it is a valid point that the nineteenth century ended in 1918, and the Great War with its obsolete dynastic and diplomatic fea-

[27] Erich Zöllner, *Geschichte Österreichs* (Vienna, 1966), pp. 501–2.
[28] Hans Kohn, 'A.E.I.O.U.: Some Reflections on the Meaning and Mission of Austria', *Journal of Modern History*, vol. II (1939), pp. 513–27.

tures was the last war of that century, it follows that the peace settlement would reveal the same mentality. Its principal feature in Central Europe, the triumph of national self-determination, has been criticized by E. H. Carr

> because we have been content to keep it in the nineteenth-century setting of political rights. We have failed to adapt it to the twentieth-century context of military and economic problems; and we have failed to understand that the right of nations to self-determination, like every other right, is self-destructive unless it is placed in a framework of obligation.[29]

But this was wisdom after the event. At the time, the triumph of self-determination seemed very real: the collapse of the Central Powers and of Russia had delivered from foreign rule no fewer than 60 million people – though for many of the new minorities, now 20 million strong, it was merely a change of masters. Each of the succession states burdened itself with large and disaffected minorities: several million Ukrainians, Belorussians, Jews, and Germans in Poland, as well as Lithuanians; several million Austrians and Hungarians in Czechoslovakia, not to mention Poles and Ukrainians; Austrians and Hungarians in Yugoslavia; Hungarians and Bulgarians in Romania; and Austrians and South Slavs in Italy. Admittedly, minorities are unavoidable in Central Europe whichever way frontiers are drawn, but not many vital interests demanded the inclusion of such large numbers, and the minority clauses in the treaties and the arbitration machinery of the League of Nations could not prevent much hardship and many injustices.

The peace settlement following the Allied victory was to be not only just to the various races, but also democratic; but here, too, performance fell far short of intention. Of all the countries involved in the dissolution of the Dual Monarchy, only one – Czechoslovakia – remained a parliamentary democracy in any real sense of the word until she was sacrificed to international expediency. In Austria, likewise, the destruction of political and parliamentary life in 1933–34 was in part due to outside pressures. All the others had preceded them in abandoning, one after another, the basic conditions of political freedom: Hungary, Italy, Poland, Yugoslavia.

The reasons for this development are not hard to find, but it does not add much to our understanding when we have isolated and defined them. In Hungary, the right-wing takeover has been seen as the reaction of a frightened and incensed people to Bela Kun's Soviet régime. Italy succumbed to Fascism because she was weakened

---

[29] E. H. Carr, *Conditions of Peace* (London, 1942), p. 38.

by the war, disappointed by its results, and alarmed by the sharpening class struggle in the industrial north. Yugoslavia's parliamentary system broke on the unresolved conflict of her nationalities (shades of the Habsburg Empire!). Lack of democratic traditions and the political and social backwardness of large sections of the new states are held responsible for the failure of democracy in Poland and the Balkans. All this may well be true, but each of these 'causes' operated to some degree in every one of the new nations, and it was their combination which caused the general malaise.

It may well be more profitable to ask why parliamentary democracy was successful in Czechoslovakia and (up to a point) in Austria. The first and most obvious characteristic shared by these two countries was that they possessed a modern and efficient industrial system, with an intelligent and disciplined labour force and a skilled professional class. The social revolution of 1918 had considerably enlarged and improved the social and educational services, mainly for the industrial and urban population, while – especially in Czechoslovakia – rural reform had narrowed the gap between town and country. In both countries a strong yet moderate labour movement stood guard, not only over the achievements of the revolution, but also in defence of democracy. Elsewhere in the region, the progressive influence of industrial concentrations was submerged in the general backwardness of the country or weakened by a divided labour movement. Failure to initiate (or complete) a social revolution enabled Fascist agitators to mobilize the underprivileged against progress; this was true of the unorganized petty bourgeoisie, which found itself ground between the millstones of labour and capital, and of the countryside, where all too often land reform without adequate credits merely shifted the titles from hated foreign magnates to anonymous bankers and financiers. In short, what all these factors appear to prove is that Western-style parliamentary democracy has a chance of survival only where the structure of society approximates to that of the Western democracies; which is a useful point to bear in mind when considering the political difficulties of newly-independent states in Africa and Asia.

However, the lack of genuine parliamentary traditions and of a store of democratic experience in Central and eastern Europe should not be used as an excuse for autocratic rule of a different kind. Apologists for the communist takeover after 1945 often argued that the region could only gain, but not lose, since it never had experienced democracy and political freedom. This is certainly not the whole truth, for few régimes had been strong enough to destroy all opposition, and none had won over all social groups. There were liberal bourgeois elements with access to ideas and writings from abroad, which precluded a government monopoly of opinion-making and information. There were workers' and peasants' organizations, often with international contacts, who not only looked after their members' interests, but in organizing and running their unions and co-operatives, their benefit and educational societies, were training members in such democratic skills as would enable them one day to take over a larger share of civic responsibility – for example on local government bodies, arbitration courts, and the like. In terms of power and influence these pockets of democratic activity may not have amounted to much – to little more, probably, than they do in the Soviet Union and other communist countries today; but they formed political habits which we may see at work in the struggle for greater personal and political freedom that is being waged in communist society today.

Thus the wheel has come full circle: the nations of Europe's borderlands whose desire for national independence broke up the great empires which dominated them, and who resisted all attempts at reuniting them under Western or German auspices, have proved no more amenable to Soviet designs of this nature. In some respects the present state of eastern Europe vis-à-vis Russia resembles the end-phase of Habsburg rule, with the one vital difference that the small nations are not confronted by a moribund edifice which can be toppled after an exhausting war, but by an advanced technological and military power whose domination can be eroded, and turned into good-neighbourly relations, by patient diplomacy alone.[30]

[30] For a detailed discussion cf. K. R. Stadler, 'The Disintegration of the Austrian Empire', *Journal of Contemporary History*, 4/1968, pp. 177–90.

Chapter 4

The Republic of Austria

THE END OF THE Great War saw the dissolution of the Habsburg Empire which had been thought of, in T. G. Masaryk's words, as a counterpoise to Germany, as a necessary organization of small peoples and odds and ends of peoples, and as a safeguard against 'Balkanization'. It was a dissolution not originally envisaged by Allied statesmen, who had looked upon Austria–Hungary as a conservative influence, a European necessity, a pacific force because of her internal difficulties. Nor had they called the force of nationality into being, but had 'rather reluctantly recognized it when it appeared and used it, not to win the war, but to hasten its last stages'.[1]

The wishes of the nationalities and the political strategy of the Allies brought the succession states into being and provided them with their initial impetus and dynamic. No such wish – to form an Austrian *Nationalstaat* – had ever been formulated by German Austrians; their new nationality was forced upon them by the victors, their state was, in Clemenceau's phrase, 'that which was left over' after the break-up. And since Austrians had not worked and fought for their state, it was to them a *Provisorium und Transitorium* and not the culmination of their hopes; hence there was no patriotism, no identification, no feeling of permanence. Phrases like 'the state that no one wanted', or 'the involuntary state', gained currency, and while they are at best half-truths, they nevertheless describe the situation at certain times and with certain sections of the population. Even the severities of the Peace Treaty did no more than produce a very short-lived reaction that could be called national solidarity; but it was more apparent in parliamentary debates and newspaper articles than in the relationship between the classes – and the different regions – of Austria.

In a general sense, people did not consider themselves Germans or Austrians, but Styrians or Carinthians, Tyrolese or Salzburgers (and traces of this particularism can still be detected in the present-day conflict between centralist and federalist interests). After the

---

[1] Arthur Cobban, op. cit., p. 15.

Great War, Otto Bauer wrote, 'the provinces made their own foreign policy'. In March 1919 the Tyrolese conservatives, fearing for the future of the South Tyrol, protested against another *Anschluss* declaration by the Constituent Assembly. In Vorarlberg a plebiscite resulted in an 80 per cent majority in favour of an *Anschluss* to Switzerland; and in Carinthia the Yugoslav invasion produced a mood of defiance *vis-à-vis* Yugoslavia, Germany, and even towards Vienna:

> Not for those in Ljubljana, not for Vienna,
> Not for the Serbs and not for Berlin,
> Carinthia for the Carinthians![2]

It has long been customary to look upon the Republic of Austria as the child of the Paris Peace Conference and the Treaty of St Germain, which are blamed for all its troubles and shortcomings. The fiftieth anniversary of that treaty, commemorated in 1969, produced a spate of articles in this vein, when it would be more accurate to describe Austria as the child of the Habsburg monarchy, and her difficulties, internal and external, as the consequences of past history. Of the three main aspects of the treaty, only one – the ban on the *Anschluss* – need concern us in the context of this chapter; the declaration of Austria as an enemy state, with its unpleasant economic and legal consequences, and the way her frontiers were drawn, throwing 3½ million Austrians into Czechoslovakia, Yugoslavia, and Italy, while creating resentment in the country and providing the basis for revisionist policies in the future, did not really weld Austrians into a 'community of suffering' as politicians liked to proclaim. Only the *Anschluss* question produced anything like a national front – in favour of an anti-national policy – and for this the Social Democrats have been largely held responsible by historians. That it should have been a Marxist and internationalist party which orientated the new republic towards Germany, and not the habitual Pan-Germans, calls for an explanation.

The Social Democrats and the German Question

'We in Austria have a little International ourselves', said Victor Adler, who united the Austrian labour movement and led it up to his death in 1918, at the Congress of the Socialist International in 1900. Yet, as James Joll points out,

> Social Democracy in Austria was German in its doctrine and origins. Its original strength was in the German-speaking areas. Its links with the German Social Democratic Party were of the

[2] Bauer, *Die österreichische Revolution*, pp. 161 ff.

closest kind, and its leaders continued to regret the Bismarckian
solution of the German problem which had severed them from
the rest of the German working-class movement.[3]

This, while true of Adler the party politician, is not the whole
truth, for Adler – like Renner and Bauer and a host of other intellectual leaders of Austrian socialism – was *deutschnational* in the
sense that at a time when every nationality stressed its ethnic or
cultural identity, the German-speakers, too, used *deutsch* as a distin-
guishing prefix, perhaps in the way in which one speaks of *Deutsch-
schweizer* or French Canadians. That *deutschnational* originally
meant very little else is shown by the fact that in their youth not
only the Jewish Victor Adler and Theodor Herzl, later founder of
the Zionist movement, but also Karl Lueger, the Catholic people's
tribune and mayor of Vienna, belonged to the same movement as
Georg Ritter von Schönerer, the anti-Austrian, anti-clerical, and
anti-semitic leader. The growing class differences resulting from the
rapid industrialization and the development of finance capitalism
in the last few decades of the nineteenth century converted Adler
and others to socialism, led Lueger to found the *Christlichsoziale
Partei*, and left Schönerer to provide the basis for the aggressively
nationalist parties and unions which were the forerunners of
National Socialism.

This latter development has linked the *Deutschnationalen* with
the Nazis, and many historians to this day adopt an apologetic tone
when dealing with this *deutschnational* phase of Austria's history.
But it must not be forgotten that the German-speakers were a
minority among the Habsburg peoples, that they were the culturally
(and socially) most advanced group and derived their intellectual
and literary impulses from the great cultural heritage which distinguished the Germans from all other nations in Central and eastern
Europe. Weimar, not Berlin or Vienna, was the spiritual home of
the German-speaking intelligentsia in Austria, and it was towards
Germany that the socialist leaders turned when the Habsburg Reich
broke up and left Vienna with a few Alpine provinces.

There was certainly no adulation of Germany on the part of the
leaders who came now to the fore, nor was it any longer the
Deutschnationalismus which an older generation of Austrian
Socialists like Victor Adler or Pernerstorfer had grown up in.
Bauer's background – German–Czech Jewish – made him impervious
to the blandishments of German nationalism; and his writings
reveal a strong anti-German bias which extended even to his assess-

[3] James Joll, *The Second International 1889–1914* (London, 1968), pp.
117–18.

ment of the philosophy of the German Social Democratic Party (as in his book *Bolschewismus oder Sozialdemokratie*). But as a Marxist he saw in union with Germany the final stage in an historical process, the completion of the German bourgeois revolution which had failed in 1848; coupled with the economic argument, based on the size and structure of *Restösterreich* (the German-speaking 'rest' of the old Austria), and the isolation of the young republic from her nationalist neighbours, the case for the *Anschluss* seemed incontrovertible.

Thus for Bauer – and very soon for the party as a whole – it was not 'the voice of the blood' which motivated them but sober political calculations. Professor Coolidge, Head of the U.S. Mission in Vienna, reported on an interview he had on 30 December 1918 with three socialist leaders who discussed the two courses open to Austria:

> either union with Germany which is favoured by the Socialists not so much for nationalistic reasons as because they believe the socialist cause would be strengthened by it, or a Danubian confederation. This (according to the speakers) is favoured by a majority of the people for sentimental, historical, economic and other reasons.[4]

And one month later, in a review of the Austrian situation, he gives only one reason for the Socialists' agitation for the *Anschluss* – to escape being permanently in a minority[5] – while Catholic conservatives opposed union with a preponderantly Protestant and strongly socialist Germany, and there was a 'general antipathy' towards that country.

The political motivation of the Left is clearly revealed in the Social Democratic election manifesto of February 1919:

> Our bourgeois parties loved the old Germany: the Germany of the Hohenzollern, of the Prussian Junkers, of murderous Prussian militarism. That Germany we Social Democrats hated. But now a new Germany has arisen: the Hohenzollern have been chased away, the German nation has liberated itself from the rule of Prussianism, and in the great German Socialist People's Republic the German working class is pressing forward to Socialism. . . . We want to join the Red Germany! . . . Union with Germany is now union with Socialism!

Josef Hindels, who discovered this manifesto, continues:

[4] *US Foreign Relations*, II, p. 220.
[5] ibid., XII, pp. 240–2.

The two classes of Austrian society, the bourgeoisie and the proletariat, have supported the idea of the *Anschluss* at different times whenever they thought it would serve their respective class interests. When the socialist revolution seemed imminent in Germany, the workers favoured the *Anschluss*. When reaction revived in Germany, the bourgeoisie discovered its 'German heart'. . . . National considerations, such as the linguistic community between Germans and Austrians, were of only secondary importance. The *Anschluss* question was a class issue.[6]

This is an over-simplification, for it underestimates the strength of national feeling even within Social Democracy. Renner, for instance, who as a Sudeten German was particularly given to stressing the Germanic nature of Austria, introduced the *Anschluss* resolution in the Provisional Assembly on 12 November 1918 with the following words:

. . . of great importance is the relation to our German parent body [*Stammvolk*]. Our great people is suffering great misfortune, the people whose pride it always was to call itself the people of poets and of thinkers; our German race with its humanist heritage and its regard for other peoples; this our German people is now humbled. But in this of all hours, when it would be so easy and perhaps so very tempting to disclaim all affinity, and thus to gain some advantage from our opponents in this hour, our German people everywhere shall know: we are one race and we share their fate.[7]

Against this view Bauer unceasingly argued the socialist case, as quoted by Braunthal from Bauer's private papers:

If we stay independent, then our state will be nothing but a very loose federation of small provinces, and we shall live the life of a dwarf state, cooped up in minute cantons, a life of smallness and pettiness in which nothing noble can prosper, least of all the noblest thing we know – Socialism. Hence it was my aim to join Germany so that we could participate in the exciting life of a great nation.[8]

In *Die österreichische Revolution* Bauer admitted that in his striving for the *Anschluss* he came up, not only against the Entente

[6] Josef Hindels, *Von der ersten Republik zum zweiten Weltkrieg* (Malmö, 1947), pp. 16, 19.

[7] *Stenographisches Protokoll* der Provisorischen Nationalversammlung, 12 November 1918.

[8] Julius Braunthal, *Otto Bauer. Ein Auswahl aus seinem Lebenswerk* (Vienna, 1961), pp. 33–4.

and legitimist circles scheming for the restoration of the Habsburgs, but also against German reluctance to endanger some of their disputed provinces for the sake of Austria:

> In Germany itself fears were entertained that the incorporation of Austria would jeopardize large slices of German territory in the west and in the east of the Reich. As it was improbable that the lost war would be allowed to end with a substantial increase in the population of the German Reich, Germany feared she would have to pay for the incorporation of Austria with the loss of territories coveted by France and Poland.[9]

But there were also objections to the *Anschluss* terms proposed by the Austrians. Bauer's negotiations with Brockdorff-Rantzau in Berlin in February and March 1919 aimed at a form of union which would have guaranteed Austria the status and the rights of an equal partner. As a *selbständiger Gliedstaat* (self-governing federal unit) she was to retain her diplomatic representatives at the Holy See and (at least for the time being) in the succession states; the national composition of her civil service and her officer corps was to be safeguarded, special agreements were to cover economic and financial affairs, and Vienna was to enjoy the status of second capital of the Reich, with the Reich President residing there for part of every year and the Reichstag holding one session a year in Vienna, where several Reich offices should also have their permanent seat – certainly not a document of abject surrender or model for the complete absorption and dismemberment of Austria in 1938 which also went by the name of *Anschluss*.[10]

In point of fact, Austria's demands went considerably beyond mere equality, much to the consternation of the economic and financial experts who negotiated for Germany. By the end of April the talks had reached complete deadlock, and the ban on the *Anschluss* must have come as a great relief to the Germans. Much of this material has only recently been discovered by a Polish scholar in the *Deutsches Zentralarchiv* at Potsdam.[11]

Twenty-five years later, an older and wiser man by now, Renner wrote this epitaph on the *Anschluss*:

> In 1918 the fear of famine and unemployment and the sudden contraction of the field for enterprise made nearly everyone think of the *Anschluss* as the only possible solution. There could be no

[9] Bauer, *Die österreichische Revolution*, pp. 110–11.

[10] Werner Frauendienst, 'Deutschösterreich und das Reich. Das Berliner Protokoll vom 2. März 1919', *Berliner Monatshefte*, 3/4 1944, pp. 63–78.

[11] Jerzy Kozenski, 'The Problem of an Austro-German Union in 1918–1919', *Polish Western Affairs*, viii/i, 1967, pp. 96–133.

question of nationalist chauvinism where the working class was concerned, especially since it was to a large extent of non-Germanic parentage and had hardly lost touch with the lands of its origin. . . To appreciate [Austria's] economic position is to understand the movement for the *Anschluss*.[12]

Nevertheless, in spite of its very real concern for the country, Social Democracy can be said to have contributed, between 1918 and 1933, to the lack of faith in Austrian independence which was so marked a feature of the First Republic; it thus delayed the development of an Austrian national consciousness and thereby, unwittingly, contributed to an atmosphere in which Pan-German tendencies could become a potent political force. That they removed the *Anschluss* from their programme on Hitler's seizure of power was only natural; but the hope for an all-German revolution continued in sections of the socialist underground during the German occupation and among groups of socialist exiles.

Politics and Constitution

The *Anschluss* having been ruled out, Austrians had to try and make the most of their opportunities, but the history of the First Republic does not contain many examples of the moderation, the diplomatic abilities, and the gift for compromise on which Austrians have always prided themselves. For a bare fifteen years Austria continued as a parliamentary democracy; for the remaining five years up to the *Anschluss* she was an authoritarian 'corporate' state. The revolutionary wave which had swept Social Democracy into power in 1918 – as the strongest single party and leader of the government – had ebbed by 1920, and never again until 1945 were Socialists to have a share in national government. They entrenched themselves in the industrial centres, mostly in the eastern half of the country, turning the city of Vienna into a model of a progressive, welfare-minded community, while the smaller towns and the countryside remained firmly anti-socialist and increasingly anti-democratic. The lack of a widely based democratic tradition, the resentment felt by the former privileged classes, the economic hardships suffered by both urban and rural poor, and – last but not least – foreign interference in Austrian affairs, can in retrospect be seen as having doomed the young republic.

The remarkable thing about this situation is that the attacks on democratic institutions came entirely from the political Right, and no credit was ever given to the Socialists for having stemmed the

[12] Karl Renner, *Denkschrift über die Geschichte der Unabhängigkeitserklärung Österreichs.* . . . (Vienna, 1945), pp. 18–19.

revolutionary tide which threatened to engulf Central Europe after the Bolshevik Revolution. Communist propaganda, revolutionary dreams, the example of the Hungarian and the Bavarian Soviet Republics, unemployment, hunger and cold, were a great temptation for the radicalized masses, but the Social Democrats succeeded in channelling these hopes and desires into democratic parliamentary activities. Perhaps the greatest single price the Austrian bourgeoisie had to pay for avoiding the terror of revolution and counter-revolution was the impressive amount of social legislation passed by the coalition government on the initiative of Ferdinand Hanusch, State Secretary for Social Affairs and an experienced trade union leader. This included the eight-hour day, the establishment of factory councils to be elected by the workers and representing an element of democratic participation in management, laws on collective bargaining, arbitration procedure, unemployment benefit, holidays with pay, special protection for young workers and women, and much besides. Of special interest to this day is the institution of the Chambers of Labour, of which we shall hear more later.

Inevitably, in view of the general situation, this advance on a broad front (for it also included, as well as certain nationalization measures, general welfare policies, the protection of tenants, and a reform of the educational system), like the strong position of the Socialists in the larger towns and their control of the powerful trade unions, had to be presented to the masses as first steps towards a socialist society. It was in this revolutionary period that the Austrian Socialists – who for a time left the discredited Socialist (or 'second') International and occupied a half-way position between it and the Communist (or 'third') International – acquired the reputation of a particularly radical, if non-communist, workers' party. That, in fact, 'Austro–Marxism' *sounded* more revolutionary than it *was* is evident from its record; but it still exercises a great fascination for students of the labour movement, as a recent (and very excellent) study proves.[13]

As soon as the revolutionary wave had subsided and the Socialists were no longer required to act as a brake on the masses, their parliamentary opponents combined forces and brought down the coalition government under Karl Renner (June 1920). This was succeeded by a new cabinet under conservative leadership in which all parties were represented proportionate to their strength in Parliament, but without collective responsibility or policy, until the last remaining task was accomplished: the framing of a constitution. From November 1920 onwards, Austria was governed by ever-

[13] Norbert Leser, *Zwischen Reformismus und Bolschewismus. Der Austromarxismus als Theorie und Praxis* (Vienna, 1968).

varying combinations of the Christian Social, the Pan-German, the Land League, and the *Heimwehr* parties, known as the *Bürgerblock* combination of anti-socialist bourgeois forces.

The constitution, promulgated on 5 October 1920 and largely drafted by Professor Hans Kelsen, one of Austria's most eminent jurists who now lives in retirement in Berkeley, California, confirmed Austria as a democratic federal and parliamentary republic, with political power firmly centred in the *Nationalrat*, or Parliament, with the *Bundesrat* as a second chamber representing the federal provinces or *Länder* proportionate to population, enjoying only a delaying veto. A Federal President as Head of State was elected by Parliament, but his functions were intended to be essentially representative. As the constitution was in the main a compromise between conservative and socialist concepts, it really pleased no one – least of all foreign observers, some of whom tended to blame it for the subsequent course of events in Austria.[14] As a matter of fact, it was perfectly suited to the temper of the people at the time, and capable of being reformed by agreement between the two camps, as happened in 1925, and especially in 1929. The latter reform, for instance, corrected one principal weakness of the constitution: the excessive concentration of power in the Lower House, to the exclusion of all other bodies; unfortunately, the remedy was worse than the complaint, for the new powers of the government were subsequently used against parliamentary democracy, while a weak President made no use of his new prerogatives when he should have acted in defence of the constitution. The attempt to deprive Vienna of its status as a federal *Land* (thus placing the socialist stronghold under conservative rule) was warded off, the right of the executive to issue ordinances without authority from the legislature was restricted, and the plan to substitute a simple majority for a two-thirds majority in constitutional enactments had to be abandoned. Even though the Social Democrats had succeeded in maintaining the essentials of democratic government, the earlier drafts proposed by their adversaries, and the dissatisfaction loudly proclaimed by the Fascist *Heimwehr*, indicated the strong anti-parliamentary pressures then building up, which led to the tragic events of 1934.

Of the other alleged weaknesses, the introduction of proportional representation has been the favourite butt of, especially, Anglo-Saxon critics. It may of course be possible to argue that this application of the principle of 'one man – one vote' and the equal franchise

---

[14] As, for instance, Mary Macdonald, *The Republic of Austria 1918–1934. A Study in the Failure of Democratic Government* (Oxford, 1946), which is useful, however, for the full text of the constitution and a detailed discussion.

betrays a lack of sophistication on the part of a nation; but since political systems exist to serve particular people at given times, no alternative – except possibly a corporatist constitution, which Dollfuss envisaged – was feasible then, or indeed for the Second Republic. Only since the elections of March 1970 have politicians been talking of electoral reform, perhaps along the lines of the system practised in the German Federal Republic, which retains a large measure of the proportional principle.

Another element of the Austrian constitution which has never been very satisfactory, and which is also now under discussion, is the federal principle. Since most of the federal provinces have acquired over the centuries traditions and institutions which they jealously guard, and since they provide the backbone of conservatism, it was inevitable that the new republic should become a federal state, however wasteful in manpower and expense the multiplication of legislatures and offices in so small a country would prove. The Socialists, on the other hand, were strongly centralist because they saw Vienna – a separate *Land* since 1922 – as the lever for political and social progress. The resulting compromise therefore provided the provinces with considerable administrative rights, while the state had extensive supervisory powers; the legislative rights of the provinces were not extensive; and the *Bundesrat* or second chamber, which was to have been the expression of federalist power, led a fairly shadowy existence. Since *Nationalrat* and *Bundesrat* from 1920 onwards always had anti-socialist majorities, and no central government was ever without representatives of the provinces, which sometimes even provided the Chancellor, no genuine problem arose. It is somewhat different today where the Socialist Party controls the *Land* governments not only of Vienna, but also of Carinthia and the Burgenland, and hence commands a (slight) majority in the second chamber. Here again, the elections of 1970 which resulted in a relative majority for the Socialists in Parliament – the first since 1919 – may lead to a revision of the traditional functions of the *Bundesrat* by agreement between the two principal parties, as part of a larger reform of parliamentary procedures which is in any case overdue.

We have already noted the swing of the pendulum in the October elections of 1920, when the Christian Social Party replaced the Socialists as the leading political force in the country; except for a twelve-month period in 1929–30, it was this party which between 1922 and 1938 provided the *Bundeskanzler* or head of government as well as the key Ministers in every cabinet. Since it never had an absolute majority, it was compelled to enter into coalitions with the other anti-socialist parties or groupings represented in Parliament:

Parties represented in the Austrian Parliament 1920–33

Date of Election	1 Christian Social Party	2 Social Democratic Party	3 Pan-Germans, later *Natio-naler Wirt-schaftsblock*	4 Land League	5 *Heimat-block*
1920	82	66	26	–	–
1923	82	68	10	5	–
1927	73	71	12	9	–
1930	66	72	10	9	8

The most striking feature of this table is undoubtedly the unity and discipline of Austrian labour, which not only succeeded in isolating the insignificant group of Communists, but also prevented any conservative or nationalist gains from the working classes. The bourgeois alliance, on the other hand, reveals a weakening of the Pan-German element (col. 3), once Austrian independence had become an established fact, side by side with a growing radicalization – the emergence of the *Heimwehr* as an anti-parliamentary para-military organization, sections of which contested the elections of 1930 with a separate list (col. 5). Instead of recognizing that it was the divisions in the bourgeois camp which made the business of governing the country so difficult – especially with the onset of the world economic crisis – and instead of seeking an agreement with the Social Democrats, the conservatives allowed themselves to be pushed by their extremist wings into ever greater hostility towards the Left, which finally led to the suspension of Parliament in 1933 and the armed clash with the Socialists in 1934.

Without indulging in any form of economic determinism we can safely say that what prevented a reasonably intelligent, civilized and industrious nation from settling down and making a success of their new state, what prevented the integration of the working classes in society and the acceptance of parliamentary democracy by the middle classes, was the economic insecurity under which all strata suffered, unemployment and poverty in the industrial areas backwardness in the rural regions. The real key to an understanding of Austrian politics in the First Republic lies in the country's economic situation after the dissolution of the Dual Monarchy.

The Economic Situation

Similar to the provisions contained in the Treaty of Versailles, Article 177 of the Austrian Treaty read as follows:

> Austria accepts the responsibility of Austria and her Allies for causing the loss and damage to which the Allied and Associated Governments and their nationals have been subjected as a consequence of the war imposed upon them by the aggression of Austria–Hungary and her Allies.[15]

Article 178 went on to say that the Allies accepted Austria's inability to make complete reparation, but they required her to make compensation 'as hereinafter determined'. Actually, nothing was laid down at this stage, since a Reparation Commission was eventually to go into the matter, and the clause remained, in Sir Sidney Peel's phrase, 'a lamb masquerading in wolf's clothing'. The immediate worry of the Austrian delegation was not over reparations but over the economic future of their country; as their comments on the 2 June draft put it:

> What remains of German Austria could not live. Our territory would merely consist of Alpine districts and the capital, Vienna, which with its two million inhabitants out of a total of six million, suffers far more than any other part of the Empire by its separation from the rest of the former Monarchy. This new State could only produce one-quarter of the food necessary for its population; the other three-quarters would have to be imported from abroad; it would moreover be obliged to purchase 12,000,000 tons of coal abroad each year, while its own output would not even amount to 2,000,000 tons. Besides that, this country would have to import the indispensable raw materials as well as a large quantity of industrial articles. . .[16]

Of the numerous counter-proposals of the Austrians only one was seriously considered: the granting, by Austria, of special preferential treatment to Czechoslovakia and Hungary exclusively in order to maintain at least some of the traditional economic links. Unfortunately, political animosities among the three countries prevented the realization of this modest measure of sanity, which the Allies were unwilling to make mandatory.

In this, as in other fields, the task of making an impossible system work was left to the League of Nations. We are not here concerned

---

[15] *Treaty of Peace between the Allied and Associated Powers and Austria* (Cmd. 400) (London, 1919).

[16] *Bericht*, I, pp. 74–6.

with the record of the League in its dealings with Austria; suffice it to say that within its terms of reference the League made possible the continued existence of the Austrian state, largely by means of three international loans between 1923 and 1934, and if it could prevent neither the slump of 1930 nor the permanent unemployment of some 300,000–500,000 persons, the fault did not lie with the League. But what does concern us here is the political effect of Austria's dependence on the League and on international finance.

Even though the signatories to the 1922 Protocols bound themselves to 'respect the political independence, the territorial integrity and the sovereignty of Austria', and promised not to take advantage of Austria's weakness, the fact remains that the loans were only granted on conditions which explicitly did away with budgetary sovereignty, and implicitly interfered with the freedom of political action. While the arrival from abroad of much-needed raw materials, food, and machinery, and the consolidation of the Austrian economy, could not but bring relief to the country, though at great cost to many of the poorer classes, the presence in Vienna of a *Finanzdiktator des Völkerbundes*, a Commissioner-General, whose advice on matters of revenue or expenditure no government could disregard, bred an attitude of cynical dependence on foreign loans, which were represented as acts of solidarity – though at 10 per cent interest and with better security than most loans at the time they were good business as well.

In spite of the warnings of their economic and financial advisers – John Maynard Keynes even wrote two books on this aspect of the peace settlement[17] – the Allies would not, or could not, place the new order on a sound economic basis, and Austria and the succession states were the principal sufferers. All kinds of curious arguments were produced, for a long time afterwards and even by writers fully familiar with the region, to minimize the loss; thus R. W. Seton-Watson, while admitting that Austria–Hungary had been an economic unit, denied that it had been 'a natural growth';[18] and C. A. Macartney, after describing the very substantial difficulties arising from the geographical and ethnic position of the monarchy, argued that there were many in the monarchy who were 'not convinced of its economic utility': agrarians who wanted free access to the prosperous industrial markets of western Europe; industrialists who complained that their interests were sacrificed to those of the agrarians; Hungarians who felt that they would be better off without the monarchy; and Austrians who considered themselves

---

[17] J. M. Keynes, *The Economic Consequences of the Peace* (London, 1920), and *Revision of the Peace Treaties* (London, 1922).
[18] *The New Europe* (22 April 1920), p. 33.

neglected in favour of the Hungarians. 'Much more,' he concludes, 'was heard of the natural economic unity of the Monarchy after 1918 than before it.'[19] This, surely, is making too much of the inevitable conflicts between different provinces, between agrarian and industrial interests, which are to be found in any country.

Another allegation which helped to obscure the very real loss the peoples of Central Europe suffered was that the monarchy was economically stagnating. There is just enough truth in this to make it appear plausible. By comparison with Germany or other western European countries Austria–Hungary was certainly backward in the sense that she followed rather than led the way in economic progress, and that side by side with highly-developed industries, notably around Vienna and in Bohemia, there were vast territories scarcely utilized and offering only the most primitive conditions of life. Up to the turn of the century it is true to say that 'the Monarchy possessed the prerequisites for economic progress, but it lacked a definite and consistent policy aimed at the general development of all its parts'.[20]

In his study on the Danubian states Frederick Hertz tried to prove statistically what 50 million subjects of Francis Joseph I knew from experience: that the last ten to fifteen years before the outbreak of the war were a period of great economic expansion and considerable social progress. He stated, for instance, that in the last ten years before 1914

> the national income rose in Austria by 86 per cent and in Hungary by 92 per cent. If allowance is made for the rise in prices, the increase in real income was in Austria 69 per cent and in Hungary 75 per cent. . . The pace of the increase in national income was much quicker than in Britain, or even in Germany.
>
> All nationalities of old Austria showed an almost equal percentual increase in wages and other income, except the more backward parts where wages rose more quickly than in the more advanced parts.

Whether every economist would subscribe to these figures in detail or not, the fact remains that there was no Czech, Polish, or South Slav race uniformly exploited by the Austro–Hungarians and kept on the level of primary producers; and consequently, there was no movement for national liberation based largely on economic exploitation. What they lost were

[19] C. A. Macartney, *Problems of the Danube Basin* (Cambridge, 1944), pp. 75–8.
[20] Antonin Basch, *The Danube Basin and the German Economic Sphere* (London, 1944), p. 5.

the advantages of the great internal market, of the natural division of labour between the different parts of the Empire and of the organic integration into a well-balanced whole. . . To this were added a comparatively liberal policy in regard to foreign trade, a sound currency, and a high international credit for financial trustworthiness.[21]

The importance to Austria of this large free-trading area is illustrated in a League of Nations report which shows the Empire to have been largely self-supporting, its foreign trade being less per head of population than that of any other Western state.[22]

Trade per Head, 1913, in Dollars

	Imports	Exports
Germany	39·3	36·9
France	41·5	33·9
Great Britain and Ireland	69·8	55·5
Austria–Hungary	13·8	11·8
Russia	5·2	5·7
Switzerland	95·3	70·4

This policy of self-sufficiency resulted in a low average standard of living and productivity: Colin Clark estimated the national income produced per head of working population in 1913 at 966 for Great Britain, 764 for Germany, 655 for Switzerland, 629 for France, but only 352 for Austria–Hungary, which brought her close to Italy (328) and Russia (306).[23] But the figure for the Empire can be broken down for the two parts, where the Austrian part accounted for no less than 452 units and the Hungarian for a mere 220; as Kurt Rothschild wrote, 'While the western regions of Austria–Hungary were similar in their structure to that of western Europe, the eastern regions were almost as backward as Tsarist Russia and the Balkan countries.'[24]

[21] Frederick Hertz, op. cit., pp. 218–19.
[22] W. T. Layton and C. Rist, *The Economic Situation of Austria* (League of Nations, 1925), p. 76.
[23] Colin Clark, *The Conditions of Economic Progress* (London, 1940), pp. 136, 148.
[24] K. W. Rothschild, *Austria's Economic Development between the two Wars* (London, 1947), p. 11.

To imagine, as the Austrians did, that their earnest pleading for the retention of this unity in whatever form might yet be successful, was illusory; we have seen that even Allied approval for a preferential tariff system did not produce one, and the suggestion of a common currency area comprising the same three countries foundered not only on technical difficulties. For the truth was, as Antonin Basch very wisely observed, that a return to the *status quo ante* was out of the question in an atmosphere of national enthusiasm:

> I am not of the opinion that it was possible in the new political situation simply to maintain unchanged the old customs unit of Austria–Hungary, even if it were extended to other countries, or that it was feasible to retain the existing set-up of economic administration and the entire *status quo* in regard to power. A programme of co-operation could succeed only if it took into consideration not only the purely economic points of view but also the unalterable fact that the new states were determined to develop their national economies. . . This implied a demand for the relative reduction of the predominant role of the German, Austrian and Hungarian nations in the whole economic life of Central and South-Eastern Europe.[25]

In consequence, Austrian economic policy soon had to accept the fact that regional co-operation – apart from normal trade relations – was out of the question, and that the country's only hope lay in the League and the goodwill of the Western Powers. In fact, all the great political struggles of the first few years of the republic centred in the basic problem of Austria's survival. It was in this connection that Dr Ignaz Seipel, a Jesuit and professor of moral theology, member of the last Imperial Cabinet and from 1921 on leader of the Christian Social Party, rose to a position of pre-eminence in Austrian politics. Venerated as the saviour of Austria by some, and hated as the evil genius who started Austria on the road to civil war and dictatorship by others, this ascetic and hard man, one of the most brilliant scholars and politicians the First Republic possessed, was responsible for the deep rift between the Catholic Church – which supported his policies – and the masses of socialist voters. That the Church of the Second Republic has studiously refrained from political partisanship and is now acceptable on all sides is but one of the lessons Austria has learned from the twenties and thirties.

When Seipel assumed office in May 1922, the country was in a desperate situation. His predecessors had failed in their attempts to

25 Basch, op. cit., pp. 17–18.

obtain foreign credits. The hopelessness and despair of the people, especially in Vienna, led to hunger riots with much looting and senseless destruction in December 1921, at the onset of another cold winter. Side by side with the suffering of the people, speculators and profiteers – many of them citizens of Allied and associated countries – flaunted their wealth. Inflation gripped the country; between May and August the rate of exchange for the Swiss franc rose from 1,896 to 12,218 crowns, the cost of living rose between June and July by 41 per cent, and by another 124 per cent in the following month. Two contradictory solutions were offered: the Socialists demanded a policy of self-help, to be financed by means of a capital levy on the vast fortunes which the banks and individuals had made from speculation, together with strict currency control, a long-term financial policy, a reorientation of the industrial structure, and the development of new sources of power. Only when their own house had been put in order should Austrian statesmen approach the powers for financial help; otherwise, Austria would lose what little freedom of action circumstances allowed her.

Not so Seipel. He did not believe that Austria could save herself by her own efforts: neither would the country stand for stringent economic controls; nor could the banks (with their international connections) be compelled to make the sacrifices demanded. He preferred the direct approach and informed the Allies that if they would not help Austria they must take over her administration themselves. This attempt at blackmail having failed, he did the rounds of European capitals and very cleverly exploited the rivalries and fears among the Allied Powers. He secured the support of Dr Beneš for League action by threatening renewed *Anschluss* efforts, while discovering in Berlin that Germany could offer neither diplomatic nor economic support. In Italy he ventilated the possibilities of an Austro–Italian customs and currency union, which would have made Austria into an Italian vassal state; after the *rapprochement* between Italy and Hungary such a step would have seriously altered the *status quo* in Central Europe, and Poincaré now came out in support of concerted action to assist Austria.

Two visits to Geneva, where Seipel impressed the hard-headed politicians and financial experts assembled there, resulted in the Geneva Protocols of October 1922 by which the political and economic independence of Austria and her territorial integrity were reaffirmed; Britain, France, Czechoslovakia, and Italy undertook to make Austria a loan of 650 million gold crowns; and Austria agreed to put through a programme of financial reforms and to accept control by a Commissioner-General of the League of Nations. Since the programme of reforms, known as *Sanierung*, was to make great demands on the population – the proposed balancing of the budget was to be achieved within two years by means of stringent economies – Parliament was to vote the government special powers. The storm that greeted Seipel when the terms became known can be imagined: accusations of a 'sell-out', coupled with allegations that he had been prepared to have Parliament put under the control of an international commission, hardened the political divisions in the country. Also, the League Commissioner was a bad choice. Sir Ernest Salter, then Director of the League's Economic, Financial, and Transit Section, wanted an American appointed to this post whose 'temperament and political attitude' would have suited him to bring about the active co-operation in the task of reconstruction of the opposing political forces in Austria – Christian Socials and Social Democrats. Unfortunately, the appointment went to Dr Zimmerman, a Dutchman qualified 'to supervise the technical plan, but quite unsuited for a task of political conciliation'.[26]

Almost 85,000 civil servants and employees of public services like the posts and railways were dismissed, indirect taxation increased vastly over direct taxes, and pensions and similar benefits were not allowed to rise proportionate to the devaluation of the currency. When the budget was at last balanced in 1926 and the enormous sum of 200 million gold crowns from the loan could be put into reserve, it was not allowed to benefit the Austrian economy by way of an investment programme, but had to be invested abroad. The number of unemployed kept on rising, an inevitable concomitant to this type of 'stabilization': from 127,000 in 1924 to 202,000 in 1926. But with the end of inflation, and the exchange of crown banknotes for the new schilling at the rate of 10,000 to one, the years 1924 to 1929 were nevertheless a period of boom: the gross national product increased by another 19 per cent (reaching 105 per cent of the pre-war level in 1929), industrial production increased by 40 per cent (though just failing to reach the pre-war level), and private consumption went up to 117 per cent of pre-war. It was in the sphere of foreign trade that the imbalance showed most clearly: imports were about one-third above 1913, while exports reached only two-thirds of the pre-war figures. The annual deficit in the balance of payments, ranging from 6 to 12 per cent, had to be met out of foreign loans which were easily obtainable because of the high rate of interest paid by Austria.

It was in this situation that the world economic crisis overtook Austria and once again raised the question of her viability. In fact, it was the failure of the *Creditanstalt* in Vienna in May 1931 which set in motion a whole complex of economic and political crises.

[26] Lord Salter, *Memoirs of a Public Servant* (London, 1961), pp. 178–80.

The following figures will illustrate the effect the slump had on Austria:[27]

The Effect of the Economic Crisis on Austria, 1929–37

	1929	1932	1934	1937
Industrial Production (1929=100)	100	61	70	103
Number of Employed (in 1000's)	1,740	1,392	1,200	1,259
Registered Unemployed (in 1000's)	192	378	370	321
Unemployment as a percentage of total labour force	9·9	21·4	23·6	20·3
Imports (in million S)	3,263	1,384	1,153	1,454
Exports (in million S)	2,189	764	857	1,217

The longer the crisis lasted, the more unemployed 'exhausted' their statutory entitlement to benefit and were simply left to fend for themselves; Otruba estimates that they accounted for another 40 to 50 per cent of those still on the dole, not to mention the scores of thousands of youngsters who joined the army of the unemployed (without any benefit) immediately on leaving school at age fourteen.

Even before the great crash, when the first signs of economic disturbances appeared, an attempt was made to strengthen Austro–German links by means of the famous 'Customs Union' project which had been hatched by the German Foreign Minister Curtius and by the mediocre Austrian Chancellor Schober in March 1931. It may well have been, as Jürgen Gehl has recently argued,[28] a German plot for an 'Anschluss by the back-door', but how the Austrian government thought it would get away with it – if it thought about the consequences at all – is still not clear, for the reaction of France and the Little Entente was immediate and violent, while Italy was equally opposed to seeing Austria move away from the revisionist bloc she was planning to form with her and Hungary. Although the International Court at The Hague found such a union incompatible with the Geneva Protocols by the bare majority of one, the attempt nevertheless lost Austria much goodwill. With the French counter-proposal, the Tardieu Plan, which aimed at a system of preferences between Austria, Hungary, and the Little Entente, proving equally abortive, there was nothing left

[27] Gustav Otruba, *Österreichs Wirtschaft im 20. Jahrhundert* (Vienna, 1968), esp. sections I, II.

[28] Jürgen Gehl, *Austria, Germany, and the Anschluss 1931–38* (Oxford, 1963).

for the new Chancellor, Engelbert Dollfuss, but to approach the League of Nations for help once more. The Lausanne Protocols of July 1932 provided for a loan of 300 million schillings on condition that Austria undertook to maintain her independence for another ten years beyond the twenty years stipulated in the Geneva Protocols. As it happened, Austrian independence was to last for less than six years after Lausanne, and through no fault of the Austrians.

It is only against this background of economic insecurity and social strife that the political history of the First Republic becomes intelligible, and in particular the phenomenon of 'Austro-Fascism'.

'Austro-Fascism'

The Austria of the First Republic has been referred to as 'Land ohne Mitte' ('country without a middle (class)'): sociologically, the collapse of the Empire and the inflation of the early twenties had decimated the middle classes; politically, the revolutionary events of 1918–19 and the extraordinary strength of the Social Democrats led to a polarization of politics characterized by the emergence of the *Bürgerblock* to prevent a socialist majority in Parliament; psychologically, the nation was in a state of civil dissension which at any time could – and eventually did – lead to civil war. With few exceptions, the representatives of the middle strata – the intelligentsia, civil servants, traders, and farmers – were united in a fierce 'anti-Marxism' which led directly to the Austrian form of Fascism, the 'Christian Corporate State'.

Given this common basis, the political differences between sections of the bourgeoisie appear in retrospect of little account, until the emergence of National Socialism as a serious political force in 1932 changed the whole pattern. What was basic to them all as conservatives was a kind of nostalgia for past glories: whether of 'Greater Austria' or of the Holy Roman Empire, both identified with the Habsburgs. Where the monarchist wing differed from the rest was in its pronounced anti-German attitude: the memories of 1866 still prevented a *rapprochement*; but they met again with the others in their opposition to the Little Entente, their hostility towards the 'ungrateful' Slavs and Latins, their desire for revision of the peace settlement. Whatever their particular political designation, Christian Social, Pan-German, Monarchist, or Land League, none accepted the Austrian Republic as final, and consequently their loyalties towards its institutions were divided.

It was this attitude which led to the suspension of parliamentary government by Dollfuss in March 1933, leading to the socialist rising, provoked by the *Heimwehr*, in February 1934, the dissolution of all political parties and their replacement by the 'Fatherland

Front', and the imposition of the *Christlicher Ständestaat* (or Christian Corporate State) system of government.

This raises the question of Fascism in Austria. Inevitably, the Austrian Left, which had observed the establishment of Mussolini's Fascist state and the rise of Hitler's NSDAP, called its opponents 'Fascist': 'Nazifaschisten', 'Heimwehrfaschisten', 'Kleriko-Faschisten'. To this day, scholars are divided on what to call a system that was clearly neither German nor Italian and yet showed great similarities with both. As early as 1948, Charles A. Gulick, in his monumental *Austria from Habsburg to Hitler*, used the term 'clerico-fascism'; in 1955, Ulrich Eichstädt spoke of 'Austro-fascism', followed by Ernst Nolte (*Der Faschismus in seiner Epoche*, 1963) who distinguishes between the Austro-Fascism of Dollfuss and the '*Heimwehr*-Fascism' which forced through the new state system.[29]

More recently, Hugh Seton-Watson called the Dollfuss régime 'without doubt reactionary, but it is hard to say whether it was fascist';[30] and Francis L. Carsten sees it as a 'halbautoritäre Regierungsform'.[31] It is obvious from the context, though, that both writers are thinking primarily of the *performance*, and not of the ideology or intentions, of Dollfuss and Schuschnigg and the men behind them. For in a later study, which deals with the similarities and differences of Fascist movements in Europe, Carsten calls the corporate state systems of Portugal, Austria, and Slovakia 'clerico-fascist': basically different from the Fascist systems proper because less radical, more conservative, and church-inspired.[32]

Whatever our views of the nature of the *Ständestaat* régime, there can be little doubt of the Fascist character of the *Heimwehr* which, with powerful backing from the Christian Social Party, undermined and eventually overthrew Austrian democracy, thus paving the way for the German invasion in 1938. As a 'patriotic, pro-Austrian' movement the *Heimwehr*, though orientated towards Italy, is often represented as a valiant defender of Austrian independence and favourably contrasted with the Austrian section of Hitler's NSDAP and its sympathizers in the country. This view is at best a misleading over-simplification; for even though many *Heimwehr* men fought the Nazi danger in the last phase, neither movement was patriotic in the sense that it wished to defend Austrian

[29] Cf. Ludwig Jedlicka, 'The Austrian Heimwehr', in *Journal of Contemporary History*, I/1 (1966), p. 127.

[30] Hugh Seton-Watson, 'Fascism, Right and Left', ibid., p. 191.

[31] Francis L. Carsten, *Der Aufstieg des Faschismus in Europa*, p. 271; 'a semi-authoritarian form of government'.

[32] Francis L. Carsten, 'Die faschistischen Bewegungen – Gemeinsamkeiten und Unterschiede', in *Fascism and Europe. An International Symposium* (Prague, 1969), pp. 12–13.

independence; it was simply a choice between vassalage under German or Italian rule.

At various times, and on various issues, these two strands of Austrian Fascism met, intermingled, borrowed from each other, combined or fought each other. Both showed certain national, i.e. Austrian, characteristics, which makes it difficult to be certain of the degree of 'patriotism' in each. It is commonly assumed, for instance, that Austrian Nazis desired only to be Germans. But this was true neither of the respectable, 'legal' section of the party (typified by Seyss-Inquart), nor necessarily of the underground militants, many of whom resented the complete disappearance of Austrian traditions and institutions after the German takeover. On the other hand, we have evidence of Austrian *Heimwehr* men learning Italian and visiting Italy for a first-hand experience of their Fascist ideals – and this at a time when the oppression of the South Tyrolese moved the sympathies of the whole civilized world.[33]

This inquiry into the nature of Fascism in Austria is important for two reasons. It helps to explain why the country was so bitterly divided that it could offer no real resistance to German pressure; to many victims of the system it appeared that the conflict between Hitler and Schuschnigg was but a quarrel between two dictators, in which they had no part. The other reason is that the various Fascist tendencies in Austria revealed all the features which made up the phenomenon of European Fascism, and to study them helps to understand the movement in general. We can group the various elements of Fascist ideology, perhaps arbitrarily, under the following headings: attitudes to the existing order of society and to socialism as its principal challenger; to democracy and the parliamentary system; racialism, which in this context means anti-semitism; 'revisionism' as a reaction to the peace settlement of 1919, coupled with nationalism and a curiously ambivalent attitude towards Germany.

Because it appeared to the working class as the last bulwark of a doomed capitalist order, Fascism never succeeded in making any inroads into the ranks of organized labour and their families. This applied even to the Nazis whose 'German socialism' was seen as a fraud and whose concept of the 'people's community' (*Volksgemeinschaft*) to overcome class divisions bore a fatal likeness to the more familiar patriarchal social order which the Catholic labour movement was aiming at, following the papal encyclicals *Rerum Novarum* and, latterly, *Quadragesimo Anno*. To the Austrian Left, inspired by visions of a classless socialist society which would come

[33] Cf. K. R. Stadler, 'Austria', in S. J. Woolf (ed.), *European Fascism* (London, 1968), pp. 88 ff.

about through the parliamentary and industrial struggles conducted by the Social Democratic Party, neither brand of Fascism offered an attractive alternative. The revolution of 1918 had brought the proletariat a great step nearer to its goal; now patient propaganda and political education would win over more and more of the electorate until one day the party had a majority in Parliament and could begin to legislate for the millennium. Only if the class enemy abandoned the democratic path to forestall a socialist victory would the working class also take to force and establish its own revolutionary system – thus the famous 'Programme of Linz' adopted in 1926 and frequently – and intentionally – misquoted and misinterpreted.

Towards the 'Corporate State'

Nevertheless, the bourgeois groups and parties to whom the events of November 1918 seemed a *real* revolution were genuinely frightened, and this in part explains their reaction to the socialist challenge. They found a ready instrument at hand: the numerous local defence corps, or *Heimwehr*, which had been formed in the aftermath of war to protect homes and farms from radicalized soldiers returning from the front, marauding bands of hungry up-rooted people, and criminal elements. The workers had their own workers' guards to protect factories and arsenals (and the new republic!) from counter-revolutionaries, and both sides had retained arms that had belonged to the imperial forces. Allied requests for the surrender of these arms were sabotaged as neither side considered it safe to comply. Besides, there was fighting still to be done: in defence of Carinthia and of the Burgenland; but even when things had settled down the armed formations of the Right and of the Left continued in existence, placing a severe strain on Austrian politics.

For while the Social Democrats in 1923 turned the workers' guards into a strictly controlled and disciplined para-military organization of the party known as the 'Republican Defence Corps' (*Republikanischer Schutzbund*), the various *Heimwehren* formed a federation of provincial associations without central authority or leadership. According to the political climate of a province, *Land* associations would either accept the leadership of the Christian Social Party, as in eastern Austria, or contain strong nationalist elements, as in the western provinces, where German political conspirators and military instructors, usually wanted men from the Kapp *Putsch* or from the Free Corps, held sway, amply supplied with German funds. Typical of such men was Waldemar Pabst, military adviser of the *Heimwehr*, after an earlier career on the

German General Staff, complicity in the murder of Rosa Luxemburg, and participation in the Kapp *Putsch*. Particularly close cooperation also existed between the *Heimwehr* and various Bavarian terrorist organizations like *Orgesch*, which provided money, arms, and leadership for the struggle against the 'Reds'.

While German archives, accessible since the end of the Second World War, have revealed the technique of helping kindred movements across the frontiers, more recently Hungarian archives have yielded information on treasonable activities by Austrian right-wing leaders.[34] Hungarian money was passed not only to the *Heimwehr* in Styria, but even to the central leadership of the Christian Social Party in Vienna in return for a pledge that they would remove the Socialists from the government, reduce their influence in the country, and seek a peaceful solution of the Burgenland issue with Hungary. As it happened, the coalition government broke up without any need for violent measures, but the *Heimwehr*, the monarchist *Frontkämpfer*, and – less importantly – the Nazi *Vaterländischer Schutzbund* continued as the strong arm of the bourgeois parties against the socialist opposition. Their opportunity came when, on 15 July 1927, Viennese workers clashed with the police in the course of a demonstration, and bitter street-fighting developed in which eighty-nine people were killed and many more wounded. The cause of the riot was the acquittal by a jury of the men who, a few months previously, had fired into a group of Socialists and killed a man and a boy. It is not without significance that in all previous clashes between political opponents not a single right-winger had been killed but only Socialists, and it was as a warning that their patience was getting exhausted that the workers intended their spontaneous demonstration. Even though the Social Democratic Party bore no responsibility for the course the demonstration took – except that it might have anticipated the fury of the masses and called out the Defence Corps to keep them under discipline – the crisis provided the Fascists with a cause and a slogan.

The July events of 1927 are often referred to as the turning-point in the history of the First Republic, since only then was a frightened and vengeful bourgeoisie persuaded to accept the *Heimwehr* as its protector, and large numbers of patriots flocked to its standards. However plausible this sounds, it is far less than the whole truth, for in actual fact this was the time of renewed Hungarian intrigues against the Little Entente and attempts to disturb the good relations between Austria and Czechoslovakia. At Easter 1928 the Hungarian premier, Count Bethlen, discussed with Mussolini plans for a *Heim-*

[34] L. Kerekes, 'Die weiße Allianz', *Österreichische Osthefte*, VII/5, pp. 353–66.

wehrputsch in Austria, and the Duce offered one million lire and supplies of arms to foist upon Austria a government that would take the country into the Italian–Hungarian revisionist bloc.[35] But no amount of foreign money could compensate for the basic weakness of a movement that was unpopular and divided within itself by the fierce rivalries of its leaders, until Seipel gave it official recognition and public respectability. On the diplomatic plane, a treaty of friendship was concluded with Italy in 1930, and with Hungary in 1931, but this did not satisfy Mussolini, who insisted on the removal of the Social Democrats from public life in order to increase Austria's value as the link in a Fascist-dominated Central Europe.

His chance came with the appointment, on 20 May 1932, of Dr Engelbert Dollfuss as Federal Chancellor. Though of poor peasant stock and a reasonable man in his former appointments, this physically tiny and excessively vain man yielded too easily to the various pressures put upon him: Mussolini's, his own Fascist allies', and the rising tide of National Socialism, which was decimating his own party and its partners in the regional elections of 1932. Delusions of a god-given mission made him take one fateful step after another: the suspension of Parliament after a procedural wrangle and the resignation of its three presidents on 4 March 1933, and government by emergency decree; the banning of the Republican Defence Corps in the same month, of the Communist Party in May (and of the Nazi Party in June, after a series of bomb outrages). His aim was the substitution of an authoritarian corporate system for parliamentary democracy, and for this purpose political parties were not needed: the 'Fatherland Front' which he proclaimed in May was to be the only body with political powers for all patriotic Austrians.

Only one obstacle remained: the Social Democratic Party, representing about 42 per cent of the electorate and the strongest party in Parliament. Its policy had been remarkably cautious – too cautious, most activists maintained – while the situation had worsened all around them and their own activities, their press, and their lawful assemblies had been wantonly interfered with. To their impatient members the leadership had given an assurance: that while they would hesitate to plunge the country into civil war, there were four government actions they would not tolerate but would call a general strike regardless of the consequences. The four conditions were: the dissolution of the party; of the Free Trade Unions; the occupation of the Vienna City Hall (or the appointment of a government Commissioner for Vienna); and the imposition of a

---

[35] L. Kerekes, *Abenddämmerung einer Demokratie. Mussolini, Gömbös, und die Heimwehr* (Vienna, 1966), pp. 9–10.

Fascist constitution.[36] It was part of the cunning tactics of the government that it circumvented these conditions by avoiding a head-on clash, but instead took many small measures that eroded both the ability for effective resistance and the authority of the socialist leadership. Last efforts to find a peaceful way out of the crisis failed, for Dollfuss had not only given Mussolini his word that 'the Marxists would be ejected from their last positions of power', but allowed the *Heimwehr* virtually to assume control of the provinces. One of its leaders, Vice-Chancellor Emil Fey, announced on 11 February 1934: 'We'll go to work tomorrow, and we'll do a complete job.' Against instructions from headquarters socialist activists at Linz decided in the early hours of Monday, the 12th, to resist by force an attack on their centre, and this unleashed the civil war.

It was a heroic gesture of defiance, doomed from the start, for the defensive policy of the party leadership was no match for the aggressive tactics of *Heimwehr*, army, and public security forces. Within four days all resistance ended in the few industrial regions where the Socialists had been able to get at their hidden arms depots, notably in Vienna, Lower and Upper Austria, and Styria. Officially, the number of dead was stated to be 118 on the government side and 196 among the workers. Nine death sentences on leaders of the 'rebellion' were passed, and several thousand suspects filled the jails. For the next four years Austrian Social Democracy, which had been the only effective bulwark against communism and which would have been a vital element in the struggle against National Socialism, was outlawed, its organizations disbanded, its presses stopped, and its leaders persecuted and humiliated by the authorities. Its activists soon re-formed in an underground organization, which was remarkably successful in keeping alive the movement, but they now called themselves 'Revolutionary Socialists' as against the reformist and hesitant policies of the Social Democrat leadership; while negotiating a united workers' front with the underground Communists they nevertheless kept in touch with the leadership in exile, notably Otto Bauer, who assisted them with literature and funds from Brno in neighbouring Czechoslovakia. But even the murder of Dollfuss in a Nazi *Putsch* on 25 July 1934, the mounting pressure from Germany, and the basic weakness of the government – which found itself under fire from the socialist underground on the Left, and the Nazi underground on the Right – could not convince the representatives of Austro-Fascism of the need for at least a gesture of conciliation towards the embittered

[36] Otto Leichter, *Glanz und Ende der Ersten Republik* (Vienna, 1964), p. 212. This is the only authentic account from the socialist standpoint.

and unco-operative working class. When at the height of the crisis before the German invasion Schuschnigg at last consented to see the spokesmen of the Socialists about a common front for Austrian independence, it was against the advice of most of his collaborators: their anti-socialism proved stronger than their patriotism.

Since socialism in Austria was democratic and parliamentary, and because it had achieved its power by democratic processes and used it to great advantage in Parliament, Austro-Fascism had to be anti-democratic and opposed to parliamentary institutions; this suited Mussolini and it also appealed to the insignificant number of intellectuals who felt in need of a political theory to justify their political actions. A thin mantle of ideological respectability was provided by the universalist philosopher and theoretician of the corporate state, Othmar Spann, professor of sociology at Vienna University. This Catholic neo-Romantic set out to oppose the teachings of Adam Smith and Ricardo with his own vision of the 'true state' in which the individual only counted as part of the whole and where 'formal democracy' was replaced by 'corporate (*ständische*) democracy'. This attack on liberal and socialist ideas appealed to Catholics and nationalists alike, but the Nazis soon lost interest in Spann because his concept conflicted with the totalitarian claim of their leader and his party. The corporate state became the political goal of the *Heimwehr* and provided the name for the pathetic constitutional structure which Dollfuss set up in 1934. But to the collection of soldiers of fortune, small-town advocates, and rabid philistines which made up the *Heimwehr* leadership, the only thing that mattered was power:

> Since the state authorities have proved too weak, and the parliamentary system unworkable, we shall have to consider . . . extraparliamentary means to cut the Gordian knot. If necessary, by brute force. . .

as their journal *Die Heimwehr* wrote on 10 August 1928. Their attitude was stated clearly in the 'Oath of Korneuburg', the political and ideological platform of the movement, adopted at a rally on 18 May 1930:

> . . . We repudiate western parliamentary democracy and the party state!
> We are determined to replace them with government by corporations (*Stände*) and by a strong national leadership which will consist, not of the representatives of parties, but of the leaders of the principal *Stände* and of the ablest and most reliable leaders of our movement. We are fighting against the subversion of our

Volk by marxist class struggle and liberal and capitalist economics. We are determined to bring about an independent development of the economy on a corporate basis. We shall overcome the
class struggle and replace it by dignity and justice throughout
society. . .[37]

In September 1931 the Styrian *Heimwehr* under Dr Pfrimer
attempted a 'march on Vienna', which failed because the time was
not yet ripe. But their conservative protectors saw to it that Pfrimer
and his eight associates were acquitted by a jury in the subsequent
trial at Graz. After all, the government had known of Pfrimer's
plans, and while hoping that he would desist, had been toying with
the idea of a constitutional *coup* themselves if the general election
failed to result in a two-thirds majority for the bourgeois parties.
They were bitterly disappointed, for the elections confirmed the
Social Democrats as the strongest single party in Parliament, while
the 'irresistible people's movement' of the *Heimwehr* polled less
than a quarter of a million votes and returned eight members in a
house of one hundred and sixty-five, most of them at the expense of
the Christian Socials.

Parliament is no longer the centre of political gravity. We are the
ones who make decisions now, we – the storm battalions of the
Heimwehr. The time for talking politics is past!

Thus Prince Starhemberg, leader of the *Heimwehr* and – Minister
of the Interior!

There was no clear demarcation line between the 'patriotic'
Heimwehr and the Nazis at this stage. The Styrian *Heimwehr*, for
example, got on the bandwaggon and fused with the NSDAP, while
Starhemberg and Fey allied themselves with Dollfuss whose coalition
rested on a majority of one in Parliament. But the intrigues went
on: we now know of a secret meeting, on 24 June 1932, between
Starhemberg, Pabst, the Italian *chargé d'affaires*, and the Secretary
of the Hungarian legation in Vienna. The subject of their deliberations was no less than a *coup d'état* against Dollfuss: a violent one if
Dollfuss formed a coalition with the Socialists, and a more gradualist
one if he did not. Pabst claimed that he had the approval of the
German NSDAP for a joint *Heimwehr*–Nazi move, while Starhemberg counted on further support from Mussolini, to consist of both
money and arms.[38]

We have already seen that there was no need for a plot, for
Dollfuss was in fact 'their man' and destroyed the parliamentary

[37] Ludwig Jedlicka, 'The Austrian Heimwehr', *Journal of Contemporary
History*, I/1 (1966), p. 139.
[38] Kerekes, *Abenddämmerung. . . .*, p. 108.

system without help from the Nazis, only to be destroyed by them five months later; but a final comment on Starhemberg – who more than any other man personified the nature of Austro-Fascism – may not be out of place. At a time when he was already receiving aid from Italy and was urging the Chancellor to adopt a firm line against Socialists and Nazis, allegedly to protect Austrian independence, he also negotiated with the German NSDAP and was even received by Hitler in February 1932. The documents published by Kerekes merely confirm, in this respect, what Starhemberg, that soldier of fortune, had disarmingly confessed, years earlier, in his memoirs.[39] After his brief period of stardom (1933–36) he was dismissed by Schuschnigg and retired sulking to his tent. The crisis of February 1938 presented him with his last opportunity: he offered himself to Hitler as a worthy alternative to Schuschnigg – an offer, however, which was not accepted. Having been let down by Mussolini, and rejected by Hitler, he next embraced the cause of Western democracy and was seen for a while in the uniform of the Free French air force, until he decided to quit Europe. The end of the war saw him return to claim his property – one of many similar 'victims' of Nazi aggression.

If these developments were the application of Fascist ideas in practical politics, we must now turn to the more purely emotional manifestations of the creed, its racial and nationalist elements.

Anti-Semitism and Anti-Judaism

The story of Austrian Jewry in the modern age is the history of Austrian scholarship and culture, and of the country's economic and social progress: so prominent was the contribution of the Jews once the traditional disabilities had been removed.[40] But their story is a much older and far less happy one.

The first documentary evidence of Jews in Austria goes back to the beginning of the tenth century, and in the centuries that followed they experienced the same treatment as in other Christian countries: they were herded together in ghettos, were made to wear certain distinctive garments or symbols, were barred from most professions, and fell victim to periodic outbursts of savage hate or routine persecution. In better days, they were able to render important services which were sometimes acknowledged; under the Babenbergs Vienna housed the largest Jewish community in the Holy Roman Empire, and in 1244 Frederick II, the last of that line, issued a *Privilegium* for their protection, under which the lives and

[39] E. R. Starhemberg, *Between Hitler and Mussolini* (London, 1942).
[40] For their part in Austrian history cf. Josef Fraenkel (ed.), *The Jews of Austria* (London, 1967).

property of Jews were no longer endangered by the unsupported testimony of Christians alone. By the end of the century, however, the first pogroms occurred, and they reached a climax with the Great Plague of 1348 which was blamed on the Jews.

In the beginning, the Habsburgs continued the tolerant policy of their predecessors, but with the sharpening of religious and social conflicts the Jews provided a convenient scapegoat, and accusations of collaboration with the Hussite rebels served as a pretext for Duke Albrecht V in 1420–21 to have them expelled from his domains, and many of them were killed. A contemporary Jewish manuscript describes the mass-burning of 210 Jews in Vienna in March 1421 after their refusal to submit to baptism. Half a century later, the celebrated case of Simon of Trient, boy-victim of alleged ritual murder, led to further persecution and eventual expulsion of all Jews from the Tyrol, from Styria, Carinthia, and Salzburg. But the sixteenth century saw the slow return of a few Jewish families to Vienna, since the Court could not do without their services as financiers, and in 1625 another ghetto was established, under the protection of the Emperor, Ferdinand II, who completed the victory of the Counter-Reformation in the hereditary provinces of the Habsburgs, and against the frantic opposition of the city council who accused the Jews of 'absorbing all wealth, spreading the plague, and undermining the Christian religion in town and country'. By the end of the century, and after another outbreak of the plague which the Emperor Leopold I's chaplain, Abraham a Sancta Clara, blamed on Jews, gravediggers, and witches, Vienna was once again a city without Jews.

But the disastrous consequences to trade and to his own finances compelled the same Leopold to readmit individual members of that faith who, as 'Court Jews', were protected by special privileges and acquired great influence as imperial bankers and contractors. (Thus, in 1704, Leopold owed Emmanuel Oppenheim 2 million florins, and between 1688 and 1709 Jews lent the treasury 78 million florins – the approximate equivalent of £10 million, or $24 million, in today's currency.) Even these privileged Jews had to observe all kinds of humiliating restrictions: they were not allowed to give hospitality to visiting Jews, and their prayers had to be said softly so as not to annoy their Christian neighbours. The condition of the poor Jews in their overcrowded ghettos can be imagined: they had to pay a high tax for a residence permit valid for five or ten years, after which they could be expelled or moved to a different area, and were never safe from official persecution and chicanery. There were 594 of them in Vienna in the last years of Maria Theresa's reign.

Already under her father, Charles VI, the medieval practice of forcing Jews to wear a big Star of David, in yellow cloth, on their garments had been reintroduced. His bigoted daughter continued the discrimination. Jews were forbidden to shave off their beards to mark them out from Christians. While the Empress listened gladly to the advice of certain converts, she received her Jewish factors hidden behind a curtain. Not surprisingly, she also resisted all proposals with which her son attempted to introduce a more tolerant practice. Only when he had succeeded her, as Joseph II, did a new age dawn for his Jewish subjects; in Vienna and Lower Austria ghettos were abolished and trade restrictions were removed; they were encouraged to start manufactures and were admitted to all trades and to agriculture; schools, the professions, and the arts were opened to them, and from 1788 onwards they even became liable to military service. No wonder that Austrian Jews always remembered this enlightened monarch with gratitude, even though he did not remove all disabilities and even imposed new restrictions on them as part of his policy of centralization. Thus immigration was still strictly limited, Jews still had to pay a special tax for being 'tolerated' and a special marriage tax, and could not own houses or land. They could neither acquire full citizenship nor were they allowed to import Jewish books – even the Scriptures – from abroad. The use of Hebrew was severely discouraged, as happened to all languages other than German, the rabbinical courts were abolished, and no new Jewish community organizations were admitted. To further the process of assimilation, Jews were compelled to adopt German first names and family names.

When Joseph died in 1790, the city council tried to get his brother, who succeeded him as Leopold II, to revoke the *Toleranzpatent* (which at that time involved the grand total, in Vienna, of seventy-two 'tolerated Jews' with about 500 dependants), but failed. Leopold, however, was soon succeeded by his son, Francis II, under whom the lot of the Jews worsened in some material respects, while the established and well-to-do participated in the general rise and prosperity of the bourgeoisie. Thus a new immigration office was opened in Vienna where expensive residence permits were obtainable which had to be renewed fortnightly; non-'tolerated Jews' could only stay for a month. A large number of petty (and humiliating) restrictions were issued in the period of reaction which followed the Napoleonic Wars, many of them anticipating the spirit of the Nuremberg laws, such as the ban on Jewish tutors teaching Christian children, or on Jewish midwives delivering Christian babies except in emergencies, at the request of the woman in labour, and in the presence of another Christian woman!

While all this took place, at the instigation of an obscurantist

Church, to placate the ignorant populace, Viennese society had begun to learn to live with Jews, to accept their invitations, and to invite them in return. During the war the wealthy Jews had been most patriotic and generous; at the time of the Congress of Vienna the salon of Fanny Arnstein attracted the most brilliant and prominent from home and abroad; two Jews – one of them a Rothschild – were friends and supporters of Metternich; and five Jews obtained hereditary baronies in the reign of Francis. The Jews of Vienna were allowed to have a meeting-place for prayers, later a proper synagogue, and they started their own social and charitable organizations, with the financial support of those few members of their faith who had risen in a largely hostile world. For the great majority of them – only 1,600 Jews lived in Vienna in 1830 – were still little people, small traders buying and selling largely from and to each other, a ghetto existence without walls. Since Christian master-craftsmen – and there were no other – would not accept Jewish apprentices, intelligent young Jews tended wherever possible to professional studies, to the universities, to the arts. Even before the democratic revolution of 1848, which in spite of its short-term failure marked the beginning of the liberal era in Austria, Jews had made their mark in the legal profession, in medicine, and in journalism.

In fact, it was a young Jewish doctor, Adolf Fischhof, whose impassioned speech to the assembled crowd in Vienna's Herren-gasse released the pent-up liberal and democratic hopes and aspirations and thus contributed to the outbreak of the revolution on 13 March 1848. With him, several more Jews were elected to the first Austrian Parliament, whose draft constitution provided, *inter alia*, for complete religious and civic equality for all citizens. The military defeat of the revolution disappointed these hopes, and in the ensuing period of neo-absolutism Jews were once again made to swear an oath of loyalty, as well as having their freedom curtailed. But economic liberalism proved stronger than political reaction. Vienna's Jewish community – already 14,000 strong – obtained its communal organization, a second synagogue, and a theological seminary. In the national economy as well as in the professions they became indispensable, and the results were not long delayed: they were admitted to several trades, could buy and own land, and eventually Anselm Rothschild joined the *Herrenhaus* as the first Jew in that aristocratic chamber.

The real breakthrough occurred with the constitutional enactment of December 1867 which proclaimed full freedom of religion and conscience and the enjoyment of all civic and political rights regardless of religious affiliation. This at last was the emancipation so long dreamt of, and Jews now moved into all the trades and

professions their talents and circumstances fitted them for. Above
all, they moved to Vienna in large numbers to seize the opportunities
the capital of the Empire seemed to offer in abundance. The figures
speak for themselves:

The Jewish Population of Vienna

   1856: 15,600   1869: 40,300   1880: 72,590
                   1891: 118,495
  1910: 175,318 = 8·6 per cent of the total population

They were not the only newcomers, however, in this period of
expansion. Between 1900 and 1910 the population of the city increased by 21·2 per cent; the Jewish share increased by only 19·3
per cent. The Great War, with the Russian invasion of the eastern
provinces of the Empire, caused the flight of many of their Jewish
inhabitants to Vienna, which reached a record total of 201,500
Jewish citizens immediately afterwards. From then on the numbers
of members of the Jewish faith started to decline: in 1934 there
were 191,481 in the whole of Austria, 176,034 of them in Vienna;
and by 1938, at the time of the German invasion, the numbers were
185,246 and 169,978, respectively.[41]

The social emancipation and the economic advancement of
Austrian Jewry went hand in hand with the rise of political liberalism and the capitalist economy, and inevitably, the victims of
large-scale industrialization and the increasing power of finance
capital – the urban bourgeoisie and the farmers, steeped in the
illiberal and anti-semitic traditions of the Church – turned against
the Jews as the ostensible engineers of their ruin. Simultaneously
they were accused of responsibility for unrest and revolution (as for
instance the revolution of 1848), and for causing the economic
hardship the common people suffered from, a contradiction which
survived into the anti-semitism of our own time.

It was perhaps pardonable if small craftsmen, traders, and shopkeepers could not understand that Jews were only the more noticeable among industrialists and bankers, whose activities hurt the
Jewish middle and lower classes just as much as they affected
Christians; that as entrepreneurs and financiers they were fulfilling
an important economic function and increasing the national wealth.
Nor could they be expected to appreciate the Jewish contribution
to the arts and sciences. What is less pardonable is the widespread
surrender to professional jealousy and envy in academic circles,
among people who had every opportunity of knowing better. It

[41] Erika Weinzierl, *Zu wenig Gerechte* (Graz, 1969), p. 19.

was the universities that made anti-semitism intellectually 'respectable', and the 'intelligentsia' that fed it to a troubled populace.

This total surrender to ignorance and greed found its political expression in two right-wing parties – Georg Ritter von Schönerer's Pan-German Party, which arose out of the nationality conflicts of the Empire, and in Karl Lueger's Christian Social Party, originally a movement of conservative social protest.[42] Both had a lasting influence on the young Hitler, as he admitted in Mein Kampf: his ideological debt was almost entirely to Schönerer, while in Lueger he recognized the successful rabble-rouser. The Social Democrats, on the other hand, the only philo-semitic party after the demise of liberalism, tended to dismiss anti-semitism, rather too lightly, as 'socialism for fools', which education would swiftly sweep away – a hope in which these heirs to the Enlightenment and nineteenth-century rationalism were to be grievously disappointed.

As for the Jews themselves, we have already indicated that they never formed a single class; for every Rothschild there were thousands of petty bourgeois, and scores of thousands of poor or proletarian Jews. In the long reign of Francis Joseph another twenty Jews were ennobled, and countless others succeeded in integrating themselves into society, the professions, and the 'establishment'. Before the turn of the century, more than 33 per cent of Vienna's students came from Jewish families, and their share of the legal and medical professions and of journalism is said to have been near 50 per cent. This was the time of Arthur Schnitzler and Hugo von Hofmannsthal, of Franz Werfel and Stefan Zweig, of Gustav Mahler and Arnold Schönberg, of Siegmund Freud and Alfred Adler.

But it was also the time of protest: protest against the facile acceptance of mere toleration, as that of Theodor Herzl, the founder of the Zionist movement, who had undergone his traumatic conversion to Zionism while covering the Dreyfus trial in Paris for the Neue Freie Presse of Vienna; and of protest against the social system, which led the young doctor Victor Adler to break with his upper-class liberal family and found the Social Democratic Party which he was to lead until his death. It was in this party that the great majority of Austrian Jews found their political home, and to which they gave some of its most brilliant leaders, like Otto Bauer, Max Adler, the young Friedrich Adler, and many more.

For the dismemberment of the Empire and the establishment of the Austrian Republic had not diminished the latent anti-semitism. On the contrary Jews – whether the large numbers of strange-

[42] Cf. Peter G. J. Pulzer, The Rise of Political Anti-Semitism in Germany and Austria (New York, 1964).

looking recent immigrants from the eastern provinces, or the
leaders of the powerful Social Democrats or the diminutive Communists – provided a convenient scapegoat on whom economic
hardship and post-war disillusionment could be blamed. For bourgeois parties a measure of anti-semitism became obligatory, even
and especially in the (Catholic) Christian Social Party which, after
the decline of the Pan-German movement, represented the Austrian
Right and provided most of the governments between 1920 and
1934; its first post-war manifesto proclaimed:

> We Germans gladly encounter the Jewish people and its national
> religion with full respect; we wish to see them protected, but also
> to protect ourselves. . . . In future [the Jews] will have to leave
> us to ourselves in our own concerns . . . in our national culture
> they will not be allowed to have their say except as guests. . . .
> The religious German must decisively reject baptism as an
> 'entrance ticket' for the Jews.

Thus Emmerich Czermak, chairman of the Christian Social Party,
in 1933; and it is worthy of note that while the language is moderate, at any rate compared with contemporary Nazi statements, the
opposition to the Jews is based on race, which even baptism cannot
change. In the period of the corporate state, campaigns copied from
Germany under the motto 'Germans, do not buy from Jews!' were
conducted by prominent officials of the Fatherland Front, Jews
were expelled from various organizations, and it required some
courage publicly to oppose this new trend; at any rate, there is no
record of a single prominent conservative protesting against the
revival of anti-semitism in the Catholic camp. On the contrary:
even the Catholic labour leader Leopold Kunschak, a hard fighter
and basically a decent man who was then at odds with Schuschnigg
and strenuously opposed the Fascist *Heimwehr*, is now known to
have accepted financial aid from the Reich for his *Freiheitsbund*.
According to Papen, Hitler's ambassador in Vienna, the result was
a strengthening of the anti-semitic line pursued by Kunschak's
group.[43]

In all this, the ambivalence of the Church towards Fascist ideologies again played its part, some dignitaries coming out with
openly anti-semitic statements, others remaining silent when they
should have spoken out. When challenged on the un-Christian
nature of anti-semitism, Catholic apologists sometimes contended
that they were not opposed to Jews, but to 'Jewish' materialism,
atheism, Marxism; and some bright publicist coined the term 'Anti-

[43] *Documents on German Foreign Policy*, series C, vol. 5 (London, 1966),
pp. 224–7.

Judaism' as the Christian version of anti-semitism. It was difficult to decide in March 1938, and made little difference to the Jews anyway, whether the perpetrators of pogroms acted on grounds of anti-semitism or of anti-Judaism. But here, as in other respects, Austro-Fascism had prepared the ground for the tragic end of Austrian Jewry which the Nazi occupation brought about.

'Revisionism' and Nationalism

'Revisionism' in the inter-war years aimed at undoing the work of the peace conference of 1919. In the area under discussion it meant two things, however: for Mussolini it became an instrument of Italian interests in the Danubian region, utilizing Hungarian desires for frontier revision to establish his sphere of influence there. In this scheme Austria was needed both as a territorial link with Hungary (to facilitate the illicit transfer of arms) and for additional pressure on the Little Entente, particularly on Yugoslavia. Hitler's revisionist aims, on the other hand, were rather more radical and long-term: the absorption of Austria, to be followed by the piecemeal reconquest of former Austrian lands which could be claimed on ethnic grounds or as 'living-space'. Thus neither brand of Fascism in Austria had any immediate revisionist aims; the Nazis were prepared to wait for a lead from Germany, and the Austro-Fascists for the crumbling of the existing order, in the hope that they might pick up some crumbs. Apart from nostalgia for the former Greater Austria, the Austrian Right had no real quarrel with either Yugoslavia or Czechoslovakia, but the one genuine national complaint they had – in common with all other Austrians – neither Nazis nor *Heimwehr* were allowed to voice: the problem of the South Tyrol.

Once the Austrian government had embarked on its Italian course, and Mussolini had promised massive support for the *Heimwehr*, the South Tyrol became an absolute taboo. Mussolini was, of course, aware of feelings in Austria, and at Easter 1928, when he offered the *Heimwehr* one million lire and arms provided it would try and seize power, he promised: 'When this has been done, I am prepared to negotiate with the new government improvements in the situation of the German minority in South Tyrol.'

On Grandi's advice this was specified to mean a government in which Steidle would have the decisive voice, provided the latter gave a written undertaking never to raise the issue in public, officially or otherwise. Steidle – Tyrolese himself – readily pledged his word;[44] and it was not for want of trying that his pledge was never put to the test.

[44] Kerekes, *Abenddämmerung . . .*, pp. 10, 19.

The Nazis, on the other hand, were bound by party discipline to obey Hitler's decision that a relatively small issue like South Tyrol must not be allowed to damage the good relations between the two Fascist nations. Nevertheless, there were rumblings of anti-Italian sentiment throughout the period, and they almost reached crisis proportions in 1939 when Hitler 'liquidated' the South Tyrol problem by means of a transfer of population to the Reich. Even the Tyrolese *Gauleiter* himself, according to a 'situation report' of Himmler's SD, had some harsh words for his Fascist allies:

> If there are still people in Italy who believe they need not be satisfied with the frontier on the Brenner pass and talk about a frontier in the Karwendel mountains, it might likewise occur to us to speak of a frontier at Salurn.[45]

Thus, apart from the odd indiscretion or violation of discipline, both Nazis and Austro-Fascists proved throughout this period that their national feelings *vis-à-vis* their neighbours and their desires for revision were extremely elastic concepts, means to certain political ends rather than the genuine passion of democratic nationalism of the nineteenth century. Only in respect of their attitude to Germany did National Socialists evince a genuine conviction: that it was unnatural for Austria to be separated from the Reich and that it was their duty to work for a reunion. It was on this issue that the anti-socialist partnership between German-orientated and Italian-orientated Fascists broke up, that Hitler and Mussolini between 1934 and 1936 began to face each other as rivals across the narrow strip of Austrian territory that separated them, and that the Schuschnigg administration and its Fatherland Front awoke to the need for defending Austrian independence. Unfortunately, considering the ambivalent attitude of Austrian conservatism towards 'Germandom', the Austrian Right was fighting this battle against its ruthless, German-led competitors with both hands tied behind its back.

This leaning towards the German 'folk' was common to all right-wing groups. It began in 1920 with the monarchist *Frontkämpferbund*[46] defining its ideal as 'the unification of the entire German *Volk*'. The *Heimwehr* leader Steidle wished 'to reconquer [Austria] for the German *Volkstum*'. The notorious Korneuburg Oath of the *Heimwehr*, the first serious challenge to Parliament and democratic politics, spoke of the determination of the organization 'to serve the whole community of the German *Volk*' and asked each member 'to

---

[45] National Archives, Washington, Microfilm T84 R14 40, 589.
[46] 'Ex-Combatants' League', a right-wing organization.

realize and to proclaim that he is one of the bearers of a new German national outlook'. The same ambivalence, only less excusably, governed the outlook of the conservative authoritarians. Ignaz Seipel, Catholic prelate and undisputed leader of the conservative camp, in the course of a lecture given at the Sorbonne, said: 'We are often criticized for lacking all national feeling and proclaiming ourselves Germans. Certainly, this is so, and not only among Pan-Germans; there is not an Austrian who would not say the same'. Engelbert Dollfuss, shortly after the suspension of Parliament, on 2 April 1933, addressed the Catholic Men's Guild and after warning them against 'Jewish Marxism' exclaimed: 'We are the representatives of the Christian-German people of Austria, called upon to inaugurate the rebuilding of our state in the spirit of the Christian-German *Weltanschauung.*' He was followed by Cardinal Innitzer who linked his support for the corporate state idea with a profession of his German outlook: 'We must not forget that we are Germans, members of a nation that has contributed so eminently to the culture of mankind. We are proud of belonging to the German people.' It was Dollfuss who inserted in the programme of the Fatherland Front the ominous words of Austria's mission in Central Europe 'for the future good of every German'. Within fourteen months he paid for his policies with his life.

Schuschnigg's judgement of Dollfuss – 'a Catholic Pan-German' – applied with equal force to himself; like many a Catholic of his background and time, steeped in Romantic mysticism, he saw the Holy Roman Empire behind the trappings of the Third Reich. His policies, as the new Chancellor, are rationally inexplicable. The recent publication of the German documents has for the first time made it clear that the 'July Agreement' of 1936 between Hitler and Schuschnigg, which provided for the inclusion of several Nazis in the cabinet and defined Austria as a German state, was not forced upon Schuschnigg but represented his own idea of a solution. It was in April 1936 that he first mentioned the possibility of recognizing the 'national opposition' in a closed circle of friends (one of whom immediately informed Papen), and asked his chief of cabinet for a list of suitable names. He surrounded himself with *National-betonte,*[47] Catholics like himself, who betrayed him in the hour of need, while holding out against the slightest gesture of appeasement to the outlawed Socialists and trade unionists until it was too late. Even within days of the invasion he asked Austrians, in his ill-fated plebiscite, to vote for an Austria 'free *and German,* independent and social, Christian and united', and his only reason for surrendering without a fight on 11 March 1938 was 'lest *German* blood be spilt'.

[47] i.e., men of known pro-German leanings.

Sentiments of this kind were constantly expressed in the conservative, Pan-German, and Fascist newspapers and on their platforms. What was even more ominous was that education became the chief vehicle of *Deutschnationalismus*. While an early directive, issued by the Ministry of Education in 1919, could still be excused as part of the *Anschluss* agitation –

The separation of *Deutschösterreich* from the non-German peoples of the monarchy makes it a matter of course that in future we shall present the history of our homeland more than hitherto as part of the history of Germany[48]

– syllabuses and prescribed texts continued in the same spirit at a time when wiser counsels should have prevailed. The interpretation published in 1930 of the aims of elementary education stressed the need for children to be brought up to act in the spirit of the *Volkstum* – and what was meant was German, and not a specific Austrian, *Volkstum*. Geography lessons were to deal with Austria and Germany 'as well as with Europe and overseas'. History teaching was to be built round scenes from the history of the province (*Heimat*), the fatherland, and the German people – a kind of 'territorial hierarchy of values', which permeated much of the teaching.

The teachers of senior pupils were instructed, in 1928, to stress 'the history of the Austrian fatherland and the German people'. Geography lessons were to give information about 'Austria and the other areas of German settlement in Europe'. But far worse was to come in the secondary schools where the regulations of 1927 identified Austria with the German people, omitted all reference to Austria's cultural tradition by treating it without qualification as part of German culture, and stated explicitly that the aim of secondary education was to 'train educated Germans' ('gebildete Deutsche zu erziehen'). This complete disregard for the valuable and characteristic contribution which the non-Germanic peoples – Slavs, Magyars, and Latins – made to Austrian culture played directly into the hands of those who planned their policies on the basis of German superiority. (It is reassuring to see that the post-war Education Act of 1962, while quite properly having the study of Austria at its centre, makes no mention of Germany but sees Austria as a member of a wider community; the 'hierarchy of values' is now: Austria – Europe – the World.)

[48] This and the following quotations are from Franz Göbhart, 'Schule und Nation', in *Die österreichische Nation: Zwischen zwei Nationalismen* (Vienna, 1967), pp. 52–6, 63.

The Beginnings of Patriotism

Nevertheless, this period of authoritarian obscurantism also produced some promising beginnings of a positive patriotism, on the Right as well as on the Left. Conservatives – mostly scholars, publicists, writers – began to resist the assumption that there was no Austrian character except as part of the German nation. Against the cynical Nazi slogan that the Austrian nation was but a 'hallucination', they went back into Austrian history to discover the first stirrings of a national consciousness and its recognition by the government. They discovered the term 'Austrian nation' as early as 1797 in the official *Wiener Zeitung*; in 1807 Count Stadion commented on the creation of the *Kaiserreich Österreich* with the words: 'We have constituted ourselves as a nation'; and in 1807 the edition of an 'Austrian Plutarch' preached the virtues of a national spirit over the local patriotism of the provinces. None of this was very meaningful, and every one of these mentions of 'Austrianism' can be countered with a much larger number of quotations pointing in the opposite direction. Nevertheless, it reassured and strengthened the resolve of all patriots.

From the 1920s onwards clubs and circles began to form which served the same purpose; for instance the *Österreichische Aktion*, whose head, Ernst Karl Winter, was to become deputy mayor of Vienna in 1934 – one of the few conciliatory gestures of the régime towards the Left; or the *Österreichische Gemeinschaft*, one of whose leaders was among the first casualties in Dachau concentration camp. Supported by writers and poets they particularly stressed the different psychological make-up of Austrians and Germans, crediting the former with all the qualities (of tolerance, pragmatism, etc.) which the latter were supposed to lack. Their 'discovery' of the *Österreichische Mensch*, first apostrophized by Schiller, developed by Grillparzer, and popularized by Hofmannsthal, Bahr, and Wildgans, met with the expected response: it infuriated the Nazis, provoked the Socialists (who referred to this strange creation as 'homunculus Austriacus'), and was ignored by the conservative politicians who were planning the destruction of Social Democracy.

For the real weakness of these Austrian patriots lay in the fact that they were all associated with the authoritarian régime; to the Left, which was mourning its dead and its prisoners, which saw its institutions destroyed, its members persecuted and ridiculed, patriotism appeared as a hollow farce and mockery. Instinctively they sensed what was not revealed until after the war,[49] that Doll-

[49] K. H. Sailer, *Geheimer Briefwechsel Mussolini–Dollfuss* (Vienna, 1949), pp. 23–9.

fuss had planned all along to prepare the attack on democracy behind a smokescreen of 'intensive vaterländische Propaganda'[50] for the awakening of Austrian patriotism. It was the personal tragedy of honest and well-meaning men that they appeared to be the tools of less honest and evil-minded men, that the Left was not prepared to distinguish between them and the ideologues of the régime.

Only the Communists, a very small minority in the labour movement, took the initiative in reconsidering the position of the Left vis-à-vis the Austrian tradition. Earlier communist attempts in Germany to counter the appeal of National Socialism by outdoing the Nazis in extreme nationalism had never been taken up in Austria, where National Socialism had been an insignificant force before 1931. Now, however, the international situation had changed. In 1935 the seventh world congress of the Comintern adopted the Popular Front tactics, which helped to win the French elections in the following year. Communists adopted the French tricolour, with the hammer and sickle banished into a small corner, and referred to themselves as 'les Français communistes'. The Spanish Civil War popularized the idea of patriotic unity against Fascist aggression; the time had come for a similar policy in Austria.

In the theoretical journal of the underground Austrian Communist Party, *Weg und Ziel*, a series of important articles on 'The National Question in Austria' was started in the March 1937 issue. At that time the author, Alfred Klahr, who was to die a few years later after a successful escape from Auschwitz, was a lone voice; even the editorial introduction to the first instalment was extremely cautious and still used the term 'deutsche Österreicher', for Klahr's thesis ran counter to every tradition and every mood in the labour movement.

There can be no doubt that these articles represented an advance on earlier attempts to define the characteristics of an Austrian nation, and, by laying even greater stress on the socio-economic factors than Bauer had done, removed some of the dangerous temptations to operate with spiritual and pseudo-historical concepts. On the other hand, by relying too much on Stalin's definition of the nation which lent itself to schematism and insufficient regard to the peculiarities of different national histories, Klahr laid himself open to charges of over-simplification and vulgarization: if a 'common territory' is one of the national criteria as against feudal particularism, and if it is valid in the cases of England and the U.S.A., why should it then not apply to *Grossdeutschland*? If the 'community of economic life' is a criterion of the nation as against feudal economic autarky, could this not also be said for the economic

50 'intensive patriotic propaganda'

imperialism of the Third Reich? Likewise, to prove the existence of a common culture it is not enough to list all those writers and thinkers who were born on Austrian territory regardless of their contribution to progress and national awareness.[51]

The habitual communist tendency to over-simplification led, after the adoption of Klahr's thesis by the KPÖ, to an uncritical glorification of Austria's past; Maria Theresa, Prince Eugene of Savoy, Andreas Hofer, and many others suddenly appeared in communist literature as protagonists of an Austrian nation – very much in line with the 'rediscovery' of 'the true spirit' of Russian history undertaken by the CPSU. Not surprisingly the Socialists reacted sharply:

> The Communist Party of Austria knows that any closer political co-operation with us Revolutionary Socialists is out of the question . . . as long as it peddles Austrian patriotism instead of mobilizing the labour movement for revolutionary purposes.[52]

And 'revolutionary purposes' to the Socialists meant, not the struggle for Austrian independence, possibly even in company with *Heimwehr*-Fascists and monarchists, but the united struggle of the German and Austrian working classes against Hitler and for the establishment of socialism throughout Europe.

However, even though the 'patriotic' wings of the Right and the Left were insignificant minorities at the time of the German invasion, their efforts had not been in vain. During the seven years of Nazi rule, Austrians of both camps and none learned to appreciate national as well as political freedom, and the Second Republic was to benefit from the labours of the few.

Finis Austriae

Austria did not just disappear on 13 March 1938 with the German invasion and the *Anschluss*. Given the international situation in the thirties, with two dictatorial régimes pressing on her, Austria's only – if limited – chance lay in a maximum of unity, of national solidarity. As from 12 February 1934, with the representatives of nearly half the population excluded from all responsibility, she was doomed. To this day it is still not clear how the minority régime of the Fatherland Front hoped to weather the threatening storm, and even Schuschnigg's three attempts at self-justification,[53] however

---

[51] For a self-critical analysis of this controversy cf. Franz Marek, 'Die österreichische Nation in der wissenschaftlichen Erkenntnis', in *Die österreichische Nation: Zwischen zwei Nationalismen* (Vienna, 1967), pp. 153–62.

[52] *Der sozialistische Kampf* (Paris), 29 July 1939.

[53] Kurt Schuschnigg, *Dreimal Österreich* (Vienna, 1937); *Ein Requiem in Rot-Weiß-Rot* (Zürich, 1946), English edition: *Austrian Requiem* (London, 1947); and *Im Kampf gegen Hitler* (Vienna, 1969).

revealing they are on Hitler's tactics, do not really add up to a rational case. The economic situation was still desperate, with unemployment figures reaching the half-million mark every winter; the slight upward turn of the world economy came too late to help the government, while the apparent boom of the German economy exercised a powerful attraction on sections of the middle classes. But it was principally the deterioration of the political situation in Europe that hastened the crisis.

In July 1934 Mussolini had rushed troops to the Brenner as a warning to Germany not to interfere in the affairs of Austria, still his satellite state. In September of the same year, at Geneva, and in April 1935, at Stresa, Italy and the West still declared for Austrian independence, but in October the Italian dictator embarked on his Ethiopian adventure which, for a short five years, revived the dream of an African Empire, but estranged the country from Britain and the League of Nations and drove the Duce into the arms of the Führer. And when the latter reoccupied the Rhineland in March 1936 without provoking the Locarno Powers into more than paper protests, it was clear to all concerned – and not least to Mussolini – that from now on it was Germany who would determine the orientation of European affairs. To anxious enquiries from Austria the answer now was: for your own sake, seek an accommodation with the Germans; we can't do very much more for you.

The 'July Agreement' of 1936 was the outcome, and because it committed Austria to what was known as a 'German course' it further weakened Austria's modest freedom of action and contributed to the universal pessimism regarding the country's chances. In this agreement, it is true, Germany acknowledged Austrian independence, but only on condition that Schuschnigg granted an amnesty to imprisoned Nazis, allowed German citizens in Austria to display the swastika flag and sing the German anthem, and admitted a number of German Nazi papers to be freely sold. His foreign policy was to be conducted in conformity with German interests, as befitted the 'second German state', and as a token of appeasement two men of known pro-German sympathies, though not actual Nazis, were to be taken into the government. The enormity of the surrender produced a wave of anti-Nazi sentiment in conservative circles, just as it encouraged the Nazi underground to increase its terms and plan more acts of violence, including attempts on the lives of German diplomats, to force Hitler's hand.

For since the failure of the Nazi *Putsch* in July 1934 Hitler was committed to an evolutionary course in Austrian affairs, and his ambassador in Vienna, Franz von Papen, acceptable to the régime in Vienna as an aristocrat and a Catholic, served his master well.

He now talked Schuschnigg into a meeting with Hitler to resolve outstanding problems, and this memorable event, on 12 February 1938, seems to have opened the Austrian Chancellor's eyes at last: stormed at and threatened by the Führer, he accepted his demands, which went far beyond the terms of the July Agreement, but discovered soon enough how little worth Hitler's 'concessions' were. For the removal of the two principal leaders of the Nazi underground was more than compensated for by the appointment of Seyss-Inquart and other National Socialists to government posts, the sacking of the Austrian Chief of the General Staff, and a general amnesty for all convicted Nazis. Deserted by Mussolini, despairing of any support from the West (where Britain had virtually written Austria off, and France was in a state of perpetual crisis), Schuschnigg now decided on one last gesture of defiance: the holding of a plebiscite on the question whether Austrians wished to remain independent or to join the Reich.[54]

There can be no doubt as to the outcome if the plebiscite had in fact been held, for after much hesitation even the leaders of the socialist underground and the free trade unions advised their followers to cast a positive vote – not *for* Schuschnigg, as they pointed out, but *against* Hitler. The Nazis were equally sure of the result, though they covered themselves by denouncing the rather questionable procedure and rules adopted for this momentous decision. The German reaction was predictable: Hitler fumed, put Göring in charge of operations, and signed the order to get ready for 'Plan Otto', which provided for the invasion of Austria. Meanwhile pressure was put on Schuschnigg to cancel the plebiscite, which he did after some hesitation. Now, true to form, Göring went further and demanded that the Chancellor resign and be replaced by Seyss-Inquart with a majority Nazi cabinet. After he had ordered the Austrian army not to offer any resistance to the invading Germans, Schuschnigg resigned, but a further hitch occurred when President Miklas for a while refused to appoint Seyss-Inquart. While in the provinces the Nazis rose and usurped power, Göring insisted on Seyss sending a telegram asking for German military aid to restore order, which Seyss refused to do; the telegram was sent, nevertheless, by one of the German emissaries in Vienna, and it served as an excuse for the invasion of Austria.

On 12 March German troops crossed the frontiers, soon followed by Hitler and other dignitaries, and it may well be that the complete absence of any opposition, and the tumultuous welcome the

[54] For the detailed story of these events cf. Gordon Brook-Shepherd, *Anschluss: The Rape of Austria* (London, 1963) which, for all its bias towards the Austrian régime, is still the best account in English.

Germans received from a part of the population, led Hitler to abandon earlier plans of a satellite régime in Vienna and decide on a complete merger straightaway. On 13 March 1938, ninety years to the day after the democratic revolution of 1848, instead of Schuschnigg's plebiscite there took place the solemn declaration by the German and the Seyss-Inquart governments jointly that henceforth Austria would be part of the German Reich. A new plebiscite, coupled with elections to the German Reichstag, was to approve this on 10 April, but in the meantime, with indecent haste, the powers turned their embassies in Vienna into consulates-general, thus anticipating the popular verdict. Only Russia, Mexico, Chile, and China protested against the rape of Austria.

Chapter 5

The German Occupation

THE SEVEN YEARS THAT followed the events of March 1938 were
a period of momentous change. The *Anschluss* removed the Republic
of Austria from the political map of Europe; it completely recast
the framework in which the hereditary lands, and then the federal
provinces, had existed for centuries, and revolutionized the political
and administrative system. Since all this, however, was undone in
1945, upon the collapse of the Third Reich, this part of Austrian
history is a closed chapter. But what is of continuing significance is
the effect of those seven years on the political and national consciousness of the Austrian people: it was the experience of foreign
(albeit German) rule, and National Socialist rule at that, which
enabled the Austrians at last to come to terms with their new place
in Central Europe and to affirm their national identity. In this
respect the period 1938–45 completed the phase of German history
which was associated with the revolution of 1848 and the war of
1866, and opened a new phase in which Austria no longer features;
for in the meantime an Austrian nation was born which is becoming
increasingly aware of its cultural identity and is jealously guarding
its political separateness.

This was not predictable in 1938 for, opposition to National
Socialism notwithstanding, strong influences and traditions both on
the Right and on the Left were at work, as we have seen, to counteract 'separatist' tendencies and to keep alive the vision of a democratic federal Germany in which Austrians would find a homestead
after the disappearance of the Nazi dictatorship. Just how quickly
and thoroughly this goodwill was dissipated makes a remarkable
story, which the following chapters will piece together from the
mass of documentary evidence which the Third Reich left behind.
It will be seen that disillusionment, opposition, and eventually open
resistance were caused by the national and the political policies of
the new régime: the suppression not only of the very name of
Austria, but of every Austrian tradition and institution; the ruthless exploitation of resources and their complete subordination to

151

German interests; and the totalitarian claims and practices of the Nazi Party, its terroristic methods and elaborate cruelty.

We have already seen how quickly earlier plans for a quasi-federalist solution were shelved, under which the two countries would have remained separate but in personal union, with Hitler as President of each, and an Austrian Nazi government under Seyss-Inquart gradually assimilating Austria to the Third Reich – a process known as *Gleichschaltung*. Instead, Austria was turned into a *Land* of Germany and Josef Bürckel, who had engineered the triumphant return of the Saar to Germany in 1935, was despatched to Vienna as Hitler's emissary to lead the Austrian NSDAP and to prepare the plebiscite. His special powers were a foretaste of things to come: in addition to being answerable to Hitler alone, which enabled him to exclude Reich Ministries from all direct contacts with Austria, he was also in charge of the extensive purges of the administration and of public life in general of all non-Nazi and anti-Nazi elements, which completed the process of Nazification within a few weeks. This policy, combined with the arrests of thousands of political opponents, the public display of cruelty and brute force, and a powerful propaganda campaign, produced that feeling of helpless abandon and chilling fear which led to an affirmative vote of 99·7 per cent of the electorate, and Bürckel's appointment as 'Reich Commissar for the Reunification of Austria with the Reich' was Hitler's reward for work well done, while Seyss-Inquart and his '*Land* government' were allowed to linger on, with steadily diminishing influence, into early 1940 when the organization of the separate *Reichsgaue* into which Austria had been split up was completed. Seyss-Inquart soon disappeared from the Austrian scene, and Bürckel, too, was replaced by another of Hitler's favourites, Baldur von Schirach, as *Gauleiter* for Vienna. Even though the majority of the seven *Gauleiter* were Austrians, it was the German party machine which controlled the NSDAP in Austria, and hordes of German administrators, managers, and civil servants were now in charge of affairs in every sphere of public life and of the economy, which was being rapidly geared to the requirements of Hitler's next move.

Even though the Munich Conference, which transferred the Sudetenland to Germany, gave the world another breathing-space of twelve months, the fear of war was widespread in Austria: this was not what people had expected when they welcomed the German army. The tightening of discipline in the factories, the growing shortage of food and consumer goods, and mass arrests of known anti-Nazis soon led to the first manifestations of organized opposition. When war broke out, there was no sign of enthusiasm such as

had prevailed in 1914, and the longer it lasted, the heavier the
burdens imposed on the Austrians and the greater their desire to
break away from the Reich and resume their independent statehood.
Strangely enough, the outside world has taken little notice of this
development.

Opposition in Austria

In the wealth of literature on the National Socialist era there has
so far been a curious gap: while the impact of German expansionism
on the non-Germanic peoples of Europe has attracted many historians, no attempt has yet been made to investigate the rather
special case of the German invasion of Austria. It had far too
readily been assumed that there was no problem for the historian
here in view of the long tradition of pro-German feeling in the
country, and if subsequently there was a marked cooling-off of
enthusiasm, this was because Germany appeared to be losing the
war. The Moscow Declaration of November 1943 on the restoration
of an independent Austria enabled the post-war leadership of
Austria to make a patriotic virtue out of an Allied policy decision.

This reading of developments inside Austria is quite unwarranted
and unscholarly, for it is based on assumptions and not on evidence.
Admittedly, such evidence was not easy to come by, but the effort
had to be made. Owing to timely evacuation (or deliberate destruction) of official records and archives by the retreating Germans it
was no easy task to locate and then to examine the vast quantities
of documentation which had accumulated in over seven years of
German rule. The only substantial body of material that could be
found *inside Austria* covered the activities of the 'Special Courts'
and of the 'Special Senates of the People's Court' set up to deal
with offences against the state and its wartime laws, involving an
approximate total of 17,000 cases and illustrating the extreme
severity of the National Socialist judicial system. The records of the
People's Court proper which tried the more important cases –
including several thousand Austrian anti-Nazis – and the records of
the military courts are only now in process of being made generally
accessible. A vast body of non-legal documentation, however, is
now available in the German archives captured by the Allies
at the end of the war and published in microfilm; it originated with
the Chancellery and other offices of the NSDAP, Reich Ministries,
Gestapo and military commands, and a host of semi-official bodies.
All these documents, on which the following chapters are based and
which have never been published in English, confirm that there
had in fact been consistent and widespread disaffection in Austria,
the growth of opposition movements, and finally even organized

resistance. It only remained to prove that opposition in Austria contained a *national* element as well as the political, economic, or moral objections to National Socialism which numbers of Reich Germans shared.

It is of interest, therefore, to compare our findings with those of a German historian who also tries to reconstruct from similar documents the development of public opinion in Germany.[1] Based exclusively on reports of Heinrich Himmler's 'Security Services' (SD) between 1939 and 1944, whereas we have used relevant documents of varied provenance from 1938 to 1945, this work confirms that, local grievances apart, Germans objected to, and rebelled against, precisely the same policies and practices that led Austrians into opposition, with the one decisive difference: that their objection *was an internal German affair, and offered no alternative outside Germany.* In this respect, therefore, the Austrian Resistance was not part of the German opposition to Hitler, but belonged to the general European struggle against National Socialism and Fascism, and for national freedom. Elsewhere in Europe, the German occupation revived and strengthened the national feelings of the conquered nations; in Austria it *created* such feelings and may thus be said to have completed the process which should have begun with the establishment of the First Republic in 1918.

Since it is claimed that there was a growing awareness of a separate Austrian identity – national feeling or national consciousness rather than national pride – caused by the increasing oppressiveness of German rule, an attempt must be made to define the origins of this feeling or consciousness. It is sometimes suggested that the motivation was entirely negative, that it was due to xenophobia or sheer opportunism, and that at best it amounted to no more than the kind of particularism which is prevalent in certain German regions. Alternatively, if it was a case of genuine opposition, the objections were to National Socialist policies, economic injustices, religious persecution – in short, to the manifestations of a particular ideology and not to Germany and the Germans.

While it is obviously difficult to isolate the individual elements that make up a mood or a conviction, there can be little doubt that one or the other of the factors listed played a part, perhaps a decisive part, with some people, as our documents show. Unworthy, primitive emotions have contributed to the evolution of national feelings in the past, as they are doing today in various parts of the world.

Austrians, like other humans, have their share of xenophobia. Inhabiting the heartland of a multi-national Empire, as they did,

[1] Heinz Boberach, *Meldungen aus dem Reich*. Auswahl aus den geheimen Lageberichten des Sicherheitsdienstes der SS 1939 bis 1944 (Berlin, 1965).

and an important European crossroads, as they still do today, may have given them closer acquaintance with other nationalities but not necessarily greater sympathy for them. The common people had (often highly derogatory) nicknames for some, and used quite uncomplimentary terms for the collectivity, of their neighbours. And, significantly, Germans were included among these foreigners; no distinction was made in this respect between Slavs and Magyars, Italians and Germans. What is more, except for monarchist circles with whom Königgrätz still rankled, Austrians did not – as Bavarians do – differentiate between Prussians and others. In any case, the argument about xenophobia invalidates the assumption of the German spirit of Austria.

The reference to particularist attitudes is equally wide of the mark, for the very term 'particularism' implies membership of a larger unit and a policy of resistance on the part of its members to assimilation, or *Gleichschaltung*, with the rest. A typical example of German particularism is provided by Bavaria, and it is tempting to assume that Austria is but another South German, Catholic unit with similar inclinations. The basic error in this assumption is of course the confusion between cultural and political unity. While Austria shares with Germany many aspects of the culture-pattern which is based on a common language (significant regional variants notwithstanding), her historical and political links with her northern neighbour have in the last two centuries been no more than tenuous.

It is difficult to disprove the assertion that Austria's new-found patriotism in the later stages of the war and after 1945 was an act of opportunism: Austrians, it is sometimes argued, were quite happy to become Reich citizens, to participate in the material benefits of union, and to bask in the reflected glory of great power status, so long as Hitler was successful. When the tide of war began to turn, however, particularly after Stalingrad, and when the Allies proclaimed the restoration of an independent Austria as a war aim, both events taking place in 1943, Austrians got ready to climb on the Allied bandwaggon and to present themselves as Hitler's 'first victims'.

Every nation has its share of opportunists, and economic hardships obliterate the line between free choice and harsh necessity. In addition, the National Socialist movement, although never a major force, enjoyed some popular support. It is also a fact that Austrians were among the most cruel persecutors of Jews and Slavs in eastern Europe, and that Austrian soldiers acquitted themselves as well – or as badly – as Germans; but the reasons for soldiers 'doing their duty', even in wars that are not of their making or that they may disapprove of, are too involved to shed much light on our problem.

If, on the other hand, it could be proved that Austrians presented the German leadership with special difficulties; that they resisted the process of assimilation by passive resistance or open disobedience; that the morale of Austria was the first to crack; and that the desire for independence was never extinguished and came to be the one ray of light in an ever-darkening world – then the charge of opportunism cannot be maintained. Such proof is not to be found in the wartime press of Austria, written and controlled by National Socialists, nor in the public utterances of the leaders, except by implication; if it exists it had to be found in the internal and confidential papers of the régime. This was the task the writer set himself, and the present study contains sufficient evidence to dismiss all such objections.

One final point needs to be made. Even if a case can be made out for widespread disaffection and opposition in German-occupied Austria, does this prove more than that conservatives, Socialists, and Communists – like their opposite numbers in Germany – were opposed to National Socialist policies and methods? That industrial workers were struggling for improvements in their living and working conditions, that Catholic farmers were defending their village priests and the right of their children to religious instruction, because this was what hurt them most, and not because they were anti-German? That, in short, opposition to National Socialism in Austria was motivated by political and social experiences, by moral and religious objections, and not by considerations of nationality. Put in another way: would the workers have gone slow, fraternized with foreign slave labour, or sabotaged production, if the régime had treated them better? Would the farmers have collaborated wholeheartedly if the party had not persecuted their religion? Would the professional classes have been more co-operative if they had not been offended by German arrogance? Would the military have remained loyal if Hitler had appeared to be winning the war?

These seemingly difficult questions are best answered by reference to the nature of the opposition in other countries. Even where the *national* element seemed foremost in the resistance movements, as in France, Poland, or Yugoslavia, the experience that made an individual take an active part – such as joining the *Maquis* – was usually a personal one and not an abstract notion of love of country: fear of arrest or deportation for forced labour, intolerable conditions, the display of cruelty and power led to hatred of the invader, solidarity with one's neighbours, compassion with maltreated minorities. Discontent with public policy, where it cannot find democratic expression, may lead to civil strife anywhere; but when the authority is a foreign power, political or social discontent feeds a desire for national liberation. (The Austrian Left, for instance, bitterly opposed to the policies of the corporate state régime, did not criticize Dollfuss and Schuschnigg on national grounds since they were Austrians like themselves; its social and political opposition during the German occupation, however, very soon assumed a national character.) The evidence of our documentation bears out the Austrian contention that it was the experience of foreign rule that awakened in the people of Austria a feeling of national identity which had been almost completely lacking during the First Republic.

We shall now turn to the examination first of the court records and then of the non-legal papers which provide us with the clearest possible picture of the growth of a collective feeling among a foreign-dominated people. Reconstructions of the rise of earlier nations have to be pieced together laboriously from scant evidence and augmented with speculation; here the oppressor himself is the chief witness, and the wealth of evidence is almost embarrassing.

The Judicial Terror

The special law on the 'Reunification of Austria with the German Reich' of 13 March 1938 provided the basis for the adoption of the machinery of judicial repression which had been developed in Germany since 1933. The process was first described as one of assimilating the existing Austrian law to that in force in Germany; in the meantime, as Franz Hueber, temporary Minister of Justice, leader of the Nazi jurists, and Göring's brother-in-law, wrote:

> Until we have achieved, in a few years' time, a unified and genuinely German legal system, it is up to us even now, while faithfully observing existing laws, to fill the letters of the Austrian legal code with the spirit of the great German Reich of Adolf Hitler.[2]

These words were hardly written when the Reich Minister of the Interior decreed that, by virtue of Article III of the Reunification Law, 'The Reichsführer-SS and Chief of the German Police can take any measures required for the maintenance of law and order *even outside the appropriate legal limits.*'[3] This of course covered the activities of the Gestapo and the SS – the arrest, without warrant or subsequent trial, of at least 20,000 Austrians immediately after the *Anschluss.* As far as the courts were concerned, by June 1938 the *Reichsgerichtshof Berlin* had established as auxiliaries the Special Senates (*Besondere Senate*) at the *Oberlandesgericht Wien*, while at the same time the German provisions for *Hoch- und Landesverrat*

[2] *Österreichische Richterzeitung,* Nr. 3, March 1938.
[3] *Reichsgesetzblatt,* I/1938, p. 237.

and a number of special political laws (*Sondergesetze*) were introduced in Austria, such as the *Heimtückegesetz*, which covered all
such criticism of the leaders of state and party and their policies and
institutions as might 'undermine the faith of the people in the
political leadership', and included grousing, gossip, rumour, and
scandal-mongering.

Gesetz gegen die Neubildung von Parteien, which affected lesser
members of underground groups who did not fall under the more
rigorous regulations governing cases of treason;

Rundfunkverordnungen, which were designed to stop the widespread practice of listening-in to foreign (i.e. hostile) stations and
spreading the information gleaned;

Verordnung zum Schutz der Wehrkraft, which covered all opposition to war, the discussion of responsibility for the war, the conduct
and the equipment of the armed forces, doubts in ultimate victory,
and relations with prisoners-of-war; and finally

Kriegswirtschaftsverordnungen, which included measures against
Volksschädlinge (people harmful to the state), mainly non-political
offences in connection with the rationing and marketing of goods,
but usually justified on political grounds and, by the severity of the
punishments, part of the judicial terror employed by the régime.

With the outbreak of war the ordinary *Land* courts, the Special
Senates, and the People's Court were no longer sufficient to cope
with the increasing number of political offences, and Special Courts
(*Sondergerichte bei den Landesgerichten*) were established in
November 1939 to relieve the pressure on the higher courts and to
try offences under the new laws mentioned above.

That the judiciary no longer enjoyed any real independence goes
without saying. As the Minister of Justice, Thierack, once put it:

> The old Teutonic conception of justice saw in the leader of a
> people its supreme judge. When the leader endowed someone
> with a judicial office it followed that, since his power derived
> from the leader and his responsibility was towards the leader,
> leadership and judgeship were closely related. A judge is there-
> fore the guarantor of racial survival and hence the close assistant
> to the leadership [der unmittelbare Gehilfe der Staatsführung].[4]

Accordingly, the German judicial system became one of the
weapons of the régime, to be employed against offenders of all kinds
on a scale which was unprecedented even in Germany. The former
Attorney-General of the German Federal Republic, Dr Max Güde,

---

[4] *Richterbriefe*. Mitteilungen des Reichsministers der Justiz, VERTRAULICH,
Nr. 1, 1 October 1942.

estimated[5] that some 26,000 death sentences were passed between 1933 and 1945, 16,000 to 17,000 by civilian courts and 10,000 by military courts. Of the latter, about 6,000 were carried out and, as we know from the number of applications by dependants to the Austrian Ministry of Social Affairs after 1945, at least 10 per cent of these were Austrians. Considering that (according to Güde) during the whole of the First World War only 48 death sentences imposed by German military courts were carried out, the contrast is evident. Similarly, between 1873 and 1919 in the Vienna *Land* Court 14 executions took place; between 1938 and 1945 it was 951; to which must be added at least 130 in Graz and 65 in Innsbruck, and various numbers at München-Stadelheim and elsewhere. Every few months these figures are amended as new documents are found; the statistics of the *Dokumentationsarchiv des österreichischen Widerstandes*, which probably keeps the fullest account, have by 1970 reached a figure of approximately 2,700 Austrians executed.

The significance of these figures is obvious: 'judicial terror' was a deliberate policy, and while it may serve the purposes of a tyrannical régime, it is not likely to enhance its popularity. A typical example is found in the *Sterbebuch* (record of deaths) of the *Landesgericht Wien*, which was kept by the prison padre Eduard Köck, whose job it was to give spiritual solace to prisoners under sentence of death who desired his ministrations, and to accompany them to their execution – until even this concession was stopped in November 1942. This elderly man who, in 1934, after the murder of Dollfuss, had the condemned Nazi rebels in his pastoral care, now extended his human sympathies to Communists and other victims of the régime, and in the short comments he added to the names and data of the victims often enough expressed his own feelings. The yellowing folio pages of the *Sterbebuch*, a deeply-moving record, contain hundreds of names of people in all walks of life: from aristocrats and professional men, priests and nuns, to socialist and communist workmen, foreign workers, deserters, and petty thieves; husbands and wives, fathers and sons, groups of young workers (three girls, aged eighteen, nineteen, and twenty-eight, were executed on 11 January; three youths, aged nineteen, twenty-two, and twenty-nine, on 7 February 1944); and the last entry, on 4 April 1945, a few days before the end, concerning a twenty-three-year-old boy who in company with a few others had burgled a tobacconist's shop:

His was the last death under the guillotine, in the Greater Germany ruled by the NSDAP.

[5] Max Güde, *Justiz im Schatten von gestern* (Hamburg, 1959).

This rule of terror was in no way hidden from the public; on the contrary, large red posters announced each execution to act as a deterrent. What went on behind the prison walls was also known to large numbers of people by means of messages and last letters smuggled out of jail by friendly priests, warders, and others; Herbert Steiner has published two volumes of them as a memento to a hard and cruel time.[6] While these extreme penalties undoubtedly served the purpose of deterring many people from actively supporting anti-government activities, they also created an atmosphere of fear, and of sympathy with the victims – especially where women and young people were concerned – so that the end of the Third Reich came as a relief even to non-political citizens, thus strengthening their identification with the Second Republic. That capital punishment was once again abolished, as it had been in 1919 until Dollfuss re-introduced it in June 1934, with the sole and temporary exception of thirty sentences executed in proved cases of mass-murder by the post-war people's courts in 1945–50, was part of this process of normalization.

Crime and Punishment

The study of the indictments and reports on the trials of many hundreds of political offenders, which are available in the *Justiz-palast* and the *Landesgericht* in Vienna, enables us to draw certain conclusions on procedure and scale of sentences. Most important – and dangerous to the defendants – were charges of treasonable activities, where German law distinguishes between *Hochverrat* and *Landesverrat*. The latter, involving contacts with enemy countries and the betrayal of national secrets, occurs only rarely in the Austrian files, mainly in connection with the rounding-up of pre-*Anschluss* agents of foreign powers.

Hochverrat, however, applied to the whole range of opposition activities which were deemed to endanger the security of the state and régime. The principal offence was membership of an underground political group and material or financial aid to such groups (such as offering hospitality to members, hiding illicit printing presses, or paying subscriptions). Eventually even collections for the benefit of political prisoners or their families were classified, as 'Vorbereitung zum Hochverrat', attempted treason, for, as the judges ruled in a trial of members of a socialist solidarity organization,

> effective welfare measures are proof of the solidarity and effective-ness of a political organization and as such attract new members

---

[6] Herbert Steiner, *Zum Tode verurteilt* (Vienna, 1964), and *Gestorben für Österreich* (Vienna, 1968).

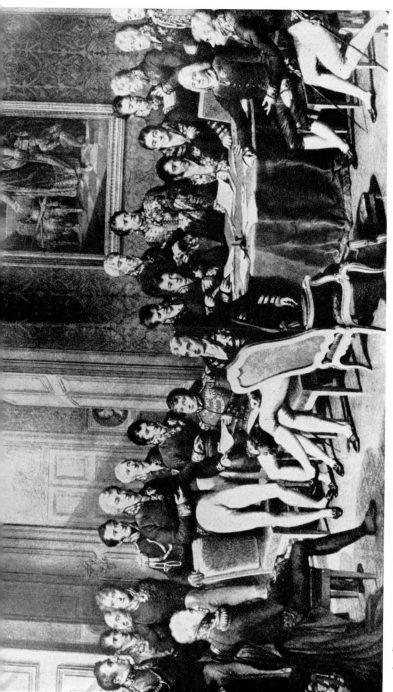

1 Statesmen at the Congress of Vienna, 1815

2 The 'Provisional Assembly for German Austria' meets in October 1918

3 Victor Adler, founder and leader of the Social Democratic Party

4 [*opp.*] Proclamation of the Republic on 12 November 1918; scene outside the Parliament building in Vienna

5 [*opp.*] The Republican Defence Corps (*Schutzbund*)

Chancellor Engelbert Dollfuss (*centre*) inspecting operations during the
February 1934 fighting

Chancellor Kurt Schuschnigg addressing a meeting in the presence
of President Miklas (*seated on left*)

Underground literature under the German occupation

9 Hitler in Vienna on 15 March 1938 (*to his right,*
Himmler; second from right, Seyss-Inquart)

11 Major Biedermann, member of the military resistance, executed in April 1945

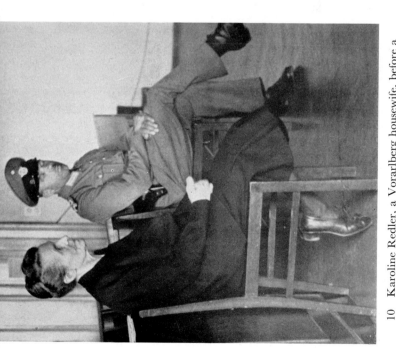

10 Karoline Redler, a Vorarlberg housewife, before a People's Court for opposition on religious grounds. She was beheaded on 8 November 1944

12   The last days of the fighting: St Stephen's in flames, April 1945

13 After the fighting: temporary graves in the streets of Vienna

14 The Viennese welcome their Russian liberators

15 Leading figures of the First and Second Republics. *Seated from left to right:* Karl Renner (first Chancellor of both Republics; President 1945–50); Leopold Figl (Chancellor; Foreign Minister, Second Republic); Theodor Körner (Mayor of Vienna; President 1951–57). *Fifth from left,* Karl Seitz (President 1918–20; Mayor of Vienna until 1934); *sixth,* Adolf Schärf (Vice-Chancellor 1945–57; President 1957–65)

17   Bruno Kreisky as Foreign Minister with President John F. Kennedy

18   Queen Elizabeth II and the Duke of Edinburgh at the State Opera
with President Franz Jonas and Madame Jonas

16 [*opp.*] The signing of the Austrian State Treaty on 15 May 1955
in the Belvedere Palace, Vienna

19   State Visit of Queen Elizabeth II and the Duke of Edinburgh, May 1969. The royal guests at Innsbruck, capital of the Tyrol

Old Vienna: typical suburban cottage where Beethoven lived towards the end of his life

Vienna between the wars: the famous Karl-Marx-Hof, typical example of municipal housing of this period

22 Vienna, the Ringstrasse

24 The Iron Ore Mountain or Erzberg, in Styria, nearly 5,000 feet high, where manganese chalybite is mined in open-cast operation

23 Kaprun, one of Austria's largest Alpine hydro-electric works in Salzburg province, with the Grossglockner mountain in the background

25   Belvedere Palace, Vienna

26   Schönbrunn Imperial Palace, Vienna

and strengthen the conviction of waverers. They also facilitate the resolve of members to act against the law since they know that the consequences of their actions will be alleviated by such benefit payments.[7]

The Gestapo reacted with the same severity whether the payments were made to a general relief organization like *Sozialistische Arbeiterhilfe* or the (communist) *Rote Hilfe*, where general political purposes could indeed be assumed, or whether collections were made on behalf of a prisoner's wife and family by his own work-mates. Since relief measures were not as a rule needed for conservative victims of the régime, this amounted to an attempt to forestall left-wing political action by striking at its very base, the 'solidarity of the workshop'.

Another tactic employed against the Left was calling all left-wing activities 'communist', thus aggravating the offence. Even where there was no evidence linking a defendant with the CP, it was either argued that 'after the outbreak of war between Germany and the Soviet Union no other (but a communist) tendency had an interest in forming an illegal organization'[8] or else that socialist workers, in donating money for political prisoners' families, 'were at least risking that this money would go to the families of Communists, and were therefore supporting the CP itself'.[9] Where in fact it could be proved that the collector was himself a Communist, or had contacts with a communist group, this was sufficient for all the subscribers to be treated as 'Communists' – and this was the fate of several thousand defendants all over Austria.

In the case of the conservative opposition the same severity was not employed towards the rank and file. While its leaders produced a remarkably large and impressive list of victims, ordinary members were usually let off more lightly; the payment of political dues or relief donations for a left-wing cause was invariably classed as 'attempted treason'; the same offence on the Right was often tried under the (more lenient) 'Gesetz gegen die Neubildung von Parteien'. This was probably due to the greater risk of industrial agitation and sabotage, especially after June 1941.

If up to 1941–42 in the great majority of cases before the Special Senates and the Special Courts the charge was treason, this no longer applied to the rest of the war when *Wehrkraftzersetzung* (the undermining of morale, detrimental to the nation's military strength) began to predominate. The longer the war lasted, and the

---

[7] OJs 40/40, Special Senate file at the Higher *Land* Court, Vienna. OJs stands for Special Senates in former Austrian territory, the second figure indicates the year in which the trial was held – 1940 in this case.

[8] OJs 231/41.　　　　　　　　[9] OJs 231/42.

slighter the chances of victory, the more barbarous the penalties imposed by the courts. Whereas originally proof had been required that a defendant wished to spread anti-war sentiment among the public, or had denigrated the armed forces either for their behaviour or their ability to win, it later sufficed to express a doubt in ultimate victory, either in private conversation or in a letter, to bring down on the offender the whole severity of the law. A party instruction to members to 'arrest' every defeatist they encountered defined as guilty of *Wehrkraftzersetzung* in accordance with the practice of the courts

> not only those who incite soldiers to mutiny and insubordination but also everyone who by spreading false news from abroad or in any other way weakens the belief in victory *of a single Volksgenosse* [compatriot].[10]

In actual fact, as hundreds of cases prove, one did not have to spread 'lies' or quote enemy sources; even defeatist comment on German news sufficed for, as one court found, 'the prediction that the Reich had already lost the war [once U.S. aircraft were able to bomb a city like Turin] is capable of undermining the defensive strength of the German people'.[11]

The Special Courts

Although the Special Courts tended to deal with the small fry among political offenders, usually individuals or families and friends, and not political groups, the files of this branch of the judiciary are of especial interest in that they reveal the moods, the grouses, and the hopes of the ordinary, non-political citizen. The activities, slogans, and perspectives of organized resistance groups can be dismissed as the natural reactions of a brave minority of conspirators; their record does not tell us very much about the feeling in the country. In the Special Courts, however, the system fought a more elusive enemy: the spoken word, the disparaging remark, the cruel joke, the latest war news from enemy broadcasts. The offenders were mostly ordinary people, workers and employers, sometimes shopkeepers, occasionally professional people, men and women in about equal numbers, few of them with a record of political activity, many with a bad record as regards their donations to the *Winterhilfe*,[12] their attendance at meetings, or other proofs of patriotic behaviour.

---

[10] *Verfügungen, Anordnungen, Bekanntgaben der NSDAP,* hrg. Partei-Kanzlei, vol. 6, 1944, p. 143.

[11] OJs 530/43.

[12] Collections for charity held every winter.

Since the number involved can be counted in thousands, the question arises how they came to be denounced. Was the ordinary Austrian a police informer or was it only a small minority of fanatics who lent themselves to these acts? The nature of the indictments provides a clue. Only a small number of denunciations was the work of professional informers (whose names were never mentioned in court). In most cases, however, a single informer – usually a party member or official of the German Labour Front – gives the names of witnesses who are then compelled to confirm the incriminating remark; or else he puts pressure on others to join him in the denunciation; in this way he escapes the odium of being alone responsible for the victim's misfortune and by making accomplices reduces his own isolation and divides the workers against themselves.

'Whispering Propaganda'

Günter Weisenborn quotes a Gestapo report[13] to the effect that propaganda by word of mouth 'constituted the most effective form of propaganda against the National Socialist state', and this was undoubtedly true of Austria. As the production of underground journals and leaflets became increasingly risky, both the resistance groups and individuals used the grapevine for spreading news (normally obtained from enemy broadcasting stations, principally the BBC), their views on the régime (often in the form of satirical poems to the tune of popular songs, or political versions of well-known prayers), or advice on how to weaken the régime (refusal to attend meetings or to donate to Nazi causes; go-slow at work through strictest observance of safety measures; solidarity with foreign workers as indeed with all opponents of the régime regardless of their politics, etc.). One defendant admitted that

> he consistently influenced all opponents of the party in a spirit hostile to the state. His intention had been to weaken the NSDAP by means of intensive propaganda. . . Even though his actions do not amount to the crime of attempted treason, they nevertheless characterize the defendant as a pronounced enemy of the state.[14]

A popular saying among workers seems to have been 'Take good care of the trees', the significance of which was not lost on the Nazis, as a court case showed in 1944:

> Josef W. said to the witness, party-member Blümel: 'It will be a sad end for all of you; you've heard that we are asked to take care of the trees. . .' Blümel knew this as a slogan of the enemies of the

[13] Günter Weisenborn, *Der lautlose Aufstand* (Hamburg, 1953), p. 153.
[14] Sg. Nr. 8703. Special Court files are numbered consecutively, e.g. Sg. Nr. 7489.

party, which he explained as meaning that trees should be preserved so as to hang the Nazis from them.[15]

There were complaints about *Piefkes*, the derogatory term –
allegedly a typical North German family name – used by Austrians
for their northern neighbours: 'Only Austrians man the West Wall
– Germans are never sent there'; 'Austrians everywhere have to take
the greatest risks – Germans get the safe jobs'; 'Wherever you look
you find a *Piefke*; one day the Führer will expel us all to make room
for the *Piefkes*'. It is immaterial that, with the apparent exception of
Stalingrad, the allegations about Austrian troops being considered
expendable were untrue; what mattered was that sufficient – and
growing – numbers of people in Austria believed them to be true.

Many other indicted utterances are positively patriotic, pro-
Austrian: 'If only the attempted assassination had succeeded –
Austria would be free again'; 'As quickly as they came they'll be
thrown out again, the whole bloody lot of them'; 'Hitler has
brought only trouble and misery to Austria'; 'We are not *Ostmärker, we are Österreicher!*'

The sufferings caused by the war, the fear of the consequences,
and the attribution of responsibility provide an inexhaustible source
of hostile utterances. The obvious injustices in the liability to military service, the crass social inequalities in the distribution of food
and textiles, and the mounting casualty lists all contributed to a
rebellious and defeatist mood.

From the evidence of the cases before the various kinds of political
courts it is clear that the longer the war lasted the greater the number of people who believed that Hitler alone was responsible for it;
who had heard (presumably from soldiers home on leave) of the
cruelties perpetrated against the populations of the occupied countries, especially in the East; and who expected a terrible end.
(Significantly, though, very little was known of the horrors of the
concentration camps and the physical destruction of European
Jewry; the closed world of the concentration camps did not offer
up its secrets until afterwards.) A few examples:

'In Poland it wasn't the Poles who killed Germans, but Germans
who tied together Poles in batches of fifty and mowed them
down.'

'Our papers are telling a pack of lies about Bolshevik cruelty
towards our soldiers. . . . As in Czechoslovakia where they wrote
the German embassy had been destroyed when not a single window was broken.'

'The Russians will win the war yet. What the poor Poles have

[15] Sg. Nr. 7381.

to suffer under the Germans is terrible . . . the Germans have always been barbarians.'

'When Germany loses the war, only the Austrians will escape alive from the Protectorate [of Bohemia], and not a single German.'

'The time will come when they will pave the streets of Europe with the skulls of these "Aryans".'

As for the principal Allied Powers, it is remarkable that most hope seems to have been placed in Britain and most fear to have been entertained with regard to the intentions of the Russians, while France was rarely mentioned and the increasing importance of the United States both as a belligerent and an arbiter of future developments was hardly understood. This at least is the evidence of our documents, especially in connection with *Rundfunkverbrechen* where the BBC is mentioned far more frequently than either Moscow or Swiss stations. Typical utterances were: 'Let the British win the war – it would be best for us and the world'; 'Compared to Churchill, Hitler is only a fool'; and 'The British are bound to win'.

Finally, morals, religious beliefs, and the position of the Church seem to have been another source of numerous indictable utterances: immorality in the youth and labour service formations, obstacles placed in the path of religious observances, and the persecution of individual priests as well as of religious orders produced many protests that often led to prosecutions before the Special Courts.

The Organization of the Resistance

Organized resistance plays its part in this study partly because it expresses the moods and aspirations of a significant minority of Austrians, and partly for the reactions it produced among the German rulers and their Austrian henchmen. Active politics in any community is the concern of a minority: the exorbitant risks involved in resistance to a tyrannical régime reduce the number of active resisters to a mere fraction of the total opposition. The majority want to survive at almost any price. Nevertheless, our documents provide evidence of attitudes and behaviour which lie halfway between passive obedience and active underground work and which must be considered *oppositional* even if they lacked conspiratorial direction and cohesion. Where did passive resistance begin? In not putting out flags when expected to do so? In not casting a vote in a farcical plebiscite, in not listening in to Hitler's broadcast addresses? In not joining the party – though pressures here varied between different professions and even from one *Gau* to the next – and in extreme necessity choosing the least political organization, like the Red Cross or the NSV, if one had to join *something*. Hans Rothfels' division of the German people into four categories – real Nazis; nominal Nazis, who joined the party for opportunist reasons or under pressure; non-Nazis; and anti-Nazis – can be usefully applied to Austria, too, where the great majority belonged to the third group, occasional opportunist or hysterical moods notwithstanding. This group is our main concern here, for unlike Habsburg loyalists or lifelong Marxists they were open to persuasion, they could be won over, and with them the régime failed as badly as with the other groups. The numerous cases of civil disobedience, of ostentatious lack of enthusiasm, and cynical disbelief, which are the subject-matter of the vast documentation available, constitute a form of resistance in view of the fact that the régime demanded total obedience and sought to enforce it with draconic sanctions.

The peculiarities of the Austrian situation made opposition and resistance more difficult than elsewhere: in a German-speaking country the invaders had opportunities for supervision and control which they lacked among Poles and Yugoslavs, or even Frenchmen and Dutchmen. For five years the reports of anti-Nazi refugees from the Third Reich had spread a profound respect for the efficiency and brutality of the Gestapo, and this was reinforced by the nature of the takeover in March 1938. Representing a minority régime, the officials of the Fatherland Front were known to everybody in their local communities, while the Gestapo captured intact the police files on the labour activists, especially the Revolutionary Socialists and the Communists; thus both the Right and the Left started with the handicap that most of their potential leaders had to refrain from underground activities lest they exposed their followers to the attentions of the authorities. (Many of the earlier losses of the Resistance were in fact due to the lack of conspiratorial experience on the part of conservatives, and to the senseless heroism and dedication of Communists.)

Austria has been remarkably slow in subjecting this period to scholarly investigation. Because, it is sometimes suggested, a country under quadripartite occupation and seeking to obtain the best possible terms from the victors could not afford to discuss openly its own role before and during the war, the role of resistance has not found the recognition it deserved. Even the first official publication dealing with the events leading up to and during the German occupation,[16] far from being a memorial to the victims, tended to

---

[16] *Rot-Weiß-Rot-Buch*. Gerechtigkeit für Österreich! Darstellungen, Dokumente und Nachweise zur Vorgeschichte und Geschichte der Okkupation Österreichs. Erster Teil (Nach amtlichen Quellen) (Vienna, 1946).

play down the problem of National Socialism in Austria and concentrated on German aggressiveness. While this was perfectly understandable at a time when it seemed politic to stress the role of
Austria as 'the first occupied country', and when questions of
political and material survival taxed her leaders to the utmost, the
promise contained in the title was never kept and no further volumes
followed this 'first part'.

Thus it was left to private initiative to write and publish accounts
of individual experiences or the share particular parties or institutions had in the opposition to the régime. These works, while
remarkably accurate, as subsequent research revealed, were not in
themselves admissible as evidence but can today be used for additional information, to explain and elaborate the evidence contained
in official documents. This applies even to Otto Molden whose *Der
Ruf des Gewissens* appeared in 1958:[17] though he quotes a large
number of documents, and augments the numerous interviews with
survivors with the experiences of his own part in the Resistance, he
lays himself open to the charge that his work is a piece of special
pleading: pro-Resistance, pro-Austrian. It was not until Dr Christian
Broda, as Minister of Justice, made the materials in the care of his
department accessible to researchers that research began to orientate
itself towards official sources; what evidence the judicial documentation still held in Austria yielded is described in a previous
section.[18] In the meantime, the U.S. government and Historical
Association jointly made available the bulk of the so-called
'Captured German Archives', while it was possible also to consult
the papers of the *Volksgerichtshof* in Berlin; material in Austrian,
German, and American hands together yielded two more books in
the series *Das einsame Gewissen* which is devoted to the scholarly
treatment of the period of German occupation.[19] This has had the
effect of influencing all other contemporary writing, which by
increasingly basing itself on genuine sources encourages the search
for more.

The Evidence of the Courts

As distinct from the Gestapo 'situation (or morale) reports' which
covered all sections of the population, the judicial documents
reveal a marked prevalence of left-wing offenders, and among

[17] Otto Molden, *Der Ruf des Gewissens. Der österreichische Freiheitskampf 1938–1945* (Vienna, 1958).

[18] Cf. also Maria Szecsi and Karl Stadler, *Die NS-Justiz in Österreich und
ihre Opfer (Das einsame Gewissen,* vol. I) (Vienna, 1962).

[19] Ludwig Jedlicka, *Der 20. Juli 1944 in Österreich* (Vienna, 1965), and
Karl Stadler, *Österreich 1938–1945 im Spiegel der NS-Akten* (Vienna, 1966)
(vols. II and III, respectively, of *Das einsame Gewissen*).

these the Communists predominate quite out of proportion to their following in the country. This latter aspect is probably explained by the fact that – at least after June 1941 – they were considered the most dangerous of all the opponents of the régime. In general, industrial workers represented a greater risk than farmers or shop-keepers: their concentration in large enterprises, their tradition of solidarity, their ability to slow down or disorganize production and transport, required harder repression than was the case with other social groups. Also, reared in the spirit of the class struggle which was part of the Austro-Marxist tradition, the Left found it natural to continue in the negative attitude towards government and authority which it had practised in fourteen years of opposition to the *Bürgerblock* and four years' struggle against the *Ständestaat*, which makes even more impressive the decision of Catholic con-servatives, reared in loyalty to the state and its constituted authori-ties, and especially of military men bound by their *Diensteid* or oath of office to engage in conspiratorial, revolutionary activities! Therefore, offences which could be overlooked in the case of a professional man, or might lead to a warning or a small fine where a shopkeeper or farmer was involved, were ruthlessly followed up and punished for the deterrent effect on the offenders' fellow-workers.

Social class affected the incidence of political offences in other ways as well: only poor people needed collections to be made at their places of work to still their hunger while under arrest or to sustain their wives and children; through the regimentation of labour (*Arbeitsverpflichtung*) they could not avoid the wrath of a local Nazi by moving, with their families, to Munich or Berlin: instead, they would hide with a neighbour or friend, and thereby incriminate him for 'illegal harbouring'. Working-class tenements are not made for hiding strangers, or having frequent visitors, un-seen; nor for receiving foreign broadcasts, unheard by neighbours. Working-class people have no 'connections' to bring into play in times of trouble; they possess nothing with which to bribe corrupt Nazis; they have no social standing, as medical men or priests have, to induce unexpected kindnesses from Gestapo men. In any conflict with the law, they had to bear the full consequences.

While social conditions and political traditions account for a large proportion of the prosecutions, in the case of the Communists an additional factor contributed to the heavy toll: it was the initial decision to continue with the traditional type of party structure, which had been barely tolerable during the inefficient Schuschnigg régime but which became suicidal under the new conditions. Follow-ing the principle of 'democratic centralism' the pyramidal structure rested on either territorial or factory units grouped together in district (*Bezirk*) organizations, several of which formed an area organization (*Kreis*), which together formed the *Land* organization. Theoretically, the Central Committee of the party should only have had dealings with the leadership of each *Land*, which in turn kept contact with the *Kreis* leaders (whom it appointed); these again selected the district leaders who looked after individual units. Thus even a police agent, or a member breaking down under interrogation, could do no more than betray the members of his own group and one other member up or down the line of hierarchy. In practice this system had never worked since the CP was driven underground in May 1933: for at each level, up to and including the Central Committee, certain functions necessitated close contact with members of other organizations, as in the press, finance, organization, factory cells, and other sections.

It is useless to criticize the Austrian Communists for their adherence to these centralizing practices, for without them the doctrinal purity and tactical unity of the party could not be maintained; in fact, it would have ceased to be a Communist Party of the style then known. Since the usual chores of devoted party workers (arranging and addressing meetings, selling party literature, etc.) were no longer feasible, the party concentrated on two organizational activities to keep its members occupied: the collection of dues from members, and of contributions to various good causes from others; and propaganda. The former activity was engaged in, not primarily for the funds raised, but for keeping alive the feeling of belonging to a living party, for keeping in touch with members, or for involving non-members in the anti-Fascist struggle. (It is pathetic to learn from the charges what trifling sums were involved in this dangerous activity: the Gestapo taking great care to discover how often a young apprentice had paid his 5 pfennigs, or a skilled worker his mark or two, and how the money had been spent.) The time and effort spent on these activities, and the danger involved, would appear to have been worthy of a better purpose; but this is even truer of much of the propaganda work of the CP.

Like the collection of funds, the production of clandestine stickers, leaflets, local journals, and central party newspapers was to some extent an inner-party substitute-activity. Considering the enormous difficulties and risks involved it is arguable that at a time when foreign broadcasts could be picked up by almost anyone who was interested, the effort might well have gone into workshop discussions, propaganda by word of mouth, and personal contacts. In the beginning, Communists and sympathizers who held foreign passports would bring an average of 500 copies of the central party paper, *Die Rote Fahne*, printed in small type on thin paper, into the country in suitcases with false bottoms. From the central delivery place – usually a shop or an office in Vienna – local couriers would carry batches of paper to their contacts in the areas, who would then pass them on to members for distribution and sale. When it became impossible to continue printing in Czechoslovakia or Switzerland, journals were cyclostyled in Vienna and carried into the districts and the provinces by couriers again. Eventually this hazardous procedure was dropped and the centre merely cut the wax stencils and dispatched them, the duty of buying and installing a primitive hand-duplicating machine, buying paper and ink, producing and stapling the journals, and distributing them falling on local organizations. It was only after the discovery of several central press sections, and the arrests of dozens of couriers that the initiative for locally written and produced journals was left to organizations, and they are none the worse for that, as we can see from numerous samples contained in the court files.

Unburdened by doctrinal assumptions about the role of the party, the Revolutionary Socialists – radicalized successors of the old Social Democratic Party of Bauer and Renner – made their decision just before the actual invasion. The recognition that it was impossible for long to maintain a national party with a central leadership and links with the lower echelons, and that to attempt to do so would involve the senseless sacrifice of all the best cadres, served the socialist movement well. The decision was to disband the central organization, assist the emigration of all whose lives were in danger or whose contacts would endanger others, while the rest should form *Gesinnungsgemeinschaften* or *Freundeskreise* (groups of like-minded people, circles of friends) which might or might not maintain loose personal – but no organizational – contacts with one another. Since only experienced and trustworthy people were to be admitted to these circles, such as could be expected to collect their own information and form their own conclusions as well as assist those in need and influence others, no central directives, newsletters, or journals were needed. (After the first heavy losses the Communists, too, seemed to move towards a similar policy when they issued the slogan '*Du* bist die Partei' – '*You* are the party now' – which was addressed to activists whose links with the leadership were broken through arrests and who were to carry on with the work. But since such contacts were constantly resumed, often through activists returning from France or Russia to Austria and certain death, the danger was in no way minimized.)

However, not even all socialist functionaries, and certainly not all rank-and-file members, approved of this decision which smacked of *attentisme* to them; and we therefore find numbers of revolutionary socialist leaders as defendants in some of the earliest People's Court trials; we discover at least one socialist organization operating between Vienna and Salzburg (and linked to a South German SPD network); and we again and again come across groups of Socialists who, for lack of a party organization of their own, link with a communist network without abandoning their political identity. Most numerous of all, however, were declared Socialists co-operating with communist factory groups, supporting relief collections and distributing literature, inevitably discovered and tried for 'assisting Communist Party activities': in the struggle against the common foe past disagreements – even the bitter controversies about the Hitler–Stalin Pact – were temporarily set aside.

As was the case with the Socialists, no attempts at rebuilding or maintaining a nationwide organization were made in the conservative camp, and for very similar reasons. Its own traditional party, the Christian Socials, had been unceremoniously abandoned by Dollfuss and merged in his Fatherland Front, and there was even less certainty about the kind of conservative party that a revived Austria should have than there was on the Left about the political future of labour. In consequence, conservative resistance groups tended to be localized, an amalgam of the trends that had made up the traditional Right: democratic conservatives (usually from the Christian labour and farmers' movements), *Heimwehr*-Fascists, monarchist supporters of Otto Habsburg, clerics, and officers of the old Imperial Army. Their aim was, generally, to keep alive the tradition of an independent Austria, to stress their *Österreichertum* against the alien, pagan influence, protect the Church and her institutions, and resist the new régime wherever possible.

There has been a certain amount of argument about the question of whether the Austrian Resistance was in fact so clearly following traditional political divisions. For reasons of conspiratorial safety, if for no other, this seemed fairly natural, and the evidence of the courts now bears it out. There did exist mixed groups, contacts between different political camps were occasionally established, and at workshop level even old Nazis were sometimes persuaded to join with the 'Reds' against the management; but the 'patriotic front of all Austrians irrespective of party' originally claimed by the Communists never existed organizationally, even though they all shared a common patriotism.

The Communist Resistance

A Gestapo *Ermittlungsbericht* (report on investigations prior to a trial), enclosed with a Special Senate file, yields this (fully accurate) description of the structure of the CP:

After a temporary cessation of activities [following the *Anschluss*] the first modest attempts at rebuilding the organization of the KPÖ were noted early in the summer of 1938. A *Landesleitung* was established in Vienna which was in regular contact with the Central Committee abroad. . . The organizational structure was subsequently changed in several ways. Originally there existed, in addition to neighbourhood cells, the factory cells which were led by the *Betriebsmänner* and had their own liaison-man with the *Bezirksleiter*. . . Between the latter and the *Stadtleitung*, the *Kreisleiter* was responsible for the contacts between the higher and the lower echelons. . .

In June or July 1939 the party organization was restructured following the trade union practice of industrial organizations: the factory cells were grouped in three sections: metal-workers, municipal workers, and the rest.[20]

(This was done in order to concentrate all efforts on the more important industrial sector; the metal and engineering industries were singled out for their importance in a war the underground saw coming; the municipal workers – especially tram-workers and the fire brigade – provided many hundred active resisters.) Of the three party leaders whom this report also mentions, the first was arrested, together with several dozen assistants, in the autumn of 1938 and died in jail before he could be tried. His two successors in turn escaped, but were eventually sent back to Austria and soon fell into the hands of the Gestapo, where one seems to have broken down under torture and betrayed all he knew, while the other was tried and executed.

The party seems to have recovered from these early blows remarkably quickly. Most districts in Vienna, and many of the large works, appear to have had functioning party organizations throughout 1939. But their activities once again called the Gestapo on the scene:

In the summer of 1939 the propagandist activities of the KPÖ, the painting of slogans, the scattering of leaflets and the distribution of literature, became once more noticeable. . . In consequence, several known Communists were shadowed and followed for months . . . until, in December, their Vienna headquarters could be located.[21]

Just before Christmas 260 activists were arrested, among them the new leader who had only shortly before returned from Paris, as well as the man in charge of the central printing section of the party

[20] OJs 215/40.   [21] OJs 181/40.

and several people responsible for contact with the provinces, which led to the wave of arrests spreading to Lower Austria and Styria. Three more leading members were smuggled into Austria, two of them from Moscow, but as they had been well-known public figures, none lasted more than a few months before they, too, in company with all those whom they saw or hid with, were discovered. The last attempt at forming a central committee was in 1942, after which there was still a great deal of communist activity but entirely auto-nomous and at last concentrated on targets that really mattered – war production, contacts with foreign labour, hiding deserters, exploiting housewives' grievances, rumour-mongering, defeatist talk.

As far as the communist underground in the provinces was con-cerned, its main centres and largest following were in the two industrialized provinces of Lower Austria and Styria. A 1939 Gestapo report describes the situation in Graz and other industrial centres where a former student of the Lenin Institute in Moscow had established a Styrian *Landesleitung* shortly after the *Anschluss*:

> The efforts of a handful of activists were extraordinarily success-ful. . . These activists met with a confident, co-operative attitude on the part of former party members and sympathizers. . . The investigations of the Gestapo Head Office [in Graz] showed with frightening clarity what little time would be required to establish an effective organization ready for action if a political crisis threatened the Reich. In addition it must be stressed that the main effort of these activists was directed towards the establish-ment of factory cells in the arms industries.[22]

The first arrests in February 1939, involving sixty-four persons, were followed by another wave about a year later when the number of victims totalled 133; they represented most of the activists in the mining, steel, and engineering centres of Kapfenberg, Leoben, Bruck/Mur, and Eisenerz.[23] Undaunted, a new leadership took over and lasted till January 1941 when the Gestapo arrested a group including an archivist, an architect, a teacher, and an actor, as well as two women and several workmen, all of whom ended on the guillotine. It is significant that the last two leading groups, those of 1940 and of 1941, contained several Socialists, and that here as in Vienna no attempts at forming a *Landesleitung* seem to have been made after early 1942.[24]

In Lower Austria, which lacks a provincial capital, resistance tended to be centred in several larger towns, notably in St Pölten, where between December 1940 and April 1941 a total of 249

[22] OJs 97/39.　　　　　　　　[23] OJs 7, 10, 133, 151/41.
[24] OJs 219/41, 327, 329 etc.; 41, 201/42.

members and supporters of a communist organization were arrested
and many executed. Here the main centre was the railway repair
shop, a particularly sensitive area, especially after the outbreak of
war, which lent itself to acts of sabotage and (through drivers and
guards) facilitated underground communications, the distribution of
literature, etc.[25]

Of the other provinces, the OJs files yield relatively little information on centralized organizations: the arrests of *Landesleitungen*
in Carinthia (in the winter of 1939–40)[26] and Salzburg (beginning of
1942)[27] and the discovery of a regional organization in Upper Austria
which was in direct communication with the leadership in Vienna.[28]

The Socialist Resistance

In spite of the precautions taken it was almost inevitable that the
majority of the leading cadres of the Revolutionary Socialists and
of the free trade union committee should be picked up after the
German invasion: many of them had been public figures before
1934, their police records for underground activities during the
Schuschnigg period were impressive, and in the few weeks of semi-
legality immediately before the *Anschluss* they had emerged into
the open as spokesmen for socialism and a united struggle against
the German threat. Many of them were to spend the next seven
years in German concentration camps, in the company of their
erstwhile persecutors of the Fatherland Front régime, and many
lost their lives. Of those that were spared in the first round-up, over
300 were picked up in the week preceding the outbreak of war: the
Gestapo, using the records of the Schuschnigg police, obviously
feared that they might cause trouble.

Those who kept some kind of organization going in the interval,
mainly to serve as a link with émigré headquarters, to arrange
hiding-places, support, and eventual escape for those in great
danger, and to provide relief for prisoners and their families, were
betrayed by a former comrade in the summer of 1939 and became
the defendants in one of the first People's Court trials and in one of
the first Special Senate trials in Austria. It was in the latter trial
that the prosecution first established the principle that the collection
of money for imprisoned *Gesinnungsfreunde* (party comrades) was
tantamount to committing treason, and that for the first time the
term 'communist' as a blanket description of all left-wing opposition
was used.[29]

Of the autonomous groups with a quasi-party structure only
three – in Vienna, Salzburg, and in the Tyrol – assumed a signifi-

[25] OJs 93/42, etc.
[26] OJs 98–109/41.
[27] OJs 560/43.
[28] OJs 218/41.
[29] OJs 40/40.

cant stature and activity, and they were in contact with one another. The group in Vienna, named after its leader, Dr Otto Haas, arose from an arrangement with an offshoot of the SPD after 1933 whereby the Austrian RS provided certain services and a link with Czechoslovakia for German socialist émigrés. Although the special usefulness of Austria disappeared with the *Anschluss*, the contacts with the South German Socialists remained, and while Haas and his friends thought little of spectacular demonstrations they still felt the need for socialist cells to discuss political developments and to collect news and information (especially about rearmament) to warn the democratic forces abroad. This kind of activity necessitated regular contacts and correspondence through couriers, and it would have required a miracle to protect it from the ever-watchful Gestapo. This miracle did not happen; but significantly, it was the enthusiasm of the Salzburg group, which insisted on a large organization and on united-front talks with the Communists, that led to the discovery of the whole network:

> In connection with the discovery, in the spring of 1942, of the Salzburg organization of the KPÖ, the existence of an organization of the RSÖ was also revealed. This illegal Marxist movement had arisen after the February fighting in 1934. . . After the *Anschluss* and a temporary standstill a new organization was formed which, in view of the changed circumstances, rejected the principle of the mass party and aimed at a cadre organization. . . In Salzburg, too, the organization of the RSÖ was rebuilt in 1939, centred mainly on the railway staffs. . . Members were recruited and dues collected which were partly used to support the dependants of political prisoners.[30]

In addition to spreading anti-Nazi information and propaganda, with the aim of 'inciting the population and preparing for industrial sabotage and social struggles',[31] the group attempted to lay in a store of small firearms (one consignment of pistols arrived from Munich hidden inside sewing-machines, and was shared out between Salzburg and Vienna); sought to make contacts with Paris; established groups all along the Austrian railways network; and was in regular touch with Vienna where Dr Haas was the central education officer for the whole organization. Only in Linz did they draw a blank, as the Socialists there refused to join a widespread organization and preferred their system of autonomous factory cells and groups of like-minded people.[32]

At the same time as the Salzburg group was uncovered (probably,

[30] OJs 560/43. [31] OJs 411/42.
[32] OJs 444/43, 411/42, 24/43, etc.

as survivors still maintain, through the agency of a Gestapo spy in
the communist group), the authorities also discovered the existence
of a widespread political underground in the Tyrol which had only
tenuous contacts with Salzburg and was primarily organized from
Berlin, where an Austrian Socialist had joined a communist-led
organization and passed his contacts on to them. From the Gestapo
reports it emerges that its emissary to the Tyrol was shadowed and
thus led the police to all the groups in Innsbruck, Kitzbühel, Wörgl,
and other places. Although even the courts had to admit that the
accused were in the majority genuine Socialists, their contacts with
a communist network damned them.[33] There were nine executions
and suicides and deaths in Gestapo detention in the Tyrol, possibly
as many as forty out of 132 arrested in Salzburg, and another five in
Vienna.

Also, simultaneously with the arrest of the communist leadership
in Carinthia came the discovery of an RS organization, three of
whose leaders were executed. What makes this case so interesting is
the fact that the accused had smuggled in anti-Nazi literature
(which extolled the virtues of democracy) from the RS émigré centre
at Maribor (Yugoslavia), which subsequently served both RS and
CP groups in Carinthia and Styria.[34]

Another Carinthian group operating in the Drau and Möll
valleys constituted itself in September 1939 and appealed to all
people regardless of party to support a 'Carinthian Freedom Front'
for the restoration of Austrian independence, while addressing
special messages to their former comrades in the Socialist Party.
Towards the end of 1939 the Gestapo learned of this, but could not
lay their hands on the organizer, as this man had in the meantime
been called up for military service and his commanding officer
refused to hand him over. The investigations against his fellow-
accused proceeded, and about a year later the State Prosecutor
demanded his arrest, only to be told that this was impossible because the man in question was fighting at the front! This case bears
out the accounts of numerous resisters whom non-Nazi officers
protected from the Gestapo – a significant illustration of the jealousy
existing between the party and the military. Normally, they succeeded only when the alleged offences had taken place before a
man's call-up; but in this case the major concerned even ignored
evidence that the accused had used his leaves for keeping in touch
with his comrades, which should have made his surrender to the
Gestapo automatic.[35] This was but one form of conservative resistance in Austria (for there were few left-wingers in the officer

---

[33] OJs 167, 181, 187, 191/44, etc.
[34] OJs 107, 139/41.   [35] OJs 158/40.

corps); other forms were to have political offenders tried by (the initially much more lenient) military courts, which at any rate saved them from torture by the Gestapo; to ignore the forming of patriotic groups under their commands and refuse transfers of opposition elements to other units; to keep key-men in hospitals longer than was necessary; and to induce complaints and illnesses by means of injections to save Austrians from even more unpleasant assignments. The near-success of the revolt on 20 July 1944 in Vienna proved what could be done in this way.

Resistance in Industry

Partly overlapping the work of socialist and communist party organizations, the systematic efforts at resistance within industry deserve a section on their own both on account of the numbers involved and because they appear, in retrospect, so much more effective and yet economical in lives. We know too much about the factors that decide modern wars to entertain any illusions about the effectiveness of industrial sabotage and go-slows, especially under totalitarian régimes, *until the military power is broken.* Nevertheless, keeping a sullen, unco-operative population under observation uses up manpower that could be otherwise employed; the existence of a determined opposition group in a factory keeps alive the tradition of social struggle and of workers' solidarity; it protects the weak – especially slave labour and prisoners-of-war – and exposes the sham 'socialism' of the régime and its contemptible instrument, the German Labour Front. With defeat in sight, the factory cell comes out into the open, voices the workers' demands, prevents the destruction or removal of plant and raw materials, and keeps production going – and all this with the feeling that one had made a contribution, however modest, and not received freedom as a gift of the victors. The self-assurance with which Austrian statesmen in 1945 confronted the Allies – who seemed to expect contrition and remorse – was based on the sufferings, the steadfastness, and the many small virtues of large numbers of their compatriots which, in their view, compensated for the misdeeds of Austrian Nazis.

The list of works in which, according to the files of the Special Courts and the Special Senates, active resistance groups existed reads like a catalogue of Austrian industry and there is no point in enumerating them.[36]

After the outbreak of war, sabotage of the war effort by means of reduction of individual effort, working to rule, bad time-keeping, waste of material and damage to tools, faulty production, and, wherever possible, destruction of valuable machinery was

[36] For details cf. Szecsi and Stadler, op. cit., pp. 69–74.

advocated. There is not much evidence of outright sabotage in the
OJs files; but then such cases would in any case have come before
the People's Courts.

The Conservative Resistance

In *Der Ruf des Gewissens* Otto Molden has provided an impressive account of the various conservative resistance groups which he
had known or about which he was able to collect information. It is
now possible to confirm his story, both in broad outline and in much
detail, on the basis of court and Gestapo documents, and to follow
up the fate of hundreds of the lesser accused whose trials by Special
Senate followed the sentencing of the leaders by the People's Courts.
For the purposes of this study it will again suffice to consider the
aims and the activities of some of the more important groups.

Of the *Österreichische Freiheitsbewegung* (Austrian Freedom
Movement) the Gestapo informed the court:

> Dr Lederer visualized the re-establishment of an independent
> Austria, its constitutional form to be decided by plebiscite. This
> was the gist of his pamphlet 'What we Want'. Another pamphlet
> his group distributed was entitled 'What the *Völkischer Beobachter*
> does not tell you'. The organization consisted of small units of
> three to four persons each, whose leaders only were in contact
> with the central leadership. In addition to a women's and a youth
> section there were plans to recruit the prematurely retired officers
> of the Austrian Federal Army for military commandos. New
> recruits were normally made to swear an oath of loyalty. One per
> cent of their income was to be paid as a contribution, out of
> which prisoners could be aided . . . Not before the autumn of 1939
> did Dr Lederer succeed in recruiting a considerable member-
> ship. . . .[37]

Actually, the Gestapo only managed to identify thirty-nine members and about sixty supporters and sympathizers; Dr Lederer and
two of his assistants were executed. So were the leaders of two other
groups – Dr Kastelic, whose *Großösterreichische Freiheitsbewegung*
aimed at a 'Greater Austria from the River Main to Trieste, based
on a corporate democracy'[38] and Dr Karl Roman Scholz, a Catholic
priest, who attracted a large number of students and women in his
organization which welcomed members regardless of their political
views.[39]

Dr Karl Meithner, a former university teacher, was among the
first to be sent to Dachau; on his release he formed a conservative

[37] OJs 260/44.   [38] OJs 239/44.   [39] OJs 307/44.

resistance group consisting mainly of academics and high-ranking civil servants, but he also sought contacts with the communist underground. At his trial his two communist contacts – already sentenced to death – steadfastly refused to incriminate him, hence the relatively mild sentence of six years; he died in prison within a few weeks, however. A survivor of the group has written a valuable account of its work, as of that of other groups.[40]

Even more interesting was the case of the *Antifaschistische Freiheitsbewegung Österreichs* (Anti-Fascist Freedom Movement for Austria) which was based on Carinthia but had useful contacts in Vienna, within the armed forces, and with the Left. Basically monarchist, it was founded by a former district leader of the Fatherland Front and its principal members included several other conservative professional men, a priest, and a non-commissioned officer of the *Luftwaffe* who seems to have been the driving force. The Gestapo accused him of having formed a cell at his air base, arranged contacts with the socialist leadership, prepared assistance for the Slovene partisans, and planned the assassination of *Gauleiter* Rainer. Of the thirty-one arrests reported by the Gestapo in 1943, we know for certain that two led to executions.[41]

Of the smaller groups, as far as their political perspectives and effectiveness were concerned, we need only mention the *Illegale österreichische kaiserliche Front* (Austrian Underground Monarchist Front), where the Gestapo succeeded in identifying forty-eight members, all rather simple people like cobblers, seamstresses, pensioners, and the like, who nevertheless were said to have produced large numbers of leaflets and to have planned to collect arms.[42] A former *Heimwehr* officer tried in vain to persuade members of his detachment of the Red Cross to form a resistance group; though he did not succeed, it is interesting to note that for three years even the party members in this detachment failed to report his efforts to the Gestapo.[43] There were numerous cases, often involving priests, where the conservative equivalent of the socialist *Gesinnungsgemeinschaften*, or circles of comrades, came to the notice of the Gestapo and led to prosecution, normally at the Special Courts if no political organization was involved; a typical sentence was fifteen months for attendance at *staatsfeindliche Zusammenkünfte* (as in Sg. Nr. 5214), meetings of enemies of the state.

Finally, the tragic case of a young Catholic in the Medical Corps who was drafted to Norway. As a confirmed anti-Nazi he first planned to escape, with several other Austrians, to England by boat,

---

[40] Felix Romanik, *Der Anteil der Akademikerschaft an Österreichs Freiheitskampf* (Vienna, n.d.); also OJs 317/44 and 302, 348, 123/44.
[41] OJs 612/43.   [42] OJs 111, 112/44.   [43] Sg. Nr. 5729.

but subsequently changed his mind and established a 'Norwegian Freedom Movement' among Austrian soldiers and Norwegian sympathizers. The intention was to assist an English invasion by isolating German units, and in the meantime to discuss the political situation and educate members. The documents available in Austria are only fragments of the case,[44] but thanks to Norwegian co-operation it was possible to piece together the rest of the story: of those arrested – twelve Austrian soldiers and twenty-seven Norwegians – three Austrians and three Norwegians were sentenced to death, five Austrians were jailed for eight to ten years, and several Norwegians received life-sentences. Our hero's last statement in court was that 'he regretted to be responsible for the death of the others but maintained he was convinced Germany would lose the war – and as long as there were Prussians there would always be terror and war'.[45]

[44] OJs 581/43.
[45] With acknowledgements to Mr Ole Berge, of the Forsvarets Krigshistorisske Avdeling, Oslo.

Chapter 6

The Growth of National Feeling

THE JUDICIAL RECORDS OF the Third Reich prove that considerable numbers of Austrians fell victim to the severities of National Socialist rule. This in itself is not surprising because it applies to all authoritarian régimes, and was probably no more typical of Austria than it was of Germany. In any case, criminality and law-breaking in any society is a marginal phenomenon in statistical terms, and no very convincing case could be built on the evidence of the courts alone. It has already been noted, however, that much of this evidence revealed anti-German attitudes and activities, and thus becomes relevant to our investigation. What was still missing was reliable information about the attitudes and feelings of individuals and social groups that were never in conflict with the law – the great majority of the population – both outside the Nazi Party and within it.

Most of this information became available when the United States published, in microfilm, her great holdings of captured German documents, while extensive searches in German archives yielded additional material. Most important sources were, firstly, the various *Lageberichte* or *Stimmungsberichte* (Situation or Morale Reports) compiled by Himmler's Security Service (SD), and by various army commands, Ministries, and party offices. Secondly, Gestapo reports and Ministry of Justice surveys and statistics supplemented the documentation available in Austria which was discussed in the preceding chapter. Both kinds contain ample evidence of the growth of a feeling of patriotic opposition, which is further borne out by the third group of papers – internal party documents, mostly from the *Parteikanzlei* (the Chancellery of the NSDAP), which shed much light on inner-party feuds and disaffection caused by conflicts with German officials and German policies. In view of the nature of the evidence it has proved necessary to group it, not according to provenance, nor to the topics it treats, but in chronological order. It will thus be possible to trace the growth of disappointment and disillusionment, of opposition and resistance, through the four periods into which the German occupation of Austria can be divided:

from the *Anschluss* to the Sudeten crisis; from Munich to the outbreak of war; from the Polish campaign to Stalingrad; and finally
on to the collapse.

'Anschluss' and Plebiscite

The four weeks between the German invasion and the plebiscite
were characterized by the most concentrated propaganda campaign
party and state had ever mounted. This was assisted by the frenzied
joy of Austrian Nazis emerging from the underground or from semi-
legality, and by the suddenness of the Austrian collapse and the
German takeover. Whereas it seemed, immediately after Schuschnigg's resignation on 11 March, that the Seyss-Inquart cabinet
would remain in being as an Austrian government in special
relationship with Germany, and that no constitutional changes
would occur until after a plebiscite had ascertained the 'wish' of the
Austrian people, Mussolini's unqualified acceptance of the German
invasion accelerated the process of dissolution. On Sunday, 13 March,
Seyss-Inquart informed the Council of Ministers that President
Miklas had handed over his office to him, and that he had received
the text of a law on the 'Reunification of Austria with the Reich'
which they were expected 'to pass without delay'. Hitler's speech
in Vienna on 15 March, in which he mentioned the several *Reichsgaue* by name (omitting even at this early stage Vorarlberg and
Burgenland, which were in fact absorbed by neighbouring provinces),
was the first indication of his long-term plans, but his edict of the
same date still provided for an *Österreichische Landesregierung*,
thus suggesting a special status for Austria within the Reich, as the
'legalistic' Nazis had confidently expected.

This '*Land* government', however, was very soon reduced to a
shadowy existence. On 23 April Joseph Bürckel, *Gauleiter* of the
Saarpfalz, was appointed *Reichskommissar* for the reunification of
Austria with the Reich; on the same day Seyss-Inquart was charged
with the duty of introducing German law in Austria. The inclusion
of Austria (now frequently referred to as *Ostmark*) in the German
Gau-system on 31 May, and the final delimitation of the Austrian
Gaue on 1 October, was followed by the *Ostmark-Gesetz* of 14 April
1939 which instituted them as *Reichsgaue* whose *Reichsstatthalter*
were identical with the party-appointed *Gauleiter*. This completed
the process of the dissolution of Austria and made the *Land* government into an insignificant institution, until on 31 March 1940 the
'*Land* Österreich' disappeared for good. Its place was taken by the
term *Ostmark* or *Reichsgaue der Ostmark*, but not for long. On
19 January 1942 Hitler's wish for the discontinuation of this term
was brought to the notice of all concerned, and subsequently the

term 'Alpen- und Donau-Reichsgaue' was suggested – but only where, for administrative reasons, the simple enumeration of *Gaue* or of *Reichsstatthalter* was impossible. It is quite obvious that by this time at the latest Hitler had become convinced of the need to remove the last reminders of a separate Austrian existence.[1]

There is ample evidence that the break-up of Austria was resented, not only by the patriotic opposition, but also by many National Socialists, either because they really believed in an Austrian 'mission' or because it conflicted with their own ambitions. It is known, for instance, that Schirach, *Gauleiter* and *Reichsstatthalter* of Vienna, entertained hopes of an economic commission of *Ostmark-Gauleiter* in view of Vienna's position *vis-à-vis* south-eastern Europe, which might have supported his ambition for the post of *Reichsminister* for South-eastern Questions. This scheme in fact foundered on the jealousy of other *Gauleiter*, but a later plan for a personal union between the *Gaue* Vienna and Lower Austria was turned down by the *Parteikanzlei* which feared that this might be the beginning of a new *Ostmark*!

Even critical eyewitnesses of the events of those first few weeks find it as difficult to criticize the passivity of a stunned and bewildered population as to communicate to others the atmosphere of hysteria and fright. Supported by the mass media, the party and its formations ceaselessly paraded the streets, held meetings, distributed food among the poor; martial music, snatches of speeches, and slogans filled the air. Lorries filled with prisoners, Jews, and anti-Nazis made to scrape patriotic slogans off pavements and walls, vague threats against all who would 'stand aside'. Deserted by the powers, Austria stood alone; the foreign press, gleefully reported by the papers, 'welcoming' the peaceful change; foremost a long interview with Ward Price of the London *Daily Mail*. After years of isolation Vienna had become the centre of interest; Germany's leaders appeared in rapid succession: Göring on 26 March and Goebbels on the 29th; Minister of Justice Frank on 2 April; leader of the Labour Front Ley on the 3rd; Economics Minister Funk and Reich Women's leader Scholz-Klink on the 4th; Education Minister Rust on the 5th; Alfred Rosenberg on the 6th; Hitler's Deputy Rudolf Hess and Church Minister Kerrl on the 7th; and finally, Hitler and Goebbels, again, on the 9th.

The German takeover proceeded apace, but there was still the plebiscite to be held on 10 April. A campaign was mounted that suggested a real contest; and its result must have been very gratify-

---

[1] For the constitutional aspects cf. Ludwig Jedlicka, 'Verfassungs- und Verwaltungsprobleme 1938–1945' in *Die Entwicklung der Verfassung Österreichs* (Graz, 1963), pp. 120–44.

ing to the new masters: 99·72 per cent put their crosses into the large circle for a Yes; nevertheless, 11,281 men and women (4,939 of them in Vienna) preferred the small circle that stood for the Noes. Bürckel's reaction was jubilant: 'We are Germans, and belong to Germany and to the Führer for all eternity'; Austria seemed to have been won over. The people of Vienna were being flattered ('This city is more than the second largest town of Greater Germany' – Mayor Neubacher); the Catholics were pacified by declarations of their bishops, including a 'Heil Hitler'-letter from the Cardinal to Bürckel; and the working classes were neutralized by a spectacular 'Reconstruction Programme for Austria' which promised work and bread for all.

With less publicity, but just as efficiently, all precautions against any possible opposition were taken. On 1 April the first trainload of political prisoners left for Dachau. In the prisons of the Gestapo thousands of Jews were awaiting their fate which, at this stage, 'only' meant deportation, compulsory emigration, 'voluntary' liquidation of their businesses, and huge donations. The federal army was thoroughly purged; of its total of 2,555 officers (only about 5 per cent of whom had been underground Nazis) it lost 17 per cent – in particular, 55 per cent of its generals and 40 per cent of its colonels – through compulsory retirement, while another 18 per cent of 'unreliable' regimental officers were transferred to administrative duties. Thirty officers were sent to jail or concentration camps, of whom six were killed or died.[2] Such men, prematurely retired, often became activists in right-wing resistance groups, just as the mass arrests provided the underground with martyrs or, after their release, with instructors and fanatical opponents of the régime.

It is still impossible to arrive at an accurate estimate of the total number of arrests. The official Austrian figure mentioned in the *Rot-Weiss-Rot-Buch* ('over 70,000') cannot be confirmed from the available documentation. We know that on 5 July 1938 Secretary of State von Weizsäcker of the Foreign Office talked to Heydrich about the bad impression made abroad by the wholesale imprisonment of 'diplomats, legitimists, and scholars' and asked him whether the majority of them could not now be released, possibly confined to a certain place and regularly reporting to the police. Heydrich agreed but claimed that four-fifths of them had already been released, which left them with fewer than 2,000 still held.[3] This would have made a total of about 10,000 *Anschluss* arrests, but the 30 September *Tagesrapport* of the Vienna Gestapo mentions a figure

[2] Kurt Schuschnigg, *Im Kampf gegen Hitler* (Vienna, 1969), p. 328.
[3] *Akten zur Deutschen Auswärtigen Politik 1918–1945*, Serie D, vol. I, pp. 509–10.

of 1,001 *Schutzhäftlinge* still in their hands, which means, with the 13,872 releases or transfers to Dachau of the preceding six months, that there had been a total of 14,873 *Schutzhäftlinge* processed by the Gestapo.[4] However, the 10–12 December *Tagesrapport* of the same office mentions a total of 20,973 *Schutzhäftlinge* since March, thus doubling Heydrich's original figure.[5] Similarly contradictory reports and statistics confirm the impression that the new rulers themselves did not know how many arrests they made. Whatever their number, they were sufficiently numerous to serve as a deterrent, to act as an inspiration to their followers, to become (in many cases) the rallying-point of discontent after their release, and to organize resistance activities.

After the parades, the sober business of government. Inevitably, the flamboyant speeches had raised expectations to a pitch which no system could satisfy. Unemployment figures dropped only very slowly, and this in spite of the large numbers of single men and women who were sent to work in the Reich. Business experienced an unparalleled boom while supplies of goods lasted; when the Germans had bought up everything which was in short supply in the Reich (e.g., butter) or which was no longer imported, shopkeepers and the general public noticed the difference. The rate fixed for the conversion of Austrian schillings was universally resented. Housing, always a key problem in Vienna, showed no improvement; although thousands of Jewish-owned flats became vacant, the influx of German officials and Nazi leaders more than took up the available space. By July 1938, discontent forced the deputy mayors of Vienna to admonish the public. Blaschke:

> Vienna, this city of two million people, had two million wishes on that historic 13 May when the *Ostmark* was liberated. If one or the other of these wishes is not yet fulfilled, remember that it is impossible to meet such a mass of wishes from one day to the next. . .

Kozich criticized those 'who would never have dreamt of such ambitious plans [as the régime had] and who are now getting impatient'. And Blaschke again turned on the *Nörgler* who felt free 'to criticize and to grumble because after only four months of Nazi rule in Vienna and in the *Ostmark* it had not been possible to fulfil every single wish'.[6]

The disappointments felt by most sections of the population were

---

[4] T84R13 39 954. (This refers to the microcopy number, roll, and frame, National Archives, Washington, DC.)

[5] ibid., 39 752. *Schutzhäftlinge* were prisoners in 'protective custody'.

[6] *Amtsblatt der Stadt Wien*, 46/28, 5; 46/30, 5.

further aggravated by the excessively bureaucratic administration and the blatant rivalry between government and party offices. *Reichsamtsleiter* Meiler from Party Headquarters, who visited Austria in the summer, was the first to notice a marked cooling-off of relations; in his secret report on the state of the party he wrote on 3 August 1938 that these unsatisfactory relations 'do nothing to improve the [already very bitter] political mood of the Austrians in the *Ostmark* caused by the measures imposed by the *Altreich*'.[7]

This was the time when resistance groups first began to appear; the euphoria of the non-political masses gave way to a critical appraisal of the new system; the right wing had recovered from the shock of losing its leaders; and the left wing felt encouraged by the mounting dissatisfaction.

From Munich to the Outbreak of War

To many people the German campaign of intimidation against Czechoslovakia was the first warning of things to come. It destroyed the hopes of those who had believed Hitler when he declared that Austria was his last territorial demand; it awakened memories of the sufferings of the First World War – and of its outcome; and it reminded people of the oft-repeated assertions of the Left that Fascism meant war. That Czechoslovakia was now the butt of Hitler's attacks affected the inhabitants of Vienna and eastern Austria in a special way, for apart from the Czech and Slovak communities there many people were of Slav ancestry or had relations there still. Between September and November the Gestapo in Vienna reported several dozen arrests for public criticism of the Sudeten Germans coupled with anti-government sentiments: the Sudeten Germans were dismissed as Nazis, the German government had instigated the riots and was spreading lies about the situation in those provinces. However, the policy of appeasement practised by Britain and France was likewise condemned; Chamberlain, Daladier, and Hitler were named together as accursed enemies of the Czechs, but the more common judgement was that 'The Führer and the Duce are both warmongers'.[8]

The Munich crisis not only served as a warning to the country at large, but it also marked a turning-point in the economic and social policies pursued in Austria as well as in the attitude of the régime towards the people. The honeymoon was over: threats replaced kind words, preparations for war took precedence over civilian

---

[7] Berlin Document Center (BDC) *Reichsleiter*, Mappe 302. *Altreich* was the term frequently used for the Reich before it became, in Nazi terminology, 'Greater Germany'.

[8] T84R13 39 898–40 014, etc.; 39 926.

needs, party organization was tightened up, German control over Austrian affairs became more stringent. At this stage it may be necessary to consider in greater detail the three principal political camps in Austria.

In the National Socialist camp a bitter struggle was raging between the old Nazi underground and the 'legal' Nazis like Seyss-Inquart. Although initially the former were rewarded with all the *Gauleiter* posts in Austria – only later were Reich Germans sent to Vienna (Schirach) and Salzburg (Scheel) – they still felt passed over by the Führer who seemed to give all the credit for the *Anschluss* to Seyss-Inquart. To put the record straight, they sent a deputation of three to Hess in Munich,[9] but not until a year later was Seyss made Reich Minister, then Deputy Governor in Poland, and eventually *Reichskommissar* for the Netherlands. It was for his policies there that he was tried and executed at Nuremberg. But the Germans also had trouble with the *Gauleiter* of Styria (who resisted all instructions from Vienna) and of Vienna (who likewise did as he pleased).[10] The candidate for the leadership of the *Gau* Lower Austria (or Niederdonau, as it was now called), Captain Leopold, who had been *Landesleiter* of the underground NSDAP in Austria, was characterized in a secret report of *Stabsleiter* Opdenhoff (later deputy *Gauleiter* of 'Oberdonau') as 'treulos, unkameradschaftlich, unwahrhaftig'.[11] This was based, in part, on Bürckel's estimate of the man; what the party leaders in Vienna thought of Bürckel and his associates from the Palatinate was reported to the Party Chancellery in June 1939:

. . . Bürckel and his *Pfälzer* don't understand us and won't meet us. Bürckel breakfasts with his *Pfälzer* in the morning, he sits with them at lunch, in the evening he goes drinking with them, and at night he is again in the same house with them. I don't need to say anything about the inadequacies of most of his *Pfälzer*. . . .[12]

The rank-and-file also caused much trouble. *Reichsamtsleiter* Meiler in his report of 3 August complained about former underground Nazis who

. . . demand highly-paid jobs, for which their training does not fit them. . . As soon as they are put in a job they start making demands. The work they do, however, is in no way commensurate

[9] Institut für Zeitgeschichte, München (IfZ Mü), PS 812.
[10] BDC, RL, Mappe 302.
[11] ibid., Mappe 304; 'lacking in loyalty, comradeship, and truthfulness'.
[12] IfZ Mü Fa–91/3 Fasz 12 Bl 670.

with their expectations. Once appointed to a job they develop delusions of grandeur. . .[13]

But the Gestapo saw this issue in a different light: they suspected, not without reason, that the discontent of 'old fighters', their being passed over in promotions, their general dissatisfaction, was due to the passive resistance practised by the (conservative) bureaucracy; and once war had broken out, these same people saw to it that reliable National Socialists, instead of being promoted, were posted to Poland.[14]

As in all political parties, there were idealists and opportunists in the NSDAP; and like all extremist parties it attracted fanatics and psychopaths, fools and criminal types. Idealists often resigned, and sometimes ended up in a resistance group; activists resented the preponderance of Reich Germans and tried to keep alive an Austrian element in the party; while psychopaths and criminals, if fortunate, could indulge in their hobbies quite legitimately in the SA and SS, and later on in occupied territories or in extermination camps; if unlucky, they ended up alongside their victims in the jails and concentration camps of the Third Reich.

There is evidence of all this in the *Tagesrapporte* of the Gestapo: the activities of Otto Strasser's *Schwarze Front* and other *national-revolutionäre* organizations; appeals to Bürckel to prevent the replacement of the Austrian leader of the underground Hitler Youth by a German; individual protests by old National Socialists.[15] On the other hand, we learn of the trigger-happy praetorian guards of the régime; of an SS-man who was killed while burgling a Jewish flat; and of a platoon of n.c.o.'s of the SA who were arrested while helping themselves to Jewish property; and many more cases of corruption, delinquency among members of the Hitler Youth, and the like.[16] This in itself proves nothing, of course; but, understandably, the opponents of the régime made the most of such cases when they learned of them and used them as ammunition in their 'whispering campaigns'. At this stage, however, the elation that victory brought was still unimpaired.

The Working Classes

Handicapped by the fact that National Socialism in Austria had never penetrated into the industrial working class, the new leadership failed to find the right approach. Their very language betrayed them as outsiders: a mixture of condescending paternalism, old

---

[13] BDC, RL, Mappe 302.
[14] T84R14 40 648, 760.
[15] T84R13 40 087; 39 943, 926, 764, 744; T84 R16 43 269.
[16] T84R13 39 737, 734; T84R15 43 173, 42 092; T84R14 41 132; etc.

clichés about both employers and employees being 'workers', assertions that the 'socialism' in the party's title was as important as its
nationalism, even threats against employers who thought they could
now do as they pleased. The trouble with this sort of argument was
that the Austrian working class had heard it all before; from the
spokesmen of governments, from independent ('yellow') trade
unions, from *Heimwehr*-Fascists, from the pillars of the corporate
state; and had refused to desert their 'Marxist-Jewish' leadership.
Only one tactical move was new: members of the Republican
Defence Corps (*Schutzbund*) who had been dismissed from their
posts in 1934, were solemnly reinstated; the mayor called them
'upright men', tribute was paid to the achievements and the proud
tradition of the Austrian labour movement. (At the same time
confidential Gestapo reports never failed to stress facts like 'took
part in the February fighting'; 'member of the Socialist Youth
since leaving school'; 'brought up in a fanatically Marxist home',
etc., as incriminating data for consideration by the courts.)

Social Democratic activists, unemployed since 1934, humiliated
by petty restrictions, forced to rejoin the Church (and take Holy
Communion!) on pain of losing a municipal flat or a study grant for
a child, went back to work dutifully attended rallies on May Day,
and joined the German Labour Front, the Nazis' substitute trade
union; but did nothing else. As events were soon to show, they
simply bided their time. The new masters resented this ingratitude
and began to utter warnings and threats. Neubacher, mayor of
Vienna, declared that those who refused to acknowledge the progress already made 'did not deserve to live in such times' (March
1939). Deputy Mayor Richter warned those 'who sought to undermine the state in the most infamous way, even though this state
provided them with work and bread . . . when the time comes,
these subversives will experience the whole weight of National
Socialist justice' (January 1939). And Deputy Mayor Kozich even
used the threat of the concentration camp against those who 'would
not work', that is, the opposition to directed labour: 'we shall keep
them safely in healthy and airy places' – a euphemism well understood by his listeners (October 1938).[17]

For in the meantime the institution of factory councils (*Betreibs-
räte*) was replaced by *betriebliche Vertretungen*, appointed by
management in consultation with the Nazi cell or Labour Front, in
a purely advisory function. In July 1938 the German law 'Zur
Ordnung der deutschen Arbeit' was introduced in Austria, which
annulled all the achievements of generations of labour pioneers; not
only were strikes forbidden and direction of labour made compulsory,

[17] *Amtsblatt der Stadt Wien*, 47/9, 2; 47/3, 4; 46/43, 5.

but the elaborate machinery of consultation, self-help, and auto-didacticism, the pride of Austrian labour, was completely and finally destroyed. The working class could be made to obey, but not to like the new régime.

As has already been mentioned, it was the Sudeten crisis of September 1938 which released all the pent-up disappointments and fears, and which also produced the first evidence of working-class reactions. In the artillery barracks at Kaiserebersdorf a labourer tells a group of soldiers that he regularly listens to Radio Moscow, and that he intends to go over to the 'enemy' when war breaks out. An inspector at Vienna power-station is arrested for suggesting the removal of all portraits of Hitler 'to avoid trouble in the near future' – obviously in anticipation of war and a German defeat; while a labourer at the same place shares his fate for telling all and sundry that, as he had always said, Hitler wanted war. Another worker is arrested at the Western Railway Station for consoling his travelling companions – all drafted to work in Germany – that they won't be away long, for 'communism is bound to come'.[18]

Alfred Rosenberg's 'Ideological Office', in its own situation reports (*Weltanschauliche Lageberichte*), also blames 'social conditions which can still not be called satisfactory' for opposition activities: in Upper Styria, for instance, resistance in several villages made it impossible to start up local groups of the Hitler Youth or League of German Maidens (BDM); in the Tyrol and in Salzburg the opposition concentrated on creating a war-psychosis; in Lower Austria the main target of the anti-Nazis was the German Labour Front; and so on.[19] Even allowing for the zeal of the party ideologues, there must be some truth in all these accounts, coming as they did from rival organizations of the régime.

What worried the authorities more than anything else were acts of industrial sabotage. On the strength of the Gestapo reports alone for the period up to the outbreak of war there seem to have been at least several dozen cases, none of them of any great importance, but more likely acts of individual protest: the cutting of a conveyor-belt in a new section of the great Wienerberger Brickworks resulting in the loss of two days' output, and the introduction of iron clamps in a clay-pressing machine a week later, stopping production for another four days. Further cases included the cutting of telephone

---

[18] T84R13 39 906, 953, 40 031.
[19] Berichte zur weltanschaulichen Lage für Kanzlei Rosenberg, henceforth quoted as WLB (Rosenberg), 1939. XIV. 57. Such 'reports on the ideological situation' sometimes emanated from lower party echelons; these are quoted as WLB, with dates and office of origin, if known.

and electricity cables on the eve of the occupation of the Sudetenland and on the occasion of a great speech by the Führer, thus
depriving a whole rural area of this experience; attempted
incendiarism at a great engineering-works; deliberate damage to
expensive new machinery at a rubber-works; the blocking-up of a
borehole at Zistersdorf oil-wells; and so on.[20] In several cases the
arrest of the likely saboteurs was reported: 'eight labourers known to
be Communists'; an agricultural worker; and the like. The damage
inflicted on Hitler's war-machine was minimal and hardly worth
the risks taken; but psychologically such acts helped to keep up the
spirits of the opposition. Of much greater political importance,
however, were the organized groups which continued the traditions
of the Austrian labour movement.

Social Democrats and 'Revolutionary Socialists'

Whereas conservative opponents of the régime had the local
church as a meeting-point, where they felt at home and among like-
minded people, the Left had no such spiritual solace and emotional
outlet. Instead, they sought and found strength in the glorious past
of their movement and especially in the achievements of 'Red
Vienna', the socialist administration of the city, which they now
idealized. Only four years previously, on the collapse of Austrian
Social Democracy, the activist wing had condemned the reformism
of the leadership, had deliberately chosen the title of 'Revolutionary
Socialists' (RS) for the underground successor-organization, and had
opened 'united front' negotiations with the Communist Party. A
number of former Social Democrats had in fact gone over to the
Communists who, for the first time since 1919, had become a
political force in the underground Left. It was only now, under
conditions of extreme oppression, that much of the organizational
rivalry and ideological disputation became irrelevant, and real co-
operation among various groups began. This is also the reason why
no clear distinction between socialist and communist resistance can
be made: solidarity with the victims of the régime, the joint struggle
for improved conditions, and the rejection of Nazi propaganda
united old Social Democrats, the 'new men' of the RS, and the
Communists.

The basis on which the underground was able to operate was the
fact that it enjoyed at least the passive sympathies of the great
majority of the population in Vienna and eastern Austria. There,
at least three out of every four had belonged to the party or the
'Free Trade Unions', had spent their childhood in the 'Red Falcon'
movement, had played football or chess, bred rabbits, or collected

[20] T84R13 40 007–8; 39 921, 901; T84R15 42 999, 43 004.

stamps, under the auspices of a socialist organization, lived in a low-rent municipal flat (or hoped for one), received a gift of baby-wear for every new-born child, and paid monthly dues for eventual cremation to the burial fund 'Die Flamme'. The emotional 'home-lessness' of the Austrian working class after the dissolution of the party and its countless subsidiary organizations in February 1934 left a vacuum which the Fatherland Front was quite unable to fill, and for which the Nazis had only very few substitutes to offer, such as 'Strength-through-Joy' outings and excursions, and the activities of the Hitler Youth for the younger generation.

In consequence, the daily reports of the Gestapo and the situation reports of the Security Service (SD) for Vienna, which are fairly complete for the period from mid-1938 to mid-1940, are full of arrests for public declarations of loyalty to the old Social Democratic Party, pride in having belonged to the 'Republican Defence Corps', and contempt for the NSDAP and its formations. At the same time, socialist activists who returned from abroad were arrested and the sentences imposed by pre-1938 courts were confirmed – the period of wooing the Socialists was over.[21]

The fate of some socialist resistance groups has already been mentioned in the preceding chapter. In spite of all the precautions taken, the central leadership of the RS was arrested soon after the *Anschluss* (while the rest of the leadership was arrested in the week before war broke out; this great swoop by the Gestapo, in which the files of the Schuschnigg police served as a dossier of potentially dangerous opponents, took more than 300 activists to Buchenwald concentration camp). Not all the existing groups obeyed the advice of their leaders and abandoned organizational activities, as we know from Gestapo reports; other arrests were of couriers and participants in various cadre activities such as collecting and forwarding infor-mation and assisting people in illegally leaving the country.[22] For the great majority of Social Democrats and Revolutionary Socialists, as well as for socialist trade unionists, the rule now was to act on their own, to keep in touch with trusted friends only, to concentrate on winning the confidence of their fellow-workers and neighbours, to counteract Nazi propaganda by spreading information gleaned from foreign radio stations, to support every good cause, and to avoid identifying themselves in any way with the régime.

The Communist Party

In theory, the Communist Party of Austria (KPÖ) had adopted similar tactics, except that they attached far greater importance to

---

[21] T84R16 43 279–387; T84R15 43 246, 248, 061.
[22] T84R13 40 078, 018; 39 912, 886, 879, 864, 853.

agitation and propaganda activities – the famous *Agitprop* – and to the maintenance of a party apparatus with strong links with the International. The former undoubtedly corresponded with the desire of many left-wingers for political activity of a kind which only the Communists offered; hence the large percentage of Socialists and non-party workers among the victims of the régime. The latter practice was part of the communist conception of the role of the party in the class struggle.

The first Gestapo reports on communist 'agents' are dated 7 and 10 September 1938; both refer to people who had returned from the Soviet Union to assist the party in Austria – the first of a large number of 'returnees' who not only went to their own certain deaths, but implicated dozens of others in the weeks and months in which the Gestapo patiently shadowed them until they had uncovered the whole network.[23] (In defence of this policy it is now argued that these brave people could not bear to live securely in Russia, or in the West, and that they badgered the party authorities to allow them to return to their comrades. Even if this be true, and they were not just ordered to return to Austria, as others had been sent to Spain to fight in the Civil War and yet others were later sent to join Tito's partisans, they were mostly so well known that their arrival made them a grave risk for the underground movement.)

On 22/23 November the Gestapo reported the arrest of Josef Csarmann, chief of the KPÖ in Vienna, and of thirty-four others who, 'in the course of several months of close observation of Csarmann', were identified as his accomplices. Among them was an even more important man – Bruno Dubber of Hamburg, wanted by the People's Court for 'high treason' since 1936 and now head of the party organization for the whole of Austria. Papers found on the various accused (and presumably confessions made under torture) revealed the structure of the party and its contacts in the provinces. The central office abroad was in Zürich at that time; a Swiss citizen was arrested at a secret *Anlaufstelle* (reporting point for couriers and mail depot) – a shoemaker's shop near the city centre – in whose suitcase behind a false bottom were hidden one thousand copies of a Central Committee resolution 'The struggle for the liberation of Austria from foreign rule', five copies of the Comintern weekly *Rundschau*, and instructions for Dubber to form a united front of all anti-Nazi Austrians.[24]

The arrest of the first forty-seven party functionaries was a blow from which the KPÖ recovered very quickly. By mid-1939 communist activities had become so numerous that the Gestapo was

[23] ibid., 40 057, 011, 041.
[24] ibid., 39 797, 167–8.

forced to take action, and in a great swoop arrested another 206 leading activists including the new chief, Ludwig Schmidt, who was later tried and executed. (Dubber died in jail after terrible tortures before he could be sentenced.) Two other party leaders, though known to the police, managed to escape; one returned later and was killed by his captors; the other died fighting as a partisan with Tito in Styria shortly before the end of the war.

The communist tactics were to join any organization 'where the masses are' – that is, where membership was often compulsory (as in the German Labour Front, DAF) or which people joined under pressure to avoid having to join the Nazi Party (such as the Nazi Welfare Organization, NSV, or the Red Cross, or Air Raid Precautions and similar bodies). Whereas the Socialists continued to advocate the boycott of *all* Nazi organizations, the KPÖ not only risked its members becoming tarred with the Nazi brush, but even sent picked men into the NSDAP, the SA, and – especially – the Hitler Youth. This latter activity, traditionally known as *Gegnerarbeit* (infiltration of hostile organizations), provided the Gestapo with numerous surprises: a communist group in Vienna 17 contained a member of the SA; a group of the Young Communist League in Vienna 12 numbered a sub-leader of the Hitler Youth among its members; and one of two young men who attempted to hoist a red flag over a radio-works on the eve of May Day – one of those spectacular propaganda stunts designed to keep up morale, which led to the discovery of ten members of the factory cell – was 'Labour Safety official of the DAF' for a number of works. And finally the grotesque case of a young man who, in February 1934, had fought in the monarchist *Jägerkorps Ottonia*, had then become supervisor of a Hitler Youth sportsground, and was now arrested for permitting Communists the use of the premises for secret meetings![25]

Of the communist literature produced at that time, the Gestapo carefully listed the title of every periodical, and the headings of leaflets, with a short summary of the contents. The originals are rarely enclosed with Gestapo reports, but always with the court files, so that it is possible to reconstruct the party line of the time. This was an amalgam of social struggle, anti-war protest, and patriotic sentiment, designed to appeal to the largest possible number of anti-Nazis. 'Anti-Fascists and war-resisters' are asked to unite in the 'struggle for a free Austria'. Slogans like '*Reichsdeutsche hinaus!*' and '*Österreicher freigeben!*' stress the national element, as does a May 1939 leaflet in favour of an 'independent Austrian Republic', which addresses itself to the local patriotism of the Viennese:

[25] T84R13 39 977, 923; 43 142; 39 952.

Von einer Weltstadt zur preußischen Provinz?
Wiener!
Seid ihr mit dieser Entwürdigung eurer Stadt einverstanden?[26]

That they did not approve was to become increasingly obvious to the party and the Gestapo. (What actually happened behind the scenes, where Viennese patriots encouraged by Schirach and others tried to preserve what was left of Vienna's cultural assets after the expulsion of the Jews, has recently been described with a wealth of inside information.[27])

Catholics and Conservatives

For the Catholic-conservative camp the period between the *Anschluss* and the outbreak of war was a time of terrible confusion and troubled consciences. To the activists of the Fatherland Front, National Socialism seemed the negation of everything they had stood and fought for, and resistance to the new régime a moral duty. However, since they were also conservatives and Catholics, an act of rebellion against a constituted authority which enjoyed the blessing of the Church required a large measure of independence and courage. That in the end so many of them took great risks in opposing the régime, even when, in 1939, it could appeal to their patriotism ('Now that we are at war, all differences must be forgotten in the defence of our homeland') and in June 1941 to their anti-communism ('He who is against us is the ally of Bolshevism'), is greatly to their credit. That the great majority of them 'did their duty by their country' and made their peace with the new masters except when they attacked their Church and their priests cannot surprise us.

The Catholic Church in Austria had been a reactionary, anti-democratic, and pro-Fascist institution throughout the period of the First Republic; it had been one of the architects – and main bene-ficiaries – of the Christian Corporate State of Dollfuss and Schusch-nigg. One of the few measures of the new régime really popular with the working class and the liberal bourgeoisie had in fact been its determination to put the Church and its servants in their place. The curious situation arose that the new rulers in Vienna fought a *Kulturkampf* which went far beyond anything which was practised in the old Reich,[28] and some of our documents express the indigna-

[26] T84R15 43, 106; 'Get rid of the Germans – release Austrian prisoners'; 'Once a metropolis, now a province of Prussia. People of Vienna! Do you approve of this debasement of your city?'
[27] Fritz M. Rebhann, *Finale in Wien. Eine Gaustadt im Aschenregen* (vol. IV of *Das einsame Gewissen*) (Vienna, 1969).
[28] Cf. Jakob Fried, *Nationalsozialismus und katholische Kirche in Öster-reich* (Vienna, 1947), pp. 29, 18.

tion of Austrian Nazis over Reich Ministries and offices accepting the protests of the Austrian Church and intervening on its behalf. After Hitler had decided that with the absorption of Austria the Austrian Concordat had lapsed, while the Reich Concordat did not automatically apply to the *Ostmark*,[29] the way was clear for Austrian anti-clericalism to remove in a few months such church privileges as it had taken the Reich five years to reduce or abolish, and to go even further, as a special issue, in May 1939, of Alfred Rosenberg's confidential report jubilantly announced: 'The measures taken are often of decisive importance . . . and in their clarity go considerably beyond similar measures in the old Reich.'[30]

They included the abolition of all church schools, the practical ban on church youth guilds, the dismissal of all ordained teachers, the closure of three out of the four theological faculties, and much more. The driving force behind this policy was *Gauleiter* Bürckel, of whom Schirach was to say at the Nuremberg Trial that his policy *vis-à-vis* the Church amounted to persecution, whereas his, Schirach's policy, had been to stop all anti-Church propaganda and demonstrations.[31]

The attempts of the Catholic hierarchy to establish a *modus vivendi* with the régime having failed, all negotiations and contacts ceased in September 1938. On 7 October, after a special service at St Stephen's, some 8,000 young men and women assembled in front of the archbishop's palace and chanted *their* version of the popular slogans of the day: 'Erzbischof befiehl, wir folgen dir'; 'Wir danken unserem Bischof'. 'Christus ist unser Führer'; 'Heil Christus, Heil Bischof'. On the following day Hitler Youth and SA stormed the palace, devastated the contents, broke 1,200 window-panes, stole a quantity of valuables, and threw a curate out of a window. A great anti-Church mass rally on 15 October put the official seal on this latter-day *Kulturkampf*.[32]

Its aims were to get the maximum number of people to leave the Church and declare themselves *gottgläubig* (believers in God) instead, to withdraw their children from religious instruction at school, and to refuse church weddings and burials. The introduction of a church tax coupled with the anti-clerical tradition of the labour movement resulted in an estimated 300,000 members leaving the Church,[33] while in Vienna alone in all types of schools approxi-

[29] T84R14 41 75 728.

[30] *Mitteilungen zur weltanschaulichen Lage*, WLB (Rosenberg), May 1939.

[31] *Der Prozeß gegen die Hauptkriegsverbrecher vor dem Internationalen Militärgerichtshof Nürnberg 14. November 1945 – 1. Oktober 1946* (Nuremberg, 1949), vol. XIV, pp. 452, 486–7 (henceforth quoted as IMT).

[32] WLB 24, 21 October 1938; T84R13 39 896.

[33] Erich Zöllner, op. cit., p. 524.

mately 50 per cent of all Catholic pupils stayed away from lessons in religion, and of 24,701 marriages in Lower Austria only 6,548 were solemnized in a church.[34]

The first conspiratorial groups are discovered by the Gestapo, and not all of them are of the calibre described by Otto Molden.[35] Here, more significantly, earnest young men of no great political experience or ambitions; groups of middle-class people of profound conservative views and habits; people with a special sense of duty or mission like the founder of the Austrian boy scout movement; circles of grammar-school boys or young students – mostly extreme right-wing, like the members of an illicit group modelled on the German *Stahlhelm* organization; and disillusioned members of the Hitler Youth: none of them really hurt the régime in any way, except that they kept the Gestapo and the courts busy; but the fact that they refused to conform and to support the new system, that they clung to the vision of an independent Austria, was their contribution to the downfall of the Third Reich and the resurrection of Austria.[36]

It was during this period that the political and ideological fronts began to consolidate themselves. But before we can survey this development under conditions of war, mention must be made of yet another group which was the principal victim of National Socialism – the Jews of Austria.

The Jewish People

Austrian Jewry as such was both socialist and conservative, assimilationist and Jewish-nationalist, free-thinking, liberal, and orthodox. Its working-class members were, of course, solidly behind the Social Democratic Party, and so were many of its intellectuals and middle-class members who provided Austrian socialism with its most brilliant leaders and thinkers, administrators, writers, and artists. But wealthy Jews, inevitably, sided with the bourgeois parties which represented their class interests, and it is probably true – though this cannot be proved – that after 1934 many Jews looked upon the Fatherland Front régime as their only protection against the threat of National Socialism.

The chronicler of Austrian history between 1938 and 1945 is at a special disadvantage in dealing with the Jewish citizens of Austria in that their fate is not usually treated either in formal court records or in Gestapo and SD reports, but is part of a greater scheme which culminated in the 'final solution'. This is a special study which

[34] T84R14 40 915, 723; WLB Gau Niederdonau, 3 November 1942.
[35] *Der Ruf des Gewissens.*
[36] T84R15 43 065; R13 40 069-74; 30 807; 40 083-4.

remains to be written.[37] All we can do here is to note such individual cases as appear in the Austrian documentation, and to reflect on the attitude of the non-Jewish Austrians, a mixture of cruelty and greed, of indifference and ignorance, of helpless compassion, and – very occasionally – practical assistance.

When on 12 March 1938 the world of bare tolerance collapsed in which the 190,000 Jews of Austria had lived, there remained but one organization which in spite of its bad record of anti-semitism seemed to offer moral support, and a refuge for those who had no religious links with Judaism. Of the 1,942 admissions to the Catholic Church between March and September, 1,702 were Jews, but the *Paulus-Werk* which was devoted to the evangelization of the Jews was banned in August.[38] Gestapo reports complained about the *judenfreundlich* (pro-Jewish) tone of parish magazines, which were promptly confiscated, and of church sermons whose authors were warned and threatened; investigation reveals, however, that in the great majority of cases the 'adulation of Jewry' complained of refers to the Jews of the Old Testament, and it is open to doubt whether the congregations identified Solomon or David with their humiliated and maltreated Jewish neighbours. Parish priests were accused of falsifying records for the purpose of securing *Ariernachweise* (i.e., evidence of 'Aryan' descent) for part-Jews, and one was arrested with his sister and accused of having performed eighty baptisms of Jews.[39]

Jews whom the police records named as left-wingers were systematically picked up and ordered to leave the country within a given period; socialist leaders like Dr Ellenbogen, a man of seventy-five, who was arrested as he talked to two other old men in the street, were not often given the same choice. Political activities were doubly hazardous if people were, and *looked*, Jewish; yet there were several arrests on this score. In addition to official persecution, Jews also suffered from the greed of their neighbours, and the Gestapo repeatedly reported acts of private pressure on Jews to vacate their flats; burglaries, thefts, and robbery with violence were the order of the day.[40]

The *Reichskristallnacht* of 9 November 1938, the first nationwide pogrom organized on the occasion of the assassination of a German diplomat in Paris by a young Jew, hit Austrian Jewry especially hard; of the total of 20,000 Jews arrested in Greater Germany,

[37] For a first account cf. Jonny Moser, *Die Judenverfolgung in Österreich 1938–1945* (Vienna, 1966).
[38] WLB (Rosenberg), No. 26, No. 20.
[39] T84R16 39 956; R13 39 874; R16 43 262.
[40] T84R13 40 058, 048, 041; 39 972, 757, 993, 947, 915.

6,547 were Viennese, and 3,700 of them were deported to Dachau.[41] But this orgy of sadism and destruction also produced a reaction which the régime had not expected: the *Lagebericht* of the *Reichssicherheitshauptamt* in Berlin (RSHA) for the first quarter of 1939 notes a certain lack of enthusiasm among the Viennese for anti-Jewish policies. If Jews had still not resigned themselves to their fate it was due in part to the attitude of the Western Powers and in part to the sympathy they still enjoyed in Vienna.

After the mood of depression among the Jews following the *Anschluss*, the great political tensions [presumably of the Sudeten crisis] have aroused certain hopes among them. This was in part due to the attitude of the population towards the Jews, which was noticed in the period under review. . .[42]

By May 1939 Vienna alone had lost 84,000 of its Jewish citizens, or 48 per cent according to the 1934 census. For Austria as a whole, the figures now were:

Gau Vienna: 91,480 *Volljuden*, 22,344 first- and second-grade *Mischlinge*;
Other *Gaue*: 3,073 *Volljuden*, 4,341 first- and second-grade *Mischlinge*,

a total of 121,238. But even this exodus was not quick enough for the anti-semites; the Jewish community estimated an average of 7,000 'legal' emigrants per month, with a steadily declining number of 'illegal' emigrants since the 'neighbouring states watch their frontiers very closely and return all caught illicitly crossing the frontier';[43] and soon after the outbreak of war mass deportations to the newly conquered Polish provinces began.

[41] ibid., 814, 710. 'Crystal Night' because of the glass littering the streets after the breaking of the windows of Jewish shops and homes.
[42] T175R10 2511 681 ff.
[43] T84R14 40 605; R15 43 113, *Volljuden* – Jews proper; *Mischlinge* – persons of mixed descent.

Chapter 7

The War: From Poland to Stalingrad

UNLIKE THE OUTBREAK OF war in 1914, which was accompanied by enthusiastic scenes in the capital cities of the belligerents, this time the reaction was sober and realistic. The fact that the generation of the First World War was still alive may have contributed to this lack of a warlike spirit. In Austria, which had never really recovered from the consequences of the war, and especially in Vienna and eastern Austria with its socialist, anti-war convictions, the invasion of Poland and the Anglo-French declaration of war created a feeling of great anxiety and depression. The first reaction of people was to blame the leaders of state and party; the SD report of 12 September notes a 50 per cent increase of *Heimtücke-delikte* in Vienna. Defeatist and anti-war utterances follow: 'In Poland they shoot down all our planes . . . The English are going to turn Berlin into a heap of rubble', says a painter in St Pölten. In Amstetten a railwayman tells a group of soldiers *en route* to the West that the Allies have broken through the *Westwall* in twelve places; he claims to have heard this in a foreign broadcast, for he did not bother to read the papers which were only telling lies (a Social Democrat). A fitter at the carriage-works in St Pölten says to colleagues who have received their call-up papers that he would not obey – or in any case would never fire on an enemy soldier (a devout Catholic).[1]

The attempt on Hitler's life at the Munich *Bürgerbräu* on 8 November 1939 was much discussed. The Gestapo noted the following reactions among the population: relief that the Führer had been spared and desire for revenge on the opposition (party members and sympathizers); the hope for 'better luck next time'; 'the work of the clever English'; an act of revenge of the Jews; the suspicion that the whole thing was a hoax 'arranged by the government'. We know today that the would-be assassin, Georg Elser, acted entirely on his own out of a mixture of pacifist and communist emotions, but few people were prepared to believe this. At the engineering-works in Steyr a number of people were arrested who

[1] T84R14 41 112; R13 40 168–9, 159.

explained the attempt as the reaction to the oppression of Catholicism. Most people seemed to connect Catholics and monarchists with the event, especially since 'sudden arrests of people of this kind took place all over the *Ostmark*'; such as the ninety-eight members of the Tyrolese *Kampffront* (Fighting Front).[2]

The receptivity for Nazi ideas, which the Gestapo claimed to discover among the workers as a result of the Hitler–Stalin Pact and the smooth co-operation in Poland, does not appear to have lasted long, if it existed at all.

The 'daily situation reports on the home front' issued by the Inspector of the Security Police and the Security Services (SD) contain plenty of evidence to the contrary. On 25 October they note that while the workers in rural areas are loyal, they are frequently the opposite in industrial areas and in Vienna where they say 'the Führer and the party wanted this war, and the people did not.' Now, however, party members are kept at home and the people are sent to the front. 'Old men are sent out to fight,' says a shopkeeper to a group of customers, 'while young men with party badges strut about the streets.' And a joiner calls old-time Nazis 'bastards who won't join up'.[3]

After the insults, violence and threats. At the Schwechat labour exchange a woman is *forced* to remove a swastika from her coat. A fitter in Wiener Neustadt silences a Nazi who enthuses about a speech by Hitler, and in Vienna a labourer threatens a group of Nazis: 'You wait: you'll hang when the Communists take over. I'll remember your faces.' The director of the Steyr savings bank, who has called Hitler and the *Kreisleiter* 'Drecksäue' (dirty swine), is arrested and made to parade the streets with a board suspended from his neck 'on which his base deed is described' – the first evidence of the revival of the medieval pillory, which the régime subsequently was to use a great deal.[4]

On 13 March 1939, one year after the *Anschluss*, the SD in Vienna reports:

It cannot be denied that the anniversary of the *Anschluss* did not produce the lively response in the population which one would have expected. Also, the instruction to put out flags was obeyed far less than [in the past].[5]

Austrians versus Germans

The SD-man who wrote this report may have consoled himself that this lack of enthusiasm was not the result of a change of mind,

2 T84R16 43 289; R14 40 801–2, 769, 775.
3 T84R14 41 098; R15 40 968; R13 40 094; R15 42 572.
4 T84R14 41 477; R15 42 492; R14 41 145.   5 T84R13 40 406–7.

but due to a more serious mood caused by the war. In reality, a new foe had arisen which was of far greater significance than the grumbling and grousing of malcontents: the first stirrings of national feeling. As was noted before, anti-German sentiments were often expressed in vulgar and offensive terms ('deutsche Schweine', 'dreckige Deutsche'); Germans in Austrian cities were often insulted, pushed around, deliberately sent out of their way, refused service and accommodation; were blamed for simply everything the speaker happened to dislike; while the past – the Austrian past – was idealized. In extenuation it could presumably be argued that inflamed nationalism has always been an exhilarating, noble thing only in patriotic lyrics, and an unpleasant and cruel experience in practice. Nevertheless, seeing the Germans as foreign invaders, who had moreover involved Austria in a war, helped to make the restoration of an independent Austria once again seem more desirable.

Sometimes the political slogan is spiced with wit: 'Finish the war! Throw the big-mouthed Prussians out! *Bierleiter Gauckel ins Trinkerasyl!*' – a pun on the *Gauleiter*'s name and his fondness for liquor, on a leaflet. More seriously, a rhyme chalked on military trains:

> Die Reservisten aus Polen sind da –
> Wo ist die SS und SA?[6]

'Those Prussian *Hunde* have started this war,' says a labourer collecting his meagre meat ration. A soldier on leave complains of the treatment of Austrian troops by the 'Prussian big-mouths'. 'Austrians are treated as expendable, to be shot down in front; North Germans stay in the rear.' On 12 January 1939 the SD admits that 'hostility towards the Reich and Reich Germans' is on the increase in Vienna; but similar opinions are reported from all over the country: 'We are Austrians; we didn't need those bloody Germans' (Eferding and Baden).[7]

The SD admitted readily enough that Reich German officials and managers 'do not hit the right note when dealing with the [Austrian] people'. This became especially irksome when supply difficulties led to shortages of food and consumer goods, to the closure of workshops through lack of labour or raw materials, to rising prices and poorer quality. The first food shortages occurred in October 1939, and the SD stated baldly that in the opinion of people conditions compared very unfavourably with those prevail-

[6] 'The reservists have returned from the Polish Front – but where were the SS and SA?'

[7] T84R14 41 477; R16 43 521; R13 40 126; R 15 42 623; R14 41 475; R15 42 574; R14 41 291.

ing in the Great War, while opponents pointed out that not all could be well with the economic plans if after two months of war there were not enough potatoes to go round. To prevent queues outside shops, someone had the bright idea one day to put a whole queue of women outside a fish shop in a police bus, drive them to a distant part of the city, and drop them there. This caused a great outcry, but even though the experiment was not repeated, women got very angry in the markets, faced with empty stalls or being offered substitutes – rolled oats instead of *pasta*, unacceptable to the Viennese palate. The SD describes one such scene: 'The Führer is responsible for this war. What has this war got to do with us?' A sixty-five-year-old woman who tried 'to defend the Führer and the Reich' was chased away.[8]

Shortages of this kind were not serious enough to hit more than the poorer classes – especially since 'officers, soldiers, and civilians with the party badge' were able to do their shopping in Slovakia, as the Security Officer of the SS in the Danubian area complained on 18 October 1939. On 9 December the SD admitted that the new income tax changes were the third since the *Anschluss* which adversely affected smaller incomes in the *Ostmark*. Now it was the turn of the middle classes: as from 1 January 1940 the German property tax and the German farm tax system were introduced. Small entrepreneurs, whom the Nazis had promised to protect, were now squeezed out at a rate 'much higher in many, perhaps in most, cases than in the *Altreich*', as if it was official policy 'to injure industry in the *Ostmark*'.[9] Traders and small manufacturers also complained about discrimination; the SD reports them as saying: 'Laws are made in Berlin, obeyed in Vienna, read in Munich, and ignored in Berlin.' The often surprising frankness of SD reports is probably due to genuine disappointment over the way things are going – and also a critique of Reich decisions made over the heads of the Austrian Nazis. Thus the conclusion of a 15 February 1940 report:

> It needs to be stressed again and again that such Reich measures are bound to draw attention to a very considerable (though certainly not genuine National Socialist) section of *Altreichsdeutsche*, party members and non-members, here who have all the attributes of conquerors, and in this way increase those unnecessary tensions which exist.

Even the summer months, and a string of victories, did not bring much alleviation, and on 14 August the mood in Vienna is described as 'still depressed': people anticipate another winter of

[8] T84R14 41 262, 081–2, 399.   [9] ibid., 40 853, 688–9; 41 376, 211.

war with trepidation, and are ready to believe every rumour: an impending attack on Yugoslavia, far greater losses of aircraft than are admitted, much more serious damage done by British bombers, etc.[10]

War and War Guilt

A chorus of hostile comment accompanies developments on the military fronts, as the Gestapo records show: 'Hitler has no business to be in Vienna and in Prague.' 'I don't need Danzig – do you? Whoever wants it can stick his own head out for it.' 'Danzig – a case of rape: just as if France asked for Hamburg.' 'What does he want Poland for?' 'I won't fight the Poles if I'm called up; they haven't done anything to me.' And: 'I'll be the first to desert. Of course, I should fight for ourselves, for Austria, but not for those in the Reich ... Austria will be free one day.'[11]

After the end of hostilities in the East, the SD claimed, morale had improved even though reactionary circles were now talking of attacks on the neutral countries and of the entry of the U.S.A. into the war. The actual invasion of Denmark and Norway 'impressed the opposition', but they said victory over such weak countries was nothing to boast about. The attack on the Netherlands produced one courageous act:

> Führer Adolf Hitler, Berlin. Please spare Holland and Belgium. In our hardest times the Dutch received us like their own children. Anna Hovorka.

For this telegram, which referred to relief work after the Great War, the sender – a Catholic schoolteacher – was suspended from duty. But the German war-machine moved on, and soon the Netherlands and France were overrun.[12]

Britain's refusal to sue for peace made a deep impression all over Austria: 'The Fourth Reich will come – the English will win the war' (Vienna). 'The English have never yet lost a war' (Herzogenburg). 'England, come and help us!' (leaflets near Mistelbach). And a civil engineer in the air force remembers that 'we kept on winning battles in the Great War, and yet we lost in the end'.[13]

The end of the fighting on land is the right moment to consider the attitude of Austrians towards the *Wehrmacht*. Again much of the evidence points to feelings common to all armies: complaints about officers, food, and accommodation; about the injustice of the

[10] ibid., 41 262, 277; R13 40 207–8.
[11] T84R13 40 174; R16 43 330; R13 40 160, 147; R15 42 616.
[12] T84R13 40 280, 268, 228–9.
[13] T84R15 42 048, 572, 395, 215.

call-up which kept younger men at home; about one's own unit being used for all the most dangerous jobs while others waited safely in the rear, etc. The only difference was again that here the 'enemy' was not just an officer, but (in most cases) a *German officer*; that the favoured units were *German* ones; that more Austrians were called up than Germans – and that even among Austrians, members of the party and its formations were often spared:

> An die Front mit dir, du Ostmarkschwein,
> SA, SS – die bleibt daheim![14]

(a sticker in Vienna on 24 October). It is immaterial whether these criticisms were justified or not, so long as enough people believed in the complaints or in the number of Austrians killed in Poland, which a leaflet put at 13,000.[15]

While the SD is full of praise for the military spirit shown by Austrians, certain unpleasant features cannot be ignored: 'noisy scenes' at the recruiting centres, 'exaggerated complaints' about young Germans not being called up in sufficient numbers, and 'derogatory remarks' about *Altreichsdeutsche* as a result of a remark by the Führer that Daladier would 'get to know his *Ostmärker*' and of hostile rumours, based on letters from the front and reports by men on home leave, that Austrians were manning the most dangerous positions in front of the *Westwall*.[16]

According to the SD, the huge propaganda machine of the Reich was not doing a good job: one notices the writers' grim satisfaction whenever they can criticize one of the minions of Joseph Goebbels, whether they be journalists, radio commentators, or in charge of the film industry or the stage. More and more people were listening to foreign broadcasts and were hoarding and passing on enemy leaflets dropped from planes in spite of the risks this involved. Again the BBC emerges as the most popular station, and even the Gestapo admits the quality of the RAF's *Wolkiger Beobachter* with its mixture of news, jokes, cartoons, and satirical verses. It is obvious to the security people that, with the frontiers hermetically sealed, the underground derives its slogans and information for its 'whispering campaigns' from enemy broadcasts; its leaflets often give their wavelengths and times so that more people can hear the enemy for themselves.[17]

---

[14] 'Fight at the front, *Ostmark* swine, SA and SS stay at home.'
[15] T84R15 43 413; R14 40 744.
[16] T84R14 40 857, 742; T77R312 114 3562 ff.
[17] T84R14 41 073; 40 630–1; 41 046; R16 43 754; R15 540; R14 41 171; etc.

The Industrial Scene

The outbreak of war was accompanied by a flood of regulations which, as elsewhere, subordinated everything, people and materials, to the great tasks ahead. These *kriegswirtschaftliche Verordnungen* (edicts regulating the war economy) affected high and low alike, but in varying degrees; and the disadvantages from which working people suffered in belligerent countries were due to their social position – lack of reserves, of 'connections', of *savoir-faire* – and not to any evil intent. In any case, their political and trade union organizations were able to defend their interests.

Not so in Austria during the German occupation (where conditions were even worse than in the Reich because of the traditional weakness of the economy). Dismissing the facile argument that things were bad for the workers because Fascism was the tool of monopoly capitalism, it is wholly inexplicable why the régime should have been so excessively hard on the very people who after all provided it with its instruments of war. It would be tempting to think that this was due to the acknowledged hostility of the workers; or because deterrents really worked; or because the Reich was so desperate that it could not help antagonizing its working population. But none of this really explains the policy of ruthless oppression, of cruelty and humiliation, of bombastic promises and very poor performances (at least on the home front). There is such a wealth of evidence in these documents to reveal the fraudulence of the 'socialism' of the Nazis, that they stand condemned out of their own mouths.

At the same time, the position of the compilers of the SD reports is rather puzzling. Where they do not fight their factional battles, they can be remarkably objective, analytical, and at times even sympathetic to working-class grievances. This was no attempt to curry favour, for their reports were secret; on the contrary, they were often likely to offend by their frankness. On the other hand, where real resistance was involved, they showed no sympathy or 'softness' – although quite a few of Himmler's men, anticipating (or parallel to) their master's own efforts, made contact with the Allies or even with the Resistance months before the end. We are left with the impression that the anonymous men who penned these reports were Austrian National Socialists who were sadly disappointed by the way things were going in the country which *they* had hoped to lead before the Germans took over; that they hoped to affect policy by their often accurate analyses; but that they remained Nazis at heart and as such accepted the barbarism of the régime.

On the other hand, the militancy shown by large numbers of

workers – involving sometimes dozens or even hundreds of men and women in a single factory – is quite surprising after all that had gone before. The DAF is of course quite helpless, and the management calls in the Gestapo when men disobey instructions, ignore the ten-hour day and leave work at the usual time, beat up foremen and abuse officials, practise ca'canny and achieve only 40 to 50 per cent of their target. The DAF complains to the Gestapo:

> In the factories Communists agitate quite openly and propose passive resistance against the war legislation. Communist slogans are painted on the walls, such as 'Down with Hitlerism!' or 'Workers of the world unite!' The decent elements among the workers are quite powerless against these people.

And again: 'It is particularly industrial workers who infect other sections of the population with their own grievances.'[18]

The grievances were real enough, and the militancy understandable. 'It should be mentioned that the city's electricity-workers were always very radical, and were well looked after, in the "red" era, by their unions', whereas now labourers earn RM 28 to 30 a week, 'which is not enough to set up house'. Short-time at Vöslau leads 'to real economic hardships, which explain the workers' protests'. Textile wages were always low in Austria, but under the Nazis even dropped below the dole:

> These workers – who are mostly anti-Nazi – claim that under the former government they received a dole of 22 schillings when they were unemployed, on which sum they could support a family, better than on their present wages.

Workers engaged on private building and in quarries are not included in the system of bad-weather compensation, nor do they receive a short-time supplement; 'the discontent of these compatriots, who include fathers of families, is understandable'. Again the *Systemzeit* (i.e., the former political 'system') comes in for praise when the desolate situation of 5,770 unemployed school-leavers is considered; whereas 100,000 schillings was once spent on training centres and canteens for them, 'today it is impossible to obtain a grant to send eighty girls to a school for dressmaking', and the Land Service offers 'no guarantee of decent accommodation for boys and girls'.[19]

Similar admissions (formulated as explanations to the RSHA in Berlin for the unrest among the workers) are made in connection

[18] T84R13 40 168, 176, 164–5; R16 43 681; R14 40 714, 594.
[19] T84R14 40 669–71, 715, 637–8, 638; 41 409–10. Labour service on the land – *Landdienst*.

with social insurance and the cost of living; thus on 13 December
1939 in a comment on the introduction of the Reich insurance
scheme, which was more expensive with smaller benefits than the
old Austrian scheme:

> After decades of trade unionism the workers of the *Ostmark* are
> very well versed in the field of social insurance. Any drop in
> standards, be it in benefits or administration, is sharply criticized
> and affects political morale adversely.

And on 22 January 1940 this comparison with conditions in the
small and stagnating republic:

> The workers have not got over the fact that, compared with the
> time before the *Anschluss*, they have suffered a reduction in real
> wages. They have not got over the fact that many social services,
> as for instance health insurance, have deteriorated.

Social inequality leads to blatant injustices: labourers and other
low-income groups cannot afford to buy all their rations, particularly butter, which is then sold freely on Saturdays to those who can
afford it. Cheap footwear and clothing is rationed – and often unobtainable – but shoes over RM 40 and clothes over RM 180 are off
the ration.[20]

All this is not the fault of the system, argues a clever SD-man in
Baden, but is due to war breaking out before the *Ostmark* had been
fully integrated in the German economy. The effect of those shortcomings is that grumbles and complaints frequently end with the
words: 'We are not Germans but Austrians; we did not ask for the
Anschluss.' And as for the excuse of the 'premature' outbreak of
war, *vox populi* replies through a joiner at Ternitz: 'Why did you
start the war if you haven't enough food for us?' Of course, as the
local *Landrat* explains, wages at the man's factory are low, and the
workers are very discontented; after all, 'the whole area has for
years been a citadel of the Social Democrats'. Nor is it worth the
women's while to go to work; of the 200 females under forty-five
who have been called up, he has only got 10 per cent so far; whoever can prefers a rushed wartime wedding and the dependant's
allowance to industrial work at low pay under wartime conditions.[21]

The cure for lack of willingness to work was the feared *Zwangs-
verschickung* (i.e., direction of labour), but this caused the régime
even more trouble and unpopularity. The three fullest accounts we
have are from Vorarlberg, between November 1939 and March
1940. A request for 400 women from a munitions factory in Berlin

[20] T84R14 40 655–7; 41 420; R13 40 500, 419.
[21] T84R14 41 291–2; R15 42 317, 276, 153.

to the labour exchange in Bregenz is impossible to meet; so far, they had only got eighty, and some of these had to be escorted by the gendarmerie, because 'it was well known how badly other women had been treated who had been sent to a spinning-mill in Neubeuren, and now they feared similar treatment in Berlin'.

Since mostly single girls were involved, their parents used what influence they had, and before long it was said that only girls from poorer families were forced to go. In March 'about twenty young girls are in jail at Feldkirch for refusing to go to Berlin'.[22]

At the same time, the number of acts of sabotage increased sharply; between January and August 1940 we find several dozen cases in the SD reports, mostly from Vienna and eastern Austria. Not all of them read very convincingly; some of the damage may well not have been deliberate but due to indifference, carelessness, or simply fatigue; but it is known that dictatorial régimes of all persuasions need 'acts of sabotage' to cover up their own incompetence or to justify their terroristic system. Certainly deliberate, and of greater long-term significance, were political protests and organized resistance groups.

The Opposition on the Left

It is again fortunate that the daily reports of the Vienna Gestapo are fairly complete for the first twelve months of war, which makes it possible to reconstruct the life and the moods of the people. As conditions deteriorated, pride in the spirit and the achievements of Austrian labour increased, as did contempt for the new régime. 'The Nazis are safely in the rear and only talk big', says a carpenter; 'I won't lift a finger for this terror-régime, only for the Social Democrats.' 'Long live Stalin!' says another, 'I am a Socialist, and shall remain one.' The leaders of 'red' Vienna are still remembered: their achievements ('just look at those municipal flats') and their fate under Dollfuss ('Breitner and Seitz were innocent, and yet they were jailed'); 'We Social Democrats will come to power again.' These loyalists have no doubt about the future: 'Austria will be taken away from the Reich, things can't go on like this.' The SD explains working-class discontent:

> *Former Social Democrats* protest more and more frequently against the increased efforts demanded of workers. They declare, *and use this argument in their propaganda*, that it is incompatible with socialism to pretend that increased working hours and production targets do not matter.[23]

[22] T84R14 40 752, 41 393; R13 40 376–7.
[23] T84R13 40 135, 112; R15 42 622, 934; R14 41 251.

The significance of this item, apart from the light it sheds on industrial relations, lies in the recognition of the Social Democrats as an active and distinct political group, and their views on war events, economic matters, other political groups, and the Nazis themselves are quoted throughout the war in innumerable reports. Moreover, the views quoted are always identical, whichever part of Austria the reports cover – a testimonial to the political education the workers had received in the labour movement. The Communists, too, in the bitter controversies surrounding the Hitler–Stalin Pact, attack socialist criticism of Soviet policy and of the KPÖ's tactics of entering 'Fascist organizations' in their underground journals, quoting *RS-Schriften*, of which, however, there is no evidence in the files. In fact, the only socialist publications the SD quotes are two leaflets of the Austrian–South German organization of Otto Haas and Waldemar von Knöringen which confirm what we have already learned about the tactics of the socialist underground and which give the first indication of a significant change of perspective: '. . . Austrians, too, victims of Hitler's aggression, must be given an opportunity to decide for themselves whether they want to stay within the Reich or not . . .'[24]

This was in April 1940, but participants in the socialist Resistance maintain that the working class, at least, had already made its decision in favour of independence.

Those who joined the Communist Party soon found themselves involved in feverish activities. For the KPÖ the opportunities which the outbreak of war offered were soon balanced by the need to explain the pact, the attacks on the Western democracies, Soviet shipments of war materials to Germany, the surrender of German and Austrian anti-Fascists to the Gestapo (including Franz Koritschoner, founder-member of the KPÖ, refugee in Russia, and a victim of the purge), the attack on Finland, and many more such unpalatable developments. It was this wave of *agitprop* material after August 1939 that drew the attention of the Gestapo to the new leadership of the KPÖ and led to the arrest of Ludwig Schmidt and 165 others in Vienna. Among these were the liaison officers with the organizations in Lower Austria and in Upper Styria, which were then destroyed through mass arrests; the total for Lower Austria by February was 148; in Styria, Kapfenberg alone accounted for 130.[25]

The satisfaction of the Gestapo was short-lived; after a short interval of a few weeks communist propaganda material was again distributed in many places.[26] Nevertheless, this was the last big

[24] T84R13 40 237–9.
[25] T84R16 43 492, 494; R15 42 455; R14 41 201; R15 42 896.
[26] T84R13 40 548, 318.

gesture of defiance, for from now on it became increasingly difficult to replace leading cadres, find new hiding-places, resume contacts with people who had barely escaped the last round-up. A communist account mentions a few more underground centres, mostly led by men who had been brought back from abroad, but none of them lasted more than a few months, and all were tried and executed. After this, communist activity was sporadic, but none the less heroic and costly: at least 2,300 activists are claimed to have been killed or executed.[27] It is idle to speculate how many of those lives could have been spared if different tactics had been employed; the more extreme a movement, the greater its need of martyrs.

Church and Laity

If one went by the evidence of the daily Gestapo reports alone one would be tempted to believe that there was little organized Catholic resistance in the first few months of war. Most of the reports deal with spontaneous protests by farmers, mainly directed against the anti-clerical measures of the régime; with the courageous example set by village priests; and with the loyalty of members of Catholic youth clubs. Later situation reports and court files, however, prove that there was a great deal of organized resistance going on at the time – but the Gestapo, while keeping suspects under observation, was too busy with its *Karteiaktion* against the Socialists, and the arrest of one communist centre after another, to bother with intellectual groups who were less of a risk at *this* stage.

What the Gestapo reported about the first few months was not very impressive; leaflets, stickers, and chain letters with patriotic slogans in Vienna, Innsbruck, Linz. Otto Habsburg, the *bête noire* of the Nazis, appears as the last hope of many conservatives, a sort of Robin Hood to rid the people of their oppressors. Many conservative groups are referred to as *Legitimisten* or monarchists; it is not always clear whether this is accurate or merely a smear-term, like 'Communists' on the Left. Arrests at first include small groups of seven (Kufstein), fourteen (Schwaz), or four (Vienna); then a group of sixteen young people, led by a chaplain, is discovered in February and accustomed to working for 'an independent Austria', while a 'legitimist' group of forty-one is mentioned in April (both Vienna). In the summer of 1940 the People's Court reports to the Ministry that seventeen proceedings against right-wing groups are pending, while in Innsbruck 109 members of a 'legitimist' organization

---

[27] Franz Marek, 'Im Kampf gegen den deutschen Faschismus', *Weg und Ziel*, December 1954.

called *Kampffront* were being interrogated, thirty-five of whom faced trial for *Hochverrat*.[28]

But the most serious losses the conservative camp suffered in this summer of 1940 were the arrests of the poet-priest Karl Roman Scholz and his associates in the Austrian Freedom Movement, who were reactionary Romantics dreaming of the resurrection of a Greater Austria and inspired large numbers of (mostly young) people to keep up their love of country and to work for freedom.[29] In addition to what Otto Molden has discovered about this group and what the court files contained,[30] we now learn that these idealistic intellectuals also planned military action and sabotage, and that they sought contacts with the Allies through the French Mission in Budapest. A similar attempt, via the British consul in Zagreb, is reported of the Greater Austria Freedom Movement of Dr Kastelic, which had a military section consisting exclusively of experienced soldiers who were to seize power at the time of 'the military defeat of the Reich, which they took for granted'. Another group, Dr Lederer's Austrian Freedom Movement, is reported to have been negotiating an amalgamation with the other organizations. Scholz, Kastelic, and Lederer died under the axe.

In the countryside, opposition took less intellectual, but equally dramatic, forms; in *Kreis* Mistelbach the party decided to punish a 'bastion of clericalism', the village of Wultendorf. Preceded by a band, party officials and SA marched through the village and beat up all those who did not show respect to the flag. 'Punitive expeditions' against Austrian villages, a beating-up to achieve 'proper respect'! It did not work; a month later, in the same *Kreis*, the party called a meeting which was attended by fifteen persons – out of a total population of one thousand. Altogether, political meetings were only attended by party members and others 'who do not need to be influenced'; the rest stayed at home. Similar reports came from all over Austria. In the Tyrol, anyone who gave evidence against a defendant was called a 'nark' and ostracized by the people; the few Nazis among the teachers in the villages were treated as enemies and sometimes even denied milk and butter by the farmers.[31]

But we also find evidence of the part played by the pro-Nazi element among the Austrian clergy. There had always been a section

---

[28] T84R13 40 112, 144, 577–8; R15 42 635, 469, 445, 432; R14 41 264–5; IfZ Mü NG–682 T938 a.

[29] T84R15 42 119–23, 072.

[30] Otto Molden, *Ruf des Gewissens*, pp. 69–83; Szecsi and Stadler, *Die NS-Justiz . . .*, pp. 75–7.

[31] T84R14 41 073, 052–3, 030; 40 838; 41 441.

of the clergy who were National Socialists in all but name; *Deutschnationalismus*, anti-semitism, and anti-democratic opinions led a number of them to serve the new régime as *Gauredner* (i.e., as public speakers on the *Gau* panel), as spies in religious orders, as informers on their colleagues. One of them, in Upper Austria, told the SD how the Church tried to prevent the call-up of young priests: it sent older parish priests away on leave so that their younger colleagues had to take their places. (He also denounced the monks of St Florian for secretly distributing Schuschnigg's last book, *Dreimal Österreich*, among the clergy.) After the attacks on Innitzer a few of them were beginning to see the error of their ways; a village priest near Vienna, *Gauredner* in 1938, was now barred from giving religious instruction, denounced by his local *Landrat*, and warned by the Gestapo *Leitstelle* Vienna. That the few cases we come across in the reports represent a distinct swing of opinion among pro-Nazi Catholic circles is confirmed by a December 1940 situation report of the SD, which signalizes the defection of yet another group of earlier supporters.[32]

These circles, priests and laymen, had been in bitter opposition to Schuschnigg and had hoped and worked for the *Anschluss*. Now, however, they intended to see Göring and explain to him that

> unless there were a radical change in official policy towards the Church, the Catholics of the *Ostmark* would never make their peace with the [Nazi] movement. On the contrary, Catholics who had already found their way into the party would be alienated from it.

This, the SD informed the RSHA in Berlin, was the new tactic of the Church in Austria: since it could not prevail alone against party and state, it hoped to recover some of the lost ground via the Reich Church Ministry. In the *Ostmark* the Church was subjected to the commands of party and state, against which it formerly dared not even protest, but now it had the impertinence to threaten Vienna with Berlin! The significance of this development is clear: the régime was beginning to lose the support of its Trojan Horse inside Austrian Catholicism, and while no direct gain necessarily accrued to the opposition, this disappointment inevitably strengthened the centrifugal forces.

Sectarians, Minorities, and Jews

A régime that was prepared to offend against the most deeply-felt emotions – or at least the traditions – of most Austrians, could

[32] T84R14 40 577; R16 43 321; R14 40 605–7.

not be expected to spare the feelings of minorities. Even here, though, the struggle of the German 'Confessional Church' had its repercussion in Austria; the first case, in December 1938, was that of a pastor from Flensburg who had been banished from Schleswig–Holstein, was now suspected of contacting anti-state groups in Vienna, and was sent back to the Reich. The first confiscations of evangelical parish magazines occurred in March 1939, and from then onwards Protestant clergy and their sermons were subjected to the same scrutiny and criticism as their Catholic colleagues.[33]

It was not Protestantism as such, though, but Protestant sectarians who were to suffer the full weight of persecution – partly because the Gestapo suspected them of anti-state activities and opinions as a result of their international connections, especially with America, and partly on account of their conscientious objection to military service. Of the various groups we meet in the documents, like the Seventh Day Adventists and the Jehovah's Witnesses, only the latter seem to have survived the first waves of arrests. The irrational cruelty used against essentially harmless and utterly non-political people is quite remarkable – except that it is held against them that they either boycotted the *Anschluss* plebiscite or cast negative votes. Their refusal to obey the call-up led to the first death sentence in Austria on 22 December 1939, when a Witness from St Pölten was tried by a military court and shot. An OKW publication, *Kriegs-kriminalstatistik für die Wehrmacht* ('War-time Criminal Statistics for the Armed Forces'), for the first twelve months of war gives the numbers of cases of *Wehrkraftzersetzung* for each quarter: 159–250–330–348, and explains that these increases are due to Jehovah's Witnesses, against whom there were 152 actions in all; and they also accounted for 112 out of the 117 executions carried out inside Germany. (Where a *Reichskriegsgericht* found for the accused and acquitted them, the Gestapo took them straight from the court and put them into concentration camps, as happened to a railwayman from St Pölten and a foundry-worker from Krems.) The courage they showed there, and the cheerfulness with which they faced torture and death, has been described by many of their fellow-prisoners.[34]

National minorities, too, particularly if they were Slavs, experienced the rigours of a racist régime. In the census of May 1939 people were asked to state their *Volks- und Sprachzugehörigkeit* (their ethnic and linguistic affiliations), which resulted in a 43·4 per cent increase over 1934 in the total non-German-speaking population

[33] T84R13 39 732–3.
[34] T84R16 43 433; R14 41 500; T77R805 5 537 704; T84R15 42 173, 088.

in Vienna alone. The result shocked the SD, but in actual fact very little had changed, and the total number of people involved – 4·9 per cent of Vienna's population – was surprisingly small for a city of this kind. For this group of 94,014 was made up of 41,395 non-Germans and 52,619 persons of non-German mother-tongue but declaring for *deutsches Volkstum*. Instead of being pleased by the preference shown, the SD dismissed it as 'opportunism', especially since there was no doubt that even if Czechs, Slovaks, and Croats considered themselves Viennese, their sympathies lay elsewhere: 'The sympathies of the majority of the Czechs in Vienna are with the Western Powers' (December 1939). 'Bad morale is particularly noticeable in the tenth district of Vienna. This is due to the large number of Marxist Czechs who live there' (January 1940).[35]

In the Burgenland and in Styria it is the Croat minorities who are worrying the régime. Not only do Burgenland Croats, who are already in process of being *eingedeutscht* (of becoming German), suddenly rediscover their *Volkstum*, but Pan-Slavism and rumours of their intended deportation make them prepared to listen to communist propaganda. In the Croat village of Güttenbach in Styria, on the other hand, the arrest of the village priest leads to a riot, threats against pro-Nazi Croats, and 'anti-state utterances'.[36]

As for the Slovenes in Carinthia, theirs was probably the hardest lot of all, especially in the later stages of the war, and we shall meet them in subsequent documents. What is significant in all this is the fact that these minorities had been loyal Austrians (as they had proved in the Burgenland and Klagenfurt troubles from 1918 to 1921) and that the bad treatment they suffered under the Nazi régime merely confirmed and strengthened their Austrian orientation. That gipsies in spite of their 'Aryan' origin suffered a fate comparable to that of the Jews was to be expected, since the official commentary on the Nuremberg Laws, drafted in 1936 by Hans Globke, proclaimed that 'artfremdes Blut in Europa' ('blood alien to our race') meant Jews and gipsies. Their deportation from Austria, which began with 2,500 men, women, and children in April 1940, and which resulted in their physical destruction, has so far produced only one slight study.[37]

To these 'alien' groups resident in Austria must be added the growing army of slave labourers, labour volunteers, and prisoners-of-war. Germany and Austria had always used seasonal and migratory workers from the inexhaustible reservoir of eastern and south-

---

[35] T84R14 41 331–2; 40703; 41 486, 400.
[36] ibid., 40 819, 607; 41 305, 437.
[37] T84R13 40 255. Selma Steinmetz, *Die österreichischen Zigeuner im NS-Staat* (Vienna, 1966).

eastern Europe. The demands of Hitler's war-machine increased this trickle to a stream of millions of foreign workers, who were to become a serious political and security liability in the later stages of the war. What is generally referred to as 'slave labour' was recruited from the 'Protectorate' of Bohemia and Moravia (1939), Poland (1940), and Yugoslavia and Russia (1941). At the same time, *volunteers* from Slovakia, Hungary, and other countries not yet at war enjoyed a higher status and better conditions, while the third group, prisoners-of-war, especially those from the Slav countries, were mercilessly exploited and cruelly treated.

The relations between farmers and their labourers are nearly always problematical; and when these labourers are practically without rights and protection, exploitation and ill-treatment often follow. Yet it emerges from our documents that many farmers – and indeed whole villages – 'adopted' and protected 'their' prisoners-of-war and foreign labourers, much to the annoyance of the party who declared them to be 'of inferior race'. What helped, especially in the case of Poles, was their 'auffällig zur Schau getragene Religiosität'.[38] which frequently led to a united front of Austrian and Polish Catholics against the party, while among industrial workers solidarity with foreign labour was a socialist and anti-Nazi demonstration.

Of the many hundreds of cases the SD reported we need only list the principal objections the régime had to the way foreign labour was treated: full equality with local labour; sharing quarters and meals; being taken to church services, football matches, and dances; inciting local workers to disobedience; forming discussion groups and listening to foreign radio stations; familiarity with local girls and women. As early as December 1939 Polish prisoners-of-war arrive at Fischamend airfield, and soon the local population is

> indignant over [their] alleged ill-treatment by the military. The civilian workers employed there have on several occasions loudly and publicly protested against the treatment they receive.

When Polish prisoners were marched through Deutschkreuz, on 17 December, 'this caused a great stir among the population, and people felt pity for them since their footwear was in very bad shape and some even walked barefoot.'

Passers-by at Moserkreuz give cigarettes to prisoners engaged in road-building; they are said to be the same people 'who will not support the official *Winterhilfe* collections'. The village priest of

[38] 'Ostentatious show of religious feeling.'

Göpfritz and a woman are arrested for organizing a collection of food for 'their' prisoners.[39]

> In January 1940 the SD notes identical complaints from many parts that German [i.e., Austrian] agricultural workers, German farmhands, in most cases regrettably side with Polish civilian labour against their masters, the German farmers. It is manifest that in these strata class feeling is stronger than 'volksmäßiges und Rasseempfinden'.[40]

The miners of Wolfsegg-Traunthal register 'with malicious joy' the difficulties their management has with Poles, even when the latter steal explosives! In Upper Austria, too, the SD notes the growth of working-class solidarity; the Poles have overcome their initial shyness and stir up their 'German' fellow-workers against their employers, while 'Marxist and communist circles' seek contacts with prisoners-of-war and slave labourers.[41]

At a party meeting in a small village in Lower Austria the speaker, an officer of the SA, noticed a group of Polish prisoners in his audience. He remonstrated with the n.c.o. in charge of the group (who had intended to do them a good turn and break the monotony of their life), but was told 'he was after all an Austrian, and in Austria the treatment of P.o.W.s was *gemütlicher*'; the prisoners were *his* responsibility and *he* decided where they were to go. Another n.c.o. likewise refused to take orders from a party *Kreisamtsleiter* who protested against the local population being invited to a theatrical evening given in a camp near Attersee, saying that his *Wehrmacht* command had raised no objections, and no civilian was giving him orders! The Nazi soon settled this by threatening to arrest everyone who attended the show, which had to be cancelled.[42]

Not all party members and functionaries were equally fanatical. The same report that deals with the abortive show quotes the *Ortsgruppenleiter* and the *Frauenschaftsleiterin* of a small village near Vienna as having collected clothes and money for their prisoners; each Pole received 10 marks and some clothing: 'Those who would not contribute were shunned by the population.' Near Eisenstadt, a group of prisoners were presented with 10 litres of wine and one hundred cigarettes by the local *Zellenleiter*, the burgomaster, and the village priest, to celebrate Christmas Eve. On the Esterházy estate, Seehof, every Sunday the hundred Poles there marched in formation to a private service in church, and *en route*

[39] T84R14 40 615e; 41 514; 40 628; R16 43 542.
[40] 'feeling for folk and race'.
[41] T84R14 41 455–6, 404 303–4.   [42] ibid., 41 515, 149–50.

were treated to wine and beer by anti-Nazis. Since church services have always been connected with charitable acts, it is only natural that small acts of kindness are reported from all places where there were prisoners or slave labour, and priests were often implicated. To the party, this was 'national-würdeloses Verhalten' ('undignified behaviour, unbecoming to a German'), and the kindness shown by officials and by the population unintelligible.[43]

Inevitably, the régime tried to counter this by means of more and stricter regulations: a ban on alcohol, on visits to inns and other meeting places, and on relations between 'Germans' and *Fremd-stämmige* (foreigners). Sexual relations between prisoners-of-war and 'German' girls and women were to be punished by shooting the man and cutting off the girl's hair, and in many cases putting her in a pillory or parading her through the streets with an offensively-worded placard round her neck. This last measure often met with disapproval, which is strange in view of the force of sexual jealousy; but it did little to stop the practice. While Polish males tended to be very cautious, women were less so; the SD learned from Upper Austria in February, and from Lower Austria in March, that even members of the party and its formations were having relations with Polish women.[44] It is probably correct to assume that at least as many people approved of the official measures in this respect as broke them; but there is sufficient evidence to show that deliberate cruelty and humiliation of prisoners and foreign labour did not pay, but helped to strengthen the aversion of decent people to National Socialism.

This was also the time which saw the end of Austrian Jewry, brought about by the policy known as the 'final solution': their expulsion from villages and small towns, which proudly proclaimed themselves *judenrein* (i.e. 'cleansed' or 'purged' of all Jews) on the departure of the last family; their concentration in the larger towns, and then in ghettos within these towns; banishment from public places and transport, with shops open to them only at certain hours: dismissal from their jobs, expulsion of their children from all schools; and over and above all, the tragic uncertainty about their future and the daily dread of new blows and insults.

Our documents illustrate very little of all this, and even less of the reactions of their fellow-citizens. The full story can be found in Gerald Reitlinger; the bare facts of the Austrian situation in Jonny Moser;[45] and the subsequent defence of this policy in the trial of

[43] ibid., 41 186, 397, 383-4.
[44] ibid., 41, 241-3, 303-4, 202; R13 40 468, 338.
[45] Gerald Reitlinger, *The Final Solution* (London, 1953); Jonny Moser, op. cit.

Eichmann and other 'murderers by remote control'. Nevertheless, what the Gestapo discovered and the SD reported deserves to be quoted in the context of this study for the dim and intermittent light it sheds on the Jewish fate. 'Thank God for the war', said a Jewess in September 1939, 'things will be better for us: we can stay here after all.'

This hope was soon dispelled, for if Jews could no longer be forced to emigrate, they could now be deported to the newly-conquered lands in eastern Poland. On 20 October the first transport of a thousand men left Vienna for Nisko/San. 'The most hair-raising rumours circulate among the Jews', the Gestapo reported about the beginning of the 'Resettlement'; 'the rest of the popula-tion knows hardly anything at all about this operation.' For a long time Germans and Austrians were disbelieved when they pleaded ignorance of the fate of their Jewish neighbours. Now we know that even the remnants of Jewish communities believed that it was only a question of resettlement; after all, on that first transport each man was allowed to take 300 marks, clothes, and tools; and they were promised that women and children would follow by the second transport. Those remaining in Vienna faced the first winter of war in great poverty; destitution spread, as even the SD admitted, for people had used up their reserves (or had them taken from them, or blocked).[46]

Not many expressions of sympathy or acts of solidarity are reported: shopkeepers who sell food to Jews outside permitted hours ('Sie sind ja auch Menschen')[47] or fruit (to which Jews were not entitled), or allow them into their cafés to find warmth and com-pany. A small tradesman says: 'Neither the Jews nor England and France are to blame for the war, but Germany which first attacked Czechoslovakia and then Poland.' A shopkeeper is arrested because he has indignantly torn up the pornographic anti-semitic weekly *Der Stürmer*, and a tailor for saying 'We are facing a great food shortage, and that will be the end of Hitler. In a year *the Jews will be in power again*, and this will be our salvation.'[48] Even allowing for the fact that the Gestapo did not learn of the many secret acts of kindness, or just plain human decency, which did occur, the fear of punishment for any overt sympathy for the Jews was simply too great. (The secret diary kept at Dachau by Hans Vogl, member of a Tyrolese resistance group and subsequently beheaded, mentions 'a seventy-four-year-old masterbuilder from Vienna in our group

[46] T84R14 40 174; 41 022; 43 421; 40 584.
[47] 'They're also humans, after all.'
[48] T84R16 43 439; R13 40 491; R15 42 822, 616, 595.

whose crime was to find living accommodation for a Jewish woman!')[49]

There was a gap of about sixteen months between the first deportations to Nisko and Eichmann's February 1941 order to ship all Viennese Jews to the *Generalgouvernement Polen*. Some 5,000 left in February–March, nearly 5,000 in October–November (destination Lodz), while more than 5,000 were sent to Riga and over 10,000 to Minsk between November 1941 and October 1942.[50] But the sad remnants of Austrian Jewry still frightened the Nazis. In his 'table talk' on 24 July 1942 Hitler said that 'the removal of the Jews from Vienna is the most urgent job, for Vienna is the city most given to *meckern* [criticize and complain]'.[51] Even as late as September 1943 the *Gauschulungsamt Niederdonau* proclaimed:

> There can be no talk of a final settlement of the Jewish question so long as Jews – living in mixed and 'privileged' marriages – with importunity and protected by law cohabit with Germans and produce children, not to mention the problem of the *Mischlinge*. According to the latest statistics 102 Jews live in mixed marriages in Niederdonau. . . It is still possible to observe a far too lenient, compassionate attitude towards the Jews on the part of many *Volksgenossen*, and interventions even by leading *Parteigenossen* on behalf of *Mischlinge* are a fairly frequent experience of officials dealing with Jewish questions.[52]

One hundred and two *Volljuden* in a total population of perhaps 1·7 million in Lower Austria as a menace to the community!

The last document concerning the Jews is dated 5 February 1945: the Reich Ministry of Justice informing the State Attorney in Linz that because of the military situation in the South the jails in Graz would have to be emptied. Harmless offenders would be sent home, but on no account would prominent prisoners, political activists, Jews, and *Judenmischlinge 1.Grades* be set free; they were to be sent to Linz (presumably to be used as hostages). If, however, this transfer could no longer be effected, these persons were

> to be handed over to the police for their 'removal' ['Beseitigung'] or, if this is no longer possible, to be 'rendered harmless' ['unschädlich machen'] by shooting. All traces of the *Unschädlichmachung* to be carefully obliterated.[53]

[49] 8 August 1943; by courtesy of the widow.
[50] Information supplied by Jonny Moser.
[51] Henry Picker, *Hitlers Tischgespräche im Führerhauptquartier 1941–42* (Stuttgart, 1963), pp. 471–2.
[52] WLB No. 24, September 1943, p. 16.
[53] IfZ Mü NG 030.

A document of this kind, originating with a Reich Minister and penned by a high-ranking civil servant, may well tell future generations more about the nature of National Socialism than many a learned treatise: the language of the professional killer ('beseitigen'); treating human beings as vermin ('unschädlich machen'); and finally the cowardice of the bully ('sorgfältige Beseitigung der Spuren').

A Catholic historian, Professor Erika Weinzierl, has attempted to piece together the story of the 200,000 Austrians of Jewish and mixed blood about whom our documents are so reticent.[54] After a discussion of the roots of anti-semitism in Austria she describes in detail the inhuman treatment, the deportations, the extermination of innocent people. Of the 67,601 Austrian Jews who were sent to camps, only 2,142 survived. Even those who had succeeded in emigrating or escaping often fell into the hands of the Germans again and were either executed on the spot (as for instance in Serbia) or deported to camps; she estimates their number at about 15,000. When the war ended, Vienna was a city practically without Jews; and since then only another 5,000 have returned to join the 6,000 survivors. The loss to Austria's cultural and economic life is visible on all sides; but far more worrying is the thought that a crime of such magnitude could be perpetrated against so little opposition.

[54] Erika Weinzierl, op. cit., esp. pp. 70–92.

Chapter 8

Decline and Fall

THE BATTLE OF STALINGRAD, the destruction of the German
Sixth Army under von Paulus, can be seen as the turning-point of
the war: there were no more great victories on the Eastern Front
after the winter of 1942–43; Africa was lost and Mussolini over-
thrown; the invasion in the West, the 'Second Front', was followed
by the revolt of 20 July 1944; and there were few even within the
party to whom the fall of the Third Reich did not come as relief
from intolerable conditions and who preferred a 'terrible end' to a
'terror without end'. Only the military machine, augmented by the
remnants of the defeated armies of Germany's allies, by the SS,
and the militarized Hitler Youth, still went on fighting, leaving
behind a trail of scorched earth to mark its lines of retreat, shooting
deserters and defeatists, and still hoping against hope that it might
yet be needed by the Western Powers to resume its crusade against
Bolshevism.

A situation of this kind provides the acid test for a people's
loyalty; and by this test Austria was soon found wanting. Not that
there were not enough Austrians who fought for the Reich up to
the last moment: as soldiers at the rapidly changing fronts; as
guards policing the rear, denouncing, terrorizing, and killing their
opponents; as judges and jurors sending men and women to the
guillotine or before firing squads. They thought they had nothing
to lose, but they were wrong; they underestimated the readiness of
people to forget and to forgive the harm done to others.

As the ferociousness of the régime increased, so did the impotent
despair of its victims and the determination of the organized Resistance. It is interesting to note that the documents on which the
following section is based reveal an increasing concentration on
those theatres of war which adjoined Austria or where Austrian
troops were largely involved; the Reich and its global connections
are of no interest to Austrians. Their concern is with their own
country and its sons; Russia, Italy, the Balkans; the battles fought,
the men killed or taken prisoner, the armies retreating to Austria;

the province of the Third Reich adopts a provincial attitude and ignores the fate of the Reich.

The Eastern Front and Stalingrad

As the enormities of the fighting in the East began to sink in, people took refuge in wishful thinking. 'The Bolsheviks won't be too hard on us Austrians', is a widespread conviction in 'clerical' villages in Lower Austria. 'This wretched war', a priest writes to a mother who has lost her son; 'how many people are already cursing the damnable ambition of one man!' And prayers at the end of sermons are for an early peace and the safe return of the men, but 'never a mention of victory or the Führer'.[1]

The relatives of men killed at the front react bitterly to the attempts of the party to exploit their sacrifice for political ends; since they blame the Nazis for the war, they ignore *Politische Leiter* when they come to condole with them, or they attack them, and they boycott memorial meetings of the party 'because my son would not have wanted this'. But all the traditional church services, prayer processions, and wakes are held and attended by the whole village, while at the – simultaneous – party meeting the officials are left to themselves.[2]

The fall of Stalingrad, where only 90,000 men are captured out of the original 330,000 men there, increases the despair and anger of countless families. Already on 8 February 1943 the SD reports the widespread conviction that Stalingrad was mostly held by Austrians, the Führer is criticized for having 'driven Austrians to their deaths' there, and the hope is expressed that many Austrians have been taken prisoner, for people widely believe 'that the Soviets treat Austrians better' (than Germans). The consensus in clerical circles is that 'the best thing would be an early peace... where Austria would receive preferential treatment'. This conviction is so general that rumours are spread and readily believed which reproduce alleged statements by Churchill, the Pope, and Otto Habsburg; the latter is said to have claimed: 'I can't save you from famine, but I can save you from bombing attacks' – an allusion to recent attacks on Munich and the fear that Austrian cities would be the next targets.[3]

In March, the SD reports from Upper Austria that the workers at Lenzing say: 'Only the party bosses and the capitalists profit from victory, never the workers. We are always cheated and can risk our lives for others'. And in May a sombre picture is given of morale in the whole province:

[1] WLB Niederdonau, Nos. 18 and 19, August and September 1942.
[2] T81R6 13 243–50.   [3] ibid., 13 319–20, 378–9, 385, 437, 057–9.

The mood of the people is still characterized by general war-weariness and hopelessness. Especially among farmers and industrial workers there is no longer any belief in our final victory. An official of the *Kreisfrauenschaft*, who travels around a great deal, says: 'To judge by conversations on the trains and in buses, there are only pessimists left.'[4]

The disaffection spreads to the army, as the following reports from Lower Austria show. A private promoted lance-corporal refuses to put on his stripes because, as he says before the military court, 'the Führer was persecuting the Catholic religion'. A sergeant pleads in a letter from the front for the release of his village priest whom the Gestapo has arrested. It is noted that soldiers on leave call on the priests – even if formerly they never bothered with them. In the district of Melk rumour has it that

> prisoners at Stalingrad are separated out: *Altreichsdeutsche* are shot at once, while Austrians are put into good camps with adequate food. *Altreichsdeutsche* are said to maintain that the loss of Stalingrad was due to Austrian troops.... In the event of defeat, Austria would be exceptionally well treated.[5]

– a conviction which the Moscow Declaration of November 1943 on the restoration of an independent Austria was soon to support. Even Stalin seems to have been told of the difference between the attitudes of Germans and Austrians, for at the Teheran Conference soon after he is reported to have said to Churchill and Roosevelt that he did not distinguish between Prussians and other Germans; 'Only the Austrians call out: "I'm an Austrian", when they surrender, and our troops accept this ...'[6]

These rumours about Russian kindness towards Austrians seem to have had a surprising side-effect: the discovery by the Germans of the mass-graves of Polish officers in the wood of Katyn, whom the Soviets were alleged to have killed, produced the opposite effect to the one the German propaganda machine sought to achieve. In May 1943 the SD reported from Upper Austria that the opposition blamed the executions on the Germans. A priest is quoted as saying: 'The greater the German propaganda concern about Katyn, the more people I meet who are convinced that Germans were responsible.' And another priest is alleged to have said: 'People who have the deaths of hundreds of thousands of Jews, Poles, Serbs, and Russians on their consciences, have no right to protest when others do

---

[4] ibid., 13 057–9, 399.
[5] WLB Niederdonau, 2 May 1943; No. 24, September 1943.
[6] *International Affairs* (Moscow), August 1961, p. 122.

a small part of what they themselves practise all the time.' And in Lower Austria many of the people of Krems 'simply will not believe [that the Polish officers were murdered by the Russians] but hold that Russian responsibility is given by the Germans as an excuse'.[7] Considering that the authorities which were here given the benefit of the doubt were not British or American, for whom Austrians always felt respect and admiration, but Russian Bolsheviks who had for years been denigrated and denounced, and considering, moreover, that the opinions quoted were those of priests and peasants, morale had indeed reached a very low level.

In the spring of 1943 a Swedish journalist, Arvin Fredborg, Berlin correspondent of *Svenska Dagbladet*, visited Austria and published an account of his experiences which at the time sounded most reassuring: five years of Nazi rule, he claimed, had revived an Austrian consciousness. Austrians were beginning to ask themselves whether a common language really made a people, and were drawing a line, not only between themselves and National Socialism, but between Austrianism and *Deutschtum*. When he returned to Berlin in March 1943 he was convinced that at least Vienna, but possibly the provinces as well, was already politically lost to the Reich.[8] Our documents confirm that he was right – if only in the sense that strong minorities held the views he cited while the general current of opinion moved in the same direction.

Already in the previous summer Lower Austria had been troubled by a new wave of anti-Reich sentiment:

> The unhappy conflict between German tribes has again assumed a special virulence – which enemy propaganda cleverly exploits and exacerbates. Unfortunately even party members, and especially women, spread this *Stammeshass* among the people. Several *Kreise* were compelled to call special meetings to combat this *Preussenhass*.[9]

And the same source reports, in March 1943, the wide circulation of an anti-German version of 'Heut' kommen die Engerln auf Urlaub nach Wien', an immensely popular and somewhat sentimental *Wiener Lied*, which the Nazis rightly claim as 'an expression of the *preussenfeindlich* attitude' to be met everywhere and especially violent now, with the word 'Prussian' denoting every *Altreichsdeutscher*. This goes so far that near Mistelbach a farmer's daughter is sharply criticized because she expects a child from a *German* soldier, but no one worries about the twelve women in the same

---

[7] T81R6 13 209; WLB Niederdonau, No. 25, October 1943.
[8] Arvin Fredborg, *Behind the Steel Wall* (London, 1944), pp. 243, 97, 200.
[9] 'hatred of other (German) tribes, and of the Prussians'.

district who expect children from aliens! And by October the rumour circulates in the *Gau* that the Führer had given the *Ostmark* to the *Reichsdeutsche;* like the South Tyrolese and other *Volksdeutsche*, Austrians would be resettled in different parts so that Germans could settle in Austria.[10]

With morale being so low, the propaganda efforts of the régime assumed a special importance, but again the SD was not satisfied with them. After the heavy air raids on German cities in the winter of 1942–43, Austrians – who had so far been spared a similar experience – objected to the frequent accounts of the warm reception Dr Goebbels was claimed to have received in the stricken cities. Vienna found these stories 'incredible', for the poor people would have other worries. Salzburg reacted bitterly to a boast that 'even greater barbarities ... could not shake us' with the comment that this might well be true of the 'big shots' who did not share the common people's sufferings; while it ridiculed the story that American bomber crews were composed of criminals released from penitentiaries. . . .[11]

At this stage of the war it was a great deal easier for the Allies to reinforce their material superiority with telling propaganda lines. The security organs attached great importance to enemy propaganda, and we are treated to detailed descriptions of the British effort (especially with 'white' and 'black' propaganda) and analyses of their programmes. *Gauleiter* and *Kreisleiter* are supplied, in 'Confidential Memoranda', with the main facts so that party officials can prepare their replies to enemy arguments (which it is naturally assumed people will either have heard on the enemy radio or read on enemy leaflets – in spite of the draconic punishments for these offences!):

Bolshevism had reformed itself, it is no longer quite so terrible. At the last moment the British and the Americans will save us from Bolshevism.

[In the case of an Allied victory – argument sometimes used by workers:] We can't do more than work, therefore we shan't be any the worse off.

They'll only hang the Nazis.[12]

[10] WLB Niederdonau, No. 18, August 1942; No. 22, March 1943; No. 25, October 1943.

[11] Quoted in *The US Strategic Bombing Survey, European Documents*. Folder 64 br (17), Ref. 2004 BN, Folders 1 and 2, National Archives, Washington, DC.

[12] T81R2 63 435; R3 62 375–6; R2 64 218; R3 62 316–18, 479–81.

It says a lot about the degree of disaffection if a régime has to
include in its briefs for propagandists suitable replies to the suggestion that 'only' its supporters will be hanged.

Italy and Yugoslavia

The Allied landing in Sicily made a deep impression in Austria –
especially since Italians were traditionally distrusted and not rated
very highly as soldiers. Whitsun 1943 was a sad time in Linz, 'no
festive spirit anywhere'; instead, people were 'nervous, tense, without confidence'; victory seemed unobtainable because the Germans
'could not last a third winter in Russia'. From Graz the RSHA reported the existence of three schools of thought in Styria: firstly,
the unteachables, who believed Sicily was a German trap for the
Americans; secondly, the realists, who thought Sicily could be won
again, albeit with enormous German reinforcements; and thirdly,
the 'indifferent and the opposition' who saw the successful invasion
as the beginning of the end.[13]

Various comments on developments in Italy led to many trials by
Special Senates. What people were accused of were expressions of
relief that the war would now soon be over, fairly accurate forecasts
of the further course of the war, and violent denunciations of the
party. By this time the rot is beginning to affect party members, as
we can see from court files and surveys from Lower Austria. Zwettl
reports that even *Block- und Zellenleiter* and *Ortsbauernführer* only
wear the swastika when they call on officials; 'Grüß Gott' increasingly replaces 'Heil Hitler'; and elsewhere 'the businesses of party
members are already being boycotted'.[14]

Events in Italy also revived the South Tyrol issue. This had
always been a highly emotional problem for Austrians, and it was
the peculiarly bad luck of both the Dollfuss and the Hitler régimes
that they were unable to do anything about it. When Mussolini
sacrificed Austria to Hitler in March 1938, the German dictator in
turn abandoned the South Tyrolese, and a year later the voluntary
Aussiedlung, or removal of the population, was decided upon. The
question of where to send them produced suggestions like Burgundy,
the Ukraine, and Polish Galicia, but it was left to an Austrian Nazi,
the pre-*Anschluss Gauleiter* Frauenfeld, now operating in Taurien
and the Crimea, to propose the Crimea as a suitable place for settlement. When Himmler's race specialists discovered that the Crimea
had been the home of the *Krimgoten*, Hitler immediately approved
the plan; he could see no physical or psychological difficulties:

[13] T81R6 13 066–7, 070–1, 075–6, 14 074.
[14] 7 OJs 599/43, 8 OJs 198/44, 6 OJs 608/43; WLB Niederdonau, Nos.
24, 25, September, October 1943.

'Sie brauchen ja nur einen deutschen Strom, die Donau, hinunterzufahren, dann seien sie schon da.'[15]

Ever since 1938 the Gestapo had discovered leaflets and stickers protesting against the betrayal of the South Tyrol; they were mostly conservative in origin, but the Communists, too, in their patriotic phase, appealed to the 'Tiroler Landesbrüder' and invoked the memory of Andreas Hofer. In 1940 all those who proclaimed themselves as enthusiastic Nazis in announcements in the press were sent leaflets reminding them of this 'national issue', and the Carinthian underground appealed to the South Tyrolese: 'Do not opt for resettlement.'[16]

Nevertheless, for a variety of motives some 80,000 South Tyrolese went north, where they were first fêted but soon forgotten once they had been found jobs. Many of them would not fit into their new environment, left their jobs and went round begging, became abusive and drifted away or into the police reserve. The bulk of the farming community never left their homes since the progress of the war prevented their resettlement *en bloc*, and this was just as well; in the meantime Badoglio had gone over to the Allies and the Germans were planning the annexation of northern Italy roughly to the extent of the former Habsburg Empire. For the Second Austrian Republic, however, there remained a new version of the South Tyrol problem, exacerbated by the National Socialist interlude.[17]

In the area adjacent to Italy, where for centuries German has met Slav, nemesis was likewise beginning to overtake the masters of the Third Reich. The speedy conquest of Yugoslavia in 1941 had left large areas untouched by war and considerable sections of the armed forces undefeated. But next to the Serb and Croat nationalist forces a new popular force was being organized by the Communists – the partisans; and their operations in the areas recently attached to the Reich, and beyond the frontiers, in the old borderlands with their Slovene population, soon involved a decision on the part of Austrian patriots whether they were prepared to co-operate with people who were communist-led, who had laid claims to Austrian territory and were likely to do so again, and who could be expected to upset the delicate balance between Carinthians of German and

---

[15] Henry Picker, op. cit., p. 429. 'They need only sail down a German river – the Danube – and there they are!'

[16] T84R13 40 018, 307; R14 40 819; R15 42 772.

[17] T84R14 40 589; R13 40 549; T81R3 62 695. For the South Tyrol problem cf. Conrad F. Latour, *Südtirol und die Achse Berlin–Rom 1938–1945* (Stuttgart, 1962); for Nazi diplomatic relations with Italy cf. T81R167 305 919, R175 316 376; and for post-war plans Louis P. Lochner, *The Goebbels Diaries* (London, 1948), pp. 383, 345.

Slovene speech. It is to their credit that Austrian resistance organizations in Carinthia and Styria decided that the partisans were
allies in the struggle against National Socialism; and in innumerable
reports and dozens of court cases against men of the Right as well
as of the Left collaboration with Tito's forces is in fact the principal
charge.

The only military resistance there was in Austria before 1945 was
in the mountain areas of Styria and Carinthia. It began in 1942,
and because initially it involved mainly Slovenes and some volunteers from the KPÖ, it is often neglected in accounts of the Austrian
opposition. This is unjustified, for most of the Slovenes were Austrians by nationality (and from choice, as their record in the time of
the First Republic, and again after 1945 in their rejection of Yugoslav claims, proved). Later they were joined by Yugoslav instructors, deserters, farmers threatened by the Gestapo, and political
activists who were forced to flee from their home-towns.

The most detailed account of events on this unquiet border is
contained in a 'History' of the *Rüstungsinspektion des Wehrkreises
XVIII* for the period October 1940 to May 1942. We read of the
troubles in connection with resettlement and removal, the arrest of
priests, and the increasingly difficult life of the people. After the
outbreak of war with Russia communist and Slovene nationalist
tendencies are said to have coalesced, a guerrilla war developed
with bands emerging from the woods to attack isolated farms and
later whole townships, German units, and depots, and to commit
acts of sabotage.[18] At this stage retribution was mild (compared
with Lidice, Oradour, and Filetto): for a police officer killed by
partisans ten 'Communists' were shot in September 1941. Soon
after, the party Chancellery banned the term 'partisan' which had
gained currency and which sounded too 'heroic'; it was suggested
that only terms like *Banditen, Heckenschützen*, etc., should be used.
Occasionally *Gegenbanden* ('counter-bands') were formed which,
in addition to police and Nazi agents, contained former partisans
who, presumably, were compelled to use their knowledge of their
one-time fellows' haunts and tactics. At the same time, however,
even 'loyal' Slovenes were expelled from their homes and farms,
humiliated, and treated as potential enemies.[19] The incredibly
stupid policy adopted by the Germans in the whole of the Balkan
region, not only towards Slavs but even towards *volksdeutsch* communities, added to the confusion and the mutual hatreds, and it is
hard to see what other policy but that of expulsion could have been
adopted by the Yugoslavs.

[18] T77R750 1 984 714–15, 723–4, 733, 751.
[19] IfZ Mü NO-2845, NO-3144; T8R26 3 575; T175R10 2 511 844.

The Second Front and the Officers' Revolt

The successful landing of Anglo-American forces on the Nor-
mandy beachheads on 6 June 1944 seems to have been taken as the
beginning of the end by considerable sections of the Austrian population. Even Hitler's *Wunderwaffen* (miraculous weapons) did not
impress the public, as we learn from a number of SD reports: the
constant bombardment of London with the famous V–1 'without
any apparent effect on the war' made people doubt their value.
Also in July Kaltenbrunner sent a morale report to Bormann, in
which he wrote: 'Only a small proportion of the people maintain
their confidence'; Innsbruck was saying that the Russian advance
'proceeded with the speed of *our* former lightning-victories'; and in
Vorarlberg and Tyrol the propaganda campaign of anti-Nazi
elements was steadily increasing. A week later the SD called the
mood of the people 'more depressed than ever'; they asked how
much longer 'we could stand this'. The depression of the Nazis was
the hope of their enemies; the Church was said to be responsible for
the conviction among the farming community that the re-establishment of an independent Austria was imminent, while Lower
Austria reported 'communist' activities from all its industrial
centres.[20]

The *Wehrwirtschaftsoffizier* of Army Command XVII (Vienna)
complains in May that discipline in industry leaves much to be
desired. The introduction of the 72-hour week has not led to
increased output. On the contrary, in June he notes a drop in
average production per hour; and a great increase in illnesses,
applications for special leave, and pure absenteeism ... as well as
a worsening of discipline. And in September he quotes the Gestapo
for a noticeable drop in output among both 'German' and foreign
labour. 'This reduction is due to *the general political development*
and to insufficient control of the workers. In one section of the
FOW-works 75 per cent of the work turned out proved to be
faulty.'[21] It is obvious that, next to general exhaustion of men and
machinery, the slogan of the Left was beginning to bear fruit:
'Work as little as you dare, as badly as you can, as wastefully as
possible!' But the 'general political development' mentioned in the
report is a reference to the events of 20 July 1944, the attempt on
Hitler's life.

It seemed a day like any other.

The *Wehrmacht* report admitted the loss of Saint-Lô to the

[20] T81R6 13 467, 495–6, 513, 494; WLB Niederdonau, No. 28, August
1944.
[21] T77R750 1 984 898, 879, 994.

advancing Anglo-American forces but claimed the destruction of ten enemy tanks and sixteen aircraft, while in the whole of France 151 'terrorists' had been killed. Throughout the night London had been under heavy attack by doodle-bugs. Elsewhere, Livorno had fallen to the enemy, Lvov was held against the Russians, and American bombers had attacked Munich and other German cities. 'The population suffered losses.'

The Vienna edition of the *Völkischer Beobachter* proclaimed editorially that everything now depended on the people's loyalty and steadfastness, since the Reich had not much else to pit against the material superiority of the enemy. In another contribution it was claimed that what was at stake was not merely Germany but the future of Europe, while an academic from Berlin was allowed to pay tribute to the contribution Austria had made to the history of the *Volk*. The Schirach family announced the death, in an air raid, of the *Gauleiter*'s seventy-two-year-old mother at Wiesbaden, which explained Baldur's absence from Vienna, while Scheel, *Gauleiter* of Salzburg, was away at Heidelberg addressing an academic gathering, in the course of which he called German scholars 'Generals of the intellect' and defined as the only value of the universities 'their contribution to victory'. It was a strange coincidence that both *Gauleiter* with army commands in their provinces were away on that day, thus avoiding the supreme test of their 'loyalty and steadfastness'.

For this was the day when, between 1700 and 1800 hours a top-secret order signed by Field Marshal von Witzleben went out from the Bendlerstrasse, the Berlin headquarters of the military conspiracy, to Army Commands XVII (Vienna) and XVIII (Salzburg), as to all other commands, breaking the news:

The Führer Adolf Hitler is dead.

An irresponsible clique of party leaders behind the front lines has attempted to take advantage of the situation to stab the hard-pressed soldiers in the back and usurp power for their own purposes. . . .

It went on to claim that the government had appointed Witzleben Supreme Commander and entrusted him with full powers to deal with the emergency. This included placing the party, the security services, the SS, and all civilian authority under his command. Ten further edicts spelled out the details: all Nazi leaders and officials were to be arrested, concentration camps and Gestapo offices to be occupied, the armed SS to be absorbed in the army, or disarmed, its leaders to be arrested.

Unfortunately, the Führer was not dead, Goebbels was not captured, the Gestapo headquarters and the central radio station were not occupied, and thus the régime was able to nip in the bud what had been the most dramatic attempt of many to overthrow the tyranny. Colonel Stauffenberg's plan had been as ingenious as it was risky: to utilize a general mobilization order which he himself had devised, against 'internal disorders and invasion by airborne forces' (code name: Valkyrie), against the political leadership. This required the removal of Hitler as well as a network of contacts inside the armed forces, which included in addition to Witzleben a number of generals and dozens of colonels, majors, and other officers. This military conspiracy, however, was but a part of a larger opposition grouping which ranged from the extreme conservative Goerdeler through socialist and Catholic trade unionists like Leuschner and Kaiser to the 'red' Count Helmut Moltke and the left-wing Socialist Reichwein. Both in their plans for a de-Nazified Germany and in their quest for allies Austria – whose hostility to the régime was well known to them – played a large part. Their preparations had in fact been so successful that the *coup* – which failed in Germany – succeeded only in two places outside: and one was Vienna.

While the Austrian Resistance was at one with the Germans in wishing to hasten the end of the Third Reich, it was on the question of the future of Austria that they came to a parting of the ways. The German resisters, while honest anti-Nazis, were German patriots and as such tended to show as little sympathy for what they considered separatist wishes as for the interests of Germany's neighbours. Understandably, the foreign political concepts of the conspiracy as laid down in numerous memoranda in 1939 and 1940 met with little response in Allied circles: they are permeated with a nationalist (and often militarist) spirit, the Versailles settlement is rejected out of hand, and the German claim to leadership in central and eastern Europe is upheld. A typical example is provided in the approach made by von Hassell to the British government early in 1940. It was essential, he argued, that the war be ended before Europe was 'destroyed and Bolshevized', and in view of the Soviet menace a viable Germany was essential for the recovery of Europe; hence Austria and the Sudetenland would have to remain inside the Reich, Poland should accept the German frontier of 1914 and France the frontier of 1937. The German invasion of Denmark and Norway ended this particular contact.

Another attempt was made via the Vatican, where Josef Müller claimed to have obtained British terms for a post-Nazi Germany which, according to his testimony, included a plebiscite in Austria. Vatican circles were said to have an open mind on the future of

Austria, though they were informed of hopes for a South German, Catholic monarchy (presumably entertained by Habsburg loyalists). In a highly suspect report on the events of 20 July 1944 originating with the SS the Pope himself is said to have favoured, after the Polish campaign, the continuance of the Austrian and Sudeten *Anschluss*.

Inevitably, every new German aggression strengthened the Allied resolve against Germany, but Goerdeler stuck to his foolhardy optimism; a 'peace plan' of May 1941 still contained German claims to Austria, the Sudetenland, and Memel (as well as the frontiers of 1914 against France and Belgium and the return of the colonies!). Even two years later, in the summer of 1943, in a memorandum to the dissident generals, he argued for the imperial frontiers of 1914 – with a possible compromise with France over Alsace-Lorraine – plus Austria and the Sudetenland; and as late as July 1944, when most other conspirators had become reconciled to the idea of unconditional surrender, he still believed in a negotiated peace.[22]

Thus, to the men of 20 July, Austria was part of the Reich and should remain so. Not so to the various resistance groups inside Austria whose desire for the restoration of Austrian independence met with increasing (if still passive) support from former Nazis and Pan-Germans, who had been bitterly disappointed by the course events had been taking since 1938. Without actively indulging in opposition, although this also happened in many cases, many of the younger idealists who had been attracted by the notions of Germany's role in Europe, or by the pledges of the Nazi Party, strongly resented their colonial status and the obliteration of every native tradition. Their sullen resentment, their refusal to report suspicious activities, repeatedly played into the hands of the opposition groups, especially in the armed forces.

Goerdeler and his fellow-conspirators were well aware of these feelings in Austria. They established secret contacts with Austrian politicians who were now forced to live in the Reich, and they visited others in Vienna, Salzburg, and elsewhere. In Vienna it was the Catholic labour leader Lois Weinberger who arranged for contacts with conservatives and Socialists, but he made it clear from the start where he and his friends stood:

> We shall do everything in our power to help you, and shall be glad when you have succeeded; we shall be grateful and won't let

[22] On the Austrian policies of the conspiracy cf. K. R. Stadler, 'Zwischen Reich und Republik', *Salzburger Nachrichten* (19 July 1969), and 'Die Offiziersrevolte gegen Hitler und die Unabhängigkeit Österreichs', *Die Zukunft*, 20/1969.

you down, but you must let us become again what we have been
for so long: *Austrians!* As such we shall be of greater service to
Germany and to other nations than we could be even as a model
province of a Reich whose name has been besmirched . . .[23]

Adolf Schärf, leader of the Socialist Party after 1945 and subsequently elected President of Austria, tells the dramatic story of
his first meeting with the German Socialist Leuschner:

> In the early summer of 1943 an unknown man called at my law
> office and introduced himself as Wilhelm Leuschner, former
> Social Democratic Minister of the Interior in Hesse. After I had
> examined his credentials – a necessary measure in those days – he
> revealed to me that in the autumn of 1943 the Nazi régime would
> be overthrown. Representatives of several parties had agreed on
> a new Reich government, in which Goerdeler would be Chan-
> cellor and Leuschner Vice-Chancellor. The line he took was this:
> if Austria backed the German revolution it could be confidently
> expected that in the coming peace the *Anschluss* would be safe-
> guarded. He had come to speak to me about the share of Austria's
> Social Democrats in this venture.

The two men talked for about three hours, and Schärf listened
with fascination. So far there had been no indication of the ultimate
plans of the Allies where Austria was concerned; the Moscow Declaration on the restoration of an independent Austria was not published until five months later. Yet Schärf continues:

> Suddenly I interrupted him. I will not deny that ever since I got
> to know and to love the intellectual treasures of the German
> people I considered Weimar, and not Austria, to be my homeland.
> But during my conversation with Leuschner it came to me like
> a revelation . . . and I said: 'The *Anschluss* is dead, Austrians
> have been cured of their love for the Reich. . . . I can foresee the
> day when the *Reichdeutsche* will be driven out of Austria as the
> Jews were driven out before . . .'[24]

Urgent enquiries from Seitz (whom Leuschner had also seen), Karl
Renner, and other socialist leaders revealed that they all felt alike;
in fact, Seitz was to hesitate a long time before agreeing to act as
Politischer Beauftragter of the military régime and then consented
on the understanding that this would in no way prejudice his attitude to the *Anschluss*.

[23] Lois Weinberger, *Tatsachen, Begegnungen und Gespräche* (Vienna,
1948), p. 135.
[24] Adolf Schärf, *Erinnerungen aus meinem Leben* (Vienna, 1963), pp.
166–8.

The accounts provided by Schärf, Weinberger, and others are amply corroborated by the numerous statements the Gestapo obtained from its prisoners in Berlin, and by the notes and correspondence it discovered. The significance of it all lies in the fact that men who had grown up in the *deutschnational* tradition of Austrian Social Democracy, or felt close affinity with Christian Democracy in Germany, had nevertheless by mid-1943 at the latest come to the same conclusion; five years after its destruction the Republic of Austria seemed more attractive than it had ever been while it existed.

Nevertheless, whatever the future might hold, the conspirators needed the Vienna Army Command (for reasons of strategy) and a number of prominent civilians representing the conservative and socialist camps (to avoid all appearances of a military dictatorship) – the *Politische Beauftragte*. In return, and to keep Austria in the Reich, an Austrian was to be given a place in the new government, as several drafts of cabinet lists showed which fell into the hands of the Gestapo. The Catholic element, and particularly Kaiser, wanted the post of Education and Cults reserved for ex-Chancellor Schuschnigg, but seems to have met with some opposition in view of his Austro-Fascist record; hence the very last list, of July 1944, only contained the words 'an Austrian' for an unspecified cabinet post. Schuschnigg, of course, knew nothing of this; the prisoners at Oranienburg concentration camp were too closely watched for contacts with the outside world. His appointment would in any case have led to bitter divisions inside Austria, as would his return to Austrian politics after the war; he took the honourable course of moving to the United States where he stayed until his retirement from a professorship at St Louis University in 1967, and now lives in retirement in Austria. But it is safe to say that the appointment of Schuschnigg or any other man would have made no difference to the will of the Austrian opposition to break away from the Reich.[25]

Where the military side was concerned, Army Command XVII in Vienna was in good hands, even though the head of the conspiracy there, Colonel Marogna-Redwitz, chief of the local *Abwehr*, had been moved shortly before the appointed day. A young captain, Karl Szokoll, who had been instructed in his role by Stauffenberg himself, had prepared everything so circumspectly that when the 'Valkyrie orders' arrived troops silently moved into new positions, occupied key buildings and strategic points, and got ready to deal with SS or party opposition. Meanwhile Nazi and SS leaders who happened to be in Vienna were summoned to 'urgent talks', and

[25] For the most up-to-date account of the conspiracy cf. Peter Hoffman, *Widerstand, Staatsstreich, Attentat* (Munich, 1969).

they all duly appeared at Command Headquarters where they were disarmed and detained. All but one accepted their fate without protest; the SS General even offered to co-operate with the new rulers. To judge by his performance at the Nuremberg Trial, *Gauleiter* Schirach would probably have done likewise had he been there – until the news came from Berlin that Hitler was alive after all, that the Valkyrie orders had been cancelled, and the traitors killed or captured.

Szokoll, incidentally, succeeded in avoiding arrest, since his had been a relatively subordinate role in the hierarchy, but he was to play an important part a few months later in the plans to surrender Vienna to the Russians before the party had a chance to turn it into a 'fortress'. The revenge of the régime was savage; among the first executions in Berlin was that of the Austrian Robert Bernardis, a close collaborator of Stauffenberg. He was followed by Marogna-Redwitz, while several other Austrian officers spent most of the remainder of the Third Reich in jail. Of the civilians named as *Politische Beauftragte* in one of the earliest dispatches from Berlin, most were arrested and taken to concentration camps; they included Karl Seitz, the former Social Democratic mayor of Vienna, and Joseph Reiter, peasant leader in Lower Austria, both still immensely popular with their respective following, and others in Salzburg and Innsbruck. On the other hand, Austrians played a significant part in crushing the rising: Lt-Colonel Pridůn of the General Staff and Skorzeny, the 'liberator of Mussolini', of the SS in Berlin, while Kaltenbrunner, Chief of the Security Services, directed the hunt after the conspirators.[26] Nothing had happened in Salzburg, where both the *Gauleiter* and the Commanding General were away and the contact-man of the conspiracy, a German colonel, had recently been posted. In any case, with most of the regular troops fighting Yugoslav partisans away in the South, and the SS dominating the scene because of the proximity to Hitler's head-quarters at Berchtesgaden, the chances of a success there had been slight. The only odd – and typically Austrian – note was struck by the acting commandant who was playing dice with his fellow-officers in a local hotel and did not allow the news of the attempt on the life of the Führer to interfere with the game!

To the opposition in Austria – as to Churchill in Britain – it was but an admission of the inevitability of defeat. The attempt on Hitler's life made by German generals illuminates the untenable military situation of Nazi Germany,

[26] For the fullest description of the Austrian side of the conspiracy cf. Ludwig Jedlicka, *Der 20. Juli 1944 in Österreich* (Vienna, 1965).

said a leaflet of the *Österreichische Freiheitsfront*. With the Atlantic Wall breached, and the desperate attempts of the régime to mobilize its last resources, the time had come to act: 'Austrians! Men! Women! Save your honour! Your lives! Your homes!' But there were few comments overheard by the Gestapo, and apparently no prosecutions (except, of course, of those directly implicated in the conspiracy and of politicians whom the régime still feared).

The real significance of the event for Austria lay in the fact that the conspiracy contained a 'special Austrian element of considerable strength', as Ludwig Jedlicka put it in his study, 'which ultimately aimed at the re-establishment of an Austrian state'. It was a most creditable achievement for the Austrian Right and it helped the opposition to clarify their position *vis-à-vis* the Reich.

Nazi Justice at Work

It is still not possible to present a complete picture of the terrorist practices of the judiciary in Austria. While war itself, and wartime legislation, increased the opportunities for law-breaking, the tremendous increase in the number of prosecutions and the cruel sentences passed can still only be illustrated from incomplete statistics. Several stray documents from the files of the OKW concerned only the military side; thus a list of cases of *Landesverrat*, enclosed with a secret order from Keitel dated 1 April 1939, for the years 1937 and 1938 which gives the numbers of Austrians and Sudeten Germans indicted:

Landesverrat	Number of prosecutions	Germans	Involving Other Nationals
1937	525	652	147
1938	1,304	1,502	519[27]

These numbers refer only to cases which were ready to be brought to trial; 'the numerous arrests made in the course of the occupation of Austria and *Sudetendeutschland* are only included in small part'. The military *Kriminalstatistik* for the first year of war has already been quoted, which mentioned 112 death sentences against Jehovah's Witnesses and the increase in the number of cases of *Wehrkraftzersetzung* from 159 in the first quarter to 348 in the last.[28] Even more significant, however, is a War Ministry statistic which allows us to compare cases and offences involving *Wehrmacht* personnel, soldiers and civilians, in the first quarters of 1940 and 1942, respectively, and reveals that the number of prosecutions, acquittals,

[27] Including 71 Austrians and 133 *Volksdeutsche* from Czechoslovakia.
[28] T77R233 973 595; R805 5 537 704ff.

and death sentences roughly trebled in the course of these two years (death sentences in brackets):[29]

	1 Jan.–31 Mar. 1940	1 Jan.–31 Mar. 1942
Defendants	12,029	32,225
Acquitted	1,290	3,002
Sentences for military offences	10,739 (129)	29,223 (347)
of which:		
Wehrkraftzersetzung	250 (26)	943 (56)
Desertion	214 (84)	711 (291)
Civil offences	7,617 (23)	23,940 (109)

The rest of the papers are of civilian origin, and they also start in 1942, the year when Roland Freisler became President of the People's Court in Berlin. Freisler, feared by the opposition in the Third Reich, has since been revealed to the whole world as a sadistic monster in the film of the trial of the conspirators of 20 July 1944, which Hitler had caused to be made for his private delectation and which was discovered after the war. To compensate for a dubious political past – he was chairman of the Workers' and Soldiers' Council in Kassel in 1918 – he distinguished himself in his career in the Ministry of Justice and came to the notice of Hitler, who called him 'a Bolshevik in his bearing and nature'.[30] On his appointment to the top post in the hierarchy of judicial terror he wrote an obsequious letter to Hitler which promised sentences that 'the Führer himself would have passed', and which he signed as 'Your political soldier'; and to Minister of Justice Thierack he sent a long statement in the course of which he claimed that of all treasonable behaviour among Germans communist activities were pre-eminent, and these again occurred in the most concentrated form in certain parts of the *Alpen- und Donaugaue.* [31]

He was assisted by an *Oberreichsanwalt*[32] of very similar calibre, Lautz, who survived the war (unlike Freisler, who was killed by an Allied bomb during a trial) and has spent his retirement suing the German state for an increased pension. He it was who bore the responsibility for most of the inhuman sentences passed on mem-

[29] ibid., 5 537 302, 484, 395, 235.
[30] Picker, op. cit. (March 1942), p. 223.
[31] IfZ Mü NG – 176.
[32] *Oberreichsanwalt* – Senior Public Prosecutor and Reich Attorney-General (not to be confused with the British and American usages of the word); subordinate to him were the *Generalstaatsanwälte* – Public Prosecutors General – and below them were *Oberstaatsanwälte* – Senior Public Prosecutors; *Ermittlungsrichter* were investigating judges.

bers of the Austrian Resistance. We first meet him in Vienna in
May 1942 in conference with the *Generalstaatsanwälte* operating
in the *Ostmark*, where he complains that the Gestapo in Vienna
takes up to a year to complete its inquiries into the more important
resistance groups, especially of the communist underground, and
then the *Ermittlungsrichter* and *Oberstaatsanwälte* take another
two to four months; in the meantime the prisons are full to bursting
and can no longer take in all the prisoners. He gave instructions to
cut out the second stage and send the files to him immediately the
first report was completed. That his subordinates approved of the
tougher line adopted since the outbreak of the war with Russia goes
without saying:

> The *Generalstaatsanwälte der Ostmark* agreed unanimously with
> the line that the crime of high treason, committed particularly
> by Communists since the war with Russia or continued since
> before the war, should lead to considerably stiffer penalties than
> hitherto, and that death sentences should be demanded of the
> courts in all cases involving even the lowliest [communist]
> leaders.[33]

In February 1944 we meet him again in a report to the Minister;
after congratulating himself on the fact that the 'not inconsiderable
numbers of enemies of the state' had not succeeded in combining
their isolated groups into large organizations, he reports on the situation in Austria:

> The number of new cases has on the whole been as before; in the
> *Alpen- und Donau-Reichsgaue* there has been a further, if insig-
> nificant, drop in cases of communist *Hochverrat*.

Because of administrative difficulties, exacerbated by enemy air
attacks, he has been compelled to let an increasing number of
cases be tried locally – but the *Generalanwälte* were warned not
to interpret this as an encouragement to clemency![34]

The remaining documents are from the Ministry of Justice and
illustrate various aspects of the situation in Austria. An internal
memorandum dated 4 June 1943 also reveals some discrepancies
between the practice of local courts (which were more amenable to
pressures and interventions) and that of the People's Court itself:

> It is the practice of the People's Court that any kind of commu-
> nist *Hochverrat* since 22 June 1941 is punishable by death. . . .
> But the *Oberlandgerichte* have as a rule felt able to pass death
> sentences only in cases where the accused has been found guilty

[33] ibid., NG – 823, pp. 2, 4.   [34] ibid., NG – 671, pp. 1–2.

of some activity beyond mere membership of the Communist Party and the payment of subscriptions. . . .

Recently difficulties have arisen in the *Alpen- und Donaugaue* where *Gauleiter* Dr Jury of Niederdonau and *Gauleiter* Dr Scheel of Salzburg have frequently intervened and asked for clemency in cases where there was obviously some local appeal to them. . . . Both stated that [in Austria] there had not been enough time for the social benefits of National Socialism to become effective and to win the confidence of the working class, and that many active and valuable elements of the previously Marxist working class, had not been recruited in time into the party and its auxiliaries. Clemency was desired in cases of compatriots who had acted in a spirit of misguided idealism.

We further learn that no similar demands had been made by Schirach (Vienna) or Uiberreither (Styria), that even Jury had so far had no success, and that a grand total of three commutations – and the risk of a generally softer line – had aroused the zeal of this particular bureaucrat.[35]

Miscellaneous statistics further illustrate conditions in the Third Reich: prisons full to overflowing, and this in spite of concentration camps, Gestapo and military prisons, and penal labour: 194,552 inmates in November 1944, almost twice the peacetime number of 108,685;[36] a total of 10,412 executions between 1939 and the end of 1943;[37] and many similar revealing aspects. Inside Austria, on 27 April 1943, 866 men and seven women were serving sentences for *Hochverrat*. On 30 November 1944, 11,146 men and 3,109 women populated the regular jails in the principal cities.[38] In February 1945, as we have already seen, the evacuation of prisons threatened by the approach of enemy forces was begun and led in some places to the deliberate killing of Jewish and political prisoners.[39] Anticipating this order, the director of Stein prison, assisted by a committee of political prisoners, prepared the release of all his charges contrary to instructions, but the plan was betrayed, *Volkssturm* (a kind of Home Guard) and SS surrounded the jail and mowed down and killed 386 prisoners and one warder. The director and three of his loyal officers were tried by court-martial and executed on 6 April 1945.

This event, referred to as a 'revolt' by the régime, sealed the fate of all prisoners under sentence of death in neighbouring Upper Austria where the *Gauleiter* ordered their execution on 9 April.[40] It

---

[35] ibid., NG – 594, pp. 1–3.   [36] T178R9 3 664 541ff.
[37] *The US Strategic Bombing Survey* . . ., vol. 1, p. 88.
[38] T178R9 3 664 607–8.
[39] IfZ Mü NG – 030.   [40] ibid.

was a particularly tragic coincidence that at the same time the Vienna *Landesgericht* had released its prisoners serving normal prison sentences, but obedient to instructions had its forty-six *Hochverräter* transferred to Stein, where the SS killed them in a prison yard on that day.[41]

Last Efforts on the Left

In spite of the increasing terrorism of the régime, the remaining years after Stalingrad were a time of great losses and mounting confidence among the working people of Austria. Whatever illusions some sections might have entertained about the nature of the régime had been brutally dispelled, and now the hated enemy itself was on the defensive. The great mass of former Social Democrats found no difficulty in sympathizing with the Western Powers, where Socialists and trade unionists occupied cabinet posts and seemed a guarantee of a post-war order of social and international justice. Communists, on the other hand, intensified their efforts to come to the aid of the Soviet Union in what small measure they could, in close and now often harmonious co-operation with other groups and individuals.

This was also the time when the large socialist network under Otto Haas, and the socialist–communist organization *Robby*, were discovered; another united-front organization in the Vienna fire brigade was found to have forty-five members, two of whom were executed – both officials of the KPÖ – two 'died' in jail, and the sentences imposed on the rest reached the total of 267 years. Several situation reports from Lautz to the Minister give an idea of the numbers involved:

On 21 May 1942 the Gestapo in the *Ostmark* were working on the following 'Marxist cases':
(1) a communist railway group in Vienna, 74 accused;
(2) a Czech group in Vienna, suspected of incendiarism and use of explosives, 70 members;
(3) a communist factory cell in Vienna, 44 accused;
(4) a communist youth organization [*Soldatenrat*], 22 arrests, 60 to come;
(5) KPÖ *Niederdonau*, 40 accused; and
(6) 170 'Revolutionary Socialists' in Salzburg.[42]

The same report quotes the Gestapo for the statement that another 1,500 persons in Vienna are suspected of communist activity, but for lack of personnel and of accommodation in its jails it could only pick them up in small numbers!

[41] Szecsi and Stadler, op. cit., pp. 25–6.   [42] IfZ Mü NG – 823.

From Graz Uiberreither in January 1943 appeals to the Minister of Justice to hurry up with the trials of Communists as a deterrent to their mounting activity, and Thierack replies that he has instructed Kaltenbrunner to round up all Styrian Communists at once. In the meantime Lautz once again complains that the 244 Communists brought in in the last few months are only a small proportion of the *Hochverräter* known to the Gestapo, but lack of accommodation and the prospect of serious disruption of essential war-work through mass arrests have delayed action. Though Lautz speaks of Communists, he admits that most of these 244 – workers in important factories and services, such as the seventeen 'functionaries' and forty-six members at Siemens-Schuckert – were active in the *Rote Hilfe*, in other words were collecting and contributing to funds for political prisoners and their families, an activity which involved many non-communist workers. Not before February 1944 was Lautz able to report that the number of new cases of communist *Hochverrat*, 'which had remained about the same since the end of 1941', was at last declining; the Gestapo and the court had done their work. Among the more interesting cases were twenty-nine members and helpers of the latest attempt to form a communist Central Committee; two of the three leaders arrested early in 1943 had committed suicide while under arrest; and twenty-five members of factory cells of the KPÖ in Vienna who had continued supporting the party long after their workmates had been arrested and sentenced – a demonstration of loyalty and solidarity which even Lautz found 'remarkable'.[43]

The chaos of 1944–45 enabled many old-time Communists to return to Austria from abroad, to desert from penal units and the army, and join up with former contacts, to play their part in the final weeks of the struggle.

Ecclesia Triumphans

In the context of this study we are not concerned with the Roman Catholic Church as such, with the debatable policies of Pope Pius XII and the hierarchy in Germany and Austria. Apart from a number of openly pro-Nazi bishops, and their opposite numbers in the anti-Nazi camp, the great authority of the Church was employed in supporting the existing order, in confirming the legitimacy of the war ('defence of the fatherland'), and in preaching the virtues of obedience and duty. Only when religious principles were attacked did the Church as such take a stand; but one looks in vain for protests against the humiliation, persecution, and destruction of Jewry from the bishops who protested – admittedly, at considerable

[43] ibid., NG–343, NG–683, NG–671.

risk – against 'Neo-paganism', the immorality of *Lebensborn*, and euthanasia.

Our concern here is with individuals *in* the Church who set an example to their fellow-citizens, however limited in scope and effect, and with the objective role *of* the Church, as the one visible area not totally dominated by the régime and as such increasingly attractive to anti-Nazis. In the last phase of German rule in Austria the Church became the rallying-point of all but the most free-thinking resistance groups, and the officials of the régime recognized this. The bulk of our documentation consists of *Weltanschau-liche Lageberichte* of the *Gau* directorate Lower Austria and covers the period from 1942 to 1944, as well as *SD-Berichte* from Upper Austria 1942 to 1943, both agrarian provinces, Lower Austria notorious for its 'clericalism', Upper Austria for its hard line against the Church; yet the situations described are identical. Even allowing for the fact that these reports were written by the Nazi zealots who needed to justify their existence and give proof of their vigilance, and that for every courageous act and for every rebellious village there were probably countless others who did obey, the cumulative effect of these reports and the innumerable prosecutions before the lower courts all confirm a state of ferment and disaffection.

Our first impression is of a *living Church* which, far from hiding in catacombs or retreating into quietism, uses every means at its disposal and every right still granted by the authorities to influence its members (and immunize them against Nazi indoctrination): popular and academic lectures on a wide variety of subjects; musical evenings, orchestras, and choirs; the cultivation of old country customs and festivals. Even Nazi festivals like harvest festivals and heroes' days are quietly 'usurped' and burials 'taken over'. Great care is taken that church events take a dignified form; 'great luxury' at weddings in church, the report notes, but the meanest clothes at the registry office.[44]

The second impression is of the *loyalty* of members to their Church, their generosity especially in rural areas: 'Whoever gives 30 or 40 pfennigs for the NSV, donates the same number of marks to the Church.' In most places young people's meetings are held at church to coincide with Hitler Youth meetings, and they are ex-tremely well attended. At Zuggers the BDM unit and its leader only appeared at the Nazi sports festival after the Corpus Christi pro-cession was over (in which they had taken part), while at the com-pulsory roll call only five out of eighteen members attended – the rest were at church.[45]

[44] WLB Niederdonau, No. 21, December 1942.
[45] ibid., No. 18, August 1942.

The third impression is of Nazis retreating before the religious influence; the 'weak links' in the movement, as the reports call them. Party members present their godchildren for confirmation – but not without first having removed the swastika! They delay cancelling their church membership with excuses like the announcement of the names of apostates from the pulpit; they take part in pilgrimages and ask for church weddings and burials.[46]

And lastly the reverence shown to the Church by army officers. In Baden the commanding officer always raises his hat when he passes a church; in Melk a prelate is buried in the presence of the town commandant and his family and all the officers of the pioneer battalion and their wives. And before inspecting the garrison at Eisenstadt the divisional commander, a general, is received by the town priest and a deputation of nuns![47] In March 1943 an act of 'sabotage' is reported in connection with a big party meeting near Tulln for which a *Reichspropagandaredner* was billed and a hall with 500 seats and standing-room for another hundred was prepared. Only seventy persons attended, while 500 persons went to a 'special advent service' at church put on for the occasion. The party thought this a 'humiliating fiasco', but the parish priest said he wasn't to blame if 'people preferred the Church to a political meeting'. But there were other weak spots in the *Gau*:

> In Albrechtsberg the church-going people believe that there will soon be a revolution. In Gutenbrunn a cautious withdrawal from the NSDAP is noticeable. In Martinsberg a farmer told the *Blockleiter* that Emperor Otto [*Habsburg*] would soon be restored. He also said that Africans were people like ourselves, and they were black because they lived in the sun – information he had from a Capuchin friar . . .

Strangely enough, only six months previously the parish priest of Deutschkreuz had also been quoted with a comment on Nazi race theories; referring to the assertion that 'the white races were different human beings from the yellow and black races' he maintained that

> they nevertheless all stemmed from Adam and Eve. The whites believe they are intelligent, but there are intelligent people among the others as well. It is held that a distinction must be made [between the races]: but what about loving thy neighbour as thyself?[48]

[46] ibid., No. 21, December 1942.
[47] ibid., Nos. 18 and 20, August and November 1942.
[48] ibid., 22, 19, March 1943, 16 September 1942.

The March 1943 report also blames the clergy at Kirchberg for propagating the idea that Germany would lose the war, which is readily believed since the 'rather high casualty rate has led to a mood of depression'. Again the army did nothing to counteract such feeling; on the contrary, 'the obvious co-operation between Church and army must lead to the assumption that National Socialism is hardly understood in *Wehrmacht* circles'. This curious statement is connected with the tough times Nazis are said to have in the army. Party members and officials report

> that the German greeting – 'Heil Hitler' – is very rarely heard in the army, and, in addition, it is always the safest course not to say that one is a party member or, especially, an office-holder. *Kreisamtsleiter* serving in the army confirm that there is no trace of ideological training there.

Similarly bad news is reported from Upper Austria. The farmers observe all the usual religious and local holidays, contrary to war-time regulations; all work stops – even slave labour. The ashes of a popular shopkeeper in Oberplan, who had died in Auschwitz concentration camp, are buried in the local cemetery in the presence of two priests, four acolytes, and a 'tremendous number' of villagers, including party members (who afterwards claimed that they had only been 'curious'!). Corpus Christi Day 1943 is reviewed at great length. It almost sounds as if the régime had expected a mass rising on that day, hence a note of relief creeps into the report in spite of an 'enormous turn-out' in Linz and an 'attitude demonstratively provocative' on the part of the marchers. In the villages, more party members took part than before, including *Blockleiter*, *Politische Leiter*, and *Frauenschaftsführerinnen*; the SD notes the comment of the population: 'Now the Nazis learn to pray.' The conclusion is that the good turn-out was a demonstration against the régime: '...many people took part, not for religious reasons, but to give visible expression to their opposition [to the state].'[49]

At the same time a student faces the Special Court in Salzburg, accused of having had knowledge of the treasonable leaflet 'Aufruf an alle Deutschen' which the young Scholls in Munich (*Die weiße Rose*)[50] had produced and one of their Austrian associates had distributed 'in many hundreds of copies' in Vienna, Linz, and Salzburg. Unfortunately, the report does not tell us any more about the Austrian side of that brave undertaking than Otto Molden first described.[51]

---

[49] T84R6 14 419; 13 228; 12 231–2; 13 077 108.

[50] This was the famous 'Appeal to all Germans' issued by the 'White Rose' conspiracy.

[51] OJs 214/43; Otto Molden, op. cit., pp. 121, 218.

What we have said about resistance on the Left applies with
equal force to the conservative camp: neither was strong enough
materially to weaken the régime or disturb its military policies;
much of their opposition was based on sectional or even local
grievances; they had no clear concept of what they were aiming at,
except for 'a free Austria', which might be a monarchy, a socialist
republic, or a client state of the Western Powers. In terms of political power or material strength they counted for little. And yet,
the heroism of the few and the brutality of the régime created a
mood in the country which involved scores and hundreds of thousands of otherwise inactive people in a kind of passive resistance, in
demonstrations of loyalty to their old institutions, in a longing for
political and national freedom – a capital of suffering on which the
Second Republic is able to draw.

The Fall of Vienna

By the end of 1943 it had become obvious that unless the Russian
advance could be stopped soon, it would not be long before Vienna
became a front-line city. Since Hitler and his immediate collaborators did not believe in a successful stand against the Red armies –
whatever they told the German people, and however many people
their courts were sentencing to death for saying just this – *Gau Wien*
had to be strengthened, and this meant the removal of Schirach.
The most logical move would have been to combine Vienna with
Lower Austria, but Hitler resisted it strenuously. Bormann, Chief of
the Party Chancellery, quotes him as saying, on 15 November 1943,
that

> combining Vienna with another *Gau* was highly undesirable,
> however much the Viennese themselves might want it. If Vienna
> had its way, it would swallow up one *Gau* after another and one
> fine day we'd be faced with a *Reichsgau Ostmark* and Vienna as
> *Gauhauptstadt*![52]

This was precisely what Hitler had had in mind when, the year
before, he had forbidden the very name *Ostmark* and even the
term *Alpen- und Donaureichsgaue*, as we have seen before. In
his 'table talks' he had twice referred to this obsession of his: on
10 September 1941 his hatred of Vienna was expressed in the statement that it had been necessary 'den Zentralstaat auf Kosten von
Wien zu zerschlagen' (to break up the centralist state at the expense
of Vienna), and on 20 May 1942 he still felt he had to justify the
appointment of Bürckel to carry out the dismemberment of Austria
after the *Anschluss*, a man 'mit radikaler Konsequenz und nicht mit

[52] IfZ Mü Partei-Kanzlei Fa–91/7 Fasz 19 BI 1 477–9.

Wiener Gemurksel'.[53] Goebbels, typically, suggested two other *Altreichsdeutsche* for Vienna, but this was a non-starter with Jury, *Gauleiter* of Lower Austria, who rejected them on the grounds that this would be unpopular with the Viennese

> who had already asked (at the time of the appointment of Schirach) whether the whole *Ostmark* had not produced a man who could be entrusted with the leadership of *Gau* Vienna.... If a change of *Gauleiter* were to coincide with certain slogans which the Allies... were bound to spread to sow disunity, this would strengthen the elements deliberately sowing dissension between the Reich and Vienna.[54]

Jury's own solution was to lead Vienna in personal union with his own *Gau*; but when we next come across Schirach, nine months later, nothing has changed: the Viennese have been spared the new German bosses, Schirach still reigns in his old splendour and makes empty promises of help to Jury. Attached to this letter is an anonymous report on Schirach which was forwarded to the *Reichskanzlei* and in which his extravagant style of life is criticized. It ends with bitter scorn: 'The mood of the people is getting better every day. 1938 it was 97 per cent of the votes. Today it is hardly 3 per cent. They, too, will soon be lost if there is no remedy soon.'

The 'remedy' envisaged by certain cliques in the leadership was the 'Austrianization' of the party, and this policy was supported by no less a man than Ernst Kaltenbrunner, Chief of the Security Services and *SS-Obergruppenführer*, an Austrian by birth who now backed Frauenfeld, a pre-*Anschluss Gauleiter* of Vienna, whom he felt would be better able to win over the Viennese. His letter to Bormann, dated 14 September 1944 after a tour of inspection, is so alarmist that its purpose is clear, but with all its exaggerations it is worth quoting from. Morale in Vienna he found very low;

> the basic defeatism is susceptible to all [the bad] news from the south-east, atrocity stories, 'pro-Austrian tendencies', and, of course, every kind of communist propaganda. Personal impressions in working-class districts and suburbs... are very unpleasant.

What he felt was needed was the removal of Schirach and a better chief of staff. Himmler agreed with him and told Bormann that, not surprisingly, Schirach had no contact with the population,

---

[53] Picker, op. cit., pp. 146, 360; Bürckel is described as a man of unbending hardness, not a Viennese muddler!

[54] IfZ, op. cit., 480, 492, 485.

and in order to avoid serious trouble in this city Frauenfeld should
be appointed. After all these alarming reports the *Parteikanzlei*
decided to investigate on its own, and its *Oberbefehlsleiter*, Friedrichs, was dispatched to find out what he could. His report, known
as *Bericht Friedrichs* (BF), is a most illuminating account of the
situation in Vienna six months before the end.[55]

Another stray document from Army Command XVII describes
the situation in Vienna as of 6 March 1945, which bears out everything the underground has been claiming:

> Morale is extremely low. Everywhere war-weariness, nervousness,
> and sometimes not only defeatist but even destructive tendencies
> can be noticed, in which the heavy bombing attacks on Vienna . . .
> admittedly were a contributory factor. Belief in a final victory of
> German arms can be found in only a few . . .
>
> This mood of pessimism is fertile soil for enemy propaganda. In-
> scriptions on walls, leaflets, etc., are being used. After heavy air
> attacks it has happened that army and party aid squads have been
> publicly abused and even attacked physically. Enemy broadcasts
> are widely listened to . . . The most stupid rumours are believed
> and passed on. The announcement of new V-weapons is ridiculed
> and described as a mere *Propagandabluff* . . .
>
> The antagonism and campaign of slander against *Altreichs-
> deutsche*, kept going by enemy propaganda and furthered by
> isolated regrettable incidents, is constantly increasing. . . . [Among
> the middle and upper classes, artists, etc.] anti-state propaganda
> for the 'Free Austria Movement' is particularly active and quite
> dangerous. It is being supported both by the Western Powers and
> by the Bolsheviks, and it is based on stories of Austrian officers
> and men at the front being tired of the war, increasingly going
> over to the enemy, and even actively fighting alongside the
> enemy . . .[56]

Four days later, on 10 March 1945, the following SD report on
the situation in Vienna's working-class districts reaches Berlin. It is
perhaps the most significant document of all because it describes a
state which might well be called 'pre-revolutionary'. After allowing
for the fact that similar situations might *exceptionally* happen in
any town after a heavy air-raid, that people still under shock might
say offensive things about the party or individual leaders, but are
quickly brought to reason again, the account continues: 'But the
incidents now reported from Vienna reveal that the working-class

[55] ibid., 473–4, 528; *Kaltenbrunner–Bericht* quoted in Jedlicka, *Der 20.
Juli 1944* . . ., pp. 92–5; IfZ, ibid., 507–27.
[56] T77R1037 6 509 648.

population are in real ferment.' Since there are few safe air-raid
shelters in the outer districts, large numbers of people squeeze into
the few safe *Bunker*, in a highly excited mood, as the following
snatches of conversation show:

> They won't give in until Vienna is a heap of rubble and we've
> all been killed. Of course, *they* aren't worried: it's not *their* lives
> but ours.
> Let them make peace at last, since they can't win any more.
> *They* won't stop by themselves, *we* must stop this damned war.
> If only someone dared to make a start . . .
> But, women, keep quiet, or you'll lose your heads in the last three
> weeks.

This prophetic utterance – for Vienna was in fact liberated four
weeks later – is followed by descriptions of incidents in the working-
class districts Favoriten, Simmering, Erdberg: one *Ortsgruppenleiter* declared that he only dared walk through his district with his
pistol cocked. After the air attack on 13 February he took his
motorized squad with him, who used their guns to chase people
away from upstairs windows where they hurled abuse and obscenities at them: 'You still *dare* come here, you bastards?' (*Huren-
hunde*); and threatened them with missiles. Another declared that
in his district no *Politischer Leiter* dared show himself alone and in
uniform after an attack because he would at least be beaten up: 'I
am sure that if people had firearms we should by now have been
shot at. We have already had stones thrown at us on several occasions.' A *Stabsleiter* who turned up with a squad of volunteers to
help bombed-out people was received with 'Steinwürfen und
stürmischen Pfuirufen' ('with stones thrown at them and loud
denunciations'). He thought it was impossible to speak sensibly to
these people any more, and suspected Communists of inciting the
women (who, incidentally, play a prominent part in all these
accounts); in fact, when he tried to arrest at gun-point a bakery-
worker who had led the riot, the women formed a barrier and the
man got away. A *Kreisleiter* driving off on his motor-cycle produced
the following comments – within the hearing of an *Ortsgruppenleiter*: 'These bastards go joy-riding while we can die like beasts.
If it weren't for them, all our troubles would have been over long
ago . . .'

Nazi women are being spat at, their help is rejected: 'Get out of
here – this is all your fault, *Bluthunde, Blutsauger*.' Nazis are no
longer wanted around, even when they try to make themselves useful; the streams of abuse – and the colourful obscenities – are all
carefully noted. On Nazis in general:

They ought to be strung up on lamp-posts so that we can have
peace again.

If they hadn't come to power, we should still be living in peace.
As long as they exist, there won't be peace; they only prolong
their lives with the war.

Because of this *one man* [Hitler] we have to suffer all this. Is there
no one to rid us of him?

And where is Schirach? In times of trouble he isn't seen or heard.
While we are being killed here, this 'gentleman' has a good time
in a safe shelter.

This goes on for several pages and no doubt presents an accurate
picture of the situation. The comments of active Nazis – 'The
Russians don't need to come here – we'll be killed before' and 'A
few more such air attacks and they'll all rise against us' – conclude
this document (known as the *Klopfer-Bericht*).[57]

It appears that the *Parteikanzlei* found this report so alarming
that they asked Vienna's *Kreisleitungen* for confirmation. We only
have the reply from *Kreis* I, dated 2 April, which confirms the facts
and adds that the situation has in the meantime got worse:

> These protests and demonstrations of women seem to have been
> organized by deserters, but unfortunately no one appears to have
> been caught. In the last few days the situation in Vienna has
> become so tense that the most incredible rumours are readily be-
> lieved. No one has the courage to deny them ...
>
> I have been deeply shaken by the lack of leadership displayed
> by the *Wehrmacht* and even some of the party commands, I was
> able to observe in the last few days ... If there is no change soon,
> Vienna will be taken by the Bolsheviks ...[58]

also were only too true, for in these days the second great *coup* of
the military resistance was being prepared, a repetition of operation
Which, of course, it was. As regards the 'incredible rumours', these
'Valkyrie', with the same Karl Szokoll, now Major Szokoll, as its
organizing genius, but with one vital difference: the contacts now
were not with Count Stauffenberg in Berlin, but with the Supreme
Commander of the 3rd Ukrainian Front, Marshal Tolbukhin, now
operating near Wiener Neustadt.

Against the criminal plans of the régime to turn Vienna into a
'fortress' the conspirators planned a military rising, the kidnapping
of Schirach, who would be forced to sign an order declaring Vienna
an open city, and concerted action with the approaching Russians
to minimize the loss of lives and the destruction of Vienna. The full

---

[57] T81R648 5 452 288.   [58] ibid., 452 294–6.

story of the conspiracy has been ably reconstructed by Otto Molden,[59] whose account has since been amply confirmed, while Ferdinand Käs, the n.c.o. who sneaked through the German lines and negotiated with the Russians on behalf of the Resistance, has published a brief account of his share in the attempt.[60] Unfortunately, on the same day as Käs returned from the Russians, 5 April 1945, the Austrian lieutenant Hanslik betrayed his commanding officer, Major Biedermann, who had taken his discretion for granted when issuing orders for the first attack which was to commence on that day or the next.

The Nazis soon discovered the plans of the conspirators, arrested all those who could not be warned in time, hanged Biedermann and two fellow-officers on 8 April in a public square, and dug themselves in; but the Red Army fought its way into the city, which was free by the 10th; and since both German regular forces and their Balkan 'allies' had 'melted away', disappeared into civilian clothes readily offered by the civilian population, which wanted an end to the fighting, it was left to SS-formations to fight their way out of the town, across the Danube, and join up with other units in western Austria. By nightfall on 13 April all fighting in the environs of Vienna had stopped and for the Viennese the war was over. Even though treachery prevented the full benefit from being reaped, the advice and information the conspiracy had passed on to the Soviets undoubtedly shortened the fighting and saved many lives – especially since, independent of the military group but containing a considerable number of other officers and men, the all-party resistance front 'o–5' was co-ordinating military and political action inside the city and was thus laying the foundation for the early resumption of a democratic civilian administration, albeit under Russian military government.[61]

The few remaining situation reports on the military developments and their effects on morale both among the troops and the civilian population need not detain us here since they do not tell us anything new. It must be noted, though, that the three weeks between the fall of Vienna and the German capitulation were a time of extreme danger for resistance groups and patriots in central and western Austria: with the fanaticism of despair, retreating German units – and particularly the SS – punished all signs of defeatism, hanged people who had displayed the white flags of surrender, and shot soldiers who refused to destroy whole villages or blow up factories and bridges. The especial tragedy of losing a husband or son in the

---

[59] Molden, op. cit., pp. 218–41.
[60] Ferdinand Käs, *Wien im Schicksalsjahr 1945* (Vienna, 1965).
[61] For the full story of 'o–5' cf. Otto Molden, op. cit., passim.

last few days of a war already lost was experienced by hundreds of families, and the (mostly right-wing) resistance groups, particularly effective in the Tyrol, added their measure of courage to that of industrial workers and others who protected their factories, power- and water-supplies, and homes from wanton destruction.

Chapter 9

Liberation, but not Liberty

On Easter Sunday, 1 April 1945, Soviet troops occupied the village of Gloggnitz, in the mountains south-west of Vienna, where Karl Renner lived in retirement with his wife and daughter. We have met him before in these pages – as Austria's State Chancellor from 1918 to 1920, as leader of the Austrian delegation at the Paris Peace Conference, and as President of the last elected Parliament, which Dollfuss suspended on 5 March 1933. As the great antagonist of Otto Bauer in the Social Democratic Party, this moderate and immensely industrious man had used his enforced retirement well: apart from a short spell of imprisonment after the February fighting in 1934, and cautious contacts with the remaining socialist leaders, he devoted himself to the writing of his memoirs, of a history of the republic, and various sociological studies, which could of course only be published after 1945. But at the back of his mind there was always the thought, as he disarmingly admitted, that Austria might need his services once more, and therefore he did his best to escape attention and avoid persecution.[1]

Although the Nazis had left and the village was perfectly peaceful and co-operative, the occupation led to much rough handling of the population; so, on Tuesday, the Chancellor left home early in the morning – 'without an overcoat, with the habitual walking-stick in my hand' – to seek out the Russian command and talk to them. This piece of initiative was to have far-reaching, and wholly beneficial, consequences for Austria. As was to be expected, the local command-post did not know what to do with this strange man, and passed him on to the next higher command. And here fate began to take a hand, for among the officers there his name and former functions were indeed known, and while they promised to instruct the troops to behave, they informed him that he would have

---

[1] Karl Renner, *Denkschrift über die Geschichte der Unabhängigkeitserklärung Österreichs und die Einsetzung der provisorischen Regierung der Republik* (Vienna, 1945), p. 7. The following account is based on this memorandum. For an exhaustive study of the man and his work cf. the invaluable monograph by Jacques Hannak, *Karl Renner und seine Zeit* (Vienna, 1965).

to be passed on to 'higher authority'. At the next headquarters he was received very politely by a group of staff officers, with whom he engaged in an exchange of views which culminated in the question whether he was prepared to assist in the rebuilding of Austria if the Red Army were to help him. This tempting but politically very risky offer worried Renner a lot: he did not wish to appear a tool of the Russians, and any mandate would have to come from his fellow-Austrians; on the other hand, a chance to influence the behaviour of the Russians, to speed the end of the war and the liberation of Austria, was too good to be missed. His family having been re-assured as to his safety, he patiently bided his time.

At the next higher command, to which he was taken two days later, he was confronted with a large assembly of high-ranking officers including several generals. The time for a decision had come, and his mind was made up. To the question whether he was pre-pared to contribute to a shortening of the war, thereby helping the Red Army as well as Austria, he replied that he trusted the Soviets to have no other designs but the destruction of the German army and was therefore willing to appeal to the people to proclaim Austria's independence and return to a democratic constitutional life. He refused to submit his plans in a memorandum to the Red Army, so as not to appear as a supplicant accepting Russian instruc-tions, but offered to write a number of appeals to the Austrian people which the army authorities would of course have to approve. This he did, restored to his family at Gloggnitz, but soon they were all moved to a little château near Wiener Neustadt, as the guests of the 3rd Ukrainian Army under Marshal Tolbukhin which was closing in on Vienna, and eventually Renner – who had spent his time drafting plans and programmes for a future Austrian adminis-tration – was taken to the capital.

Not until then did he discover that others had shown similar enterprise to his: that members of the old political parties had already got together, in Vienna as elsewhere, as soon as the German army had been expelled and had established provisional administra-tions in liaison with the Russians. The battle of Vienna had in fact begun on 6 April and lasted for a whole week, district by district, until the last units of SS or retreating Germans had been expelled. But all the while the inter-party resistance organization 'o–5' had been busy on its own, clearing up nests of desperate Nazis, safe-guarding supplies, seeking out suitable persons, and preparing for a civilian administration; in his account of those tumultuous days[2] Adolf Schärf, soon to become chairman of the Socialist Party of Austria (in which the old Social Democrats and the Revolutionary

[2] Adolf Schärf, *April 1945 in Wien* (Vienna, 1948).

Socialists combined) and eventually President of Austria, described how on 12 April he was asked to join with various other politicians in setting up a provisional city government. While the three political parties the Russians were prepared to admit – the Socialists, the Communists, and the Christian Socials, who now called themselves Austrian People's Party – negotiated the distribution of offices, Renner's work had begun to bear fruit, for on 20 April he announced that the Russians had entrusted him with the task of forming a provisional government for Austria.

Whereas he had originally thought of convening a meeting of all surviving members of the last democratic Parliament (minus the eight avowed Fascists of the *Heimwehr*), the remarkable strength and undoubted popularity of the old political groupings made such a step unnecessary, and a somewhat arbitrary distribution of offices in the Provisional Government took place, with the Communists obtaining under Russian pressure rather more posts than their estimated strength warranted – seven, as against ten Socialists, nine conservatives, and three independent experts. On the same day, 27 April 1945, the leaders of the three parties also issued their famous *Declaration of Austrian Independence*, which the new government duly ratified and which in part read as follows:

> The democratic Republic of Austria is re-established and shall be conducted in the spirit of the constitution of 1920.
> The *Anschluss* imposed upon the people of Austria in 1938 is null and void.
> For the execution of this Declaration, and with the participation of all anti-Fascist parties, a Provisional State Government has been formed and entrusted, without prejudice to the occupying powers, with full legislative and executive powers.
> From the day of the publication of this Declaration of Independence all military, official, or personal oaths taken by Austrians with regard to the German Reich and its government are null and not binding.
> From this day on all Austrians are again in loyalty bound as citizens to the Republic of Austria.

The importance of this declaration lay in the annulment of the *Anschluss* and its legal consequences on the one hand, and in the return to the democratic constitution instead of to the 'state of affairs as existing in March 1938' which had been an earlier and rather careless Russian formulation and would have implied the resurrection of the corporate state system of Dollfuss and Schuschnigg. By 1 May five constitutional enactments were ready and duly promulgated which provided the framework for the new state. But in the meantime another problem had arisen which had not been foreseen by the Austrians: their relations with the Western Powers, which had been rather alarmed by the establishment in Vienna of a government which they suspected of being the Russians' puppets.

The Evolution of Allied Policy

We have already seen that for reasons quite unconnected with Austria the *Anschluss* of 1938 had been passively accepted by the principal powers, and it is equally obvious that even during the war the future of Austria was not one of their main preoccupations. As Fritz Fellner has written,

> as far as the leading statesmen ... were concerned there was no 'Austrian problem' as there was and still is a 'German problem' ... apart from the Moscow Conference of October 1943, Austria never appeared as a separate item on the agenda of any Allied conference; it was merely an element in the various plans for the reconstruction of the Danubian region, or else its rebirth was mentioned as a necessary move in the weakening of Germany ...[3]

In a broadcast talk on 12 November 1939 Winston Churchill listed Austria among the countries for which Britain had unsheathed the sword and whose cause she had made her own, but this was no statement of policy as yet. When Foreign Secretary Anthony Eden went to Moscow in December 1941, Stalin mentioned the restoration of Austria as one of the aims of Russian policy, whereas Churchill was at that time far from convinced that this was the best solution. As we know from his memoirs he entertained the hope right into 1943 that Vienna might once again become the capital of a Danubian federation – possibly even including Bavaria[4] – and U.S. Secretary for War Henry Stimson also saw no future for a small independent Austrian state.[5] But the record of the U.S. government was rather better than that: not only had the United States never recognized the *Anschluss de jure*, but as early as 27 May 1941 President F. D. Roosevelt in a broadcast address several times referred to 'the seizure of Austria' and to Austrians as the first of a series of peoples 'enslaved by Hitler in his march of conquest', while Secretary of State Hull stressed that the U.S. government had 'never taken the position that Austria was legally absorbed into the

[3] Fritz Fellner, 'Österreich in der Nachkriegsplanung der Alliierten 1943–1945', in *Österreich und Europa* (Graz, 1965), pp. 581 ff.
[4] Winston S. Churchill, *The Second World War* (London 1948–54), IV, p. 717.
[5] Henry Stimson, *On Active Service in Peace and War* (London, 1949), p. 325.

German Reich'. And at last, in the Moscow Conference of Foreign
Ministers in October–November 1943, the official policy of the
United Kingdom, the United States, and the Soviet Union was laid
down in the following words:[6]

> ... Austria, the first free country to fall a victim to Hitlerite
> aggression, shall be liberated from German domination.
>   They regard the annexation imposed on Austria by Germany
> on March 15, 1938, as null and void. They consider themselves
> as in no way bound by any changes effected in Austria since that
> date. They declare that they wish to see re-established a free
> and independent Austria and thereby to open the way for the
> Austrian people themselves as well as those neighbouring states
> which will be faced with similar problems, to find that political
> and economic security which is the only basis of lasting peace.
>   Austria is reminded, however, that she has a responsibility,
> which she cannot evade, for participation in the war at the side
> of Hitlerite Germany, and that in the final settlement account
> will inevitably be taken of her own contribution to her liberation.

According to Philip Mosely, the political adviser of the U.S. delegation, the last paragraph represented a compromise between the
Anglo-American view and the Soviet proposal under which Austria
bore 'full political and material responsibility for the war' and
would therefore be liable to reparations.[7] The subsequent difficulties
in the framing of the State Treaty, and in relations among the
Allies in general, were therefore not due to the problem of reparations – which the Potsdam Conference anyway was to decide to
waive – but to the imprecise definition of 'German assets' in Austria
to which the Allies laid claim.

The Moscow Conference had also set up the European Advisory
Council (EAC), with its seat in London, but unlike its policies for
other occupied countries, this body did not primarily concern itself
with the restoration of independence, but with the establishment of
Allied control machinery and occupation zones. In the agreements
of 4 and 9 July 1945, an 'Allied Commission for Austria' was set up,
in which each of the four powers enjoyed what amounted to the
right of veto, and the country was divided up into three kinds of
control systems: *zones of occupation* (Soviet Union: Lower Austria,
excluding Vienna, Burgenland, and Upper Austria north of the
Danube; U.S.A.: Upper Austria south of the Danube, and the
province of Salzburg; U.K.: Styria, Carinthia, East Tyrol; and

[6] *US Foreign Relations*, 1945, vol. III (Washington, 1968), p. 40.
[7] Philip E. Mosely, 'The Treaty with Austria', *International Organization*,
4 (1950), p. 227.

France: North Tyrol and Vorarlberg); *sectors of Vienna* (one for each power); and finally the *Inner City of Vienna* under joint quadripartite control, the Allied *Kommandatura*: this district, which contained the House of Parliament and all government offices, was policed by a joint force, the 'Four in a Jeep', which became the last visible instrument of East-West co-operation until 1955. With the exception of the Inner City of Vienna, then, the agreement was an exact copy of the arrangements made for Germany; and there was the same danger as in Germany of the

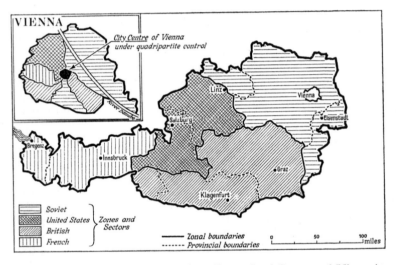

The Allied Occupation, 1945–55: Zones (and Sectors of Vienna)

Western zones breaking away from the Soviet-dominated East, which would have disappeared behind the Iron Curtain. As long as the Renner government remained unrecognized by the West, certain reactionary politicians – including Otto Habsburg – proposed policies which might easily have led to this result; fortunately, they were not listened to.[8]

At the Potsdam Conference, from 17 July to August 1945, Great Britain, the Soviet Union, and the U.S.A. agreed to waive reparations from Austria except in the case of 'German assets' in Austria. The three powers further agreed only to claim shares of 'German

[8] *US Foreign Relations*, The Conference of Berlin [The Potsdam Conference], 1945 (Washington, 1960), pp. 334 f.

assets' actually within their zones. France, too, subsequently acceded to this agreement.

But the Potsdam Conference produced no hard-and-fast definition of what constituted 'German assets', an omission which allowed the Soviet Union to place the broadest possible interpretation on this somewhat vague term. The Potsdam Conference also decided to shelve the question of extending the authority of the Renner Provisional Government (still recognized only by the Soviet Union) to the whole of Austria pending the arrival of British and American forces in Vienna.

The first detachments of Western forces arrived in Vienna on 31 July, and the Allied Council met for the first time on 11 September. Apart from adopting several measures connected with the machinery of Allied control, this meeting also voted in favour of interzonal travel throughout Austria, which had hitherto been prohibited, and of extending the right of the three political parties, which so far only the Russians had permitted in their zone, to operate throughout the country. But there was still no agreement on an extension of the authority of the Renner government to the Western zones, mainly as a result of British opposition. Forewarned by developments elsewhere in eastern Europe, Churchill had in vain tried to get President Truman to adopt a hard line *vis-à-vis* the Russians, but apart from agreeing that the Communists were over-represented in that government, and that its links with the provinces should be strengthened, the Americans concentrated on reforms rather than on the withholding of recognition, especially since representatives of the provinces were also pressing for contacts with Vienna.

To overcome Allied suspicions Renner requested, and received, Allied permission for meetings with representatives from the provinces for the purpose of broadening his government. Thus on 18 September 1945 representatives of the Western provinces met at Salzburg, affirmed their wish for a united Austria, and demanded the reconstruction of the government on a broader basis. This was followed by a conference of all provinces held in Vienna which agreed, on 25 September, on the new Provisional Government still under Dr Renner: this was now to consist of 13 conservatives, 12 Socialists, 10 Communists, and 4 independents. Even more important, in view of the forthcoming general elections and the universal fear of communist gerrymandering, was the setting-up of a commission within the communist-led Ministry of the Interior, and of similar commissions in each province, to supervise the conduct of the elections. The road was now clear for Allied recognition of the government throughout Austria; an Allied memorandum of 20

October informed Renner that they could now legislate for the whole of Austria – provided that all legislation was first approved by the Allied Council!

But the real test came with the elections of 25 November 1945 – the first since 1930, after two totalitarian régimes, with a large number of young voters without any experience of democratic procedures, and hundreds of thousands of Austrians still away, in P.o.W. camps of the Allies, or denied the vote because of their membership of the Nazi Party. Yet, of those who had a vote, over 93 per cent used it, and cast it in a fully representative way, as subsequent elections were to prove. The only unknown factor was the strength of the communist vote. While it was agreed that the CP had gained new adherents since before the war, and was now enjoying the support of the Soviet forces, the question was whether this was sufficient to make it into a serious political factor in Austria. Factory council elections in eastern Austria suggested that no more than 10 per cent of the industrial vote would go to them; and even the American forecast, based on confidential reports, gave them 10 to 15 per cent, while conservatives and Socialists would share the remainder in almost equal proportions.[9] The actual results came as a great surprise to all observers:

	Votes	Seats
People's Party	1,602,227	85
Socialist Party	1,434,898	76
Communist Party	174,257	4
Democratic Party	5,972	0
	3,217,354	165

In a significant comment after the elections, Ernst Fischer, who had been communist Minister of Education and who was expelled from the CP in 1969 following his criticism of Soviet policy in Czechoslovakia, gave the following reasons for his party's defeat: people's loyalty to their old parties; the desire for peaceful normal conditions; the solidarity of relatives, especially women, with persons prosecuted for their Nazi past; and lastly the Russian occupation.[10] At this point, as Stearman wrote,

> the Russians were forced to turn from a strategy of conquest to tactics of defense in order to hold what they had. From now on, Austria would be regarded as a hostile land instead of a potential 'people's democracy'. This new attitude soon manifested itself

[9] *US Foreign Relations*, 1945, III, p. 656.
[10] ibid., pp. 664–5.

when Chancellor Figl presented his new government to the Allied Council for approval. Although his cabinet generously included a Communist minister (Power and Electrification), the Soviet High Commissioner vetoed three ministers, all of whom had served – with Soviet permission – in the Renner Government.[11]

In addition to the Communist, the new government contained two non-party experts, six Socialists, and eight conservatives under a conservative Chancellor, Leopold Figl, and a socialist Vice-Chancellor, Adolf Schärf, while Renner moved into the office of Federal President by a joint vote of both chambers of Parliament on 20 December 1945.

Meanwhile another conflict was building up, this time on the economic front. As early as 13 September the Austrian government had rejected a Soviet proposal to set up an Austro-Soviet joint-stock company for the working of the oilfields in Lower Austria. The Soviet contributions would be made up of the equipment and exploitation right at Zistersdorf, claimed as 'German assets'. The Austrian contention, however, was that much of this was property belonging to the Western Powers which had been appropriated by the Germans after the *Anschluss*; agreement to form such a company would therefore expose the Austrians to Soviet economic pressures as well as putting them in the wrong with the West. Similar proposals made for the Danubian Steamship Company, and for a comprehensive trade agreement between the two countries, suffered the same fate, for developments in several eastern European countries had warned the Austrians of a policy of dependence on the Soviet Union.

Most accounts of these complicated triangular conflicts oversimplify the issue by contrasting the generous and benevolent attitude of the Western Powers with the greed and cruelty of Soviet practice. It should, however, be borne in mind that at that time the Soviet Union was in urgent and desperate need of compensation for the extensive damage she had suffered and of alleviation for her population which was still going short of essentials, whereas the Western Powers, particularly the United States, were in a position to adopt a more far-sighted policy as an investment for future political and economic co-operation. Thus 'the wholesale sacking of areas under Soviet control', of which Stearman writes, the dismantling of whole factories and the shipment to Russia as war booty of machinery, rolling-stock, raw materials, and other goods, was bound to conflict with the Western interest in the restoration of the Austrian

[11] William Lloyd Stearman, *The Soviet Union and the Occupation of Austria* (Bonn, n.d.), p. 36.

economy; estimates of the value of property thus removed range from the official American sum of 400 million dollars to an Austrian estimate of 1,000 million dollars.[12] Now, with the elections over and the prospects of a compliant government diminished, the Soviets took the next step with the famous 'Order No. 17' which was published on 6 July 1946 and decreed that in accordance with the Potsdam Conference decisions all German assets in eastern Austria were to pass into Soviet ownership, such assets to include

1. All property on Austrian soil belonging to Germans (natural as well as legal persons) before the *Anschluss*.
2. All property brought by Germans into Austria after the *Anschluss*, as well as all factories built with German capital in Austria after the *Anschluss*.
3. All property purchased by Germans after the *Anschluss* for which the purchase price represented the property's real value and was not the outcome of a forced sale.

To sweeten the pill, the Soviet Order emphasized that all enterprises thus confiscated would remain in Austria, conform to Austrian legislation and pay taxes, would employ Austrian labour, and produce for the Austrian market. Inevitably, the Austrian government protested to the Western Allies, who sought to have unilateral Soviet action suspended until such assets had been defined, but all to no avail. While the U.S. government, soon followed by the British and the French, renounced their claims to German assets in Austria, the Austrian Parliament rushed through a law nationalizing the three largest banks, the mining, oil, steel, machine, and metal industries, electrical and automotive plants, the Danube Shipping Company, some power installations and transportation firms – a total of over seventy enterprises, of which almost half were already under Soviet control. As was to be expected, the Russians protested against the application of this law to firms falling under Order No. 17, and the four Communists in Parliament found themselves in the ludicrous position of having to vote against a policy they had always championed.

The properties acquired by the Soviets were administered by *USIA*, the Administration for Soviet Property in Eastern Austria, and they numbered more than 400 enterprises, including about a hundred agricultural holdings. In all, they accounted for about 30 per cent of the total production of the Soviet zone and 7 per cent of the Austrian production. A sister organization, *SMV* or Soviet Mineral Oil Administration, governed the oilfields with refineries and other installations, while the third part of the Soviet

[12] ibid., p. 48.

economic complex was the *DDSG*, the old Danube Shipping Company, which comprised the bulk of the shipping in the Soviet zone and included assets in Hungary. By the end of the occupation, nearly 63,000 persons were employed in Soviet-controlled enterprises.[13] The Austrians not only contested the 'German' status of the great majority of these 'German assets', but they also complained about the ruthless exploitation of the country's resources, the neglect of adequate reinvestment or even maintenance, and the policy of starving the country of badly needed goods. It was estimated that only about 30 per cent of the output of *USIA* firms was released for the Austrian economy, while the rest – like the 60 to 70 per cent of the oil produced by *SMV* – disappeared behind the Iron Curtain; thus the second richest oil producer in Europe, after Romania, was forced to import oil for hard currency.

USIA and its sister organizations were also extremely slack in paying taxes, import duties, and insurance contributions for their employees, while at the same time running large numbers – probably as many as two hundred – retail shops which, because they paid no federal or local taxes, were able to undercut their Austrian competitors as well as provide goods not easily obtainable. Much of their merchandise, particularly cigarettes from eastern Europe, was smuggled into Austria by various gangs enjoying Soviet protection, and it took the Austrian government years to clear up these machinations of the underworld, which extended to kidnapping of persons wanted by the Russians, blackmail, and demands for protection money. The cynical comment of the Viennese, 'We've been annexed to the Balkans', was not unfounded, and it is against this background that the unceasing complaints about the size (and the behaviour!) of the occupation armies must be seen.

By the end of 1945 there were still some 350,000 Allied troops in Austria – 200,000 Russians, 65,000 British, 47,000 Americans, and 40,000 French, according to an American estimate – which produced Renner's famous metaphor of the 'four elephants in a boat'. Their maintenance cost Austria dear: not only did the Russians and the French live off the land, which further aggravated the food situation, but the Austrian government also had to supply the forces with local currency; in August 1945 it was 10 million schillings for the three Western Powers together, and 450 million schillings for the Russians alone. One of the last acts of Renner's Provisional Government was an extremely hard-hitting Note to the Allied Council on 29 November: it said in effect that the number of occupation troops was determined, not in accordance with Allied security needs, 'but

[13] For details of Soviet economic policy in Austria cf. Stearman, op. cit., ch. III, a highly critical but well-documented account.

rather according to reasons of military balance of the Allied Powers', and Austria should surely not have to bear these costs.[14]

As was to be expected, the Allied Council saw in this Note an attempt to 'sow dissension among the Allies' and rejected it rather rudely, but in actual fact the Western Powers did their best to alleviate the lot of the Austrians who were then living on an official ration of around 1,700 calories a day. The greatest single service, however, which they were able to render in this first period of occupation was to bring about a new control agreement which the four Supreme Commanders signed on 28 June 1946 and which vastly increased the Austrians' freedom of action.

The new agreement confirmed that the authority of the Austrian government now extended to the whole of the country. Restrictions on interzonal traffic were lifted and the demarcation lines between the four zones served only as boundaries of the areas of responsibility of the respective High Commissioners. The agreement also laid down that all legislation and international agreements entered upon by the Austrian government were to be submitted to the Allied Council before coming into force. Constitutional laws would require the written approval of the Allied Council. All other legislative measures and international agreements could be assumed to enjoy the Allied Council's approval provided no objection was raised within thirty-one days. From now on, in view of the Allied Council's regulation that all decisions must be unanimous, approval could be assumed failing the emergence of a unanimous objection within thirty-one days. It also meant that government measures could no longer be held up by the Allied Council for more than thirty-one days.

Thus the Austrians were slowly becoming masters in their own house while their chance of an early treaty and the departure of the occupying forces receded still further.

The Foreign Ministers' deputies having made meagre progress with their task of working out a draft treaty, their chiefs meeting in Moscow in March–April 1947 came up against one old difficulty – the problem of German assets – and a new one: the Soviet espousal of Yugoslav claims to Austrian territory in Carinthia and Styria amounting to some 2,600 square kilometres, and about 190,000 inhabitants, whereas the Western Powers insisted on the inviolability of Austria's 1938 frontiers.

The Soviet Union also supported Yugoslav reparations claims against Austria, maintaining that the Potsdam agreement not to exact reparations from Austria did not apply to Yugoslavia as that country was not a signatory to the decision. The Western Powers

[14] *US Foreign Relations*, 1945, III, p. 686.

rejected Yugoslav claims but proposed a compromise whereby Yugoslavia should retain all Austrian property actually in Yugoslavia. This was unacceptable to the Soviet Union.

The main point of difference, however, was the definition of the term 'German assets' in the Potsdam agreement. The Western Powers were in favour of the term applying to all property, rights, and interests with three exceptions: 1. Property acquired under Nazi legislation, or by force or coercion; 2. Property belonging to the Austrian state before the *Anschluss* or acquired after it and being used for the purpose of normal governmental administration; and 3. Property in which non-Germans also had a share. The only concession the Soviet Union was prepared to make was in respect of property acquired by force.

Even though a special Four-Power Commission was appointed to work out a compromise, and worked at it for five months, the concessions which the West was prepared to make to the Soviet viewpoint were rejected by Molotov at the London Conference of Foreign Ministers in November–December 1947 as totally inadequate. Yet after their next meeting in Paris, in May–June 1949, a joint communiqué announced that agreement had been reached on the outlines of a treaty. What induced this sudden burst of optimism was the fact that the Soviet Union no longer supported Yugoslavia's territorial and reparations claims, since Tito was in open rebellion against Stalin and his country had been expelled from the communist grouping quaintly known as Cominform. Hence the Foreign Ministers agreed that Austria's frontiers should be those of 1 January 1938; that Austria should guarantee the rights of her Croat and Slovene minorities; that no reparations should be exacted from Austria, but that Yugoslavia should be allowed the right to retain Austrian property actually on Yugoslav soil; that the Soviet Union (like the Western Powers) should waive all claim to so-called 'German assets' with the exception of oil interests and the Danube Shipping Company and receive instead the sum of 150 million dollars payable over six years; that the Soviet Union should also receive all the Danube Shipping Company's assets in Bulgaria, Romania, and Hungary as well as in eastern Austria; and that the Soviet Union should be allowed 60 per cent of oil production, concessions, and refineries in eastern Austria.

The Marshall Plan

Although the deputies were instructed to prepare a draft by 1 September 1949, they failed to reach agreement on German assets by that date, and even after two extensions, so that the problem once again landed in the lap of the Foreign Ministers for their London meeting in May 1950; now it was no longer Yugoslavia but Trieste and various criticisms of Austrian policy that provided the Soviets with pretexts for their delaying tactics. For in the meantime developments both inside Austria and elsewhere in western Europe had changed the nature of the East–West confrontation: despairing of Soviet co-operation in rebuilding a war-torn continent, the United States, while massively supporting countries like Austria under her Foreign Aid Programme, at a conference in Paris in the summer of 1947 launched what was to become the greatest co-operative effort at economic reconstruction ever undertaken, the European Recovery Programme (ERP), also known as the 'Marshall Plan' after the then Secretary of State, George Marshall. That this was not a mere gesture of solidarity but, in Walter Lippmann's words, an 'act of enlightened self-interest', is evident, and that it had the most far-reaching consequences, particularly for Germany, is beyond doubt; yet it is difficult to say what other course was open to the West in view of the Soviet tactics but to combine regardless of the consequences.

Where Austria was concerned, this great imaginative move came just in time. Two years after the end of the war the economic situation was still as hopeless as it had been when the fighting ceased. In spite of the trebling of Austria's visible and invisible exports between 1946 and 1947, these exports paid for no more than one-third of her imports, the deficit being covered by foreign aid: half of it was met by the U.S.A., one-quarter by UNRRA, and the rest by Britain and various relief organizations. Food still occupied a prominent place in all imports: Austrian agriculture in 1947 produced only 36 per cent of the food issued in rations – less than half of what it marketed in 1937. The remaining two-thirds of rationed food were supplied by America, a fact duly noted on the back of the monthly ration card. Large posters informed the public that four out of every five loaves of bread they consumed were a present of the U.S.A. to the Austrian government, which could use the money received for it for its own economic policies. Even the currency reform of December 1947, by which the note circulation was approximately halved and which enabled the Austrian schilling to find its level again in international trade, did no more than provide a basis for a constructive policy; but with confidence restored, the arrival of the required means marked the turning-point.

In the first year of the European Recovery Programme Austria received goods to the value of $280 million, of which the most important were food ($125 million), coal ($42 million), raw materials ($67 million), machinery ($12 million), and fertilizers and feeding stuffs ($15 million).

The proceeds from the sale of 'Marshall goods' were spent on projects of vital importance: $80 million on general reconstruction; $40 million on hydro-electrical development; $41 million on the modernization of industry; $46 million on housing; $14 million on the mechanization of agriculture, etc. The effects were highly gratifying. That year alone showed an increase of 47 per cent in industrial production as compared with 1947. By the beginning of 1949, for the first time since the end of the war, it had reached the level of 1937; but whereas the output of capital goods stood at 140 per cent of 1937, that of consumer goods was still only about 70 per cent. Better nutrition, adequate supplies of fuel and raw materials, and new machines were paying dividends on the industrial front. The output of steel had reached pre-war level, pig-iron showed an increase of 50 per cent over pre-war, aluminium and ball bearings of 200, electric bulbs of nearly 100 per cent. While heavy vehicles and bicycles were still down by 25 per cent, motor-buses had reached 100 per cent, and the 4,000 tractors produced in 1948 were thirty-eight times the number coming off the assembly line in 1938.

By mid-1949 total production exceeded the pre-war level by 26 per cent, but consumer goods still lagged behind, at 90 per cent of the 1937 figure. This was the price that had to be paid for the heavy investment policy in the capital industries and for a determined exports drive.

Though a latecomer in international markets, Austria was now back to 60 per cent of her pre-war level of exports, while unemployment was down to 3.65 per cent of the insured population – compared with 33 per cent in 1937! Despite this very real progress, the national income was estimated at the close of 1948 to be only about 80 per cent of that of 1937, and the United Nations *Economic Survey of Europe* put it even lower in its calculations of dollar income per head of population, reckoned at 170 in 1938, 96 in 1947, and 130 in 1948 – which, incidentally, was 52 dollars less than the average for Europe (without the Soviet Union).

If Austria's economic survival was made possible only by Western aid, the degree of progress was determined by her own exertions. An industrious and highly skilled working class, schooled in the voluntary discipline of its great political and trade union organizations, resisted once again, as it did in 1918, the temptation of easy-sounding extremist solutions, and accepted its share of responsibility for the country's survival. From the first blocking of savings deposits in 1945 to the currency reform of 1947 and the Wage–Price Agreements of 1948 and 1949, it made big sacrifices, even though each rise in the cost of living caused by progressive de-control was eventually met (after considerable delay) by wage increases and by various measures on the lines of the British Beveridge Plan, such as children's allowances and the first steps towards a national insurance scheme.

Inevitably, this process was accompanied by tensions which the Communist Party tried to exploit. Having successively lost all but one of their cabinet posts, as well as control of the police and many other positions in key offices, and unable to prevent the attachment of Austria to the Western camp, they concentrated on the hardships experienced by the working classes and succeeded in encouraging a group of left-wing Socialists to rebel against their party's share in this policy of 'capitalist restoration' and 'subservience to dollar imperialism'. Ostensibly in connection with the currency reform, but actually because he had voted in favour of accepting Marshall Aid which the Soviet Union subsequently denounced, the last remaining communist Minister resigned in November 1947, thus ending the three-party coalition which had been in office since April 1945; from now on until 1966 Austria was governed by a coalition of conservatives and Socialists. With negotiations for a State Treaty still nowhere near completion, the economic situation improving but producing great strains and stresses, and a new electoral roll nearly one-third larger than in 1945, the coalition faced its next great test in October 1950 when Austria's Parliament was due to be re-elected.

From the historian's viewpoint, however, the main significance of the 1949 elections lay in the way the Austrian people reacted to, and overcame, the Nazi period. After all, according to official statistics, 525,833 Austrians had been registered as former Nazis by 1947, not including several thousand other ex-party members because they had subsequently fallen out with the party, and if one adds candidates for membership, or members of organizations similarly proscribed by the Allies, a grand total of 581,915 persons found themselves in an extremely precarious position.[15] Subject to denazification, disfranchised, with the constant threat of loss of job, home, property, and freedom over their heads, there was a distinct danger that this category and their families and dependants – over 2 million people – might adopt a hostile attitude towards the Austrian state and remain sullen and unco-operative even if originally they had never been Nazis from conviction. Admittedly, Marshal Tolbukhin's army had announced on entering Austria that 'ordinary members of the Nazi Party will not be persecuted if they do not resist the Soviet army', but this was before final victory had been won. The Allied occupation, the emergence of various resistance movements, and the revelations about war crimes and concentration camps created

[15] *Österreichisches Jahrbuch* (Vienna, 1947), p. 146.

a climate of opinion in which both convinced National Socialists
and unwilling party members had reason to fear the worst.

This the government and national leadership set out to counteract. Their own record was unblemished: eight out of the eleven
members of Figl's cabinet and 118 out of 215 members of the two
houses of Parliament had either been victims of the Nazi régime or
else were active in some form of resistance work.[16] In their name
Renner defined the official attitude towards the ex-Nazis in Austria
in midsummer 1945:

> ... the number of the members and candidates of this party who
> were really motivated by the spirit of Nazism or acted in the
> interests of the party was not a very large one. The vast majority
> were victims of economic, social, or even personal coercion. All
> those who were employed in public or economic life and held a
> post of any importance or who worked for armament undertak-
> ings were forced under threat of losing their positions to become
> members of the party. They did not resist this blackmailing
> coercion; but can one expect that scientists, artists, businessmen
> of all kinds, who rarely went in for politics at all, or workers who
> were threatened by unemployment or concentration camps,
> should heroically risk their livelihood in order to avoid the
> formal adhesion to a party which dominated the public opinion
> of the country with so much zest and such astonishing initial
> success?

He added, though, that several thousand real Nazis who were suspected of serious crimes, and 'hundreds of war criminals', were
awaiting trial by the new Austrian 'people's courts'.[17]

There was still a minor difficulty to be overcome: the refusal of
the Allied Council to allow new political parties to be formed, but
after much hesitation it accepted the (socialist) Minister of the
Interior's interpretation of an article in the electoral law according
to which one hundred citizens in any one constituency may form
themselves into a 'vote-soliciting group' (wahlwerbende Partei), and
may nominate candidates. As a result, numerous 'Fourth Parties'
constituted themselves in preparation for the election, one of which,
the 'League of Independents' (Verband der Unabhängigen, VDU),
openly claimed to represent the 400,000-plus former Nazis. While
the more senior men among the returned prisoners-of-war and
among the 150,000 'folk Germans' expelled from Czechoslovakia
and other Danubian countries and recently naturalized in Austria

---

[16] Der österreichische National- und Bundesrat 1945 (Vienna, 1946).
[17] Karl Renner, Drei Monate Aufbauarbeit der provisorischen Staatsregierung der Republik Österreich (Vienna, 1945), pp. 9–10.

were expected to conform to their former political behaviour and vote conservative or socialist, the real battle was for the support of ex-Nazis and of the young voters of twenty and over, the products of Nazi education and of Hitler Youth indoctrination. Each of the 'licensed' parties tried to secure part of this vote: the People's Party with great determination, the Communists mainly 'for the record', and Socialists half-heartedly and with little expectation of success except among the young.

The wooing of the Nazi vote was not always very dignified; while the Socialists arranged public discussions which attracted a few of the earnest Nazis who were disillusioned and made a genuine effort to understand their former enemies, some politicians of the Right, especially in the provinces, appealed to the 'heroic Front soldiers' whose support they asked for in the struggle against the 'inhuman consequences of the war', for which, by implication, the Allies were blamed. Special groups of 'Front comrades', recruited from among ex-Nazis, were formed and attached to the People's Party, and eventually a secret conference was held at Oberweis to which several prominent Nazi leaders were invited, presumably to discover what their price would be for giving a lead to their former followers by supporting the People's Party. It cannot be established whether in fact twenty-five safe seats had been offered, or demanded, or important posts in the party, or party support for the repeal of anti-Nazi legislation; but the admission that former Nazi leaders still commanded a following in the country, which was implicit in the selection of the delegates, created a very bad impression.

The Socialists' reply was to give greater encouragement to all dissidents to form their several 'Fourth Parties': since they were not going to benefit from the enfranchisement of ex-Nazis, neither should their rivals. Their avowed aim was to prevent a concentration of all right-wing forces in one party which might lead to another 1934. They were not afraid that any of these groups might become a new Nazi Party, mainly because there was neither a strong Germany to back them, nor any Austrian capitalists to subsidize them, if only because after the return of the Russian-held industries 60 per cent of Austria's economy would be state-owned. Moreover, there had always been a tendency, if not a very pronounced one, towards nationalism and anti-clericalism among the Austrian middle classes and farmers, as exemplified by the *Grossdeutsche Partei* and the *Landbund* of the First Republic; and they considered it both a tactical and a political advantage to have the nationalists in parties of their own rather than allow them to influence the Centre Party. The Socialists consequently hoped that the several 'Fourth Parties', particularly the VDU, would gain enough votes to lose the People's

Party its majority and give the Socialists the chance to head a new
coalition government with the conservatives.

On first reading the election results presented a confused picture
and could be interpreted in several ways:

Election Results, October 1949
Gains (+) or Losses (−) compared with 1945:

Party	Actual Votes	Percentage of Votes	Seats in Parliament
People's	1,844,850 (+ 242,606)	44·2 (− 5·7)	77 (− 8)
Socialist	1,621,275 (+ 186,377)	38·6 (− 6·5)	67 (− 9)
VDU	489,132	11·7	16
Communist	212,651 (+ 38,394)	5 (± 0)	5 (+ 1)

Technically, it was a swing to the Right, for if in the elections of
1945 the combined Left vote exceeded the People's Party's vote by
7,000, now the anti-socialist vote exceeded the Left vote by half a
million; in practice, however, the ill-assorted team of VDU politicians, ranging from democratic national liberals and anti-clericals to
resentful unteachables who only paid lip-service to parliamentary
democracy, was not a genuine political force, as its subsequent development was to show. Of the approximately one million new
voters, about one-quarter had gone to the conservatives and another
quarter to the parties of the Left, while one-half had been secured
by the VDU (now called the WDU or *Wahlverband* of Independents), a considerable success for a first attempt (and a rather short-
lived one at that). Superficially, it looked like the emergence of
Neo-Nazism on a big scale, and like the increase in the communist
vote (camouflaged as 'Left Bloc' with the accession of the socialist
splinter group of Erwin Scharf) it boded ill for Austrian politics. In
actual fact, the VDU was soon rent by internal quarrels, resignations, and expulsions, while a communist attempt, in October 1950,
to call a general strike against a new wage–price agreement concluded between the government and the Trade Union Federation,
in which a few factories were occupied and street-fighting developed
in several places under the benevolent eye of the Soviet authorities,
was a dismal failure on account of the discipline of the great majority of socialist working-men.

While putting their own house in order, busily rebuilding their
economy, and laboriously wresting more concessions from the
Allied Council, Austrians kept an eye cocked on developments on

the international scene where negotiations for a State Treaty were becoming increasingly farcical. At the May 1950 meeting of the Foreign Ministers' deputies the Soviet delegate produced a new pretext for procrastination, to replace the former sponsorship of Yugoslav claims against Austria: the problem of Trieste, coupled with the alleged infringements of agreements on denazification and demilitarization in Austria. The far-fetched complaint about Trieste rested on the assertion that the Western Powers were continually violating the Italian Peace Treaty by maintaining troops in Trieste directly contrary to the Statute of Trieste. In view of the Western Powers' flagrant violation of the Italian Treaty it was hardly likely that they would be any more successful in keeping to the provisions of an Austrian Treaty. If the Western Allies really wanted to proceed to the conclusion of an Austrian State Treaty, it was imperative that they should honour their obligations under the Statute of Trieste. As for the other complaint, it was maintained that former active 'Fascists' were filling responsible posts in the service of the state, and the newly formed VDU was a Neo-Fascist organization, as was the so-called 'Youth Front' of the People's Party. Furthermore, preparations were going ahead in the Western zones for reviving an Austrian army, and the Austrian police and gendarmerie were being brought up to excessive strength. The delegates of the Western Powers retorted that there was absolutely no connection between Trieste and the State Treaty, and that Soviet statements about Austrian violation of the denazification and demilitarization agreements were completely unfounded. These fresh demands and complaints put forward by the Soviet Union meant that throughout 1950 none of the meetings of the Foreign Ministers' deputies produced any results whatever, and in 1951 negotiations were finally broken off and not resumed till February 1953.

Human nature being what it is, early relief over the end of the war and the collapse of the Third Reich had worn thin, and the hopes for real freedom under a State Treaty, frequently disappointed, turned into a mood of impatience with *all* the Allied Powers and insistent demands for 'liberation from our liberators' and 'a peace treaty, whatever the price'. The outbreak of war in Korea changed all this. The ominous propaganda slogan of the Communists, 'It is only sixty kilometres to the People's Democracies', assumed a new and menacing meaning, and the question on everybody's lips was, 'Shall we be next?' It was only with President Truman's announcement of aid to Southern Korea, and the prompt action by the United Nations, that confidence returned with the realization that the roughly 25,000 Western troops in Austria

(10,000 Americans, 8,500 British, and over 6,000 French, as against 44,000 Soviet troops) were a guarantee of Western solidarity. And if the Western Powers alone could not restore Austria's freedom, they were at least able to make their presence as little burdensome and objectionable as possible.

But the attempt to keep the diplomatic ball rolling was not abandoned. In March 1952 the three Western Powers submitted to the Soviet Union an abbreviated State Treaty of 8 Articles compared with the 53 Articles of the original draft, which was duly rejected by the Russians, resubmitted in September, and rejected once more by the recipients. Meanwhile the Austrian government had taken a hand in this game with a memorandum addressed to all governments with which it had diplomatic relations, complaining that Austria was receiving worse treatment than other liberated countries, even those that had fought on the German side, and suggesting United Nations intervention. On the initiative of Brazil the U.N. General Assembly actually issued, on 20 December 1952, an urgent appeal to the Four Powers to reach agreement on Austria, but the Soviet Union, the real stumbling-block, and her satellites absented themselves from the voting on the grounds that the United Nations had no authority to intervene in action taken against ex-enemy states. This particular diplomatic round ended in February 1952 with the 260th meeting of the deputies, which had to be adjourned indefinitely since the Western representatives refused to accede to the Soviet request for withdrawal of the abbreviated treaty. It was becoming ever more obvious that a new approach was needed, preferably from the Austrian side, to break the diplomatic deadlock, especially with West Germany moving into the Western Alliance; unless Soviet fears could be assuaged, Four-Power occupation would become a permanency. It was at this stage that the *neutralization of Austria* was put forward as a practical and immediate policy, after it had been mentioned, off and on, as a possible long-term goal.

For while Austrian politicians had never made a secret of their sympathies for the West, they could understand Soviet reluctance to present their rivals with a new base after the removal of Allied troops, and this without receiving any compensation.

Towards Neutrality

Therefore, Austrian minds had turned to solutions which would be acceptable to both sides, and soon the possibility of a neutral status was mooted. It was an attractive idea: to Austrians, neutrality meant Switzerland, a prosperous, democratic, and peaceful country. The first public statement came from no less a man than President

Renner, who pointed to neutral Switzerland as a model for, and possible partner with, a neutral Austria:

> Just as Switzerland is surrounded by the three great countries of western Europe, so Austria is surrounded by the five peoples of Central Europe, whose lines of communication traverse her territory. It is in the common interest of all Austria's five neighbours that their communications should be free for all, and remain so; that no one country should monopolize them for itself against the others, let alone utilize them as a springboard for military operations. . . . The two republics constitute a compact group of peoples right across Central Europe, guaranteeing free intercommunication in time of peace, constituting a peaceful barrier on the threat of war; and for us in particular holding out the hope that our people can at last enjoy the peace and tranquillity that Switzerland derived from the Congress of Vienna.[18]

This was soon followed by a resolution, unanimously adopted, at the annual conference of the Socialist Party, which declared the party to be in favour of an

> Austria – free and neutral! An international guarantee of Austria's neutrality to secure her frontiers, her freedom and independence. Admission of Austria to the United Nations.[19]

But there were warning voices as well, mostly in the conservative camp; their tenor was expressed by Lujo Toncic, afterwards briefly Foreign Minister and presently Chairman of the Council of Europe, to the effect that a neutrality statute was incompatible with membership of the United Nations, that Austrian neutrality would probably not be guaranteed by the Great Powers or anybody else who mattered, and that anyway Austria's geopolitical position at the gateway to the Danube basin placed her in quite a different category from Switzerland.[20] And in a government statement Chancellor Leopold Figl on 9 November 1946 merely affirmed that 'Austrians do not speculate on forming blocs in association with other foreign powers. . . .'

But the Socialists continued pressing the idea; Renner's successor, President Theodor Körner, declared in November 1951 that no one could impugn to a small country the suicidal delusion that it could play any part in the conflicts of the great:

[18] *Wiener Zeitung* (Vienna), 19 January 1947.
[19] *Parteitagsprotokoll* 1947, p. 134.
[20] 'Die Neutralisation Österreichs', *Berichte und Informationen* (Salzburg), 5 July 1946.

A free and independent Austria, *removed from all rivalries and not tied to either side*, but only devoted to the cause of peace, will be an asset for Europe and the world.[21]

Gradually the advantages were seen to outweigh the possible risks. In the course of a parliamentary debate on 2 April 1952 Foreign Minister Karl Gruber asserted that for Austria a policy of neutrality was a matter of course and that the government had repeatedly stated that it had no intention of joining any military bloc. This statement was supported by speakers of the two coalition parties, though warning voices were still raised lest neutrality should turn Austria into a pawn in Soviet power politics.

In June 1953 Gruber saw the Indian Prime Minister, Jawaharlal Nehru, who happened to be staying in Switzerland; while he denied that any Indian mediation in Moscow was requested, it is known that the Indian ambassador told Molotov that he considered an Austrian undertaking to keep out of military blocs and commitments adequate for Russia's needs. Molotov replied that while it would undoubtedly be of great value, it did not go far enough.[22] The Americans, on the other hand, had their own objections; Gruber complained of the 'rigid outlook' of the U.S. State Department, whose experts tended 'to over-estimate the legal aspect of international politics':

> The danger of Communist infiltration does not so much lie in legal agreements with the Soviet Union as in the latter's actual political presence ... what would be dangerous would be a conception of neutrality that allowed the Soviets to decide unilaterally whether such-and-such an Austrian action was neutral, or to intervene in Austrian internal affairs. . . .[23]

The first official discussion at Four-Power level took place at the Berlin Conference of Foreign Ministers in January–February 1954, towards the end of which Molotov proposed an additional Article in the State Treaty by which Austria undertook not to join any bloc or military alliance and not to permit foreign military bases on Austrian territory or to engage the services of foreign military advisers. The Four Powers should also undertake to adhere to this resolution. Figl accepted at once, but six days later Molotov withdrew his Article and declared himself satisfied if the Austrian

[21] *Neues Österreich* (Vienna), 13 November 1951.
[22] Bruno Kreisky, 'Österreichs Stellung als neutraler Staat', *Österreich in Geschichte und Literatur*, I/3, 1957, pp. 129–30.
[23] Karl Gruber, *Between Liberation and Liberty* (London, 1955), pp. 221–4.

government were to issue a declaration which should be appended to the treaty[24] – the result of Western protests that Austria should be free to choose military neutrality but not be forced into such a status.

The Western Powers, and especially the Americans, were altogether not very happy about the turn events were taking. Bruno Kreisky recalls a conversation he and Figl had with Secretary of State John Foster Dulles, at which the latter asked the Austrians to consider the risks involved in such a policy and described in great detail the advantages accruing to small states from belonging to powerful alliances. While agreeing in principle Kreisky pointed out that geography ruled out any policy for Austria other than the preservation of the unity of the country: 'and to join either bloc would inevitably lead to partition'; he adds: 'I had the impression that Dulles was convinced by these arguments.'[25] However, since the Soviets still linked their agreement to other, more intractable, issues, the conference ended in failure, and a new hardening of their occupation policy set in until, for reasons connected with internal changes in the Soviet Union— the dismissal of Premier Malenkov – and with the impending ratification of the Paris Agreements, Molotov made a new offer in February 1955. The Austrian government reacted immediately and reiterated its readiness to meet the Russian wishes, whereupon an invitation was extended to Chancellor Julius Raab to bring an Austrian delegation to Moscow for talks.

The result of these talks was the famous Moscow Memorandum of 15 April 1955 in which the Austrians pledged themselves, in the spirit of their Berlin Conference declaration, to join no military alliances and to permit no military bases on their territory, and to assume an international obligation 'to practise in perpetuity a neutrality of the type maintained by Switzerland'. They were further to submit this declaration to their Parliament after ratification of the State Treaty, and to seek to obtain international recognition for this declaration and a guarantee by the four Great Powers of 'the inviolability and integrity of Austrian territory'. The Soviets in turn expressed their readiness to recognize the declaration on Austrian neutrality and to participate in a Four-Power guarantee.[26] On the following day, *Pravda* spelt out the Soviet interpretation of a 'policy of independence'; it meant the neutralization of Austria 'on the Swiss model' – a complimentary reference which surprised

---

[24] Heinrich Siegler, *Austria. Problems and Achievements 1945–63* (Bonn, n.d.), pp. 27–8.

[25] Bruno Kreisky, *Die Herausforderung* (Düsseldorf, 1963), pp. 96–7.

[26] Alfred Verdross, *The Permanent Neutrality of the Republic of Austria* (Vienna, 1967), pp. 5–6.

the Swiss after years of Soviet attacks on 'unneutral, reactionary' Swiss policies.[27]

Even before leaving Moscow the Austrian government delegation sent a message to the Austrian people: 'Austria will be free. We are getting all of our country back . . .', which ensured them an enthusiastic reception on their return. On 27 April Parliament approved the report on the Moscow discussion, and on 15 May 1955 the Foreign Ministers of the Four Powers and of Austria – Messrs Dulles, Macmillan, Pinay, Molotov, and Figl – signed the Austrian State Treaty in the historic Belvedere, Prince Eugene's baroque palace in Vienna. Now the road was clear for the required legislation. On 7 June Parliament adopted a motion on neutrality and on the country's desire to be admitted to the United Nations, which the government framed as a constitutional enactment for Parliament to approve on 25 October, the day when according to the treaty the last occupation soldier was to have left the country:

> *Article I.* (1) For the purpose of the permanent maintenance of her external independence and for the purpose of the inviolability of her territory, Austria of her own free will declares herewith her permanent neutrality, which she is resolved to maintain and defend with all the means at her disposal.
>
> (2) In order to secure these purposes Austria will never in the future accede to any military alliances nor permit the establishment of military bases of foreign states on her territory.
>
> *Article II.* The Federal Government is authorized to enact appropriate legislation.[28]

The improbable had happened. For the first time since 1945 the Soviet Union had withdrawn from a country without having installed a régime of her own choice and without political agreements that severely reduced the country's freedom of action. It is still anybody's guess what caused the Soviets to make this gesture, and there has been no lack of guesses. The principal reason has been seen in a Soviet desire to prevent the ratification of the Paris Agreements which were designed as a Western defence measure with the inclusion of West Germany, and were signed between 19 and 23 October 1954. This is almost certainly wrong, for when the final Austro-Soviet Agreements were concluded in April ratification was practically assured. It is therefore also unlikely that this concession was intended as a bait for the Germans, to hold out hopes of reunification if they refused to join the Western bloc and to rearm. A far more plausible explanation is that of Bruno Kreisky, who participated

[27] Stearman, op. cit., p. 150.
[28] *Bundesgesetzblatt* Nr. 221 of 1955.

in the treaty negotiations as State Secretary for Foreign Affairs and was Foreign Minister from 1959 to 1966, and who writes that with the success of the Western policy of 'containment' Stalin's successors meant signally to end the period of Stalinist foreign policy. The new policy of co-existence involved a few concessions which would improve the Soviets' political image; as Khrushchev himself said to the Austrians, it seemed more important to him (though not to Molotov) to demonstrate Russia's willingness to negotiate than to hang on to military positions of small value. To critics of Austria's course Kreisky replied at the time of the final discussions:

> The alternative of neutrality or membership of one of the big military blocs does not exist for Austria. Our choice is much more limited; it is at best: the *status quo* or neutrality. But does the *status quo* not also amount to a kind of neutralization – neutralization by occupation? Where is there an alternative for a people which tries to be its own master under present circumstances? The neutrality which we proclaim enables us to demand its corollary: a guarantee of our independence and inviolability.[29]

But Khrushchev had his critics, too, and at the July meeting of the Central Committee of the CPSU he justified his policy by pointing to the fact that the abandonment of Soviet bases in Austria had not strengthened the military potential of their opponents; the Soviet zone of occupation had not been part of the 'socialist' order, and the 'socialist camp' lost nothing by Austria's conversion to neutrality.[30] He might have added that the concession on Austria was the beginning of a new diplomatic offensive: the reconciliation with Tito's Yugoslavia, the summit conference at Geneva, the opening of diplomatic relations with West Germany, the evacuation of Porkalla as a concession to Finland, all within weeks or months of the State Treaty.

But the West was also beginning to count the cost of Austrian neutrality.

> When the last Western troops left Austria, there remained a neutral wedge 530 miles long (from Bratislava to Geneva) which split Italy from West Germany – less than six months after they had been joined together for defense purposes in the 'Western European Union', – and which therefore split NATO and the whole Western defense in two. What the Paris Agreements had joined together, the State Treaty, at least partly, put asunder,

[29] Kreisky, *Die Herausforderung*, pp. 101–3, 111.
[30] David Dallin, *Soviet Foreign Policy after Stalin* (Philadelphia, 1961), p. 228.

writes Stearman.[31] The supply and communication lines between Italy and Germany, which ran through the Tyrol, were cut, which not only made the Italians and the Swiss nervous but had also wider strategic implications, as the Lebanon crisis in the summer of 1958 was to show.

Against these practical difficulties there were, of course, less tangible gains, listed by Dulles in the language of the Cold War in a televised conversation with President Eisenhower, as quoted by the *New York Times* of 18 May 1955:

> In the first place, it marks the first time that the Red Armies will have turned their face in the other direction and gone back since 1945, . . . Now, that's bound to have a tremendous impact in the other countries where the Red armies are there in occupation. It is going to create a desire – a mounting desire – on the part of those people to get the same freedom from that type of occupation that the Austrians have gotten. And furthermore this, this joy at their freedom which was so manifest by the Austrian people that is going to be contagious and it's going to spread surely to the neighboring countries – Czechoslovakia – for the first time there'll be an open door to freedom on the part of Hungary . . .[32]

Just what the consequences were we shall have to consider in our survey of the history of the Second Republic; but in the meantime the remaining parts of the State Treaty have to be examined against the background of Austria's economic and political development while still under occupation.

Freedom at Last

While the rest of 1953 was still taken up with futile wrangling over the abbreviated treaty text, a new complication arose from Molotov's linking the treaty negotiations with the German problem, and it took all of 1954 to shift him from this position. Progress had been made, however, in the question of German assets, where Russia now agreed to take $150 million, at an annual rate of $25 million, in goods instead of in dollars, and abandoned her earlier demands for long-term concessions in the oilfields and in Danubian shipping. The Austrian government's success, at the Moscow talks, in securing the abandonment of these terms meant the restoration of the country's territorial sovereignty and economic independence.

Hence the economic provisions of the State Treaty,[33] after the

---

[31] Stearman, op. cit., pp. 162–3.

[32] ibid., p. 169.

[33] *State Treaty for the re-establishment of an independent and democratic Austria* (HMSO, Cmd. 9482, 1955).

renunciation of all reparations arising out of the state of war, returned to Austria the *USIA*, *SMV*, and *DDSG* enterprises, oilfields,
refineries, and installations, on deliveries of goods to the value of
$150 million spread over six years, plus $2 million in cash for the
Danubian Steamship Company, plus one million tons of oil annually
(about one-third of total output) for the next ten years. Though it
was difficult at the time to believe that the Austrian economy could
meet these requirements—worth nearly 20,000 million schillings –
in actual fact treaty deliveries acted as a stimulant to production,
secured full employment and modernization, and created valuable
trade contacts with eastern Europe. This of course benefited the
nationalized sector of the economy in the first instance; after the
return of the Russian-held enterprises Austria's role as the Western
country with the largest percentage of public ownership was accen-
tuated still further: in 1963 the government controlled

95 per cent of all electricity, gas, and water undertakings,

78 per cent of transportation,

69 per cent of banks and insurance firms, and

31 per cent of industrial undertakings,

employing approximately one-fifth of the total labour force and
accounting for 23 per cent of the GNP.[34]

Though operating on a narrow margin, the Austrian economy
can rightly claim to have been the scene of a minor miracle since the
end of the war – nothing on the scale of the German *Wirtschafts-
wunder*, but the more remarkable because so unlike the record of
the First Republic. From the almost complete breakdown in the last
months of the fighting and for some time afterwards, the slow return
to a functioning economy in 1946 suffered a great setback in the
winter of 1946–47 when the severe drought of the summer not only
dashed all hopes of a recovery in agriculture, but had a disastrous
effect on electricity production; an early and hard winter and a
decline in coal imports turned this into a fuel crisis of the first
magnitude which set economic recovery back by many months. The
year 1947 was characterized by strong inflationary tendencies which
also threatened to interrupt progress in production and foreign
trade: memories of the runaway inflation of 1920–22 haunted
people's minds and tempted them to do the very things that would
bring about a repetition. But the first of the wage–price agreements
already mentioned and the currency reform combined to lead to
reasonably stable monetary foundations, on which the great advance
of the following years could be built.[35] What followed in the four

[34] Gustav Otruba, op. cit., p. 49.

[35] For a lucid, though not uncritical, account cf. K. W. Rothschild, *The
Austrian Economy since 1945* (London, 1950).

years of the Marshall Plan, between 1948 and 1951, was Austria's 'economic miracle': industrial production trebled, industrial productivity and the volume of exports doubled, and by 1949 the gross national product exceeded the level of 1937 and reached the former records of 1913 and 1929 in 1950. This was made possible by a generous infusion of foreign aid – $1,600 million between 1945 and 1955, of which the United States contributed no less than 1,400 million in direct and indirect ERP aid. This was the kind of 'investment' which Central Europe could have done with between the wars, and history might have taken a different turn. However, laying the foundations of economic viability is not necessarily jam today, and conflicts over social policy as well as the long-term effects of the Korean War made 1951–52 into a period of international crisis aggravated by the drastic drop in ERP credits. A tough budget in 1952, with increases in taxation and various charges, dearer money and cuts in public spending, succeeded in stabilizing prices at the cost of retarding industrial production and risking greater unemployment. The reaction of industrial and commercial interests to seven years of economic planning, and their demands for a more 'liberal' economy, with which Dr Kamitz, the Minister of Finance, was wholly in sympathy, clashed with the Socialists' concern for full employment, and the government resigned on 23 October 1952, a year before its term was up. Thus the general election of 1953 was fought on a very narrow front: the disinflationary, 'sound money' policy of the conservatives versus the socialist demand for an elastic budget and credit policy.

While the People's Party had the support of the American Mission for Economic Co-operation, which made the size of the allocation out of ERP counterpart funds for 1953 dependent on the progress Austria was making towards the stabilization of her financial position, the Socialist Party was massively supported by the 1·3 million-strong Federation of Trade Unions and rank-and-file militancy. An interesting pointer to the temper of the working classes is contained in the strike statistics, which show that in 1952 twice as many working hours were lost as in the previous year, and nearly four times as many workers were involved. This increase, however, was due to a 'warning strike' conducted by the building trades and directed against the cut in public works. If that strike is omitted from the total, it will be seen that no more men struck in 1952 than in the previous year, and that 13 per cent less time was lost. In other words, the negotiating machinery showed no signs of deterioration, union discipline was as high as ever, but the strike weapon was used more for political ends.

Evidence that the tide was running in their favour had already been provided in the presidential elections of the previous year. Karl Renner had died on New Year's Eve 1950, and his successor was to be elected by popular vote. Since none of the six candidates secured the required 50 per cent of the valid votes in the first round on 6 May 1951, a second ballot had to be held three weeks later. In the first ballot, apart from two freak candidates, receiving 5,000 and 2,000 votes respectively, each of the four parliamentary parties ran a candidate, and, as was expected, the communist candidate Gottlieb Fiala secured the usual 5 per cent of the votes for his party – 220,000 in all. The League of Independents, which had obtained 11·7 per cent in the general election of 1949, nominated an essentially non-political and generally respected medical man, Dr Burghard Breitner, a university professor from Innsbruck, who obtained 15·4 per cent of the vote – an expression of non-confidence in the government rather than a vote for neo-Nazism. The socialist candidate, Dr Theodor Körner, mayor of Vienna, improved on his party's performance in the general election by 60,000 votes or 0·4 per cent, and Dr Heinrich Gleissner, the People's Party candidate, dropped 120,000 votes, or 4 per cent, though still heading the poll with 1,720,000 votes. The great question was where the votes cast for the four least successful candidates would go in the second ballot, and the result of 27 May was a great surprise, for it showed that in addition to the communist vote, which may be considered to have gone wholly to him, Körner also received half the votes given to Breitner in the first ballot. Thus Austria's first post-war President, Karl Renner, was succeeded by another socialist without a change in the party-political balance in the country, and it was not even necessary to reconstruct the government still headed by Leopold Figl, of the People's Party.

Although under the Austrian constitution a President is not a very powerful figure in normal times, a good deal of prestige attaches to his office, and in a political crisis his advice cannot be disregarded, as events were soon to show.

Altogether eleven parties and organizations contested the elections of 1953, though only five of them nominated candidates in all the twenty-five electoral districts, others, such as the Slovene Christian Democrats and the monarchists, who fought in Carinthia, or the Patriotic Union, which contested two districts in Vienna, admitting their purely local or insufficient strength. However, only four parties succeeded in gaining parliamentary representation, the same as in the last general election of 1949, except that this time the Union of Independents had formed a *Wahlpartei* together with several small splinter groups (WDU), while the Communist Party even went beyond the 'Left Bloc' camouflage of the 1949 election and formed an electoral alliance called the People's Opposition (VO) together with Professor Dobretzberger, a Catholic fellow-traveller and former Schuschnigg Minister, and a sect of dissident Socialists. Compared with 1949 the electorate was larger by almost 200,000, so that to hold its own each party had to show an increase of 4½ per cent. The results as compared with those of 1949 can be seen from the following table.

Austrian General Election Results, 1953

Party	Votes obtained 1953	Compared with 1949	Percentage of total vote		Seats in Parliament
			1953	1949	
Socialist	1,819,000	+ 195,000	42·1	38·7	73 (+ 6)
People's	1,780,000	− 64,000	41·3	44	74 (− 3)
WDU	473,000	− 16,000	11	11·7	14 (− 2)
VO	228,000	+ 3,000	5·3	5·4	4 (− 1)

The Socialists thus increased their vote by about 12 per cent, as against a loss of 3½ per cent each for the People's Party and the Independents, and became the strongest party in the country, if not in Parliament, where the conservatives still maintained their lead. As for the Communists, the acquisition of Dobretzberger did not yield the 12,000 votes his 'Democratic Union' polled in 1949; their increase was under 1½ per cent. Lastly, the seven splinter groups between them polled some 15,000 votes. Approximately 96 per cent of the electorate voted.

If figures have any meaning at all, these results could only be interpreted as a clear mandate for the coalition parties to continue along the path of compromise and co-operation, but with greater regard for the interests of the economically weaker sections of the population. However, the People's Party proved to be poor losers: powerful industrial and financial interests combined to remove the conciliatory Figl and replace him with Julius Raab, a much tougher man, for the purpose of creating an 'anti-Marxist' majority in the cabinet by including the WDU in the coalition, on the grounds that the combined People's Party and Independent vote showed a majority of a quarter of a million over the combined Left vote. Since the Socialists refused to co-operate with the WDU, the danger of an anti-socialist bourgeois bloc government as in the First Republic was great, but eventually, and with the strong backing of the President, wiser counsels prevailed and a new conservative–socialist coalition government was formed. The only tangible gains for the Socialists following their success at the polls were two new under-secretaryships in the government, one of them Bruno Kreisky's in Foreign Affairs; and it was substantially this team which negotiated, and obtained, the State Treaty in 1955.

We have considered two basic assumptions underlying the State Treaty and without which there could have been no treaty: Austria's readiness to adopt a statute of permanent neutrality (not mentioned in the treaty in order to stress the voluntary nature of that step), and agreement among the Allies about reparations and German assets. But there are other parts of the treaty which are worth looking at, for a better appreciation of Austria's standing in international law and of the commitments she has voluntarily entered into.

Critics might in fact contend that the treaty as a whole was backward-looking in that it reaffirmed the principal aims of the Treaty of St Germain (the ban on the *Anschluss*, the establishment of democratic institutions based on universal human rights and the specific rights of national and religious minorities, and the guarantee of the frontiers of the First Republic). They could add that the Allied recognition of Austria 'as a sovereign, independent, and democratic State' (Art. 1) was invalidated by the very same ban on the *Anschluss* (Art. 4), the provisions on the 'Rights of the Slovene and Croat Minorities' (Art. 7), and on the 'Dissolution of Nazi Organizations' (Art. 9) together with a 'Prohibition of Service in the Austrian Armed Forces of Former Members of Nazi Organizations' (Art. 12); they could even object to the continuing ban on the restoration of the House of Habsburg-Lorraine (Art 10.2), for all these are surely issues which a sovereign state must be free to decide for itself? But these are academic questions. The State Treaty was not intended as a blueprint for an ideal democratic society, but as a pragmatic basis for immediate action in the interests of peace and stability as the Allies saw them; and since the overwhelming majority of Austrians agreed with these limitations on their freedom of action, there simply is no case to answer.

Chapter 10

The Second Republic Today

TECHNICALLY THE SECOND REPUBLIC came into being on 27 April 1945, but Austrians like to distinguish between the occupation régime and the time since the State Treaty was signed on 15 May 1955, when they at last were masters in their own house. But there was no break in continuity: Austrian politics still moved along the lines determined by the party leaders after liberation; economically she still participates in the prosperity common to the Western world; and in the field of foreign relations her neutrality has proved neither onerous nor embarrassing. A quarter-century after her resurrection Austria is still totally unlike the creation of St Germain; it is as if History had been given another chance and had designed the Second Republic in such a way as to make amends for the uncertainty and misery of the First. And yet – and inevitably – time is not standing still, and in the period under review several new problems and developments have shaken Austrians out of their conservatism where their political institutions are concerned, and their facile assumption that economic progress could be assured by a policy of muddling along. The ending of government-by-coalition in 1966 and the experience of four years of one-party government have led to a revaluation of Parliament and plans for the overhaul of democratic processes, while increased concern about the competitiveness of the Austrian economy, particularly *vis-à-vis* the Common Market, paid a high dividend in the elections of 1970 to the party which claimed to stand for modernization. No change, however, seems needed in foreign policy where relations with East and West continue satisfactory, and this in spite of the courageous interpretation of Austria's obligations at the time of the Hungarian Revolution in 1956 and the Czech troubles in 1968. In the following pages we shall deal, in turn, with political and economic developments and problems at home, and with Austria's standing abroad.

Government and Politics

In the fifteen years since the last Allied soldier left the country Austria has had five general elections and two presidential elections;

whereas the latter were due to the deaths of the incumbents, in the case of the former it was increasing difficulties, mainly over economic policy, which caused two premature dissolutions. It may be a sign of growing confidence that even during the election campaign of 1970 an extension of the life-span of Parliament, from four to five years, has been discussed.

The general election of 1956 was conducted in an atmosphere similar to the one prevailing in 1945: defensive rather than offensive, averse to drastic measures and social upheaval, and once more the People's Party benefited from it, although it just missed an overall parliamentary majority by one seat.

The General Election of 1956

Party	Votes	Percentage gain or loss since 1953	Seats	Gain or loss since 1953
People's	2,000,068	+ 11·00	82	+ 8
Socialist	1,873,250	+ 2·85	74	+ 1
Freedom	283,713	− 40·00	6	− 8
Communist	192,432	− 15·66	3	− 1

On the face of it these results can be read as illustration of the trend towards the two-party system, for although the Freedom Party (the former WDU) made a short-lived recovery in 1959, it has been declining ever since, while the decline of the Communist Party (even with its 'Left Socialist' appendix) has gone on without a break. Another feature of this election was the emergence of the floating voter. The approximately 200,000 WDU-voters who had given their support to the ÖVP this time could not be counted on as regular voters, for when President Körner died in January 1957, it was the Socialist Party chairman and Vice-Chancellor in the Raab cabinet, Dr Adolf Schärf, who made the running in the presidential elections of May 1957 with 2·26 million votes against 2·16 million for the combined ÖVP-FPÖ candidate Dr Denk. The theory then was that Austrians instinctively preferred the highest offices neatly balanced – a 'red' President when there is a 'black' Chancellor, and presumably vice versa. (It did not work out in 1970, when the Socialists gained the Chancellorship as well; and it seems unlikely that the electorate will replace the popular President Jonas when he comes up for re-election, after a six-year term, in 1971.) The incumbent always enjoys additional advantages, for when Schärf was renominated for a second term, in 1963, he faced the very popular (though ailing) ex-Chancellor Julius Raab. Although the FPÖ refrained from nominating a candidate and advised its supporters to return blank ballot-papers, and there was only one other candidate, of the short-lived European Federalist Party, who polled 4 per cent of the vote, Schärf was re-elected with 55 per cent of the total vote against 41 per cent for Raab.

The relative failure of the Socialists in the 1956 elections caused them to rethink their role in Austrian society, resulting in a new statement of principles, and to undertake certain reforms in the party machine. Thus when Chancellor Raab sprang a surprise election on them in 1959, they were well prepared, and this time the swing of the pendulum went their way.

The General Election of 1959

Party	Votes	Percentage gain or loss since 1956	Seats	Gain or loss since 1956
People's	1,927,600	− 3·6	79	− 3
Socialist	1,953,566	+ 4·1	78	+ 4
Freedom	335,949	+ 15·5	8	+ 2
Communist	142,598	− 25·9	–	− 3

Against the solidity of the two major parties, the high fluctuations among the opposition are worthy of note. A 15 per cent increase for the Freedom Party would seem ominous if it meant a solidly (or even overwhelmingly) Neo-Nazi vote, which of course it did not; it was in large measure a protest vote against the huge party machines and as such unreliable from one election to the next. The Communists' failure to maintain their parliamentary representation was the price they paid for their support of the Soviet suppression of the Hungarian rising. The Socialists, once again – as in 1953 – emerging as the strongest party in the country, were still one seat behind the People's Party in Parliament as a result of an electoral system which distributes seats among the *Wahlkreisverbände*, or groups of constituencies, not on the basis of the number of electors, but on population, thus favouring rural areas with larger families over urban constituencies. Nevertheless, as the losers of this election, the conservatives had to abandon any plans they might have had of forming a coalition with the Freedom Party against the Socialists; the new coalition, on the contrary, saw a strengthening of the socialist element in that Dr Bruno Kreisky, who since 1953 had been Foreign Under-Secretary, was now appointed Foreign Minister and his office, for nearly forty years a department of the Chancellery, was again raised to the status of an independent Ministry.

What no one could foresee at the time, however, was that this would be the last success of the Socialists for about ten years and

that they were in fact facing a critical period in their history. True
enough, they also won the presidential elections of 1965 after the
death of Schärf, when Franz Jonas, mayor of Vienna, succeeded by
the very narrow margin of 1·38 per cent, or 65,000 votes, against
the People's Party's ex-Chancellor Dr Gorbach. (Since the Freedom
Party had not put up a candidate, the result proved once again that
parts of the national liberal camp will rather vote 'red' than 'black'.)
But the Socialist Party's weakness was only in part due to their own
uncertainty about their function in a mixed economy, which forced
them to be simultaneously government and opposition in all questions involving social policy. Nor is it true to say that it was the
'conflict of generations', with younger men pushing up and being
held in check by old machine-politicians; but it is undoubtedly true
that the machine needed shaking up, as the example of Franz Olah
was to prove before long. Since the parliamentary elections of 1962
and 1966 showed the same trend, we can consider them together.

The General Election of 1962

	Votes 1962 (in thousands)	compared with 1959	Seats	compared with 1959
ÖVP	2025	+ 98	81	+ 2
SPÖ	1961	+ 8	76	− 2
FPÖ	315	− 21	8	no change
KPÖ	135	− 7	0	no change

The General Election of 1966

	Votes 1966 (in thousands)	compared with 1962	Seats	compared with 1962
ÖVP	2191	+ 166	85	+ 4
SPÖ	1929	− 32	74	− 2
FPÖ	149	− 166	6	− 2
KPÖ	19	− 116	0	no change

On both occasions the People's Party benefited from its record
as Austria's leading party since 1945, the quality of its leadership,
its image as the party of cautious progress and no experiments. The
Freedom Party suffered from the fact that parliamentary procedure
makes it very difficult for a small party to make an impact on the
country, from the very mixed qualities of its leadership, and finally

because in the battle of the giants it seemed an irrelevancy. The drop in the communist vote in 1966 was not due to complete extinction of this particular species but to a belated 'united-front' gesture: apart from one *Wahlkreis*, where they felt fairly confident and put up the party's secretary-general, Franz Muhri, they advised their supporters to vote the socialist ticket. Instead of rejecting this offer – a kiss of death in a country remembering ten years of Soviet occupation – the Socialist Party accepted it, albeit without offering any *quid pro quo*. This was one reason for their electoral débâcle, for their opponents did not hesitate to make political capital out of this temporary comradeship.

But far more serious was the case of Franz Olah, chairman of the Austrian Federation of Trade Unions, member of the Socialist Party's executive, and Minister of the Interior at the time of his fall. A man with a good record as a resistance fighter, prisoner of the Nazis for seven years, and of working-class origin, which accounted for his popularity in the trade unions, he had succeeded in building for himself a position of personal power and developing a style of politics which was authoritarian and quite unlike anything which Austrian socialism had ever known. The weakness of inner-party democracy, the breakdown of communications between the leadership and the rank-and-file, and even lack of vigilance at the top made it possible for this Perón-like politician to shake the party in its very foundations. Even his removal could only be achieved in stages: he was relieved of his functions in the trade unions for circumventing the control machinery in the spending of union funds, withdrawn from the government, expelled from the party and his union, and finally sued for misappropriation of funds, on which a court found him guilty. A man of ambition, Olah did not retire into private life, but representing himself as an anti-communist patriot persecuted by crypto-communist rivals in the leadership, founded his own 'Democratic-Progressive Party' (*Demokratisch-Fortschrittliche Partei*, DFP) which in 1966 collected some 150,000 votes, mostly, it may be assumed, at the expense of the Socialist Party.

With the Socialist Party in complete disarray both in its own organization and in the image it presented to the country, the People's Party was free to use its overall majority in Parliament as it pleased. Yet, and this is significant for the hold the coalition had on the public, it offered to take the Socialists into a coalition on terms which the latter were unable to accept. Thus twenty-one years of government by coalition came to an end, and Chancellor Dr Josef Klaus was the first conservative leader in Austria after 1945 to form a purely conservative administration. This, a normal event in most other countries, seemed revolutionary in Austria, and while some

may have feared a revival of the bourgeois bloc policies of a Seipel
or Dollfuss, others celebrated the decision as the coming-of-age of
Austrian democracy. In actual fact, very little changed. Government
in Austria is an elaborate business, and what goes on in Parliament
and in the Cabinet Room is but the tip of an iceberg; the prepara-
tory work is all done in consultation with interested parties – capital
and labour, producers and consumers, organized in chambers,
leagues, unions, and federations. As it turned out, single-party
government under Klaus was no better and no worse than most of
its coalition predecessors, and the political observers who maintained that after this experience Austrian politics would never be
the same again came in for a considerable shock when the results of
the 1970 elections were declared. Not only had the electorate failed
to give Klaus the absolute majority which he had made the condition for continuing in office, it had also, in spite of its alleged dis-
taste for coalitions, made the two parties so nearly equal that it is
difficult to see how the country could be governed without one; and
lastly it had given the Socialists a clear, if modest, lead over their
rivals.

The Election of 1970

A lot has been made of the changes in personnel, policy, and image
which have helped the Socialist Party to win this election.[1] In
Kreisky the party has undoubtedly found an attractive and intelligent leader (he spent the war years in exile in Sweden), who as a
former Foreign Minister has had experience of office and knows
the world. It is said of him that he aims at turning the old type of
workers' party into a progressive, left-of-centre people's party, open
above all to the new managerial and technical intelligentsia to
whom democratic planning and modernizing the country would
hold a special appeal. To prepare for the elections, teams of experts
in various fields, 1,400 in all, prepared detailed programmes for
economic, technological, educational, and social reform, and the
campaign itself, largely a one-man show, owed more to American
presidential elections than to traditional methods, and heavy bor-
rowings from modern election tactics abroad – like artists and
scholars, jet pilots and actors, declaring for Kreisky – have stressed
the unorthodox and experimental approach. The People's Party was
clearly caught napping, and even though in the end it, too, produced its programmes for the seventies and arranged pop sessions
for young voters, the initiative remained with the Socialists. What
made these elections so remarkable, though, was the serious tone of

[1] For an interesting analysis cf. F. Parkinson, 'Austrian Socialism Today'
(Home and Foreign Policy) in *The World Today* (March–April 1964).

the argument, the lack of personal invective, and the general feeling that, whatever the outcome, both sides could be trusted to observe democratic rules – not a small thing in a country which has experienced civil war and dictatorship in the recent past.

The General Election of 1970

Party	Votes	Gain or Loss since 1966	Seats	Gain or Loss since 1966
People's	2,078,010	− 113,099	79	− 6
Socialist	2,235,905	+ 306,920	81	+ 7
Freedom	254,363	+ 11,793	5	− 1
Communist	45,689	+ 28,053	—	—
Democratic-Progressive	17,405	− 131,123	—	—
National Democratic	3,484	+ 3,484	—	—

(For further details see below pp. 295–6.)

In a country known for the relatively stable electoral behaviour of the population even a shift of around 6 per cent has the effect of a political landslide, especially when it leads to the first socialist Chancellor in the history of the republic (apart from Renner, appointed in the extraordinary circumstances of 1918 and 1945). The elections have again confirmed the movement towards a two-party system first noted by Charles A. Gulick, that wise observer of Austrian politics from Berkeley, as a 'trend or long-term drift', if we mean by it that (i) not more than two parties at any given time have a chance to gain power; that (ii) one of them gains a majority and stays in office without help from a third party; and that (iii) over a period of time two parties alternate in power.[2] Austria has only reached the first stage in this process: the elimination of the smaller parties as a serious political force. A glance at election statistics since 1949 shows that in the course of these twenty-one years the percentage of the total vote gained by all the smaller parties together has shrunk from 17·3 to 6·9 per cent, while the combined conservative–socialist vote has increased from 82·7 to 91·3 per cent. This may or may not be a good thing, but in practice it means that Austrians increasingly have only one choice open to them: the choice between conservatism and socialism, whatever these terms may mean today, and in the foreseeable future.

Apart from the general trend, the small parties are also hampered by the electoral law which stipulates that a party must have

[2] Charles A. Gulick, 'Austria's Socialists in the Trend toward a two-party System: An Interpretation of Postwar Elections', *The Western Political Quarterly*, XI/3 (September 1958), pp. 539–62.

gained a 'basic seat' (*Grundmandat*) in any one of the multi-member constituencies before its total vote is taken into account – a significant modification of the assumed equality of votes in proportional representation. Without this stipulation the Communists, with a little luck, should have gained two seats, and the FPÖ even ten. Another feature of the present arrangement of 'grouped constituencies' (*Wahlkreisverband*), each of which contains one or more federal provinces, has already been mentioned: the weighting in favour of large-family rural areas against small-family urban areas, which in 1953 and 1959 resulted in parliamentary majorities for the ÖVP on a minority of votes. This time it again disadvantaged the Socialists who, for the same percentage of the total vote that secured the conservatives 85 seats and the absolute majority in a house of 165 members in 1966, received only 81 seats. It will not surprise anyone if electoral reform will rank fairly high on Kreisky's list of priorities.

Detailed analysis of the election results has revealed that the 'new look' of the Socialist Party – efficient, modern, no longer at war with the Church or orientated exclusively towards the industrial working class – has enabled the party not merely to appeal to the young voters, but also to penetrate into the professions, the better-off middle classes, and even into the farming community. Already in possession of three governorships (*Landeshauptmann*), of the federal provinces of Vienna, Burgenland, and Carinthia, the Socialists would have won Upper Austria and Styria as well if these had been *Land* elections instead of parliamentary elections, and practically drew even with the People's Party in *Land* Salzburg. Even in the last remaining conservative strongholds they reduced their opponents' lead from 40 to 23 per cent in Vorarlberg, from 33 to 21 per cent in Tyrol, and from 13 to 4·5 per cent in Lower Austria. What these new conquests and opportunities will do to the *socialist* nature of the party is anybody's guess, and the Austro-Marxist spokesmen are already raising their voices as the guardians of the party's conscience against abandoning socialist principles; facile talk about emulating the British Labour Party or about an Austrian version of 'Scandinavian Socialism' is countered with references to the ideological and organizational state the German Social Democratic Party is said to be in. It is an open secret that in this debate the provinces – pragmatic, unconcerned with theory – are making a stand against the party in Vienna, inheritors of a proud 'red' tradition, against the ideologues and the old party machine, and they believe that Kreisky is their man. The demotion of Dr Pittermann, former Vice-Chancellor and chairman of the parliamentary party, and the advancement of numbers of intelligent young technocrats to party and parliamentary offices, would seem to be the first moves in this direction.

If the Socialists still have to sort out relationships between party and trade union leaders, between Vienna and the provinces, and between 'traditionalists' and 'modernizers', the People's Party, too, has its internal difficulties. Organized as a federation of three vocational groups, the *Bauernbund* (Farmers' Federation), the *Wirtschaftsbund* (Employers' and Trades People's Federation), and the *Arbeiter- und Angestelltenbund* (Workers' and Employees' Federation), the party has reflected the weight and influence of a particular group at any given time: while the farming element was perhaps most influential at the time of Leopold Figl, and the business community in the Raab era, it would seem to be the turn of the ÖAAB now, which not only looks back on the traditions of Christian Socialism, but is the only section of the party given to serious thinking about the future. Although technically in competition with the Socialists, for working-class votes and members, many years of co-operation with the SPÖ in the (supra-party) trade unions, the Chambers of Labour, and the elaborate system of consultation and conciliation machinery have created an atmosphere of respect and trust. Not surprisingly, the ÖAAB was less than enthusiastic about single-party government under Klaus, and would have welcomed a return to a 'grand coalition' now.

The Freedom Party went into the elections under singularly inept leadership: by promising to oppose a 'red' Chancellor and to join a coalition with the ÖVP only, they had not only misjudged the temper of the electorate, but also revealed themselves as just another right-wing party. The result was a policy unconvincing to conservatively inclined people, who could see no reason for not voting ÖVP straightaway, and unattractive to voters keen on social issues, who for lack of an alternative voted SPÖ. Thus the FPÖ vote can be assumed to represent the hard core of the survivors of the old nationalist, anti-clerical, and anti-socialist camp, sufficiently 'national' for the respectable ex-Nazi, but not radical enough for the extreme lunatic fringe which found its home in the National Democratic Party, a replica of the neo-Nazi NPD in West Germany, which was only able to put up candidates in eight constituencies out of twenty-five.

Franz Olah's DFP, which stood in twenty constituencies, was almost literally wiped out, losing nine in every ten of its 1966 supporters. From the start it had been a one-man show – it was significant, for instance, that even at the time of Olah's expulsion not a single branch of the SPÖ or of the ÖGB declared for him; all he collected was a group of disappointed local officials and a good deal of diffused but unorganized opposition to socialist leadership. His subsequent contacts with monarchist and neo-Nazi groups, and his conviction for fraud, may well have led most of the original protest vote back into the socialist camp. But quite apart from his personal shortcomings and the lack of a plausible policy, Austrians have probably lost all taste for a 'Führer' and prefer parties that fit into the existing scheme.

Lastly the Communist Party, whose apparent increase in votes was due to there being candidates in all twenty-five constituencies instead of only one as in 1966. Its decline is irreversible: Soviet policy in Czechoslovakia not only brought to a head the smouldering discontent in the membership, it also led to the expulsion of Ernst Fischer, noted author and critic and one-time Minister of Education, and to numerous resignations from the Central Committee and other party offices. Together with the loss in recent provincial elections of its last two members of *Landtage* (or provincial legislatures), one in Carinthia and one in Styria, it has reached rock bottom, and with its policy of uncritical support of Soviet policy (as for instance over Israel) it is difficult to see how it is ever going to be accepted as a *genuinely Austrian party*. While individual Communists, especially in the trade unions or as shop stewards, may still be respected – and re-elected – as spokesmen of working-class discontent, the KPÖ has ceased to be a political force, and the aggressively anti-communist 'Declaration of Eisenstadt', issued by the Socialists before the elections, has destroyed all hopes of a united front on the Left.[3]

Contrary to expectations, the outcome of the negotiations between the two major parties was not another 'grand coalition' but a socialist minority government. Whether this was due to the ÖVP refusing to acknowledge defeat and demanding parity with the SPÖ, or to victory at the polls having gone to the heads of the Socialists who were eager to show what a purely socialist administration could do, it will be no easy time for Kreisky, faced as he is with an anti-socialist majority of three (84 : 81) in Parliament. Quite properly the Federal President refused to go against the trend revealed in the elections by calling upon the losers – ÖVP and FPÖ – to form a government; and a 'red–blue' small coalition was out of the question because of the FPÖ's pre-election pledges.

The new administration will therefore have to act very circumspectly if it is to avoid a series of parliamentary defeats, and Kreisky's declared intention is to find the necessary majorities as he

[3] For a useful survey of the historical development and the programmes of Austria's political parties cf. Klaus Berchtold, *Österreichische Parteiprogramme 1868–1966* (Vienna, 1967).

goes along – sometimes from the ranks of the ÖVP and at other times (and more probably) from the FPÖ. He is in a good position tactically, for the country will not welcome another election very soon, and if a charge of obstruction can be brought against his opponents to add to their present disarray it will improve his party's electoral prospects.

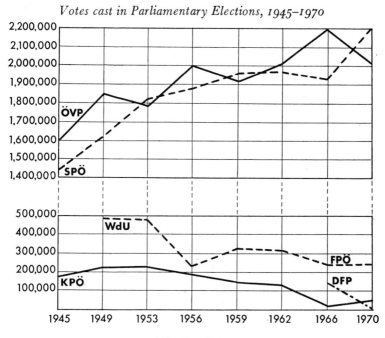

Votes cast in Parliamentary Elections, 1945–1970

The Parties:

ÖVP – *Österreichische Volkspartei* (conservative)
SPÖ – *Sozialistiche Partei Österreichs* (socialist)
KPÖ – *Kommunistische Partei Österreichs* (communist)
WdU – *Wahlverband der Unabhängigen* (national liberal), later re-constituted as:
FPÖ – *Freiheitliche Partei Österreichs*
DFP – *Demokratisch-Fortschrittliche Partei* (Franz Olah)

N.B. – In 1966 Franz Olah, former socialist Minister and trade union leader, who had been expelled from the party, formed his own DFP, thus contributing to the weakening of the SPÖ and (indirectly) to the end of government by coalition. Also in 1966, the KPÖ contested only one constituency and recommended its supporters elsewhere to vote SPÖ.

Seats obtained in Parliamentary Elections, 1945–1970

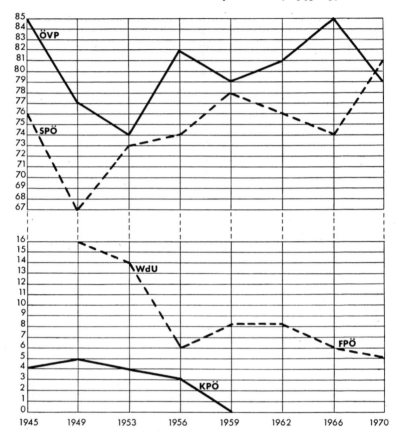

But government and politics in Austria are by no means the exclusive concern of Parliament and political parties; we have here yet a third layer of policy-making consultative institutions established by law and with compulsory membership for all professional and vocational groups, the so-called 'Chambers'; and because there is nothing like it in other advanced countries, and they are a key element in the Austrian political system, a closer examination is called for.

'Chambers' and other 'Organized Interests'

As early as the 1840s, in the first wave of industrialization, the need was felt for the government to have the advice of the growing body of entrepreneurs and traders, to deal with them as a group and issue regulations accordingly. Therefore, the 'Chambers of Commerce and Industry' were established by law in 1848, both to represent the interests of their members and to serve the public interest. Together with a steady increase in their rights and duties came the privilege of representation in the *Reichsrat* or Parliament, and the system worked so well that it was taken over by the republic, which divided these chambers into four sections: commerce, trade, industry and finances, and transport. But now there was a significant addition: the representatives of organized labour also wanted an institution with the statutory right 'to give expert opinion on draft legislation concerning economic and social questions, and to make proposals for changes', and in consequence the 'Chambers of Labour' were set up. After the war, the Second Republic immediately restored both types of institution – those representing economic interests, like the Chambers of Commerce, or of Agriculture, and those representing individuals, like the Chambers of Labour, of Lawyers, of Physicians, etc.

In spite of the statutory nature of these Chambers, membership of which is compulsory, they are independent bodies. The government only sees to it that the Chambers keep within the law; it has no right to give directives to them. The Chambers have two main fields of activity: autonomous functions, which comprise all those activities which concern the common economic interest of their members; this includes giving expert opinions on parliamentary bills and advising Parliament and governmental authorities on practically all matters touching interests of the business community; and delegated functions: in a number of cases the Chambers have the legal authorization to assist in fulfilling or even to fulfil tasks which are normally done by public authorities. This helps the latter in performing their tasks and also guarantees that such matters are dealt with in a way that ensures that public interests are duly taken into account.

In the case of the Economic Chambers this means that in certain functions they are supervised by the Ministry of Trade and Industry, that they are responsible for examinations and the granting of diplomas, and that they – and not the Ministry – maintain a network of foreign trade representatives in about eighty foreign cities.

There are nine regional Economic Chambers, one in each of the federal provinces, as well as a Federal Chamber with co-ordinating, national, and international functions. Total membership approaches 290,000 and divides on occupational lines into six sections: small-scale production, industry, commerce, finance with credit and insurance, transport, and tourism, many of their subdivisions going

right back to medieval guilds, corporations, and 'brotherhoods'.
Every five years each of these Chambers elects its own officials; not
surprisingly, the ÖVP 'Economic Association' secured nearly 85 per
cent of these offices in the last elections, while the SPÖ 'Free Economic Association' obtained just under 9 per cent.

As the counterpart of the Economic Chambers the Chambers of
Labour look after the interests of manual and non-manual employees, and the question can legitimately be asked what difference
there is between them and the trade unions; especially in view of the
fact that practically all officials and 'councillors' of these Chambers
are trade unionists. The answer is obviously the difference between
the statutory body which is consulted by government, examines
impending legislation and proposes new legislation, and has access
to Ministries and authorities, and voluntary associations like the
labour unions which jealously guard their independence and must
be prepared to use their strength, if need be, even against a government. Thus the Chamber of Labour is not a substitute for free trade
unions, but an extremely useful complement, leaving questions of
wages and conditions to the unions, which of course do all the
'collective bargaining', and concentrating on economic policy as a
whole. Its well-staffed departments for social policy, economic
science and labour law, for the protection of young workers, consumers, and employees in trouble over social insurance benefits,
engage in research, observation of the working of legislation, advisory work, and publication, as well as being extremely active in
educational work of both a vocational and a liberal kind.

Like their counterparts on the employers' side, the Chambers of
Labour are self-governing institutions in each of the nine provinces,
although the Vienna Chamber acts as their centre, and every five
years 'councillors' are elected for each Chamber, the number depending on the strength of the labour force in a province. Of the
total of 810 'councillors' at the 1969 elections, the Socialists obtained 560 or 68 per cent, the ÖVP Workers' Association 23·5 per
cent, the Communists 2·6 per cent, the FPÖ 5 per cent, and non-
party lists under one per cent. It may, of course, be argued that
there is no good reason (except tradition) for having party lists in
these elections at all; on the other hand, the better organized (and
the more successful at elections) socialist or Christian workers'
groups are, the greater the pressure they can bring to bear on the
SPÖ or the ÖVP for specific working-class demands. Apart from this
consideration there is little else to justify the procedure (for in the
representation of the interests of their constituents, 'councillors' and
shop stewards of all groups are very much alike) – except possibly
the desire 'to show the flag' or to test their party's popularity.

This applies with even greater justification to the election of shop stewards under the Factory Councils Act, in which the Austrian Federation of Trade Unions (ÖGB) is more prominently involved. It is no exaggeration to say that of all the *Interessenverbände* or 'organized interests', the ÖGB is the most important for social (and hence political) peace in the country. After a fairly late start in the 1870s, due to repressive legislation, Austrian trade unionism developed in close harness with the Social Democratic Party, whose leader, Victor Adler, referred to party and unions as 'Siamese twins'. Neither the German nationalist nor the Christian workers' associations could ever match the strength and effectiveness of the socialist or 'free' unions, and this state of affairs continued in the First Republic until, in 1934, Dollfuss forcibly amalgamated the socialist unions, after the removal of their leaders, with the Christians and founded the 'Unitary Trade Union' (*Einheitsgewerkschaft*), soon to be superseded by the Nazi Labour Front (*Deutsche Arbeitsfront*, DAF) after the *Anschluss*. The lessons of disunity and of totalitarian rule were not lost on the survivors of the old movement, and when a number of them met together, in the last days of the fighting in Vienna in April 1945, they were determined to restart on a non-party basis, and the ÖGB was the result.

Almost two-thirds of Austria's labour force are unionized. They belong to one or the other of the sixteen 'industrial' unions which form the ÖGB, ranging in strength from the 16,000 of the artists and musicians' union to the 280,000 of the metalworkers' and miners' union. Between the four-yearly federal congresses a federal executive of forty-six members nominated by the sixteen constituent unions in proportion to their strength conducts the day-to-day business of the federation, while each union has its own executive to look after its members' interests. In structure the ÖGB comes nearest to the German Trade Union Federation (DGB), though the Austrian federal executive enjoys far greater powers. Politics, inevitably, pervades the union movement in the sense that there is rivalry for union offices between the four recognized political groupings – socialist, Christian, communist, and non-party; and the Socialists hold the lion's share of such offices, though care is taken to have the smaller groups represented on executives and similar bodies if only because of the greater effectiveness of unanimous decisions – or at least of agreement between Socialists and Christians. This is important for the two main concerns of the trade union movement: collective bargaining and pressure for improved social legislation.

All wages in private undertakings and in the nationalized industries are regulated by thousands of collective agreements. They are negotiated by the trade unions – often on an industry-wide basis –

with the appropriate employers' organizations. Besides wages, the collective agreements regulate also such working conditions which are not already regulated by the extensive provisions of Austrian social legislation. Most Austrian collective agreements are valid not only for single companies, but for whole industries. It is up to the shop stewards in a company to negotiate for additional company benefits. Collective agreements are in most cases concluded for an indeterminate period, with a period of notice of two or three months. At present a collective agreement operates – until notice is given – for an average of about eighteen months.

Social legislation in Austria is well developed. An important part is the comprehensive system of social insurance. All earners of wages or salaries are insured in cases of sickness, accidents at work, unemployment, and old age (pension). In all branches of social insurance the insurance premiums are paid jointly (50 :50) by employers and employees; only the premiums for accident insurance are paid in full by employers. Holidays with pay for workers and salaried personnel are regulated by law. The minimum vacation is eighteen workdays a year and rises after longer employment up to thirty workdays. Special protective regulations exist for young working people below the age of eighteen years (prevention of piecework and night-work), for expectant mothers, and a number of hazardous occupations. The working week now stands at forty-three hours, to be reduced within the next four years to forty hours. The result of this kind of effective bargaining is a high degree of industrial peace: in 1967, for instance, the time lost in strikes per employed person was two minutes, compared with 6 in West Germany, 55 in the United Kingdom, 102 in France, and 2,040 in Italy!

But however satisfied the unions may be with their achievements, they are nevertheless very worried about the long-term economic problems of the country.

The Economic Situation

On the face of it, Austria's economic position and prospects seem satisfactory. The structural changes brought about, first by the requirements of the German war economy, and then by the general reorientation made possible by the European Recovery Programme, can leave no doubt as to the country's economic viability. According to the March 1970 Report of the Austrian Institute of Economic Research, 1969 had been the most successful year since the onset of the western European recession in 1965, with the gross national product rising, in real terms, by 6·4 per cent. Unlike 1960 and 1964, this result was based not on the domestic boom but largely on exports, and on an industrial expansion almost double that of the economy as a whole. While this is satisfactory as far as it goes, it nevertheless pinpoints the basic problem: the exposure of an economy operating on a very narrow margin to fluctuations in the world economy. Thus the lean years of 1965 to 1967 reflected not only internal movements (such as the change from coal to other sources of energy), but even more the contracting market for Austrian goods abroad and increased competition from lower-priced imports in several fields where whole sectors of industry were unable to compete owing to structural weaknesses. The industrial growth-rate, which had stood at 7·8 per cent in 1964, dropped to 3·7, 3, and eventually even 2 per cent, until a slow recovery set in again in 1968. That the Austrian economy should be especially vulnerable is inevitable, but the question is whether all is being done to maintain the country's competitive position *vis-à-vis* the outside world. While the trade unions attempt to secure for the working population a fair share of the national cake, both in terms of wages and social benefits, they have so far seemed unable to convince a succession of conservative Ministers of Finance that their main concern should be the provision of means for structural improvements. Increased pressure from Austria's trading partners – especially the Common Market countries – and the likelihood of a form of association with the EEC in the near future – make this a matter of some urgency.

Nevertheless, after the recession had been overcome the Austrian economy showed signs of an improvement which is still being maintained. In the first stages of the upswing, foreign demand for Austrian products – particularly from West Germany – proved to be the motor of the economy. On this domestic scene inventory replenishment contributed to this movement, but local demand for finished goods recorded only about the same growth-rate as in 1967. Virtually all sectors of the economy participated in the expansion, which led to a rise in imports while maintaining the export boom.[4]

For many years industry and construction have played a leading role in the Austrian economy. In 1968 these two sectors accounted together for about 47 per cent of the gross national product, virtually unchanged from 1964. Industry alone contributed in the former year around 36·5 per cent to the GNP. During the same 1964–68 period commercial activity increased in relative importance and today it accounts for 13·7 per cent of the gross national product. The growth of the public services sector is reflected in the rise of its share in the grand total from 9·3 per cent in 1964 to 11 per cent

[4] Bankers Trust Company, London, *A Survey of the Economy of Austria* (London, autumn 1969), from which the following data are taken.

in 1968. Agriculture and forestry is the only branch of the economy that has stagnated, resulting in a drop of its contribution to the GNP from 9·4 per cent in 1964 to 7·1 per cent in 1968.

The gross national product by sectors of origin
(in millions of U.S.$)

	1968
Agriculture and Forestry	804
Industry	4,138
Construction	1,146
Electricity, etc.	319
Transport	700
Commerce	1,554
Banks, Insurance, etc.	581
Public Services	1,246
Other Services	861
Total	11,349

This trend is also illustrated in the distribution of the labour force over the various sectors:

Percentage distribution of the labour force over the sectors of employment:

	1961	1968
Agriculture and Forestry	22·8	19·5
Manufacturing and Industry	46·5	45·6
Commerce and Transport	16·4	19·6
Liberal professions, domestic service	7·9	8·0
Public services	5·3	5·8

One of the major problems is agriculture. At present, agricultural production covers around 85 per cent of the domestic need for foodstuffs. In 1968, labour productivity in this sector rose by about 3·5 per cent, while at the same time the number of persons employed fell. In reaction to a deteriorating price–cost relationship, investment expenditure in agriculture declined in 1968 by about 14 per cent. With regard to the forestry sector, gross revenue is estimated to have decreased by 7 per cent. Agriculture still ranks high, however, among the sources of national wealth:

Gross value of the production of selected Austrian industries
(in millions of U.S.$)

	% change 1965–1968
Foodstuffs	+ 18·6
Chemicals	+ 30·3
Textiles	+ 7·6
Machinery, iron and steel industry	+ 18·3
Iron and metal fabricating industry	+ 1.7
Paper	+ 15·4
Electrical goods	+ 20·0
Petroleum	+ 19·2

The continuing economic expansion has not failed to have its effect on the labour market. During the last few months of 1969 the falling rate of unemployment has consistently moved at a lower level than in the corresponding months of 1968. Unfilled vacancies were reported on the increase while the number of foreign labourers in Austria had risen steadily, amounting for the whole of 1969 (as reported in the press) to nearly 65,000 – the largest number ever employed in Austria. Four out of five of these came from Yugoslavia, and one in eight from Turkey.

As for the nature of Austria's foreign trade, machinery and transport equipment are the two leading import items, accounting in 1968 for about 30 per cent of the total. As a result of the relative decrease in raw-materials imports and the absolute decline in foodstuff imports compared with 1965, chemical goods today hold third place on the list. Since 1965 purchases abroad of electrical machinery and equipment have increased particularly rapidly, viz. by about 36 per cent. Imports of metal goods and petroleum and petroleum products have also shown significant rises.

On the export side, iron and steel is the single most important item, accounting in 1968 for about 12 per cent of the total. Machinery held second place, followed by textile goods. Compared with 1965, chemical exports have shown a very considerable growth, viz. by 65 per cent. During the same 1965–68 period, foreign sales of electrical equipment rose by about 36 per cent, while textile exports also experienced a significant expansion. Of particular significance, however, is the pattern of Austria's foreign trade, which has serious political implications:

The pattern of foreign trade (in percentages)

	1968	
	Exports	*Imports*
Europe	85·00	88·6
European Community	40·3	57·4
(of which W. Germany	23·4	41·4)
EFTA	23·7	18·4
Eastern Europe	14·8	9·8
Other Europe	6·2	3·0
North America	6·0	3·8
Latin America	1·5	2·6
Asia	4·7	2·6
Africa	2·3	2·1
Australia	0·5	0·3

Austria has been a member of the European Free Trade Association since that organization started its operations in 1960. The above table shows, however, that notwithstanding the relative increase in trade with the EFTA partners that this membership has induced, the European Community remains Austria's most important market. The very strong ties with West Germany are particularly noticeable. As Germans form, moreover, by far the largest contingent of foreign tourists, Austria tends to be especially vulnerable to the economic conditions in that country.

The final results for 1969, published in the press in February 1970, have modified this picture only slightly. It was a record year for exports, with a 21·3 per cent increase over 1968, which in view of a relatively modest increase in imports reduced the foreign trade deficit by 18·8 per cent. 85·7 per cent of all exports still went to other European countries and 7·5 per cent to the Americas. Although the greatest expansion took place with EFTA countries, in absolute figures the ratio between the three main blocs is still very much the same:

Austrian trade in 1969 (in percentages)

	Exports	*Imports*
EEC	41·4	56·5
EFTA	24·5	19·5
Eastern Europe	13·5	9·7

Fortunately for Austria, modern mass-tourism just about covers the trade balance: with an average registration of 6 million foreign visitors in Austrian hotels per annum spending some 10,000 million schillings, 85 to 95 per cent of the trading deficit is met. But the attractions of 'wine, women, and song' are an insecure foundation for a country's economy, and critics comment bitterly that unless the necessary structural reforms are undertaken, Austrians will become a nation of waiters and ski-ing teachers. This is becoming ever more urgent as the consolidation of the Common Market system proceeds and Austria will find herself increasingly edged out and her products rendered uncompetitive.

This is the reason why Austria's relationship with the European Community has remained a political issue both inside the country and abroad. We have already commented on the facile optimism of some who believed that Russian opposition to Austrian membership could be overcome once the market authorities were prepared to make some concessions to meet the letter of the State Treaty. According to Alfred Verdross, however, the great majority of writers agree that a permanently neutral state is not allowed under international law to become a full member of EEC, since according to Article 224 the EEC treaty remains in force in time of war. If, therefore, the Council of Ministers of EEC were to decree a unilateral ban on exports in the event of a war in which the member states did or did not take part, Austria would have to comply if she were a full member of the community, thereby violating her duties as a neutral state because – as has been shown – the laws of neutrality forbid a unilateral ban on exports in time of war. If, on the other hand, Austria decreed a bilateral ban on exports she would violate the EEC treaty, which provides for a homogeneous economic area. Moreover, Austria would be paralysing her own foreign trade and jeopardizing her very existence. Hence a permanently neutral state must not accept economic commitments in time of peace which would hinder the fulfilment of its duties in time of war.[5] The Soviet government advanced political arguments in the ensuing debate. On the occasion of a visit to Moscow in October 1959 Kreisky was warned by Gromyko that Austrian membership of the EEC amounted to a violation of her neutrality and would be opposed by the Soviet Union 'with all legal means'. According to Der Spiegel the Soviet Foreign Minister answered Kreisky's question what these 'means' would be with the threat that Russia would conclude no further treaties with Austria, would abstain from all international agreements to which Austria was a party, and might even reconsider the State Treaty of 1955.[6]

Patient explanations that it was merely a form of association and

[5] Verdross, op. cit., pp. 16–17.
[6] 'EWG–Anschluss. Prost', Der Spiegel, 28/1962.

not full membership that was sought may have convinced the Soviet leaders, but they did not stop the flow of notes, *démarches*, and threatening articles in the press.

Following Britain's application for membership in 1961 the Austrian government pursued a line of seeking a 'multilateral' association in concert with Sweden and Switzerland.

The Vienna Conference of Foreign Ministers of Austria, Sweden, and Switzerland held in October 1961 came out in support of an association with the Common Market. It 'confirmed its view that neutrality is no obstacle to association in an acceptable form with the EEC', and Kreisky expressed the hope that the Common Market leaders would meet the neutral states halfway and ensure a form of association that would not infringe their rights and duties. This of course provoked an immediate Soviet warning: association with the EEC was out of the question for Austria because it was but the first step towards an economic *Anschluss*, and for all neutral states because the EEC aimed at a West European confederation under the aegis of the United States.[7] However, de Gaulle's 'no' to Britain brought about the switch to a 'unilateral' solution, which was still rejected by the Russians. The state visit to Moscow of Chancellor Gorbach in June 1962 was in part designed to allay Soviet fears. Khrushchev once again spelled out the reasons for his government's negative attitude:

> We take this attitude because this Community disorganises European trade, declares economic war on other countries and undermines the independence and sovereignty of the small states connected with it, undermines their ability to determine their national policy for themselves.[8]

The conflict spilled over into domestic politics. Whereas the People's Party was favourably inclined towards an organization dominated by men like de Gaulle and Adenauer, many Socialists referred to the Common Market as a capitalist, 'bourgeois' body which threatened to deepen and perpetuate the European split, and obviously preferred the 'pink' EFTA with its strong labour governments and movements. This was where the matter was allowed to rest until the departure of de Gaulle from the French political scene restored a measure of flexibility to the EEC and the arrival of a socialist-led government in West Germany made possible another approach. Renewed negotiations between Austria and the Market authorities starting in December 1969 on the basis of an interim

---

[7] O. Afanasyeva, 'A Threat to Neutrality', *International Affairs* (Moscow), December 1961, pp. 85–6.

[8] *Soviet News* (London), 2 July 1962.

agreement which would provide for a lowering of tariffs up to 40 per cent were interrupted by the change of government in Austria; but there is no reason to assume that Kreisky would depart from the line laid down recently in his party's paper 'that Austria could never become a member of EEC, or at any rate not until EEC had grown into a great *all-European* community, which was only possible after a far-reaching agreement between East and West.'[9]

This article was written in reply to yet another warning from Moscow, where *Pravda* had stated that 'any kind of association' between Austria and the Common Market, which only 'served the hegemonistic interests of German monopoly capital', would violate Article 4 of the State Treaty forbidding every political or economic union between Austria and Germany. And thus we are back to the question of Austrian neutrality.

Neutrality, the U.N., and Foreign Policy

The international position of present-day Austria is characterized by her status as a country which has opted for permanent neutrality and has had this decision accepted by the Great Powers and most other members of the United Nations. Although this course originally met with a certain amount of criticism, which ranged from charges of neutralism and opportunism to accusations of cowardice and desertion, both her experience after 1918 and her position in 1945, under Four-Power occupation on the dividing-line between the Western and communist worlds, made neutrality both desirable and inevitable. After the break-up of the Habsburg Empire the Allied ban on the *Anschluss* meant that in the interests of the new balance in Europe Germany was not to be compensated for her losses elsewhere, and particularly not in the sensitive area of the Danube region. In a way this decision to keep Austria out of a power bloc can be seen as anticipating the idea of neutralizing a state in her geographical position. On the Austrian side, too, the notion of using neutrality as a means of reducing tension was demonstrated by the Tyrolese offer to neutralize their province if this would satisfy Italian security needs and keep the South Tyrol united with the North, while the Vorarlberg vote in favour of union with Switzerland revealed a similar trend.

The subsequent history of the First Republic did little to enhance the status of nominal sovereignty in the eyes of Austrians;[10] and the time after 1945, with the constant danger that inter-Allied conflicts

---

[9] *Arbeiter-Zeitung* (13 March 1970), p. 2.
[10] For early discussions of a neutral status for Austria cf. Gerald Stourzh, 'Zur Geschichte der österreichischen Neutralität', *Österreich in Geschichte und Literatur*, V/6 (June 1961), pp. 273–88.

like the Berlin Blockade and the war in Korea might spread to Austria and bring about a 'German situation', led to an imaginative rethinking of Austria's position and in consequence to the adoption of neutrality. How does this decision appear today, fifteen years afterwards?

No one can tell the extent to which the neutralization of Austria contributed to the momentous events of 1956 in eastern Europe: the troubles in Czechoslovakia, the establishment of the reforming Gomulka régime in Poland, and the revolution in Hungary (which, significantly, aimed at release from the communist bloc and a neutral status similar to Austria's; unfortunately, the Western Powers were too preoccupied with the Suez crisis then to pay much attention). It is far more likely that it was the Twentieth Congress of the CPSU with its denunciation of Stalin and the proclamation of a new, 'liberal', policy which started this movement. But it can be assumed that easier access to a pro-Western if neutralized Austria has contributed to the weakening of monolithic power – and thought processes – among East Europeans, especially in view of the way in which Austria interprets her obligations as a neutral.

Already in May 1955 Kreisky had written:

> We shall have to determine the exact nature of our neutrality. It will be as different from the neutrality of Switzerland and Sweden, and resemble it as much, as the geographical and historical profile of these two states varies from the Austrian or resembles it. After the special nature of its imperial past, and the small-power status of the First Republic, Austria will now have to plan its own type of neutrality.[11]

Since Swedish neutrality is not embodied in the constitution or guaranteed by the powers, but should more probably be called 'freedom from alliances' (*Allianzfreiheit*), the only possible comparison is between Austria and Switzerland, and here Alfred Verdross, the doyen of Austria's international lawyers, has come to the conclusion, after an exhaustive study of the history, theory, and practice of Swiss neutrality, that Austria's commitments correspond exactly to the Swiss model.[12] They include the duty to observe the legal rules of neutrality in all wars between other states; the right and also the duty to defend her territory against external aggression ('permanent neutrality is of necessity armed neutrality'); the duty not to accept obligations which might lead her into a war (such as alliances, or the granting of bases to other states); the right to ask other powers to guarantee her territory; and, finally, complete freedom to organ-

[11] Quoted in Kreisky, *Die Herausforderung*, p. 112.
[12] Verdross, op. cit., pp. 10–21.

ize her internal and foreign policies as far as this would not conflict with the foregoing duties. There is, however, no duty of ideological neutrality, as was established by the Swiss and the Norwegians at the outbreak of the Second World War.

While there is complete agreement on all these points among Austria's politicians, their practical application has on occasion led to controversy, notably in connection with the EEC (the European Common Market), the establishment of a federal army, and the conflict between political freedom and *raison d'état*. There is no argument about the 'duties of abstention' – the supply of war material or the granting of loans to belligerents – or the 'duty of impartiality', should a country's geographical position and economic interests necessitate the continuance of trade with belligerents, as was the case with Switzerland from 1939 to 1945 when she established her trade with both sides on the basis of the average volume in time of peace (the so-called 'principle of the *courant normal*'). It follows, however, that a permanently neutral state cannot under international law become a full member of EEC, since the integrated economy which the Treaty of Rome seeks to establish cannot be dissolved in time of war – and has in fact important political and military implications in the context of western European defence.

Hence, successive Austrian governments have attempted, in common with Switzerland and Sweden, to arrive at a special treaty arrangement with the EEC which would neither violate nor impair neutrality. These moves started in 1962, but have so far been no more successful than Britain's, at one stage being held up by Italy who used her veto to put pressure on Austria over the South Tyrol conflict. From the other side come periodic warnings that the Soviets would consider Austrian membership a violation of the State Treaty and of the neutrality statute, which is undoubtedly a correct view, but since no responsible politician asks for full membership anyway, the threats are only meant to ensure that the 'arrangement' is kept as loose as possible. Internal politics enters the issue only occasionally; to the Freedom Party with its weakness for all things German, the EEC is the next best thing to an *Anschluss*, while Communists and left-wing Socialists see in it an instrument of neo-imperialism. The great mass between feels no emotional attachment to the EEC, but sees it as a (largely successful) concern with which Austria has to come to satisfactory terms; sometimes the Socialists feel compelled to warn against illusions on the Right that membership of the Common Market would be an automatic cure for Austria's structural economic weaknesses, and that Russia's warnings need not be taken seriously.

A controversy of a different kind has arisen over the question whether Austrian neutrality needs to be 'armed neutrality'. Whereas the lawyers say that under Article 5 of the Hague Convention of 1907 all neutral states, whether permanently so or not, must resist all attacks on their territory, and that Austria has pledged herself to 'maintain and defend' her neutrality 'with all the means at her disposal', the noted physicist Hans Thirring[13] has argued that Austria is under no obligation to maintain an army, for the State Treaty merely contains a list of the weapons Austria is *not* allowed to have (such as A-B-C weapons, submarines, or guided missiles!), while the Neutrality Act – which, as an Austrian and not an international law, could be changed by a two-thirds majority of Parliament – does not specify what 'the means at her disposal' must be. The Professor goes on to plead for unilateral disarmament and a special treaty with Austria's six neighbours; but without necessarily following him all the way, there are numbers of people who seriously doubt the usefulness of the Austrian army with its 33,000 conscripts, both as an instrument of defence and as a token of Austrian neutrality. This feeling is strongest on the Left, where the pacifist traditions of the labour movement still prevail and where both the cost and the spirit of the army are often attacked, whereas the extreme Right, true to type, believes in an even bigger and better army to inculcate discipline and manly virtue in the young men under its care.

Rather more complex is the problem of ideological and political partisanship in a neutral country. The government statement of 26 October 1955 referred expressly to the fact that 'the basic rights and freedoms of the citizen will be in no way infringed' by the neutrality law and added:

> Neutrality binds the state, not the individual citizens. The intellectual and political freedom of the individual, in particular the freedom of the press and of speech, are in no way affected by the permanent neutrality of a state. Permanent neutrality does not involve ideological neutrality.[14]

There was some controversy, though, before this statement could be formulated, for Chancellor Raab, while claiming that 'Western Christian principles' and 'the spiritual adherence to the Western world' formed the basis of his neutrality, nevertheless advised the press and radio to exercise restraint: 'There is no use today rebuking some Western state for its colonial policies, or tomorrow conducting

---

[13] Hans Thirring, *Mehr Sicherheit ohne Waffen* (Vienna, n.d. [1963]), p. 14.

[14] *Wiener Zeitung* (27 October 1955).

a propaganda campaign against the East . . .' His socialist fellow-Ministers objected to this gag on the freedom of the press, and Minister of the Interior Helmer bluntly declared that 'because of her culture, her character, and her ten-year struggle against communism Austria belonged in the camp of the free Western world'. Two days after the government statement a correspondent covering the Foreign Ministers' Conference in Geneva was reportedly ordered to cancel his broadcasts after attacks in the communist press, and the outside world was wondering whether some kind of 'Austro-neutralism'[15] was being developed by the same man who had denied in a newspaper interview

> that Austria in its internal affairs intends to become some sort of half-way house between democracy and totalitarianism. Our state is a democracy, firmly based on freedom of speech and assembly, free elections, and respect for the rights of the individual.[16]

While conservative Ministers have always tended to be more circumspect in their criticism of Soviet and East European policies, in actual fact there was little difference in practical politics between the major parties. A Soviet offer in November 1955 of a loan of 800 million schillings at 3 per cent interest from funds accumulated in the Soviet Military Bank, though favoured by some economists, was successfully vetoed by the Socialists who opposed any new financial commitments to the Russians. On the other hand, a U.S. long-term credit of 387 million schillings at low interest rates was agreed in February 1956, with Raab praising the United States, without whose assistance the 'old continent would have fallen to communism'. The expulsion of the headquarters staff of the communist-led 'World Federation of Trade Unions' from Vienna for violations of Austrian law, and the decision to apply for membership of the Council of Europe, made it apparent that, in Stearman's words, 'the Communist concept of Austrian neutrality was not being followed by the Austrian Government'.[17]

The real test of Austrian neutrality came with the Hungarian Revolution in October 1956. From the start, members of the government expressed their sympathy with the rebels, called upon the Soviet government to help bring about an end to the fighting, and extended every possible help to casualties and refugees. Socialist Members of Parliament, especially the youthful Peter Strasser, went to Budapest to help Hungarian efforts to restart the Socialist Party suppressed by the Communists, and great quantities of medical and

[15] Stearman, op. cit., pp. 171–3.
[16] Julius Raab, 'A Neutral Austria', *The Observer* (London), 10 July 1955.
[17] Stearman, op. cit., p. 174.

other non-military aid reached the freedom-fighters. With massive
concentrations of Soviet troops, often within sight of the border, the
Austrians, as guardians of 170,000 Hungarian refugees and with
fewer than 30,000 poorly equipped and only partly trained soldiers
at their disposal, could well have been forgiven if they had yielded
to furious Soviet admonitions and threats; but for them, only
recently freed themselves, it was a case of *tua res agitur*. They
showed the same spirit at the time of the invasion of Czechoslovakia
by troops of the Warsaw Pact states in 1968; and the Soviets seemed
to have learned to live with Vienna's interpretation of the true
meaning of Austrian neutrality which, as Kreisky foresaw, is significantly different from that practised by countries like Sweden
and Switzerland:

> Swedish neutrality is unlike Swiss neutrality in that it is neither
> part of the constitution nor guaranteed in any form by the Great
> Powers. Nor is it a commitment undertaken in treaties with one
> or more states. It is rather the intention of Sweden to conduct its
> affairs in times of peace in such a way that in times of war its
> neutrality can be recognized in international law.... If there is
> thus legally some affinity between Austrian and Swiss neutrality,
> Austria's membership of the United Nations and of the Council
> of Europe makes its foreign policy resemble that of Sweden.
> Hence one can assume that a *specifically Austrian variant of
> neutrality* will develop alongside Swiss and Swedish neutrality.[18]

In actual fact, the resemblance to Sweden has of late become rather
less obvious, though it is a long way yet – and it may never be
travelled – to neutrality of the Finnish type.

Austria had first applied for admission to the United Nations in
1947, but a Soviet veto, based on the fact of Allied occupation, prevented this until after the country's sovereignty had been fully
restored by the State Treaty. Since 1955 the world organization has
grown from a membership of 59 to 126, and this includes most of
the African states and others admitted as a result of the process of
decolonization. In this situation, neutrality – that is, independence
from Great Power blocs – confers a certain prestige and facilitates
mediation in the framing of resolutions and work in committees.
This is particularly evident in the less publicized activities of a
social, economic, and humanitarian nature, though on occasion
Austria, too, had to stand up and be counted on controversial issues
such as the Middle East problem or racial policies in southern
Africa.

[18] Bruno Kreisky, *Die österreichische Neutralität* (Aktuelle Probleme
unserer Zeit Nr. 5) (Vienna, 1960), p. 9.

It would be unrealistic to assume that a small country could hope to mediate between the super-powers on major issues. The most it can do is to avoid being drawn into the vortex of one or the other and to offer its services in avoiding open clashes and submitting compromise texts, as was the case in the 1969 General Assembly debate on the Soviet draft of a resolution on security. In the last few years Austria has been able to contribute to the strengthening of the control powers of the International Atomic Energy Organization (IAEO), whose headquarters are in Vienna, to the preparations for the world conference on human environment, and as chairman of the committee on the peaceful uses of space. Admittedly, in all these questions Austria found herself on the side of both the U.S.A. and the U.S.S.R., whereas Sweden has recently tended to adopt a line independent of, and sometimes even opposed to, one or both of the Great Powers. Swedish membership of the disarmament committee in Geneva gave her the chance to act as the voice of conscience and commonsense, and her critical attitude over Vietnam is well known – luxuries which Austria does not yet feel she can afford, both on account of her interpretation of neutrality and her geographical position.

On joining the United Nations Austria made it clear that she could not participate in military sanctions decreed by the organization, though she has since applied economic sanctions against Rhodesia. An illustration of the kind of dilemma she may from time to time find herself in was provided at the time of the Lebanon crisis in the summer of 1958 when internal difficulties induced the Lebanese President to appeal for military aid. As a result, American planes from West Germany flew, with Austrian permission, over the Tyrol to the Near East. However, because of the emergency situation in Lebanon, some flights were made without the necessary authorization, which led to an Austrian protest and an American apology. Eventually, peace was restored and a special meeting of the U.N. General Assembly called upon the Americans to withdraw their troops and supplies from the country.

An American application to the Austrian government to grant the right of overflight for their transport planes returning to Germany was granted on 17 October 1958 on the grounds that the evacuation had been recommended by the U.N. (including Austria) and that it was a contribution to the lessening of tension in the Near East.[19] While this was felt to be fully compatible with the requirements of neutrality, a policy of 'impartiality' (as was at one time thought to be favoured by some politicians) was definitely not, as a government *démenti* of 15 November 1961 showed:

[19] *Wiener Zeitung* (17 October 1958).

Reports have recently appeared in the Press that in the event of war certain Austrian politicians were toying with the idea of allowing the belligerents the free use of Austrian air-space and territory in order to avoid being compelled to do so by force; and that agreements to this effect were to be concluded with the NATO and Warsaw Pact countries. The Federal Government wishes to state categorically that none of its members has ever issued any such statement, and that in the event of war it has no intention of granting transit rights to any foreign air or ground forces whatever, as to do so would be a contravention of Austrian neutrality[20]

– or committing suicide to avoid some other form of death!

Crises of this kind in no way detracted from the status Austria was slowly acquiring; her example did not pass unnoticed in countries where similar problems were crying out for a solution. At the Laos Conference of fourteen nations which opened in Geneva on 16 May 1961 Prince Norodom Sihanouk of Cambodia appealed to Laotians to form a provisional national government and adopt a neutral status to end their political conflicts:

> *A very highly placed personality of the Socialist block has suggested the formula of an Austrian-style neutrality and a high Western personality has agreed with this declaration.* Since diplomatists always like to lean on precedents, why should not our diplomatic efforts attempt to apply in Laos the same excellent results obtained in Austria?[21]

In the same year it was disclosed that the Soviet government had officially asked the Austrian government if it would be prepared to provide the United Nations with permanent headquarters in Vienna. Needless to say, the Austrians would have been only too pleased, and not mainly for reasons of prestige, but of security. The idea had originally been mooted by Khrushchev in New York after hostile demonstrations had greeted Fidel Castro of Cuba and other unpopular heads of government, and he suggested Vienna, Geneva, or even Leningrad. Later, in Vienna for his meeting with President Kennedy he privately mentioned his preference for Vienna to Chancellor Gorbach, and this was subsequently raised at an official level by the Soviet ambassador[22] – a proposal which surprised the Austrians, as Kreisky admitted, though it cannot have been entirely unwelcome.

[20] Quoted in Heinrich Siegler, *Austria, Problems and Achievements 1945–1963* (Bonn, n.d.), p. 36.

[21] *The Manchester Guardian* (17 May 1961).

[22] *The Manchester Guardian* (7 June 1961).

If Austria could not house the United Nations, she was compensated, as already mentioned, with the IAEO and later with the UNIDO (United Nations Industrial Development Organization) headquarters, the latter as a result of the sympathy Austria had acquired among the developing nations. Her earlier reticence gone, she will probably accept nomination in the near future for one of the non-permanent seats on the Security Council, where she may well have to cast a vote in delicate divisions; but after Sweden and Finland she should have no difficulty in reconciling her obligations with membership of that body. Her recent election to the Executive Committee of the World Health Organization (WHO) was a welcome move in this direction. So far Austria has taken part in two major U.N. actions by supplying first a military hospital and then a police force in Cyprus, and more recently by sending personnel to serve as U.N. observers on the Suez Canal, without the propriety of these decisions being questioned. Thus, empirically, a problem that seemed almost insoluble at the beginning is being solved by a shrewd mixture of skill and tact.[23] And this applies to the whole conduct of Austria's foreign affairs.

Reviewing the international situation at the end of the sixties Foreign Minister Waldheim, addressing the Austrian Society for Foreign Policy and International Relations in 1969,[24] struck an optimistic note: U.S.–Soviet disarmament talks at Helsinki, plans for a European security conference, and a shift in the United Nations from confrontation to cautious co-operation in certain fields. Without belittling the problems that still await a solution – Vietnam and the Middle East in particular – there had at any rate been a certain easing of the tension in Europe, and Europe was the legitimate centre of Austria's foreign political activities.

In spite of the division of Europe into two ideological camps, Europe was still a geographical and historical entity, and any long-term European policy must aim at 'a gradual *rapprochement*, the rebuilding of co-operation and the utilization of the available intellectual potential of the whole continent'. In her geopolitical system, Austria, as a neutral country with a Western-type social system, must avoid being considered its last outpost by the West, or as part of a hostile Western grouping by the East. Various post-war plans for the political unification of Europe have had only limited success; it is clear today that economic co-operation does not lead

[23] For an account of early deliberations on this question, and the subsequent record of Austria in the United Nations, cf. Wolfgang Strasser, *Österreich und die Vereinten Nationen* (Vienna, 1967).

[24] Kurt Waldheim, *Bilanz der österreichischen Außenpolitik* (Vienna, 1969).

to political unity. Austria, of course, welcomes and supports every initiative towards European unity within the limits imposed by her neutral status. She has thus joined the Council of Europe, OECD, ECE (Economic Commission for Europe), and other organizations; she is a member of EFTA; and tries to obtain a viable economic arrangement with the Common Market while supporting, in the United Nations, every move tending to strengthen European co-operation.

Even the problem of the South Tyrol, which has proved intractable for the last fifty years, seems nearer a solution. A 'package deal' and 'calendar of operations' recently agreed between the two governments and approved by an (albeit slender) majority of the local People's Party provides for Italy to take a number of measures – approximately 130 – to extend the autonomy of Bolzano province and meet some of the most urgent wishes of the Tyrolese over the next four years, while Austria recognizes the competence of the International Court to adjudicate in disputes arising from the Gruber–de Gasperi Paris Agreement of 1946 and promises to inform the United Nations, after completion of the 'calendar', that the Austro-Italian conflict is settled. Austria does not surrender her *Schutzfunktion*, the right to interest herself in, and speak up for, the Tyrolese, embodied in the Paris Agreement, to help them retain their ethnic and social 'substance'.

Preoccupation with European affairs, however, does not rule out an awareness of world problems. Even a small and neutral country must 'show the flag', and this is best done inside the United Nations and other international organizations. The Austrian efforts to make Vienna the venue of international meetings and the seat of U.N. agencies (like the International Atomic Energy Organization and UNIDO) do not serve considerations of prestige but contribute to the country's security. With the completion of an ambitious Conference Centre and a headquarters building for the various international organizations Vienna will be recognized as the third centre (after New York and Geneva) of the United Nations. Austrian foreign policy cannot aim at spectacular successes; its achievements lie in domestic stability and prosperity and the image it enjoys abroad.

The start of the Strategic Arms Limitation Talks (SALT) in Vienna between the U.S.A. and U.S.S.R. on 16 April 1970 coincided with the climax of negotiations for a new Austrian government. Differences in foreign policy between the two parties are of shades and nuances and not fundamental, yet Kreisky, both during the election campaign and since, has indicated the issues on which his administration would differ from its predecessors. There was first the question of South Tyrol, where he felt the former government had been over-hasty in accepting a compromise *without international guarantees* and containing the promise of reforms which would be decreed and not negotiated in the Italian Parliament. A socialist-led government will presumably wish to cultivate the good relations existing with Italy – especially since the SPÖ has always rejected extremist demands for South Tyrolese 'self-determination' – but it will nevertheless watch the working-out of the package deal very closely.

On European integration Kreisky reiterated his conviction that no chances of Austrian participation must be missed, but 'there are limits imposed on us by the State Treaty and our neutrality. Neither East nor West must ever be allowed to have any doubt that we mean to stand by our pledges'. On relations with the Soviet bloc, his rule was 'normalization', but not 'fraternization', and as for Germany, while capital investment in Austria would be welcomed, it had to be on the basis of genuine co-operation and not of quick profits and a shut-down in a time of recession, as happened during the First Republic. The Communists were quick to note the omission of several of their pet subjects, the Soviet-sponsored European Security Conference amongst others, but it is certainly unwarranted to anticipate any significant changes in the direction of Austrian foreign policy since 1955, especially in view of the fact that Kreisky himself had played such a leading part in its formulation. That he appointed as his Foreign Minister Dr Rudolf Kirschschläger, a career diplomat and non-party man who had been his Chief of Cabinet at the Foreign Ministry, underlines still further the continuity of Austrian foreign policy.

Epilogue

WE HAVE NOW FOLLOWED the story of the Austrian people over the past thousand years and have seen how history and geography, the dynastic interests of rulers and the pressures of peoples, combined to produce a type of people with a culture and tradition unmistakably their own, which owe little to a particular 'racial' origin and much to the interaction of diverse influences. Twice this nation seemed on the point of extinction, in both world wars and immediately after, either to be submerged in larger empires or else wished away by perfectionist academics. Yet today it still exists, consolidated and undisputed, because it has at long last discovered its identity and accepted its role in the comity of nations.

Alfred Cobban has drawn our attention to a curious but short-lived vogue among political scientists during the Second World War: the denial of the right of small nations to exist as separate entities in the modern world. Whereas the Great War had been fought for the right of national self-determination, there was now a strong feeling in both Britain and America that the collapse of international peace had been brought about by the 'Balkanization' of Europe. 'The idea of nationality as a basis for independent statehood is obsolete,' wrote G. D. H. Cole in 1941.

> In the case of great states surrounded by smaller neighbours it is inevitable, if state sovereignty is to remain the basis of political relationships, that the great states should seek to engulf their neighbours, and the small states be kept alive, if at all, only when they are in the position of buffers between the great.[1]

In the following year two American writers expressed similar views. As 'great differences in military strength between states within the same power zone' constituted 'a political hazard to the whole international community', a number of small states would have to sacrifice their independence, wrote one;[2] and the other thought it

---

[1] G. D. H. Cole, *Europe, Russia and the Future* (London, 1941), pp. 13, 101.
[2] N. J. Spykman, *America's Strategy in World Politics: the United States and the Balance of Power* (New York, 1942), p. 463.

unlikely 'that the small sovereignties destroyed by the Nazis can be restored. It is doubtful that the small nations of Europe will rise from their servitude to Nazi tyranny as small nations.'[3]

However lofty the sentiments of socialist and liberal supporters of democratic confederation or of world government, the spokesmen of the small nations would not hear of them and preferred the pledge, contained in the Atlantic Charter of August 1941, that 'sovereign rights and self-government' would be restored to those who had been forcibly deprived of them. It was not that Czechs or Norwegians had any illusions about their countries' ability to exist without friends and allies and some forms of international co-operation; what they did feel was that federations or groupings of whatever kind could only succeed if they were based on confident, united, and independent nations of whatever size.

Both in 1919 and in 1945, Austrian independence was used as a device for weakening Germany. Now that the German problem has assumed quite a different form and character, the fate of Austria has become a secondary factor; but in the new framework of inter-national relationships the emergence of a non-aggressive, national consciousness in Austria can be seen as a stabilizing factor in Central Europe. Occasional lapses apart, this is also the view of German politicians and historians who, while still smarting under the divi-sion of Germany into 'BRD' and 'DDR', accept the 'confirmation and finalization' of the separation of 1866 in the decisions of 1945. As Werner Conze writes:

> Over a hundred years the Germans have become accustomed to a separate Austrian state. However much criticized and fought over it may have been in the past, it causes no pain [today be-cause] old links and common interests can freely and constantly be renewed across the frontier.[4]

Much of the present denunciation of national feeling, while understandable as a reaction against its excesses, is based on a failure to distinguish between a legitimate national claim to international recognition, and aggressive – usually racist – national policies. By failing to make this distinction clear the historian confuses the issues, as when Arnold Toynbee in a recent tract[5] calls nationalism a 'death-wish' in this atomic age and defines it in such a way ('exemplified in the present member-states of the United Nations')

[3] R. Strausz-Hupé, *Geopolitics: the Struggle for Space and Power* (New York, 1942), p. 191.
[4] Werner Conze, *Das deutsch-russische Verhältnis im Wandel der modernen Welt* (Göttingen, 1967), p. 59.
[5] Arnold Toynbee, *Change and Habit* (Oxford, 1967).

that all differences between established nation-states and young
nations struggling for unity and recognition, between advanced industrial states and developing nations, are ignored for the sake of an
unrealistic perfectionist policy.

But a more plausible criticism can be made of the assertion of
particularist claims when these conflict with the interests of the
larger whole. This issue has recently arisen over nationalist movements in Britain, Canada, France, and Switzerland, and it is usually,
and rightly, placed in the context of the nature of government and
of our social perspectives. Leaving aside the authoritarian, *étatiste*,
view of the political Right, it could be argued that the *étatisme* of
the democratic Left is similarly old-fashioned and dangerous, however persuasive some of its arguments appear to be. For in fact it is
the role ascribed to the state – as the larger, more efficient, more
'democratic' institution – which lies behind much of the current
controversy between centralism and federalism. A good example of
this is a recent article by Paul Johnson, in which 'progress' is defined so narrowly as to raise the question of its relation to democracy:

> In a democracy progress is a function of the paramountcy of
> central government. In the United States, the greatest obstacle
> to human betterment is the existence of States' Rights, which
> underpin the power of the rich, the obscurantists and the racists.
> The backward areas thus prolong their backwardness and inhibit
> the progress of others; any improvement is left to the restricted
> powers of the Federal Government.[6]

The statement about the United States may or may not be true,
but it could also be argued that the concentration of power in one
centre might produce as many ills as it may seek to cure. Size is no
guarantee of quality, but smallness not only enables 'the small in
spirit, the provincially greedy, the corrupt wheeler-dealers, the
clerical bigots, the language fanatics, the anti-sex men, the censors'
to flourish and dominate: it also brings out human qualities and
establishes relationships which the larger organization thinks it can
manage without, or suppresses. In search of a well-ordered, efficient,
and benevolent social organization our latter-day reformers ignore
the dangers of manipulation, the loss of initiative, the decline of
personal commitment and participation in the democratic process
which is a characteristic of modern industrial society. It could
surely be argued that national awareness on the part of a small
ethnic group under pressure from a larger organization is today not

[6] Paul Johnson, 'Nationalist Cloud-Cuckoo Land', *New Statesman* (26
July 1968).

necessarily or always 'a retreat from the real world into a narrow, selfish concept of closed societies, hag-ridden by historic grievances, dwelling on their separateness and exclusivity', and that its spokesmen need not be people

> anxious to put a brake on progress, retreat into the past, erect frontiers, emphasise and strengthen the differences of race, creed, speech, culture, origin; for them the family, tribe, clan is a comfortable womb, a defence against an external world whose only limits are the planetary dimensions or now, indeed, the universe.

Paul Johnson was in fact writing about Celtic nationalism in the United Kingdom, and he may or may not be right about its supporters; in the context of this study, however, the argument has a familiar ring, for this was the Pan-German reply to the Austrian case.

In a world where integration (as distinct from co-operation) is more talked about than achieved, a good case can be made out for the recognition of national claims as long as these do not conflict with the need for supra-national institutions. Just as the firmness of a structure depends on the strength of its component parts, so a healthy international order will depend on the soundness of its constituent members.

In defence of a national consciousness it can in fact be asserted that a recognized national identity is an integral part of man's self-respect and thus makes for better citizenship; that only someone who is firmly rooted in his own nation can appreciate the strength of feeling of members of other nations; that only a united nation can establish a consensus on policy and conduct, and thus work a democratic system where government and opposition are not irreconcilable enemies but alternating political forces; and lastly, that a divided nation invites foreign intervention; centrifugal forces involve outside interests, for divided loyalties encourage territorial ambitions on the part of neighbouring states.

Towards Full Nationhood

This is the state Austria would appear to have reached today, after two international wars and one civil conflagration, two authoritarian régimes, under Dollfuss and Hitler, and the threat of a third, under Stalin. In consequence, all forms of political extremism are shunned; and for once it is not only the relative wellbeing of all classes, the prosperity and stability of the country, on which the remarkable strength of national unity is based.

Most remarkable of all, however, is the weakness of Pan-German sentiment in the country; if it were not too rash a prophecy one

might almost speak of its virtual disappearance. This is not to say
that there are no pockets of right-wing extremist sentiment, usually
connected with the old nationalist athletics clubs; nor that a certain
nostalgia for the good old days of the Third Reich has completely
disappeared among those who were its beneficiaries. What seems
more significant, however, is the extent of integration of former
National Socialists in the community. If, understandably, the VDU
seemed at first an association of resentful outsiders, its successor, the
FPÖ, appears to be fully integrated in the Austrian political structure, a refuge for former Pan-German (and Nazi) elements as well
as for the traditionally liberal, anti-clerical groups, and increasingly,
especially among the younger generation, an attractive alternative
to the vast machines of the two great parties. The small percentage
of the total poll which this grouping secures is somewhat misleading,
for pro-German elements have found a political home in the large
parties as well; nevertheless, it is an indication of the increased
acceptance of Austria's separate statehood, whatever voters may
think of their cultural and ethnic identity. The FPÖ's formula: 'We
affirm our acceptance of Austria as a separate state, but consider
ourselves as belonging to the German ethnic and cultural community'[7] is, however, bitterly criticized by 'patriotic' circles in both
major camps.

Officially, both the *Österreichische Volkspartei* (ÖVP) and the
Sozialistische Partei Österreichs (SPÖ) are orientated exclusively
towards the Austrian state and reject any idea of a closer relationship with Germany or any other state. But they do not insist on
acceptance of the notion that Austrians are a nation separate and
distinct from the German nation: the pragmatic nature of Austrian
post-war politics leaves such academic questions to personal decisions. The Socialists have quietly buried their dispute with some of
their former leaders like Friedrich Adler and Julius Braunthal who
elected not to return from exile because they opposed the 'patriotic'
party-line, whilst the conservatives, never very strong on political
principles or ideas, slipped quite naturally into the role of *the*
patriotic party. But like the Socialists whose (mostly intellectual)
Marxist wing occasionally proclaims its rejection of 'Austrian
nationalism', the conservatives, too, have their intellectuals hanker-
ing after outworn concepts; with them it is the mystic *Reichsidee*
with its strong appeal to Catholic Romantics.

Reference has already been made to Otto Habsburg, the Austrian
pretender, and his 'monarchist' or 'legitimist' supporters; their

---

[7] 'Wir bejahen die Eigenstaatlichkeit Österreichs, bekennen uns zur
deutschen Volks- und Kulturgemeinschaft . . .' *Richtlinien freiheitlicher
Politik in Österreich*, FPÖ (Vienna, 1957).

plans for a 'Greater Austria' – the restoration of a Habsburg Empire albeit reduced in size to Austria and Hungary and reinforced by 'loyal' Croats, Slovaks, and others – contributed to the political troubles of the First Republic in its early years and became an irrelevant issue in its period of stabilization. With the destruction of parliamentary democracy the monarchists once again experienced a short-lived boom, since Schuschnigg needed all the support he could muster, only to be cruelly persecuted in the period of the German occupation. Otto Habsburg's attempts to get himself restored by the Western Powers after 1945 were pathetically unsuccessful, and with the consolidation of the parliamentary régime in Austria his chances today are lower than ever. Little notice is taken of his occasional visits, as a private citizen, to the country of his birth, except on the obscure fringes of reactionary politics.

His tactics have therefore been directed towards building up his image as a fighter for European unity, with a strong anti-Russian bias and in company with extreme right-wing circles, presumably in the hope that an increase in stature and a reputation as a 'European statesman' may benefit his propaganda inside Austria. Unfortunately for him the need to appeal to reactionary forces leads him to stress historical views and interpretations which run directly counter to the newly formulated national interests of Austria. Thus in his first post-war book he proposes to use the crown of the Holy Roman Empire, 'representing the tradition of Charlemagne, ruler over a united occident', as the symbol of a united Europe,[8] and in his second book apostrophizes the Germans as the *Reichsvolk schlechthin* (the 'people of the Reich *par excellence*'), whose mission over a thousand years as the standard-bearers of the Reich has 'entered their flesh and blood, is rooted deeply in their soul'.[9]

Germans as Europe's 'cardinal people', looking back on a millennium of their Reich – which ignores Austrian developments since 1804 and 1806 as well as 1866, 1914, and 1938 – is not what appeals to Austrians today, and sentiments like these disqualify for attention in Austria. In any case, ordinary people are not normally given to taking much notice of abstract propositions, and their feelings are formulated in quite different ways.

Since empirical sociology is still a very young discipline in Austria, available data on the national consciousness of the population are rather scarce and not very conclusive. Only one major effort in this direction was made in 1965, and its results – like those of opinion polls anywhere – are bitterly disputed by interested parties.

The inquiry conducted by the *Sozialwissenschaftliche Studien-*

[8] Otto Habsburg, *Soziale Ordnung von morgen* (Vienna, 1957), pp. 166–8.
[9] Otto Habsburg, *Im Frühling der Geschichte* (Vienna, 1961), pp. 174–5.

gesellschaft proceeded in two stages, the second serving to explore in depth the opinions discovered in the first. One of the introductory questions: 'If you had a free choice where to live, which country would you prefer – Switzerland, Germany, Austria?' produced the following answers (in percentages):

Switzerland	16	Austria	64
Germany	14	No opinion	6

Significantly, these answers correspond to the political sympathies of the sample: conservative and socialist voters identify most closely with Austria (73 per cent and 75 per cent) and least of all with Germany (9 per cent, 8 per cent), while in both camps 14 per cent chose Switzerland. FPÖ supporters, however, showed a marked preference for Germany (56 per cent), followed by Austria (28 per cent) and Switzerland (12 per cent).

To the question whether Austrians were a nation, 48 per cent of the sample replied in the affirmative, while 23 per cent said Austrians were slowly beginning to consider themselves a nation. Fifteen per cent found they were not (the majority of them FPÖ supporters) and 14 per cent probably found the question too difficult. But only 9 per cent agreed with the statement 'Austria would like best to join Germany', while 73 per cent denied this flatly.[10]

Some by-products of this and other inquiries are worth mentioning. It was discovered, for instance, that most people look upon speakers of *Reichsdeutsch* as foreigners and tend to keep their distance. (It is a well-known fact, on the other hand, that this feeling is not reciprocated by Germans – probably because they never *feared* Austrians and tend to look down upon them as *gemütlich* incompetents. A historian of the cinema has pointed out that in Nazi war films the funny parts were usually taken by Austrians, or possibly Bavarians: bibulous or gluttonous privates, comic sergeants, stupid country yokels, etc.) Young Austrians look upon Germans as loud-mouthed, boastful, 'efficient, but lacking in warmth', the best soldiers in the world; significantly, they do not think nearly as highly of the military prowess of their own people.

Feelings of this kind among young people are the result of two influences – the school and the family. Another inquiry concerned itself with the image of Austria in the minds of the young generation: their impressions of Austria's past, her size and her leaders, her achievements and her enemies.[11] The findings were highly significant:

[10] Rupert Gmoser, 'Wie denken Herr und Frau Österreicher über Österreich', in: *Die österreichische Nation: Zwischen zwei Nationalismen* (Vienna, 1967), pp. 37–47.

[11] Ernst Gehmacher, 'Wie bildet sich ein Nationalbewußtsein?', in: *Die österreichische Nation. . . .*, pp. 29–36.

those with only an elementary education tended to a very positive (and highly exaggerated) evaluation of Austria's greatness and her contribution to progress – obviously the result of the over-simplification and the laudatory tenor of patriotic history teaching. The slightly better educated knew about the historic links between Austria and Germany and were therefore more accessible to German nationalist concepts – 'a little knowledge of history favours Pan-German sentiments' (p. 33) – whereas among students and lovers of history a clearer understanding of Austria's special status and nature prevailed. It is the view of opinion researchers, however, that the mass media with their descriptions and films of international sporting events are doing more to strengthen national identification than do other influences, and every Olympic medal or new international record has a greater impact than all the history books and perorations of politicians put together.

What complicates the discussion about the Austrian nation is the view that Austrians have already moved on to the next higher stage – that of an 'international nation' – and that they therefore need not consolidate their present position. This argument was anticipated by Guido Zernatto, one of the few talented writers and poets of the Schuschnigg era, then a kind of Austrian 'nationalist' and as such opposed to German nationalism. To him, a patriot and devout Catholic, Austria's 'German mission' was not a national, but a cultural and intellectual, mission. In his American exile he appears to have moved on to larger *guiding principles*, to which nations would be subordinated; as the editor of his posthumous study *Vom Wesen der Nation* interprets him:

> What gives Austrians their own special quality, consonant with their history, is their supranational outlook and way of life. Were they to lose these, they would not be progressing to a state of nationhood, but falling back into one.[12]

This is not very helpful, for it avoids the question of Austria's present position, as does Karl Renner's famous dictum: 'Austrians are on the way to becoming a nation of cosmopolitan type.'[13]

A more helpful interpretation of recent Austrian history and its effects on national attitudes is offered by Christian Broda, Austrian Minister of Justice; referring to the First Republic he writes:

> It took a long time before we all accepted the basic assumptions of the state in which we lived. It was not until the conquest of

[12] Wolf In der Maur, Introduction to: Guido Zernatto, *Vom Wesen der Nation* (Vienna, 1966), pp. 61 f.
[13] Quoted *Wiener Zeitung* (23 October 1946).

Austria in 1938 and seven years of foreign rule that the path was clear for an Austrian state consciousness (*Staatsbewusstsein*). . . . But in the ten years of Allied occupation we laid the foundation for a national consciousness (*Nationalbewusstsein*), which prepared the ground both psychologically and politically for our Declaration of Neutrality in 1955.[14]

This, in fact, clinches the argument; Austrian neutrality was warmly welcomed by most out of conviction or opportunism: the conviction that it was the only proper role for a state of Austria's tradition and geographical position to play; opportunism, because it conjured up visions of a second Switzerland, peaceful, prosperous, and respected. And the few who opposed it did so because they understood that this was the end of all dreams of union with the Reich, that the neutrality statute was a safer barrier against all encroachments than the ban on the *Anschluss* had been in 1919; and that behind the protection neutrality offered them the Austrian people were now in a position to grow into a united nation.

Thus, after a chequered history great in its achievements and terrible in its falls, after much hesitation and indecision, the Austrian people have at last discovered their identity and become, not just a state, but one of the Nations of the Modern World.

[14] Christian Broda, *Die veränderte Gesellschaft und die neuen Aufgaben der Sozialisten* (Vienna, 1966), p. 23.

Bibliography

A. Books

M. Abrash: 'War Aims toward Austria-Hungary; the Czechoslovak Pivot', in *Russian Diplomacy and Eastern Europe 1914–1917* (New York, 1963).

Akten zur Deutschen Auswärtigen Politik 1918–1945 (AdAP), Serie D. (Baden-Baden, 1950).

R. Albrecht-Carrié: *The Unity of Europe: An Historical Survey* (London, 1966).

N. Almond & R. H. Lutz: *The Treaty of St. Germain* (Stanford, 1935).

M. Balfour: *The Kaiser and his Times* (London, 1964; New York, 1968).

Bankers Trust Company, London: *A Survey of the Economy of Austria* (London, autumn 1969).

A. Basch: *The Danube Basin and the German Economic Sphere* (London, 1944).

O. Bauer: *Die Nationalitätenfrage und der Staat* (Vienna, 1908).

—— *Geschichte Österreichs* (Vienna, 1911).

—— *Die österreichische Revolution* (Vienna, 1965; after the original of 1923).

—— *The Austrian Revolution* (London, 1925).

—— Introduction to: Victor Adler, *Aufsätze, Reden und Briefe* (Vienna, 1929).

E. Beneš: *My War Memoirs* (London, 1928).

K. Berchtold: *Österreichische Parteiprogramme 1868–1966* (Vienna, 1967).

Bericht über die Tätigkeit der deutschösterreichischen Friedensdelegation in St. Germain-en-Laye (Vienna, 1919).

H. Boberach: *Meldungen aus dem Reich.* Auswahl aus den geheimen Lageberichten des Sicherheitsdienstes der SS 1939 bis 1944 (Berlin, 1965).

W. Böhm: *Konservative Umbaupläne im alten Österreich* (Vienna, 1967).

J. Braunthal: *Otto Bauer. Eine Auswahl aus seinem Lebenswerk. Mit einem Lebensbild Otto Bauers* (Vienna, 1961).

Ch. Broda: *Die veränderte Gesellschaft und die neuen Aufgaben der Sozialisten* (Vienna, 1966).

E. H. Buschbeck: *Austria* (London, 1949).

E. H. Carr: *Conditions of Peace* (London, 1942).

F. L. Carsten: *The Rise of Fascism* (London and Berkeley, Calif., 1967).

—— *Der Aufstieg des Faschismus in Europe* (Frankfurt, 1968).

—— 'Die faschistischen Bewegungen – Gemeinsamkeiten und Unterschiede', in *Fascism and Europe. An International Symposium* (Prague, 1969).

W. S. Churchill: *The Second World War* (London and Boston, 1948–54).

C. Clark: *The Conditions of Economic Progress* (London, 1940).

A. Cobban: *National Self-Determination* (Oxford, 1944).

G. D. H. Cole: *Europe, Russia and the Future* (London, 1941).

W. Conze: *Das deutsch-russische Verhältnis im Wandel der modernen Welt* (Göttingen, 1967).

W. Daim: 'Die Nation – in österreichischer Sicht', in *Die österreichische Nation: Zwischen zwei Nationalismen* (Vienna, 1967).

D. Dallin: *Soviet Foreign Policy after Stalin* (Philadelphia, 1961).

Documents on German Foreign Policy, series C, vol. 5 (London, 1966).

U. Eichstädt: *Von Dollfuss zu Hitler* (Wiesbaden, 1955).

R. Endres: 'Das Zeitalter der Reformen' in *Unvergängliches Österreich* (ed. Karl Ziak) (Vienna, 1958).

F. Fellner: 'Österreich in der Nachkriegsplanung der Alliierten 1943–1945', in *Österreich und Europa* (Graz, 1965).

A. Fredborg: *Behind the Steel Wall* (London, 1944).

J. Fried: *Nationalsozialismus und katholische Kirche in Österreich* (Vienna, 1947).

J. Gehl: *Austria, Germany, and the Anschluss 1931–38* (Oxford, 1963).

E. Gehmacher: 'Wie bildet sich ein Nationalbewußtsein?' in *Die österreichische Nation: Zwischen zwei Nationalismen* (Vienna, 1967).

R. Gmoser: 'Wie denken Herr und Frau Österreicher über Österreich', in *Die österreichische Nation: Zwischen zwei Nationalismen* (Vienna, 1967).

F. Göbhart: 'Schule und Nation', in *Die österreichische Nation: Zwischen zwei Nationalismen* (Vienna, 1967).

K. Gruber: *Between Liberation and Liberty* (London, 1955).

M. Güde: *Justiz im Schatten von gestern* (Hamburg, 1959).

Ch. A. Gulick: *Austria from Habsburg to Hitler* (Berkeley, 1948).

O. Habsburg: *Soziale Ordnung von morgen* (Vienna, 1957).

—— *Im Frühling der Geschichte* (Vienna, 1961).

J. Hannak: *Karl Renner und seine Zeit* (Vienna, 1965).

C. H. Haskins and R. H. Lord: *Some Problems of the Peace Conference* (Cambridge, 1920).

F. Hertz: *Nationality in History and Politics* (London, 1944).

J. Hindels: *Von der ersten Republik zum zweiten Weltkrieg* (Malmö, 1947).

A. Hitler: *Mein Kampf* (Munich, 1925).

P. Hoffmann: *Widerstand, Staatsstreich, Attentat* (Munich, 1969).

I.M.T.: Trial of the Major War Criminals before the International Military Tribunal Nuremberg 14 November 1945–1 October 1946 (Nuremberg, 1947).

A. Inkeles: 'Some Observations on Culture and Personality Studies' in *Personality in Nature, Society and Culture* (ed. Kluckhohn and Murray) (New York, 1956).

Introducing Austria, Statistisches Zentralamt (Vienna, 1968).

L. Jedlicka: *Der 20. Juli 1944 in Österreich* (vol. I of *Das einsame Gewissen*) (Vienna, 1965).

—— 'Verfassungs- und Verwaltungsprobleme 1938–1945' in *Die Entwicklung der Verfassung Österreichs* (Graz, 1963).

The Jews of Austria (ed. Josef Fraenkel) (London, 1967).

J. Joll: *The Second International 1889–1914* (London and New York, 1968).

R. A. Kann: *The Multinational Empire* (New York, 1950).

F. Käs: *Wien im Schicksalsjahr 1945* (Vienna, 1965).

L. Kerekes: *Abenddämmerung einer Demokratie. Mussolini, Gömbös, und die Heimwehr* (Vienna, 1966).

J. M. Keynes: *The Economic Consequences of the Peace* (London, 1920).

—— *The Revision of the Peace Treaties* (London, 1922).

C. Kluckhohn: *Culture and Behavior* (New York, 1962).

B. Kreisky: *Die österreichische Neutralität* (Aktuelle Probleme unserer Zeit Nr. 5) (Vienna, 1960).

—— *Die Herausforderung* (Düsseldorf, 1963).

C. F. Latour: *Südtirol und die Achse Berlin–Rom 1938–1945* (Stuttgart, 1962).

W. T. Layton and C. Rist: *The Economic Situation of Austria* (League of Nations, 1925).

O. Leichter: *Glanz und Ende der Ersten Republik* (Vienna, 1964).

V. I. Lenin: *Selected Works* (Moscow, 1936).

N. Leser: *Zwischen Reformismus und Bolschewismus. Der Austromarxismus als Theorie und Praxis* (Vienna, 1968).

D. Lloyd George: *War Memoirs* (London, 1936).

—— *The Truth about the Peace Treaties* (London, 1938).

L. P. Lochner: *The Goebbels Diaries* (London, 1948).

C. A. Macartney: *Problems of the Danube Basin* (Cambridge, 1944).

M. MacDonald: *The Republic of Austria 1918–1934. A Study in the Failure of Democratic Government* (Oxford, 1946).

F. Marek: 'Die österreichische Nation in der wissenschaftlichen Erkenntnis', in *Die österreichische Nation: Zwischen zwei Nationalismen* (Vienna, 1967).

W. P. Metzger: 'Generalizations about National Character: An Analytical Essay', in *Generalization in the Writing of History* (ed. Louis Gottschalk) (Chicago, 1963).

D. H. Miller: *My Diary at the Conference of Paris* (New York, 1924).

K. R. Minogue: *Nationalism* (London, 1967).

O. Molden: *Der Ruf des Gewissens. Der österreichische Freiheitskampf 1938–1945* (Vienna, 1958).

J. Moser: *Die Judenverfolgung in Österreich 1938–1945* (Vienna, 1966).

Nationalism. A Report by a Study Group of Members of the RIIA (London, 1963).

E. Nolte: *Der Faschismus in seiner Epoche* (Munich, 1963).

Österreichisches Jahrbuch (Vienna, 1947).

Der österreichische National- und Bundesrat 1945 (Vienna, 1946).

G. Otruba: *Österreichs Wirtschaft im 20. Jahrhundert* (Vienna, 1968).

Papers relating to the Foreign Relations of the United States. 1919. The Paris Peace Conference (Washington 1942–); *1945* vol. III (Washington, 1968).

H. Picker: *Hitlers Tischgespräche im Führerhauptquartier 1941/42* (Stuttgart, 1963).

Protokoll des Parteitags der SPÖ (Vienna, 1947).

P. G. J. Pulzer: *The Rise of Political Anti-Semitism in Germany and Austria* (New York, 1964).

F. M. Rebhann: *Finale in Wien. Eine Gaustadt im Aschenregen* (vol. IV of *Das einsame Gewissen*) (Vienna, 1969).

G. Reitlinger: *The Final Solution* (London, 1953; New York, 1961).

K. Renner: *Der Kampf der österreichischen Nationen um den Staat* (Vienna, 1902).

—— *Denkschrift über die Geschichte der Unabhängigkeitserklärung Österreichs und die Einsetzung der provisorischen Regierung der Republik* (Vienna, 1945).

—— *Drei Monate Aufbauarbeit der provisorischen Staatsregierung der Republik Österreich* (Vienna, 1945).

—— *Österreich, St. Germain, und der kommende Friede* (Vienna, 1946).

—— *Die Nation: Mythos und Wirklichkeit* (Vienna, 1964).

Richtlinien freiheitlicher Politik in Österreich, FPÖ (Vienna, 1957).

F. Romanik: *Der Anteil der Akademikerschaft an Österreichs Freiheitskampf* (Vienna, n.d.).

K. W. Rothschild: *Austria's Economic Development between the two Wars* (London, 1947).

—— *The Austrian Economy since 1945* (London, 1950).

Rot-Weiß-Rot-Buch. Gerechtigkeit für Österreich! Darstellungen, Dokumente und Nachweise zur Vorgeschichte und Geschichte der Okkupation Österreichs. Erster Teil (Nach amtlichen Quellen) (Vienna, 1946).

K. H. Sailer: *Geheimer Briefwechsel Mussolini–Dollfus* (Vienna, 1949).

E. Salter: *Memoirs of a Public Servant* (London, 1961).

A. Schärf: *April 1945 in Wien* (Vienna, 1948).

—— *Erinnerungen aus meinem Leben* (Vienna, 1963).

K. Schuschnigg: *Dreimal Österreich* (Vienna, 1937).

—— *Ein Requiem in Rot-Weiß-Rot* (Zürich, 1946).

—— *Austrian Requiem* (London, 1947).

—— *Im Kampf gegen Hitler* (Vienna, 1969).

H. Seton-Watson: *Nationalism and Communism* (London and New York, 1964).

—— 'Super-national Monarchy and National State', in *Die Auflösung des Habsburgerreiches* (ed. R. G. Plaschka and K. Mack) (Vienna, 1970).

C. Seymour: *The Intimate Papers of Colonel House* (London, 1926).

—— *American Diplomacy during the World War* (Baltimore, 1934).

G. Brook-Shepherd: *The Austrian Odyssey* (London, 1957).

—— *Anschluss: The Rape of Austria* (London, 1963).

H. Siegler: *Austria. Problems and Achievements 1945–1963* (Bonn, n.d.).

N. J. Spykman: *America's Strategy in World Politics: the United States and the Balance of Power* (New York, 1942).

K. R. Stadler: 'Austria', in *European Fascism* (ed. S. J. Woolf) (London, 1968).

—— *Österreich 1938–1945 im Spiegel der NS-Akten* (Vienna, 1966).

—— *The Birth of the Austrian Republic* (Leyden, 1966).

J. Stalin: *Marxism and the National and Colonial Question* (2nd edn., Moscow, 1936).

E. R. Starhemberg: *Between Hitler and Mussolini* (London, 1942).

State Treaty for the re-establishment of an independent and democratic Austria (HMSO, Cmd. 9482, 1955).

Statistical Handbook of the Czechoslovak Republic (London, n.d.) (1940?).

Statistisches Handbuch für die Republik Österreich, Statistisches Zentralamt (Vienna, 1969).

W. L. Stearman: *The Soviet Union and the Occupation of Austria* (Bonn, n.d.).

H. W. Steed: *Through Thirty Years* (London, 1924).

H. Steiner: *Zum Tode verurteilt* (Vienna, 1964).

—— *Gestorben für Österreich* (Vienna, 1968).

S. Steinmetz: *Die österreichischen Zigeuner im NS-Staat* (Vienna, 1966).

Stenographisches Protokoll über die Sitzungen der provisorischen Nationalversammlung für Deutsch-Österreich 1918 und 1919 (Vienna, 3 October 1918).

H. Stimson: *On Active Service in Peace and War* (London, 1949).

W. Strasser: *Osterreich und die Vereinten Nationen* (Vienna, 1967).

R. Strausz-Hupé: *Geopolitics: the Struggle for Space and Power* (New York, 1942).

M. Szecsi and K. Stadler: *Die NS-Justiz in Österreich und ihre Opfer* (vol. I of *Das einsame Gewissen*) (Vienna, 1962).

J. L. Talmon: *The Unique and the Universal* (New York, 1965; London, 1966).

A. J. P. Taylor: *The Habsburg Monarchy 1809–1918* (London, 1967 edn.).

H. W. V. Temperley (ed.): *A History of the Peace Conference* (London, 1921–).

H. Thirring: *Mehr Sicherheit ohne Waffen* (Vienna, n.d. [1963]).

A. Toynbee: *Change and Habit* (Oxford, 1967).

Treaty of Peace between the Allied and Associated Powers and Austria (Cmd. 400) (London, 1919).

H. R. Trevor-Roper: *Jewish and other Nationalism* (London, 1962).

The US Strategic Bombing Survey. The Effects of Strategic Bombing on German Morale, 2 vols. (Washington, 1946–47).

A. Verdross: *The Permanent Neutrality of the Republic of Austria* (Vienna, 1967).

Verfügungen, Anordnungen, Bekanntgaben der NSDAP, hrg. Partei-Kanzlei, vol. 6 (Munich, 1944).

G. S. Viereck: *The Strangest Friendship in History* (London, 1933).

K. Waldheim: *Bilanz der österreichischen Außenpolitik* (Vienna, 1969).

S. Wambaugh: *Plebiscites since the World War* (Washington, 1933).

E. Weber-Kandl: *Hitlers Österreichbild*, phil. dissertation (Vienna University, 1965).

L. Weinberger: *Tatsachen, Begegnungen und Gespräche* (Vienna, 1948).

E. Weinzierl: *Zu wenig Gerechte* (Graz, 1969).

G. Weisenborn: *Der lautlose Aufstand* (Hamburg, 1953).

A. G. Whiteside: *Austrian National Socialism before 1918* (The Hague, 1962).

Z. A. Zeman: *The Break-Up of the Habsburg Empire* (London, 1961).

G. Zernatto: *Vom Wesen der Nation* (Vienna, 1966).

E. Zöllner: *Geschichte Österreichs* (Vienna, 1966).

B. Articles

O. Afanasyeva: 'A Threat to Neutrality', *International Affairs* (Moscow), December 1961.

W. Frauendienst: 'Deutschösterreich und das Reich. Das Berliner Protokoll vom 2. März 1919', *Berliner Monatshefte*, 1944.

Ch. A. Gulick: 'Austria's Socialists in the Trend toward a two-party System: An Interpretation of Postwar Elections', *The Western Political Quarterly*, XI/3, September 1958.

L. Jedlicka: 'The Austrian Heimwehr', *Journal of Contemporary History*, vol. I, no. 1 (1966).

P. Johnson: 'Nationalist Cloud-Cuckoo Land', *New Statesman*, London, 26 July 1968.

R. A. Kann: 'Karl Renner (December 14, 1870–December 31, 1950)', *Journal of Modern History*, vol. 23, no. 3, September 1951.

L. Kerekes: 'Die weiße Allianz', *Österreichische Osthefte*, VII/5, Vienna.

A. G. Kogan: 'The Social Democrats and the Conflict of Nationalities in the Habsburg Monarchy' *Journal of Modern History*, vol. 21 (1949).

H. Kohn: 'A.E.I.O.U.: Some Reflections on the Meaning and Mission of Austria', *Journal of Modern History*, vol. II December 1939.

J. Kozenski: 'The Problem of an Austro-German Union in 1918–1919', *Polish Western Affairs*, 1/1967, Poznan.

B. Kreisky: 'Österreichs Stellung als neutraler Staat', *Österreich in Geschichte und Literatur*, I/3, 1957, Vienna.

F. Marek: 'Im Kampf gegen den deutschen Faschismus', *Weg und Ziel*, December 1954, Vienna.

T. G. Masaryk: 'The Future Status of Bohemia', *The New Europe*, 22 February 1917.

Ph. E. Mosely: 'The Treaty with Austria', *International Organization*, 4/1950.

F. Parkinson: 'Austrian Socialism Today' (Home and Foreign Policy), *The World Today*, March and April 1964.

J. Raab: 'A Neutral Austria', *The Observer* (London), 10 July 1955.

H. Seton-Watson: 'Fascism, Right and Left', *Journal of Contemporary History*, vol. I, no. 1 (1966).

—— 'Nationalismus und Nationalbewußtsein', *Österreichische Osthefte*, 8/1, January 1966, Vienna.

K. R. Stadler: 'Die Offiziersrevolte gegen Hitler und die Unabhängigkeit Österreichs', *Die Zukunft*, 20/1969, Vienna.

—— 'The Disintegration of the Austrian Empire', *Journal of Contemporary History*, 4/1968.

—— 'Fünfzig Jahre Vertrag von St. Germain', *Österreich in Geschichte und Literatur*, XIII/8, 1969, Vienna.

—— 'Zwischen Reich und Republik', *Salzburger Nachrichten*, 19 July 1969.

G. Stourzh: 'Zur Geschichte der österreichischen Neutralität', *Österreich in Geschichte und Literatur*, V/6, 1961, Vienna.

C. Journals and Newspapers Used

Amtsblatt der Stadt Wien (Vienna)
Arbeiter-Zeitung (Vienna)
Berichte und Informationen (Salzburg)
Berliner Monatshefte (Berlin)
Bundesgesetzblatt (Vienna)
International Affairs (Moscow)
Journal of Contemporary History (London)
Der Kampf (Vienna)
Der sozialistische Kampf (Paris)
The (Manchester) Guardian (Manchester)
Neues Österreich (Vienna)
The New Europe (London)
Österreich in Geschichte und Literatur (Vienna)
Österreichische Richterzeitung (Vienna)
Österreichische Zeitschrift für Aussenpolitik (Vienna)
Polish Western Affairs (Poznan)
Reichsgesetzblatt (Berlin)
Richterbriefe (Berlin)
Salzburger Nachrichten (Salzburg)
Soviet News (London)
Der Spiegel (Hamburg)
Weg und Ziel (Vienna)
Wiener Zeitung (Vienna)
The World Today (London)
Die Zukunft (Vienna)

D. Sources of Unpublished Material

Archives of the Ministry of Justice, Vienna

Bundesarchiv Koblenz
Document Center, Berlin
Dokumentationsarchiv des österreichischen Widerstandes, Vienna
Haus-, Hof- und Staatsarchiv, Vienna
Institut für Zeitgeschichte, Berlin (East)
Institut für Zeitgeschichte, Munich.
Institut für Zeitgeschichte, Vienna
Library of Congress, Washington, D.C.
National Archives, Washington, D.C.
The Hoover Memorial Library, Stanford, California
The New York Public Library

Index

337

Printed in Great Britain by
Western Printing Services Ltd, Bristol